# THE NEW MIDDLE AGES

BONNIE WHEELER, *Series Editor*

*The New Middle Ages* is a series dedicated to pluridisciplinary studies of medieval cultures, with particular emphasis on recuperating women's history and on feminist and gender analyses. This peer-reviewed series includes both scholarly monographs and essay collections.

## PUBLISHED BY PALGRAVE:

*Women in the Medieval Islamic World: Power, Patronage, and Piety*
  edited by Gavin R. G. Hambly

*The Ethics of Nature in the Middle Ages: On Boccaccio's* Poetaphysics
  by Gregory B. Stone

*Presence and Presentation: Women in the Chinese Literati Tradition*
  edited by Sherry J. Mou

*The Lost Love Letters of Heloise and Abelard: Perceptions of Dialogue in Twelfth-Century France*
  by Constant J. Mews

*Understanding Scholastic Thought with Foucault*
  by Philipp W. Rosemann

*For Her Good Estate: The Life of Elizabeth de Burgh*
  by Frances A. Underhill

*Constructions of Widowhood and Virginity in the Middle Ages*
  edited by Cindy L. Carlson and Angela Jane Weisl

*Motherhood and Mothering in Anglo-Saxon England*
  by Mary Dockray-Miller

*Listening to Heloise: The Voice of a Twelfth-Century Woman*
  edited by Bonnie Wheeler

*The Postcolonial Middle Ages*
  edited by Jeffrey Jerome Cohen

*Chaucer's* Pardoner *and Gender Theory: Bodies of Discourse*
  by Robert S. Sturges

*Crossing the Bridge: Comparative Essays on Medieval European and Heian Japanese Women Writers*
  edited by Barbara Stevenson and Cynthia Ho

*Engaging Words: The Culture of Reading in the Later Middle Ages*
  by Laurel Amtower

*Robes and Honor: The Medieval World of Investiture*
  edited by Stewart Gordon

*Representing Rape in Medieval and Early Modern Literature*
  edited by Elizabeth Robertson and Christine M. Rose

*Same Sex Love and Desire Among Women in the Middle Ages*
  edited by Francesca Canadé Sautman and Pamela Sheingorn

*Sight and Embodiment in the Middle Ages: Ocular Desires*
  by Suzannah Biernoff

*Listen, Daughter: The* Speculum Virginum *and the Formation of Religious Women in the Middle Ages*
  edited by Constant J. Mews

*Science, the Singular, and the Question of Theology*
  by Richard A. Lee, Jr.

*Gender in Debate from the Early Middle Ages to the Renaissance*
  edited by Thelma S. Fenster and Clare A. Lees

*Malory's* Morte D'Arthur: *Remaking Arthurian Tradition*
  by Catherine Batt

*The Vernacular Spirit: Essays on Medieval Religious Literature*
  edited by Renate Blumenfeld-Kosinski, Duncan Robertson, and Nancy Warren

*Popular Piety and Art in the Late Middle Ages: Image Worship and Idolatry in England 1350–1500*
  by Kathleen Kamerick

*Absent Narratives, Manuscript Textuality, and Literary Structure in Late Medieval England*
  by Elizabeth Scala

*Creating Community with Food and Drink in Merovingian Gaul*
  by Bonnie Effros

*Representations of Early Byzantine Empresses: Image and Empire*
  by Anne McClanan

*Encountering Medieval Textiles and Dress: Objects, Texts, Images*
  edited by Désirée G. Koslin and Janet Snyder

*Eleanor of Aquitaine: Lord and Lady*
  edited by Bonnie Wheeler and John Carmi Parsons

*Isabel La Católica, Queen of Castile: Critical Essays*
  edited by David A. Boruchoff

*Homoeroticism and Chivalry: Discourses of Male Same-Sex Desire in the Fourteenth Century*
  by Richard E. Zeikowitz

*Portraits of Medieval Women: Family, Marriage, and Politics in England 1225–1350*
  by Linda E. Mitchell

*Eloquent Virgins: From Thecla to Joan of Arc*
  by Maud Burnett McInerney

*The Persistence of Medievalism: Narrative Adventures in Contemporary Culture*
  by Angela Jane Weisl

*Capetian Women*
  edited by Kathleen D. Nolan

*Joan of Arc and Spirituality*
  edited by Ann W. Astell and Bonnie Wheeler

*The Texture of Society: Medieval Women in the Southern Low Countries*
  edited by Ellen E. Kittell and Mary A. Suydam

*Charlemagne's Mustache: And Other Cultural Clusters of a Dark Age*
  by Paul Edward Dutton

*Troubled Vision: Gender, Sexuality, and Sight in Medieval Text and Image*
  edited by Emma Campbell and Robert Mills

*Queering Medieval Genres*
  by Tison Pugh

*Sacred Place in Early Medieval Neoplatonism*
  by L. Michael Harrington

*The Middle Ages at Work*
  edited by Kellie Robertson and Michael Uebel

*Chaucer's Jobs*
  by David R. Carlson

*Medievalism and Orientalism: Three Essays on Literature, Architecture and Cultural Identity*
  by John M. Ganim

*Queer Love in the Middle Ages*
  by Anna Klosowska

*Performing Women in the Middle Ages: Sex, Gender, and the Iberian Lyric*
  by Denise K. Filios

*Necessary Conjunctions: The Social Self in Medieval England*
  by David Gary Shaw

*Visual Culture and the German Middle Ages*
  edited by Kathryn Starkey and Horst Wenzel

*Medieval Paradigms: Essays in Honor of Jeremy duQuesnay Adams, Volumes 1 and 2*
  edited by Stephanie Hayes-Healy

*False Fables and Exemplary Truth in Later Middle English Literature*
  by Elizabeth Allen

*Ecstatic Transformation: On the Uses of Alterity in the Middle Ages*
by Michael Uebel

*Sacred and Secular in Medieval and Early Modern Cultures: New Essays*
edited by Lawrence Besserman

*Tolkien's Modern Middle Ages*
edited by Jane Chance and Alfred K. Siewers

*Representing Righteous Heathens in Late Medieval England*
by Frank Grady

*Byzantine Dress: Representations of Secular Dress in Eighth- to Twelfth-Century Painting*
by Jennifer L. Ball

*The Laborer's Two Bodies: Labor and the "Work" of the Text in Medieval Britain, 1350–1500*
by Kellie Robertson

*The Dogaressa of Venice, 1250–1500: Wife and Icon*
by Holly S. Hurlburt

*Logic, Theology, and Poetry in Boethius, Abelard, and Alan of Lille: Words in the Absence of Things*
by Eileen C. Sweeney

*The Theology of Work: Peter Damian and the Medieval Religious Renewal Movement*
by Patricia Ranft

*On the Purification of Women: Churching in Northern France, 1100–1500*
by Paula M. Rieder

*Voices from the Bench: The Narratives of Lesser Folk in Medieval Trials*
edited by Michael Goodich

*Writers of the Reign of Henry II: Twelve Essays*
edited by Ruth Kennedy and Simon Meecham-Jones

*Lonesome Words: The Vocal Poetics of the Old English Lament and the African-American Blues Song*
by M.G. McGeachy

*Performing Piety: Musical Culture in Medieval English Nunneries*
by Anne Bagnall Yardley

*The Flight from Desire: Augustine and Ovid to Chaucer*
by Robert R. Edwards

*Mindful Spirit in Late Medieval Literature: Essays in Honor of Elizabeth D. Kirk*
edited by Bonnie Wheeler

*Medieval Fabrications: Dress, Textiles, Clothwork, and Other Cultural Imaginings*
edited by E. Jane Burns

*Was the Bayeux Tapestry Made in France? The Case for St. Florent of Saumur*
by George Beech

*Women, Power, and Religious Patronage in the Middle Ages*
by Erin L. Jordan

*Hybridity, Identity, and Monstrosity in Medieval Britain: On Difficult Middles*
by Jeffrey Jerome Cohen

*Medieval Go-betweens and Chaucer's Pandarus*
by Gretchen Mieszkowski

*The Surgeon in Medieval English Literature*
by Jeremy J. Citrome

*Temporal Circumstances: Form and History in the Canterbury Tales*
by Lee Patterson

*Erotic Discourse and Early English Religious Writing*
by Lara Farina

*Odd Bodies and Visible Ends in Medieval Literature*
by Sachi Shimomura

*On Farting: Language and Laughter in the Middle Ages*
by Valerie Allen

*Women and Medieval Epic: Gender, Genre, and the Limits of Epic Masculinity*
edited by Sara S. Poor and Jana K. Schulman

*Race, Class, and Gender in "Medieval" Cinema*
edited by Lynn T. Ramey and Tison Pugh

*Allegory and Sexual Ethics in the High Middle Ages*
by Noah D. Guynn

*England and Iberia in the Middle Ages, 12th–15th Century: Cultural, Literary, and Political Exchanges*
edited by María Bullón-Fernández

*The Medieval Chastity Belt: A Myth-Making Process*
by Albrecht Classen

*Claustrophilia: The Erotics of Enclosure in Medieval Literature*
by Cary Howie

*Cannibalism in High Medieval English Literature*
by Heather Blurton

*The Drama of Masculinity and Medieval English Guild Culture*
by Christina M. Fitzgerald

*Chaucer's Visions of Manhood*
by Holly A. Crocker

*The Literary Subversions of Medieval Women*
by Jane Chance

*Manmade Marvels in Medieval Culture and Literature*
by Scott Lightsey

*American Chaucers*
by Candace Barrington

*Representing Others in Medieval Iberian Literature*
by Michelle M. Hamilton

*Paradigms and Methods in Early Medieval Studies*
edited by Celia Chazelle and Felice Lifshitz

*The King and the Whore: King Roderick and La Cava*
by Elizabeth Drayson

*Langland's Early Modern Identities*
by Sarah A. Kelen

*Cultural Studies of the Modern Middle Ages*
edited by Eileen A. Joy, Myra J. Seaman, Kimberly K. Bell, and Mary K. Ramsey

*Hildegard of Bingen's Unknown Language: An Edition, Translation, and Discussion*
by Sarah L. Higley

*Medieval Romance and the Construction of Heterosexuality*
by Louise M. Sylvester

*Communal Discord, Child Abduction, and Rape in the Later Middle Ages*
by Jeremy Goldberg

*Lydgate Matters: Poetry and Material Culture in the Fifteenth Century*
edited by Lisa H. Cooper and Andrea Denny-Brown

*Sexuality and Its Queer Discontents in Middle English Literature*
by Tison Pugh

*Sex, Scandal, and Sermon in Fourteenth-Century Spain: Juan Ruiz's* Libro de Buen Amor
by Louise M. Haywood

*The Erotics of Consolation: Desire and Distance in the Late Middle Ages*
edited by Catherine E. Léglu and Stephen J. Milner

*Battlefronts Real and Imagined: War, Border, and Identity in the Chinese Middle Period*
edited by Don J. Wyatt

*Wisdom and Her Lovers in Medieval and Early Modern Hispanic Literature*
by Emily C. Francomano

*Power, Piety, and Patronage in Late Medieval Queenship: Maria de Luna*
by Nuria Silleras-Fernandez

*In the Light of Medieval Spain: Islam, the West, and the Relevance of the Past*
edited by Simon R. Doubleday and David Coleman, foreword by Giles Tremlett

*Chaucerian Aesthetics*
by Peggy A. Knapp

*Memory, Images, and the English Corpus Christi Drama*
by Theodore K. Lerud

*Cultural Diversity in the British Middle Ages: Archipelago, Island, England*
edited by Jeffrey Jerome Cohen

*Excrement in the Late Middle Ages: Sacred Filth and Chaucer's Fecopoetics*
by Susan Signe Morrison

*Authority and Subjugation in Writing of Medieval Wales*
edited by Ruth Kennedy and Simon Meecham-Jones

*The Medieval Poetics of the Reliquary: Enshrinement, Inscription, Performance*
by Seeta Chaganti

*The Legend of Charlemagne in the Middle Ages: Power, Faith, and Crusade*
edited by Matthew Gabriele and Jace Stuckey

*The Poems of Oswald von Wolkenstein: An English Translation of the Complete Works (1376/77–1445)*
by Albrecht Classen

*Women and Experience in Later Medieval Writing: Reading the Book of Life*
edited by Anneke B. Mulder-Bakker and Liz Herbert McAvoy

*Ethics and Eventfulness in Middle English Literature: Singular Fortunes*
by J. Allan Mitchell

*Maintenance, Meed, and Marriage in Medieval English Literature*
by Kathleen E. Kennedy

*The Post-Historical Middle Ages*
edited by Elizabeth Scala and Sylvia Federico

*Constructing Chaucer: Author and Autofiction in the Critical Tradition*
by Geoffrey W. Gust

*Queens in Stone and Silver: The Creation of a Visual Imagery of Queenship in Capetian France*
by Kathleen Nolan

*Finding Saint Francis in Literature and Art*
edited by Cynthia Ho, Beth A. Mulvaney, and John K. Downey

*Strange Beauty: Ecocritical Approaches to Early Medieval Landscape*
by Alfred K. Siewers

*Berenguela of Castile (1180–1246) and Political Women in the High Middle Ages*
by Miriam Shadis

*Julian of Norwich's Legacy: Medieval Mysticism and Post-Medieval Reception*
edited by Sarah Salih and Denise N. Baker

*Medievalism, Multilingualism, and Chaucer*
by Mary Catherine Davidson

*The Letters of Heloise and Abelard: A Translation of Their Collected Correspondence and Related Writings*
translated and edited by Mary Martin McLaughlin with Bonnie Wheeler

*Women and Wealth in Late Medieval Europe*
edited by Theresa Earenfight

*Visual Power and Fame in René d'Anjou, Geoffrey Chaucer, and the Black Prince*
by SunHee Kim Gertz

*Geoffrey Chaucer Hath a Blog: Medieval Studies and New Media*
by Brantley L. Bryant

*Margaret Paston's Piety*
by Joel T. Rosenthal

*Gender and Power in Medieval Exegesis*
by Theresa Tinkle

*Antimercantilism in Late Medieval English Literature*
by Roger A. Ladd

*Magnificence and the Sublime in Medieval Aesthetics: Art, Architecture, Literature, Music*
edited by C. Stephen Jaeger

*Medieval and Early Modern Devotional Objects in Global Perspective: Translations of the Sacred*
edited by Elizabeth Robertson and Jennifer Jahner

*Late Medieval Jewish Identities: Iberia and Beyond*
  edited by Carmen Caballero-Navas and Esperanza Alfonso

*Outlawry in Medieval Literature*
  by Timothy S. Jones

*Women and Disability in Medieval Literature*
  by Tory Vandeventer Pearman

*The Lesbian Premodern*
  edited by Noreen Giffney, Michelle M. Sauer, and Diane Watt

*Crafting Jewishness in Medieval England: Legally Absent, Virtually Present*
  by Miriamne Ara Krummel

*Street Scenes: Late Medieval Acting and Performance*
  by Sharon Aronson-Lehavi

*Women and Economic Activities in Late Medieval Ghent*
  by Shennan Hutton

*Palimpsests and the Literary Imagination of Medieval England: Collected Essays*
  edited by Leo Carruthers, Raeleen Chai-Elsholz, and Tatjana Silec

*Divine Ventriloquism in Medieval English Literature: Power, Anxiety, Subversion*
  by Mary Hayes

*Vernacular and Latin Literary Discourses of the Muslim Other in Medieval Germany*
  by Jerold C. Frakes

*Fairies in Medieval Romance*
  by James Wade

*Reason and Imagination in Chaucer, the* Perle-*poet, and the* Cloud-*author: Seeing from the Center*
  by Linda Tarte Holley

*The Inner Life of Women in Medieval Romance Literature: Grief, Guilt, and Hypocrisy*
  edited by Jeff Rider and Jamie Friedman

*Language as the Site of Revolt in Medieval and Early Modern England: Speaking as a Woman*
  by M. C. Bodden

*Ecofeminist Subjectivities: Chaucer's Talking Birds*
  by Lesley Kordecki

*Contextualizing the Muslim Other in Medieval Christian Discourse*
  edited by Jerold C. Frakes

*Ekphrastic Medieval Visions: A New Discussion in Interarts Theory*
  by Claire Barbetti

*The [European] Other in Medieval Arabic Literature and Culture: Ninth-Twelfth Century AD*
  by Nizar F. Hermes

*Reading Memory and Identity in the Texts of Medieval European Holy Women*
  edited by Margaret Cotter-Lynch and Brad Herzog

*Market Power: Lordship, Society, and Economy in Medieval Catalonia (1276–1313)*
  by Gregory B. Milton

*Marriage, Property, and Women's Narratives*
  by Sally A. Livingston

*The Medieval Python: The Purposive and Provocative Work of Terry Jones*
  edited by R. F. Yeager and Toshiyuki Takamiya

*Boccaccio's* Decameron *and the Ciceronian Renaissance*
  by Michaela Paasche Grudin and Robert Grudin

*Studies in the Medieval Atlantic*
  edited by Benjamin Hudson

*Chaucer's Feminine Subjects: Figures of Desire in* The Canterbury Tales
  by John A. Pitcher

*Writing Medieval Women's Lives*
  edited by Charlotte Newman Goldy and Amy Livingstone

*The Mediterranean World of Alfonso II and Peter II of Aragon (1162–1213)*
  by Ernest E. Jenkins

*Women in the Military Orders of the Crusades*
  by Myra Miranda Bom

*Icons of Irishness from the Middle Ages to the Modern World*
by Maggie M. Williams

*The Anglo-Scottish Border and the Shaping of Identity, 1300–1600*
edited by Mark P. Bruce and Katherine H. Terrell

*Shame and Guilt in Chaucer*
by Anne McTaggart

*Word and Image in Medieval Kabbalah: The Texts, Commentaries, and Diagrams of the Sefer Yetsirah*
by Marla Segol

*Rethinking Chaucerian Beasts*
edited by Carolynn Van Dyke

*The Genre of Medieval Patience Literature: Development, Duplication, and Gender*
by Robin Waugh

*The Carolingian Debate over Sacred Space*
by Samuel W. Collins

*The Disney Middle Ages: A Fairy-Tale and Fantasy Past*
edited by Tison Pugh and Susan Aronstein

*Medieval Afterlives in Popular Culture*
edited by Gail Ashton and Dan Kline

*Poet Heroines in Medieval French Narrative: Gender and Fictions of Literary Creation*
by Brooke Heidenreich Findley

*Sexuality, Sociality, and Cosmology in Medieval Literary Texts*
edited by Jennifer N. Brown and Marla Segol

*Music and Performance in the Later Middle Ages*
by Elizabeth Randell Upton

*Witnesses, Neighbors, and Community in Late Medieval Marseille*
by Susan Alice McDonough

*Women in Old Norse Literature: Bodies, Words, and Power*
by Jóhanna Katrín Friðriksdóttir

*Cosmopolitanism and the Middle Ages*
edited by John M. Ganim and Shayne Aaron Legassie

*Reading Skin in Medieval Literature and Culture*
edited by Katie L. Walter

*The Medieval Fold: Power, Repression, and the Emergence of the Individual in the Middle Ages*
by Suzanne Verderber

*Received Medievalisms: A Cognitive Geography of Viennese Women's Convents*
by Cynthia J. Cyrus

*The King's Bishops: The Politics of Patronage in England and Normandy, 1066–1216*
by Everett U. Crosby

*Perilous Passages:* The Book of Margery Kempe, *1534–1934*
by Julie A. Chappell

*Francis of Assisi and His "Canticle of Brother Sun" Reassessed*
by Brian Moloney

*The Footprints of Michael the Archangel: The Formation and Diffusion of a Saintly Cult, c. 300–c. 800*
by John Charles Arnold

*Saint Margaret, Queen of the Scots: A Life in Perspective*
by Catherine Keene

*Constructing Gender in Medieval Ireland*
edited by Sarah Sheehan and Ann Dooley

*Marking Maternity in Middle English Romance: Mothers, Identity, and Contamination*
by Angela Florschuetz

*The Medieval Motion Picture: The Politics of Adaptation*
edited by Andrew James Johnston, Margitta Rouse, and Philipp Hinz

*Wales and the Medieval Colonial Imagination: The Matters of Britain in the Twelfth Century*
by Michael A. Faletra

*Power and Sainthood: The Case of
Birgitta of Sweden*
    by Päivi Salmesvuori

*The Repentant Abelard: Family, Gender, and
Ethics in Peter Abelard's* Carmen ad
Astralabium *and* Planctus
    by Juanita Feros Ruys

*Teaching Medieval and Early Modern
Cross-Cultural Encounters*
    edited by Karina F. Attar and Lynn Shutters

*Religion, Power, and Resistance from the
Eleventh to the Sixteenth Centuries:
Playing the Heresy Card*
    edited by Karen Bollermann, Thomas
    M. Izbicki, and Cary J. Nederman

*Borges the Unacknowledged Medievalist: Old
English and Old Norse in His Life and Work*
    by M. J. Toswell

*Race, Caste, and Indigeneity in Medieval
Spanish Travel Literature*
    by Michael Harney

*The Gnostic Paradigm: Forms of Knowing in
English Literature of the Late Middle Ages*
    by Natanela Elias

*Jews and Christians in Thirteenth-Century France*
    edited by Elisheva Baumgarten and
    Judah D. Galinsky

*Consolation in Medieval Narrative: Augustinian
Authority and Open Form*
    by Chad D. Schrock

*Women, Enjoyment, and the Defense of
Virtue in Boccaccio's* Decameron
    by Valerio Ferme

*Medieval Ovid: Frame Narrative and
Political Allegory*
    by Amanda J. Gerber

*Games and Gaming in Medieval Literature*
    edited by Serina Patterson

*Reading Women in Late Medieval Europe:
Anne of Bohemia and Chaucer's Female
Audience*
    by Alfred Thomas

*Narratives of the Islamic Conquest from
Medieval Spain*
    by Geraldine Hazbun

*Chaucer the Alchemist: Physics, Mutability, and
the Medieval Imagination*
    by Alexander N. Gabrovsky

*Voice and Voicelessness in Medieval Europe*
    edited by Irit Ruth Kleiman

*Chaucer and the Death of the Political
Animal*
    by Jameson S. Workman

*Vision and Audience in Medieval Drama:
A Study of* The Castle of Perseverance
    by Andrea Louise Young

*The Circulation of Power in Medieval Biblical
Drama: Theaters of Authority*
    by Robert S. Sturges

*Joan de Valence: The Life and Influence of a
Thirteenth-Century Noblewoman*
    by Linda E. Mitchell

*Heloise and the Paraclete: A Twelfth-Century
Quest* (forthcoming)
    by Mary Martin McLaughlin

# THE DISNEY MIDDLE AGES

## A FAIRY-TALE AND FANTASY PAST

*Edited by*
*Tison Pugh and Susan Aronstein*

palgrave
macmillan

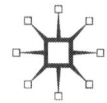

THE DISNEY MIDDLE AGES
Copyright © Tison Pugh and Susan Aronstein, 2012.
All rights reserved.

First published in hardcover in 2012 by PALGRAVE MACMILLAN® in the United States—a division of St. Martin's Press LLC, 175 Fifth Avenue, New York, NY 10010.

Where this book is distributed in the UK, Europe and the rest of the world, this is by Palgrave Macmillan, a division of Macmillan Publishers Limited, registered in England, company number 785998, of Houndmills, Basingstoke, Hampshire RG21 6XS.

Palgrave Macmillan is the global academic imprint of the above companies and has companies and representatives throughout the world.

Palgrave® and Macmillan® are registered trademarks in the United States, the United Kingdom, Europe and other countries.

ISBN: 978–1–137–55088–0

The Library of Congress has cataloged the hardcover edition as follows:

> The Disney Middle Ages : a fairy-tale and fantasy past /
> edited by Tison Pugh, Susan Aronstein.
>     p. cm.—(The New Middle Ages)
>   ISBN 978–0–230–34007–7 (hardback)
>   1. Walt Disney Productions. 2. Medievalism—Social aspects. 3. Middle Ages in motion pictures. 4. Fairy tales—Social aspects. 5. Medievalism—Political aspects. 6. Commercial products—Social aspects. 7. Medievalism in art. I. Pugh, Tison. II. Aronstein, Susan Lynn.

PN1999.W27D575 2012
384'.80979494—dc23                                             2012022503

A catalogue record of the book is available from the British Library.

Design by Newgen Knowledge Works (P) Ltd., Chennai, India.

First PALGRAVE MACMILLAN paperback edition: October 2015

10  9  8  7  6  5  4  3  2  1

# CONTENTS

*List of Figures*     xiii

*Acknowledgments and Note to Readers*     xv

1. Introduction: Disney's Retroprogressive Medievalisms: Where Yesterday Is Tomorrow Today     1
   *Tison Pugh*

## Part I  Building a Better Middle Ages: Medievalism in the Parks

2. Mapping the Happiest Place on Earth: Disney's Medieval Cartography     21
   *Stephen Yandell*

3. Disney's Castles and the Work of the Medieval in the Magic Kingdom     39
   *Martha Bayless*

4. Pilgrimage and Medieval Narrative Structures in Disney's Parks     57
   *Susan Aronstein*

## Part II  The Distorical Middle Ages

5. "You don't learn it deliberately, but you just know it from what you've seen": British Understandings of the Medieval Past Gleaned from Disney's Fairy Tales     77
   *Paul Sturtevant*

6. The Sorcerer's Apprentice: Animation and Alchemy in Disney's Medievalism     97
   *Erin Felicia Labbie*

7. *The Sword in the Stone*: American *Translatio* and
   Disney's Antimedievalism  115
   *Rob Gossedge*

8. Walt in Sherwood, or the Sheriff of Disneyland:
   Disney and the Film Legend of Robin Hood  133
   *Kevin J. Harty*

9. Futuristic Medievalisms and the U.S. Space Program in
   Disney's *Man in Space* Trilogy and *Unidentified Flying Oddball*  153
   *Amy Foster*

### Part III   Disney Princess Fantasy Faire

10. "Where happily ever after happens every day":
    The Medievalisms of Disney's Princesses  171
    *Clare Bradford*

11. Disney's Medievalized Ecologies in *Snow White and
    the Seven Dwarfs* and *Sleeping Beauty*  189
    *Kathleen Coyne Kelly*

12. The United Princesses of America: Ethnic Diversity
    and Cultural Purity in Disney's Medieval Past  209
    *Ilan Mitchell-Smith*

13. Esmeralda of Notre-Dame: The Gypsy in
    Medieval View from Hugo to Disney  225
    *Allison Craven*

14. Reality Remixed: Neomedieval Princess Culture
    in Disney's *Enchanted*  243
    *Maria Sachiko Cecire*

*A Select Filmography of Disney's Medievalisms*  261

*Select Bibliography*  263

*Biographical Notes on Contributors*  275

*Index*  277

# FIGURES

| | | |
|---|---|---|
| 2.1 | Standard T-O map schematic, c. 700 | 27 |
| 2.2 | Hereford mappamundi schematic, c. 1300 | 28 |
| 2.3 | Disneyland schematic with five original themed lands, c. 1955 | 30 |
| 3.1 | Neuschwanstein Castle | 41 |
| 6.1 | Mickey as the Sorcerer's Apprentice, magically relieving himself of undesired labor | 100 |
| 7.1 | Wart's magical "education" at the hands of the film's co-star, Merlin | 123 |
| 8.1 | Marian (Joan Rice) tends to the wounded Robin Hood (Richard Todd) | 135 |
| 8.2 | Disney's animated vulpine Robin Hood | 140 |
| 8.3 | Timothy Dalton as the Errol Flynn-like Hollywood heartthrob and Nazi agent | 145 |
| 8.4 | Keira Knightley as Robin Hood's daughter Gwen | 147 |
| 11.1 | The dwarfs' "medieval-Craftsman" cottage | 195 |
| 12.1 | Jasmine as Arabian princess | 214 |
| 13.1 | Quasi, Djali, and Esmeralda escape from Notre Dame | 235 |

# ACKNOWLEDGMENTS AND NOTE TO READERS

We gratefully acknowledge the support of our home institutions, the University of Central Florida, College of Arts and Humanities, and the University of Wyoming, College of Arts and Sciences. In addition, Alison Foster Rosenberger helped us immeasurably with the amazing depth of her Disney knowledge.

In adherence to the 1961 Report of the Register of Copyrights on the General Revision of the U.S. Copyright Law, quotations of primary texts, including films and film images, are made in accordance with the doctrine of fair use, which permits "quotation of excerpts in a review or criticism for the purposes of illustration or comment; quotation of short passages in a scholarly or technical work, for illustration or clarification of the author's observations."

To reduce the volume's documentary apparatus, all chapters cite films as listed in the filmography of Disney's works addressing medieval or quasi-medieval themes at the end of this volume.

CHAPTER 1

INTRODUCTION  DISNEY'S RETROPROGRESSIVE MEDIEVALISMS: WHERE YESTERDAY IS TOMORROW TODAY

*Tison Pugh*

Disneyland proclaims itself "the happiest place on earth," and cultural critics would do well to take this assertion seriously. Why else would millions of people visit its parks annually, not to mention the millions more who buy Disney merchandise, watch Disney films, visit Disney websites, and otherwise consume Disney products, if not to partake in some of this happiness, readily available at a price agreed upon by producer and consumer as reasonable? Success breeds suspicion, and many social theorists snipe at Disney's homogenized presentation of mainstream American (and unabashedly imperialistic) entertainment. Jean Baudrillard posits Disney as merely a simulacrum, as "a perfect model of all the entangled orders of simulation.... [I]t is a play of illusions and phantasms," and in a comparison offensive in its bathos, he likens Disney's expansive yet efficient parking lots to "veritable concentration camp[s]."[1] In his study of the mythic function of utopias, Louis Marin condemns Disneyland as a dystopia: "[Disneyland] alienates the visitor by a distorted and fantasmatic representation of daily life, by a fascinating image of the past and the future, of what is estranged and what is familiar."[2] One might well wonder when Baudrillard and Marin visited Disneyland, as most patrons appear to be enthusiastically enjoying themselves, rather than staving off the exploitative effects of anti-utopic alienation. Disney's empire, a conglomeration of exaggeration and fantasy, invites exaggerated attacks from its critics, who see dystopia and alienation where amusement bustles.

To argue that the Disney experience is pleasurable for the vast majority of its patrons, who would be unlikely to spend their hard-earned money on the dubious proposition of recreational pastimes coupled with alienation, is not to suggest that it should be exempt from critical inquiry, but to point out that the recreational desires of Disney's consumers are fulfilled through these commercial transactions. As Cheryl Mattingly affirms, "While the compelling power of Disney can legitimately be construed as a form of global domination, an emphasis on domination and on the consumer as unwitting victim underestimates the agency of the audience."[3] Even children, often presumed to be readily swayed by the Disney entertainment juggernaut, are capable of distinguishing between fantasy and reality. In an intriguing study, Alexander Bruce examines the influence of Disney's Princesses on elementary school girls and determines that even these young consumers filter out Disney's presentation of gender roles from their perceptions of themselves and their culture.[4] Whether a utopian playground or a dystopian snare, Disney—the theme parks, films, vacation cruises, and other components of the empire, as well as the man who created this entertainment conglomerate and whose name now emblematically represents its corporate interests—consistently satisfies their patrons' expectations by offering a fairy-tale fantasy of the past. "Once upon a time" and "they lived happily ever after" book-end nearly every aspect of the Disney experience, proving the protean adaptability of a fairy-tale and fantasy-land past to communicate in the present and into the future.

The essayists of *The Disney Middle Ages* explore Disney's mediation and re-creation of a fairy-tale and fantasy past, not to lament its exploitation of the Middle Ages for corporate ends, but to examine how and why these medieval visions prove so readily adaptable to themed entertainments many centuries after their creation. To study Disney's medievalisms is to confront the intertemporality of time, in which anachronism may be celebrated as a means of understanding the present rather than merely as a solecism detracting from historical "authenticity." In a world where yesterday is tomorrow today, where fantasies of the past serve as templates of possible futures at the present moment of consumer consumption, Disney's temporal play liberates its patrons from time's inexorable linearity into a world of eternal promise, no matter how coercively such delights are conceived. In this manner, Disney's historical play faces the same pitfalls and possibilities of other excurses into the past. Historiographers such as Michael Oakeshott argue that, when history is written, the creation of the present trumps disinterested assessments of the past and future: "Both future and past, then, emerge only in a reading of present; and a particular future or past is one eligible to be evoked from a particular present and is contingently related to the particular present from which it may be evoked."[5] Never an impartial endeavor, history is written to make meaning in the present, and as Hayden White observes, histories carry allegorized meanings within their narratives. He adumbrates the interpretive and ideological stakes in writing history: "Precisely insofar as the historical narrative endows sets of real events with the kinds of meaning found otherwise in myth and literature, we are justified in regarding it as a product of *allegoresis*."[6] Many of Disney's amusements play with the multitemporality of medievalism through a retroprogressive fantasy, in which the past allegorically yet elliptically makes possible illuminating lessons for today and hopeful visions for the future.

Disney frames its medieval histories with an overarching sense of play, and this narrative strategy obfuscates the serious purposes behind this play, for as numerous commentators note, Disney's fictions are often perceived as more real than the source texts or historical events they represent. Due both to this hyperreality of Disney texts and to their participation in an illusory yet sacrosanct vision of children's culture as perpetually innocent, many Disney fans adopt critical blinders when enjoying the corporation's entertainments. Elizabeth Bell, Lynda Haas, and Laura Sells catalog four primary rhetorical tropes used to exonerate Disney's media from their complicity in the ideological propagation of Western culture: "It's only for children, it's only fantasy, it's only a cartoon, and it's just good business," such voices declare, with these and other rationalizations exempting Disney from critical inquiry.[7] Disney claims for itself the realm of children's fantasy and cloaks itself within this mantle: as children's innocence is seen as a prized virtue within many discourses of Western thought, so too does Disney itself become camouflaged under a veneer of innocence, despite the commercial nature of its endeavors. Henry Giroux argues that history, innocence, and family merge in the Disney imaginary, thus rewriting history as the triumph of American middle-class values: "Disney's construction of historical memory, innocence, and family values points beyond the past while remaining firmly within it. Disney culture offers a certain notion of history that is not only safe and middle class but also indifferent to racial, class, and social conflict."[8] By combining history with innocence for the fun of the family, Disney's fanciful play with the past rewrites history for the sake of the child, yet the child is a construction of Disney discourse that reflects and refracts the corporate entity's complicity in the ideological projects at hand. This line of inquiry guides the chapters of *The Disney Middle Ages*, as the following excursus on Disney's pirates and their quasi-medievalism illustrates.

## Disney's Quasi-Medieval Pirates and Tropes of Innocence, Countercultural Conformity, and Animation

By decoding various incarnations and translations of pirates in sample moments of Disney's corpus, including the theme parks' Pirate and Princess Parties, the rides and films of Pirates of the Caribbean, and a World War II era cartoon short featuring Goofy, this introduction lays the theoretical groundwork for subsequent chapters by positing Disney's medievalisms as enabling retroprogressive and transtemporal transformations. It should be noted at the outset of this exploration into Disney's piracy trope and its historical vagaries that pirates, although active in the Middle Ages as they continue to be active today, are not an exclusively medieval phenomenon and do not serve as iconic representations of the Middle Ages in the same semiotic manner as, for example, Disney's castles and princesses. Angus Konstam documents that the earliest known pirates were the Lukkans, whom Egyptian scribes recorded as raiding Cyprus in the fourteenth-century BCE,[9] and the so-called "Golden Age of Piracy," the period of Henry Morgan, William "Captain" Kidd, and Bartholomew Roberts (a.k.a. "Black Bart"), among other notorious names, stretches between 1650 and 1730. In the Victorian and Edwardian eras, Robert Louis Stevenson, in *Treasure Island*, and J. M. Barrie, in *Peter and Wendy* (known simply as *Peter Pan* in the Disney imaginary), embellished portrayals of piracy in texts that have achieved canonical status in the field of children's literature. For Disney, however, the fuzzy temporal boundaries of piracy in suggesting a chronological period nonetheless become enmeshed with an iconic view of the Middle Ages as a time of romance, adventure, and chivalry for children, and the precise historical contours of the Middle Ages are thereby less relevant than the fantasy of piracy as a premodern phenomenon repeatedly re-created for the amusement of Disney's patrons. Disney and its media conglomerates posit not merely the emptiness of history as a critical term but the possibility of escaping the conditions of history—both past and present, as well as future—through the meta-construction of the Disneyfied subject, who transcends history, if not Disney.

For Disney's patrons, the "happily ever after" ending defines the Disney experience to the extent of corrupting all other markers of time. This trope of "happily ever after" is a temporal fantasy—a string of adverbs promising pleasure reaching into an endless future. For Disney's pirates, as for so many aspects of Disney entertainment, history is always already reconceived within a fairy-tale world of a chimerical and plastic medieval past. In many regards, Disney's medievalism simply adheres to the tropes of fairy tales, but even the medievalism of fairy tales is suspect because the timelessness of these narratives evinces a desire for a prehistory, one prior to the historical moment of their recording by such folklorists as Charles Perrault (1628–1703) and Jacob and Wilhelm Grimm (1785–1863 and 1786–1859). Fairy tales look to a simpler and "medieval-ish" past to create a time of romance, adventure, and magic, and Disney's genius was to couple this nostalgia with a liberal dose of futurism, blending the two diametrically opposed temporalities into a seamless whole. Disney's pirates wander in and out of the temporality of the Middle Ages yet remain persistently recognizable as countercultural Others, and so too do fairy-tale princesses, in a complementary manner, inhabit a vaguely realized medieval world of desire reflective of narrative and ideological continuity between yesteryear and tomorrow: someday, that prince will come. Much of Disney's play with the past, even in narratives dated before or after the Middle Ages, can be productively investigated as exemplars of Disney's medieval, or quasi-medieval, sensibility, an inherently flexible reinterpretation of history guided not by dates and facts but by an asynchronous nostalgia for fairy tales and fantasies set in the past, while inspired by an American view of the future.

This intertemporality of Disney's medievalisms invites park patrons to play with their identities as refabricated under a rubric of children's innocence. Indeed, transformations of identity are key to the Disney experience, as tourists in the theme parks are encouraged to perform personas consistent with Disney values. By donning a pair of mouse ears when passing through the gates, consumers proclaim allegiance to a Disneyfied identity, one honoring the promise of perpetual childhood. Tourists wearing mouse ears and other such accoutrements demonstrate their willingness to perform Disney identities in the present moment of their vacation, and in Disney's Pirate and Princess Parties, children transform themselves into avatars of scurrilous masculinity and befrilled femininity in a present rewritten as a quasi-medieval past. "Become a Pirate and Princess in the place where Dreams come true," the advertisements proclaim; these events urge children to "embark on your quest through the Magic Kingdom Park," and thus to assume the role of an adventurer exploring the tame Disney environs as if setting forth on an epic or Arthurian journey.[10] Stuart Hall argues that identities must be examined in context of the discourses in which they are created, that "identities are constructed within, not outside, discourse," and that "they emerge within the play of specific modalities of power,"[11] and such is the power of Disney discourse to define two—and, in this instance, only two—enactments of identity for young children. The personas of both pirate and princess are rendered innocent through their rebranding as children's play, with the soft femininity of princesses tempering the untamed masculinity of pirates, yet these roles rigorously demarcate modern gender roles through a fantasy of an eternally premodern present.

In remarketing piracy as a virtue of children's innocence rather than a countercultural vice of adult evil, Disney proves the power of its construction of children's innocence as its defining corporate tactic. To accomplish many of its financial objectives, Disney needs children: its marketing efforts speak to the child, and also to parents and grandparents seeking to create lasting memories for their offspring. But Disney must create the children it needs, and so the corporate entity fosters a vision of the innocent child that dovetails with its marketing and media objectives. As Jacqueline Rose points out, the concept of the innocent child is a cultural fabrication designed to preserve ideological fantasies of adult sexuality:

> Freud is known to have undermined the concept of childhood innocence, but his real challenge is easily lost if we see in the child merely a miniature version of what our sexuality eventually comes to be. The child is sexual, but its sexuality (bisexual, polymorphous, perverse) threatens our own at its very roots. Setting up the child as innocent is not, therefore, repressing its sexuality—it is above all holding off any possible challenge to our own.[12]

To argue that Disney's Pirate and Princess Parties are implicated within regimes of adult sexuality may appear to exaggerate the meaning of this play, but such sexuality is merely repressed as children are introduced into gender roles of masculine pirates and feminine princesses. It is, of course, parents who provide the economic means for children to join this quasi-medieval play of pirates and princesses, and in the continual return to the fantasy of a medieval land of fairy tales and piracy, adults sate their own nostalgic desires to relive childhood through their children. The intertemporality conducive to the play of young and innocent pirates and princesses is designed for children, yet serves adult needs to conquer time's inexorable march, if only momentarily.

Disney's play with identities of innocence may perpetuate traditional archetypes of gender, yet it does so while relying on the possibility of quarantining the meaning of such archetypes through their deployment as play. Even very young children realize that they cannot grow up to be pirates and princesses—that they cannot grow into adulthood while simultaneously returning to a quasi-medieval past—and in this manner Disney's play with history unites with its play with identity: the transformations of identity performed by young pirates and princesses occur within the present reconceived as the past, and can thus ostensibly be contained within that past. Disney's Pirate and Princess Parties have been on hiatus for several years, yet various other opportunities for children to play with their identities remain, such as the Bibbidi Bobbidi Boutique, which, in addition to princess makeovers for young girls, also offers "The Knight Package" for young boys, which, as the website proclaims, "includes hair styling as well as a mighty sword and shield."[13] Not coincidentally, if ultimately unsuccessfully, the theme parks' Pirate and Princess Parties made possible the reenactment of Disney's blockbuster narrative of pirates and princesses: the film franchise of *Pirates of the Caribbean*, the first episode of which concludes with young blacksmith Will Turner (Orlando Bloom) winning the hand of his fair lady Elizabeth Swann (Keira Knightley) because he has successfully performed the role of a pirate.[14] As for Elizabeth, surely, the distinction between a governor's daughter in a Caribbean paradise and a princess is slight, and the most critical of their shared features is their success in achieving "happily ever after" endings, which conclude in the eternal innocence of a romance as yet unconsummated.

Here too arise the quasi-medieval qualities of Disney's narratives set in the past, as describing the piracy of Pirates of the Caribbean (both the theme-park ride and the film) as endeavors in medievalism should be grossly anachronistic yet proves more useful in assessing their historical themes than pinpointing precise historical dates. As is well known, the Caribbean was discovered by Western explorers beginning with Christopher Columbus in 1492, long after the European Renaissance was well under way. Disney's Caribbean pirates are nonetheless freed from any historical specificity by the unvanquishable allure of a premodern sensibility that celebrates and reformulates the genres of medieval romance and fairy tale into postmedieval narratives. As Erin Mackie suggests of the liminality of piracy, "Like the pirates themselves, the trope of piracy has always been highly mobile, a marker of the very instabilities of those lines that define social and ethical standards";[15] pirates also destabilize temporality by signifying an ill-defined and quasi-medieval era of adventure prior to the present yet without the moorings of a precise historical date. With regard to the temporal setting of *Pirates of the Caribbean*, the film mentions a few historical details that date its narrative action to the postmedieval period, including references to the pirates Morgan and Bartholomew and to Hernando Cortez's exploits among the Aztecs. These real-life tidbits do not establish a historical milieu for the film; rather, they imbue it with a sense of nostalgia for a time prior to modernity that allows for piracy to serve as a trope of masculinity as yet untamed by civilization.

The quasi-medievalism of *Pirates of the Caribbean* is most evident in the film's fantasy and romance plotline, one that couples identities of innocence with a thematic rebranding of the countercultural ethos of piracy as morally praiseworthy. Screenwriters Terry Rossio and Ted Elliott, whose interest in fairy-tale themed films is evident in works such as Disney's *Aladdin* and DreamWorks's *Shrek*, describe their film as a "swashbuckling Gothic romance";[16] one could therefore see hints of a doubly refracted medievalism in the film's rewriting of gothic novels' reconstruction of medieval horrors, but the film's medieval roots ironically become more apparent in Elliott's misplacement of his story within the realm of the Romantic era and the countercultural influence of George Gordon, Lord Byron. In discussing his heroine and her romantic interest, Elliott discerns a plotline that is decidedly postmedieval: "Elizabeth is the protagonist, representing the idea of the romance of the pirate. The romantic illusion of the outlaw is a very common concept in our society; in fact, the underpinning of all romances is the anti-hero, the Byronic bad boy. That's what Elizabeth is looking for."[17] Elizabeth, the innocent and virtuous protagonist, is looking for love in this quest romance, but surprisingly, Elliott's assessment of his film's generic roots is mostly incorrect because Captain Jack Sparrow (Johnny Depp), who might be construed as the film's "Byronic bad boy," is not Elizabeth's love interest. He is indeed a pirate, yet his transgressions are subordinated to the plot's overarching focus on the quest for love, as Sparrow makes explicit when he rejects the search-and-rescue of romance, telling the young hero Will Turner: "I see. Well, if you're intending to brave all, hasten to her rescue, and so win the fair lady's heart, you'll have to do it alone, mate. I see no profit in it for me." This rejection of romance ironically promises the audience that the film is indeed a romance, and Will Turner, the humble but devoted blacksmith, metamorphoses into Elizabeth's "knight in shining armor" as the plot unfolds.

Quite simply, a "Byronic bad boy" is an unsuitable protagonist for a Disney film requiring a morally unambiguous hero. As Martha Driver and Sid Ray posit, "The Middle Ages has always been a 'site of heroic fantasy,' producing a wide range of heroic character types who quest and battle for various causes,"[18] and certainly, in terms of the film's play with the romance tradition, Will Turner's character, a blacksmith-*cum*-pirate, testifies to the ready adaptability of medieval heroisms for subsequent temporal periods. The Renaissance and the eighteenth century, for example, are not "sites of heroic fantasy" in the same manner as the Middle Ages, and so even narratives such as *Pirates of the Caribbean*, which are set in times subsequent to the Middle Ages, can productively be considered for their exploitation of medievalisms to generate the heroism necessary for their storylines. For, as Rossio further explains, the overarching genre of *Pirates of the Caribbean* is not Byronic romance but fantasy: "Now this may be a 'pirate movie,' but what the audience is going to respond to is the fact that they get to go into this fantasy world.... I think it would have been very dangerous to try to make just a 'straight' pirate movie."[19] *Pirates of the Caribbean* elaborates on the promise of a "straight" pirate movie by merging romance heroism with a medieval fantasy of chivalric love for its protagonists, yet one stripped of any moral ambiguity that might undermine its overarching air of innocence.

For a Disney romance to blossom, the film must redeem piracy as a virtue, thereby realigning a countercultural and villainous lifestyle as morally sound. Elizabeth's father, Governor Swann (Jonathan Pryce), muses on the moral valence of piracy at the film's conclusion: "Perhaps on the rare occasion [when] pursuing the right course demands an act of piracy, piracy itself can be the right course?" Elizabeth earlier declared, in a scene depicting her as an innocent young girl, "I think it'd be rather interesting to meet a pirate," and her innocent childhood desire finds its fulfillment in Will Turner. Despite her father's disappointment in her amatory interest—"After all," he sniffs, "he is a blacksmith"—she asserts her lover's new identity: "No, he's a pirate." Jack Sparrow's brand of self-serving piracy is eclipsed by Will's assumption of a pirate persona for the sake of true love, not plunder, and Will now proves himself a man through his adventuring. Jack Sparrow earlier wondered of him, "You're not a eunuch, are you?" to which Will asserted his nascent manhood: "I practice [sword fighting] three hours a day, so that when I meet a pirate, I can kill it." In transforming from craftsman to pirate, Will enacts the metamorphosis of identity made possible throughout the Disney experience: the ability to shift into quasi-medieval and fairy-tale identities of the premodern that bolsters one's performance of normative gender roles in the present. Into this film's patchwork of genres—quest romance, ghost story, and swashbuckler—must be added the Horatio Alger rags-to-riches story of the American striver who succeeds through his honesty and pluck, a theme alien to medieval romance but relatively common in Hollywood's re-creations of the Middle Ages, as in *First Knight* (1995) and *A Knight's Tale* (2001). In these instances, medieval and quasi-medieval themes are subsumed by the tropes of the rags-to-riches story, proving the inconsequentiality of temporality to Disney narratives. It is equally ridiculous yet equally accurate to assess Will's narrative trajectory as that of a medieval American, yet both descriptors fit him better than the temporally correct assessment of the character as a British subject of the seventeenth century.

In contrast to Elizabeth and Will's converging storyline of fairy-tale fantasy and romance runs that of Captain Jack Sparrow, and here viewers witness Disney's frequent theme of the successful reintegration of countercultural elements into the dominant society. Depp queerly inflects the pirate tradition in his performance, making manifest the homosociality and latent homosexuality percolating beneath the surface of pirate life, and Jennifer Geer describes Depp's Sparrow as "ambiguously gendered" such that he registers as a "fine example of an unmarked transvestite."[20] Despite Depp's provocative portrayal, Sparrow serves no purpose at the film's end other than to enable Will and Elizabeth's romance: he may be the film's most scintillating character, yet he is oddly peripheral to its deeper focus on heterosexual romance. Like piracy itself, Sparrow's countercultural disruptions to gendered and ideological normativity are easily subsumed under the film's celebration of heterosexual romance and Anglo-Caribbean (*qua* proto-American) community. Both the past and piracy allow a uniquely American vision to emerge triumphantly, if improbably, at the film's conclusion.

But why does Disney consistently return to the piracy trope? In the creation of Disney as the utopian fulfillment of wholesome American values of family, community, and patriotism, the social function of pirates within its empire appears counterintuitive to its overarching ethos. Nonetheless, by reinventing and reinterpreting reality, including unpleasant aspects of reality, Disney can re-signify virtually any countercultural element into its utopian vision. In *Walt Disney World: The First Decade*, an in-house account of the park's history, an unidentified designer outlines the ways in which Disney hones "reality" with a utopian edge:

> This brand of "spruced-up" reality is integral to the Disney Theme Shows. As a key designer said, "The environments we create are more utopian, more romanticized, more like the guests imagined they would be. For the most part, negative elements are discreetly eliminated, while positive aspects are in some cases embellished to tell the story more clearly."[21]

Although a utopia might appear more likely to necessitate the absence of pirates than their presence, many countercultural transgressions can be recoded within the Disney imaginary to conform to traditional American values. As Depp's performance makes manifest, pirates typically signify unlawfulness, drunkenness, plundering, murder, and, quite often, homosexuality, but they can nonetheless be scrubbed to fit into a Disney utopian vision. *Walt Disney World: The First Decade* awkwardly connects its paean to utopias with Pirates of the Caribbean, its boat ride through an animatronic buccaneers' bacchanalia:

> Pirates of the Caribbean, located in Adventureland's Caribbean Plaza, clearly embodies this utopian spirit. The storyline portrays a disaster—the

capture, pillaging, and ultimate burning of a seacoast town by a crew of swashbucklers who would shiver the timbers of Blackbeard. Yet scurrilous as they are, there is something loveable about these rapscallion rogues. And while their captives may fret a little, they seem to be having as much fun as the buccaneers.[22]

Another in-house Disney publication, Jason Surrell's *Pirates of the Caribbean: From the Magic Kingdom to the Movies*, agrees that the countercultural dangers of piracy, within the Disney worldview, simply connote innocence: "Imagineers turned their band of bloodthirsty brigands into more family-friendly rapscallions just out to have a little innocent fun."[23]

If pillaging and plundering can be construed as appropriate pastimes within a utopia of play and innocence, the limits of Disney's ability to resymbolize a countercultural ethos appear virtually endless. The narrative arc of Pirates of the Caribbean casts the pirates as criminals, yet they are redeemed through the animatronic and animated play of the past, and Disney's perspective on the potentially troublesome aspects of the ride as the shenanigans of "loveable rapscallions" merges with the presentation of the ride as innocent play for children. As Stephen Fjellman observes of Pirates of the Caribbean, "This softening of the message is also effected by the musical theme—'Yo ho, yo ho, a pirate's life for me'—in which pirates are equated with children just having fun."[24] In this regard, the "utopia" of piracy is constructed as a children's fantasy and a moral fable as well, as Tony Baxter, lead creative designer for Pirates of the Caribbean at Disneyland Paris, suggests: "That's the moral of the story.... The end result, the whole 'Crime Doesn't Pay' moment, takes place at the end."[25] Marin likewise observes that the moral lesson of Pirates of the Caribbean inhibits transgressive readings of the pirates: "The morality of the fable [Pirates of the Caribbean] is presented before the reading of the story in order to constrain the comprehension of the fable by a preexisting moral code. The potential force of the narrative, its unpredictability, is neutralized by the moral code that makes up all of the representation."[26] In this manner, pirates are re-signified into conformity with American apple-pie values: the morality encoded in the parks subsumes transgressive elements into its ethos of play.

As the film and theme-park versions of *Pirates of the Caribbean* indicate, the quasi-medieval "history" of piracy can be rewritten as an exemplum within the Disney imaginary, and these strategies intersect with the many ways in which Disney animates its narratives. Disney animates fairy tales in the literal sense of the verb, in the many cartoon-short and feature-length films of these narratives, but history in all of its incarnations is ready for Disney animation in a more fluid sense, of rewriting history so that it comes alive in telling an untrue tale that nonetheless speaks Disney truth. Fjellman refers to Disney's forays into historical narratives as "Distory," the purpose of which is to "tap into people's nostalgic need for a false history—for the reasonably benign makings of a community of memory."[27] When viewing Disney's animated versions of history, or most mainstream Hollywood films set in the past, one would be rather foolish to expect historical verisimilitude. Disney's reconstruction of history cloaks its ideological goals under the guise of children's entertainment, but children's entertainment also functions as a disciplinary apparatus of ideology: teaching children reinforces for adults (in their roles as parents and teachers) the governing precepts of their culture.

The power of Disney's animation to encode ideological agendas is evident in the cartoon "How to Be a Sailor," which features Goofy in a slapdash history of the world from a nautical perspective. The cartoon contains scenes set in the Middle Ages for the iconic signification of a romanticized, rather than a historical, past of piracy, but its true focus is on the present and into the future. This animated short, produced in 1943 as part of Disney's World War II propaganda, uses medieval "history" to tell a story of American exceptionalism and eventual triumph. Implicitly comparing the past to the present, the narrator denigrates the Middle Ages for its scientific failings: "In the thirteenth century, even as today, great thinkers worried about what shape the world was in. Some great minds firmly believed that if you sailed west far enough, you would sail off the edge of the world."[28] Even the slightest inquiry into medieval science and technology reveals that this assertion of historical "fact" is stereotypical rubbish deriding the intelligence of medieval thinkers: Greeks such as Posidonius, Ptolemy, and Erasthosthenes theorized Earth's circumference with impressive accuracy hundreds of years prior to the Middle Ages, and, as Evelyn Edson asserts, "nearly all medieval scholars conceived of the earth as a globe."[29] The cartoon's placement in the thirteenth century speaks to a desire to give piracy a medieval setting despite the implausibility of its historical moment, which more concerns a linear narrative of American scientific progress and military might: the Middle Ages are a necessary stepping stone in this story of American exceptionalism. To demonstrate this passage from ignorance to America, "How to Be a Sailor" begins with the prehistoric era, proceeds to an "ancient mariner" in Viking helmet and shield, and then illustrates a thirteenth-century Goofy garbed in Tudor dress. From these beginnings, the narrative reaches its climax in American military might of the mid-twentieth century and anticipates a future in which its power is unrivaled, with kid-friendly lessons on sailing topics such as semaphore code, hornpipe dancing, clipper ships, and knot tying addressed along the way.

Animated history is more concerned with ambiance than accuracy, and rightly so, for who would expect a Disney cartoon to privilege education over entertainment, history over propaganda? Within Disney's modern Middle Ages, virtually any aspect of a historical narrative can be colored as fantasy, as a world of enchantment and narrative seduction no matter the content of the tale. And so when Goofy faces mutiny and execution from his fellow sailors/pirates, the narrator's words portray the Middle Ages as inescapably romantic, no matter the humorous horror of the events unfolding: "From the earliest days, sailors were preyed upon by ... PIRATES! In those romantic days, ships often changed captains very suddenly. This colorful ceremony was called 'walking the plank' or 'feeding the sharks.'" As a pirate pushes the plank out, Goofy walks to his implied death, participating in a "colorful ceremony" of murder that has been animated and sanitized for children. Cartoon violence does not catalyze the same emotional reaction as actual violence, but the cartoon ends with a depiction of desired violence to resolve the contemporary challenges of World War II: in clothing of red, white, and blue, Goofy transforms into a torpedo and sinks the Japanese navy—whose boats are anthropomorphized with racially caricatured faces—as he speeds across the ocean into a setting sun. In "How to Be a Sailor," the threat of piracy, quarantined in the medieval past, makes possible a vision of a patriotic utopia in which the United States of America reigns unchallenged while its enemies lie humbled in defeat: so many centuries after the Middle Ages, the high seas are safe at last.

Such is the allure of piracy and retroprogressive medievalism, in that the past is often safe and sanitized, and if, in contrast, it appears barbaric and crude, it can be quarantined in the past to promote modernity as the ideal temporality of Disney's present. The contradictory impulses of Disney's play with temporality, in its harkening back to the Fantasyland of yesterday and reaching forward to the Tomorrowland of the future, shatter time's linearity. The retroprogressive impulse alternates between the poles of yesterday and the future, yet these ostensibly distinct temporalities collapse in the celebration of Disney and American values. If pirates can be re-signified into avatars of Disney ideology, stripped of any specific historical milieu and cleansed of their countercultural deviancy, and then repackaged and animated into innocent fare for children, so too can various other examples of Disney's media, as the following chapters investigate.

### The Disney Middle Ages

*The Disney Middle Ages* continues exploring retroprogressive medievalisms in the chapters of Part I, "Building a Better Middle Ages: Medievalism in the Parks," which considers the ways in which the Walt Disney Company creates experiential medievalisms for its patrons. Stephen Yandell, in "Mapping the Happiest Place on Earth: Disney's Medieval Cartography," ponders the historical development of theme-park maps. In creating this new genre, Disney's cartographers played with many tropes of medieval maps, including illuminated borders, ornamental compasses, and marginalia. In mapping the parks, Disney is less concerned with geographical reality than with the hyperreal creation of the park experience, which correlates with medieval cartographers' vision of charting the world as primarily an allegorical rather than a geographical undertaking. In "Disney's Castles and the Work of the Medieval in the Magic Kingdom," Martha Bayless examines the temporal play catalyzed by Disney's iconic castles, the dominant architectural feature of their landscapes. Bayless demonstrates how these castles are imagined as geographies of interior transformations, where one may access fantasies of the past to experience an apotheosis in the present. Susan Aronstein concludes this unit with "Pilgrimage and Medieval Narrative Structures in Disney's Parks," in which she theorizes the ways in which Disney creates an experiential narrative of pilgrimage and discovery throughout its theme parks. As sites of cultural pilgrimage, the Disney Parks rely on narrative structures and storytelling techniques to reinforce the cultural status of their multiple plots. Iconography plays a central role in this process, for by reading touchstone moments from Disney narratives, modern-day "pilgrims" decipher the meaning of these texts, thus solidifying their role in the creation of cultural meaning.

Disney's play with history constructs a sanitized vision of the Middle Ages for countless consumers, and the meanings of this continually recreated Middle Ages are the subject of the following unit, "The Distorical Middle Ages." In his "'You don't learn it deliberately, but you just know it from what you've seen': British Understandings of the Medieval Past Gleaned from Disney's Fairy Tales," Paul Sturtevant shares the results of a series of focus-group interviews investigating the ways in which Disney shapes real-world views of the Middle Ages. Disney's medievalisms are particularly relevant in how they influence conceptions of social, gender, and racial stereotypes, despite their films' recent forays into more egalitarian depictions of women and nonwhite races. In "The Sorcerer's Apprentice: Animation and Alchemy in Disney's Medievalism," Erin Felicia Labbie explores the interconnections of alchemy and animation in the medieval and the Disney imaginary. "The Sorcerer's Apprentice," a segment of Disney's *Fantasia*, portrays acts of creation in the present as dependent on revisions of the past, and this tension captures the ways in which animation itself is conceived of as a magical, yet historically simple, technology bridging yesterday and tomorrow. Rob Gossedge, in his chapter "*The Sword in the Stone*: American *Translatio* and Disney's AntiMedievalism," discusses Disney's revisions to T. H. White's *Once and Future King*. White's Arthurian legend, influenced by his perceptions of childhood and of World War II, becomes sanitized in Disney's retelling, employing the medieval for reductive moral lessons. In this manner, the quintessentially British legend in its many incarnations, including the versions of Geoffrey of Monmouth, Thomas Malory, Alfred, Lord Tennyson, and White, is rewritten as a story of and for Americans. Kevin J. Harty examines Disney's multiple retellings of the Robin Hood legend in "Walt in Sherwood, or the Sheriff of Disneyland: Disney and the Film Legend of Robin Hood." Robin Hood is a countercultural figure, one who resists the tyranny of an unjust monarchy, yet he is tamed in Disney's versions of the legend. As Harty argues, Disney's revisionings offer insight into the historical circumstances of these film's productions, from the anti-communist scares of the 1950s to the changing gendered mores of the late twentieth century. In "Futuristic Medievalisms and the U.S. Space Program in Disney's *Man in Space* Trilogy and *Unidentified Flying Oddball*," Amy Foster examines the multitemporality of Disney's 1979 cinematic tribute both to Mark Twain's 1889 novel *A Connecticut Yankee in King Arthur's Court* and to the U. S. Space Program. Walt Disney avidly supported American ambitions in space, most notably in his *Man in Space* series of the 1950s, and *Unidentified Flying Oddball* depicts a medieval past in need of the technological advances of the future to realize its potential.

The concluding chapters of *The Disney Middle Ages*, collected under the heading "Disney Princess Fantasy Faire," examine the archetypal role of princesses and gender construction in Disney's corpus. "Medieval" princesses flourish in contemporary society due to the iconic position of Disney's Princesses—Snow White, Cinderella, Aurora/Sleeping Beauty, Ariel, Belle, Jasmine, Pocahontas, Mulan, Tiana, and Rapunzel—and Clare Bradford, in her "'Where happily ever after happens every day': The Medievalisms of Disney's Princesses," traces the erratic arc of feminine agency within the Disney canon. Children's entertainment since the 1960s has increasingly focused on dismantling gendered binaries of male and female, yet, as Bradford argues, Disney's Princesses cannot claim such a progressive trajectory. Kathleen Coyne Kelly, in "Medievalized Ecologies in *Snow White and the Seven Dwarfs* and *Sleeping Beauty*," examines Disney's construction of fairy-tale ecologies in light of conservation movements of the 1930s, 1940s, and 1950s, exploring the ways that Disney's ecologies coincided with and created American views of nature. In "The United Princesses of America: Ethnic Diversity and Cultural Purity in Disney's Medieval Past," Ilan Mitchell-Smith discusses the intersections of gender and ethnicity in Disney's reconstruction of the

Middle Ages, analyzing the ways in which Disney Princesses represent a premodern world in need of an infusion of modern American values. Rather than a celebration of cultural diversity, these films assimilate ethnic difference into a unified vision of a proto-American community. Allison Craven, in "Esmerelda of Notre-Dame: The Gypsy in Medieval View from Hugo to Disney," traces this character's depictions in key retellings of *The Hunchback of Notre Dame*, noting the transformations in her gendered identity as well as the ways in which her Disney depiction marks a shift in animated technologies. The final chapter of *The Disney Middle Ages*, Maria Sachiko Cecire's "Reality Remixed: Neomedieval Princess Culture in Disney's *Enchanted*," analyzes the creation of a fairy-tale medieval past in Disney's mixed live-action and animated film *Enchanted*. The film's tagline—"the real world and the animated world collide"—showcases its investment in merging positionalities of real and fictional, of humans and animated beings, to create a commercially viable Middle Ages for the consumption of patrons in the present.

Timelessness in time: such is the allure and the paradox of Disney's medievalisms. The Middle Ages provides proof of American technological superiority, as this past also establishes a benchmark of fairy-tale fantasy against which one can measure modernity's dehumanizing impulses. Endlessly protean and endlessly malleable, medieval and quasi-medieval temporalities serve as the preeminent chronological period for creating cultural fantasies of yesterday for consumer consumption today. The appeal of the "Dark Ages" reveals the contradictions inherent in modernity, as the medieval simultaneously becomes a marker of how far we have progressed and of all that we have lost. In bottling this nostalgia, the Disney empire creates cultural artifacts that overlook the tensions inherent in retroprogressive agendas, yet such contradictions can only be contained, never quelled, as Disney's pirates, princesses, and other avatars of innocence make manifest through their play in the Disney present.

### Notes

1. Jean Baudrillard, *Simulations*, trans. Paul Foss, et al. (New York: Semiotext[e], 1983), 23–24.
2. Louis Marin, *Utopics: Spacial Play*, trans. Robert Volrath (Atlantic Highlands, NJ: Humanities, 1984), 240.
3. Cheryl Mattingly, "Becoming Buzz Lightyear and Other Clinical Tales," *Folk* 45 (2004): 9–32, at 9.
4. Alexander Bruce, "Princesses without a Prince: A Consideration of Girls' Reactions to Disney's 'Princess' Movies," *Children's Folklore Review* 28 (2005): 7–21, at 15.

5. Michael Oakeshott, *On History and Other Essays* (Oxford: Blackwell, 1985), 8.
6. Hayden White, *The Content of the Form* (Baltimore: Johns Hopkins University Press, 1987), 45.
7. Elizabeth Bell, Lynda Haas, and Laura Sells, ed., *From Mouse to Mermaid: The Politics of Film, Gender, and Culture* (Bloomington: Indiana University Press, 1995), 4.
8. Henry Giroux, *The Mouse That Roared: Disney and the End of Innocence* (Lanham: Rowman & Littlefield, 1999), 148.
9. Angus Konstam, *Piracy: The Complete History* (Oxford: Osprey, 2008),10.
10. "Disney World: Disney's Pirate and Princess Party 2010," explorethemagic.com; Web, accessed August 8, 2011.
11. Stuart Hall, "Who Needs Identity?" *Identity*, ed. Paul du Gay, Jessica Evans, and Peter Redman (London: Sage, 2000), 15–30, at 17.
12. Jacqueline Rose, "The Case of Peter Pan," *The Children's Culture Reader*, ed. Henry Jenkins (New York: New York University Press, 1998), 58–66, at 60.
13. "Bibbidi Bobbidi Boutique," disneyworld.disney.go.com; Web, accessed February 28, 2012.
14. To distinguish between the theme-park ride and the film versions of Pirates of the Caribbean, I use italics for the latter. The film pays homage to its theme-park roots in numerous scenes (e.g., pirates enticing a dog holding the key of their prison cell over to free them, a buccaneer lasciviously chasing a woman). Also, the musical motif of "Yo Ho (A Pirate's Life for Me)," originally penned for the theme-park ride, is employed often in the film.
15. Erin Mackie, "Welcome the Outlaw: Pirates, Maroons, and Caribbean Countercultures," *Cultural Critique* 59 (2005): 24–62, at 29.
16. Den Shewman, "Pirates of the New Sensibilities: Terry Rossio and Ted Elliott," *Creative Screenwriting* 10.4 (2003): 48–52, at 49.
17. Den Shewman, "Pirates of the New Sensibilities," 51.
18. Martha Driver and Sid Ray, "Preface: Hollywood Knights," *The Medieval Hero on Screen*, ed. Martha Driver and Sid Ray (Jefferson, NC: McFarland, 2004), 5–17, at 5.
19. Terry Rossio, qtd. in Jason Surrell, *Pirates of the Caribbean: From the Magic Kingdom to the Movies* (New York: Disney Editions, 2005), 119.
20. Jennifer Geer, "J. M. Barrie Gets the Miramax Treatment," *Children's Literature Association Quarterly* 32.3 (2007): 192–212, at 210.
21. *Walt Disney World: The First Decade* (Walt Disney Productions, 1982), 48.
22. *Walt Disney World: The First Decade*, 50.
23. Jason Surrell, *Pirates of the Caribbean*, 33.
24. Stephen Fjellman, *Vinyl Leaves: Walt Disney World and America* (Boulder: Westview, 1992), 228.
25. Jason Surrell, *Pirates of the Caribbean*, 65.

26. Louis Marin, *Utopics*, 254.
27. Stephen Fjellman, *Vinyl Leaves*, 60.
28. "How to Be a Sailor," dir. Jack Kinney, *Walt Disney on the Front Lines*, DVD (1944; Walt Disney Treasures, 2004).
29. Evelyn Edson, *Mapping Time and Space* (London: British Library, 1997), 3–4.

PART I

BUILDING A BETTER MIDDLE AGES:
MEDIEVALISM IN THE PARKS

CHAPTER 2

MAPPING THE HAPPIEST PLACE ON EARTH: DISNEY'S MEDIEVAL CARTOGRAPHY

*Stephen Yandell*

Can you ever really be lost in Disneyland? After all, the park offers an ordered, safe model of the world. Admittedly, opening day in 1955 found guests disoriented in a variety of ways,[1] but Disneyland has since generated phenomenal success by prioritizing guests' feelings of comfort and familiarity. Walt Disney championed these priorities at every stage of the park's development: Main Street USA, he insisted, would provide an ideal welcome by offering guests aspects of their childhood,[2] and an easy-to-reach central hub would offer a constant "sense of orientation."[3] Today, even the most unprepared guests navigate the park easily because of these features, while taking advantage of clear signage, an army of cast members, and an endless supply of brochure maps.

However, as any of the thousands who have been escorted to Disneyland's "Lost Children" station also know, getting lost on the eighty-five acre property is absolutely possible. Children lag behind in shops, and adults get separated by parade routes. The mere act of allowing people inside the gates, in fact, compromises Disneyland's perfection—and in this lies a crucial incongruity. The park's success depends largely on its appeal to the public's deep desire to feel safe, sound, and found, and yet the same success also generates crowded conditions in which people young and old find themselves lost.

Further complicating a visitor's conflicted status is the work of the Imagineers. While much of the park's immersion depends on nostalgia, some of the themed lands and attractions are designed to get one lost; being in unfamiliar, harrowing situations is part of the fun. Guests can take a Jungle Cruise in dangerous waters and zoom down a mountain on the Matterhorn Bobsled, all with the assurance that no one is at any real risk of being hurt—or lost. Guests surrender themselves to the pleasurable state of being safely lost, a balance that is carefully maintained, Imagineer Eddie Sotto explains, by the park's adherence to a key formula: "fear minus death equals fun."[4]

Guests being simultaneously lost and found is central to the work of Disney parks across the world, and as modern, or postmodern, as such a project may seem, it finds a strikingly clear analog in the Middle Ages. Specifically, this lost–found status undergirds the design of two major genres of maps: poster-sized maps of Disneyland sold as souvenirs from 1958 onward, and medieval maps produced between roughly the eighth and fifteenth centuries known as *mappaemundi* (maps of the world). Both genres invite viewers to contemplate the world more deeply, along with humanity's place in it. They both pose a world in its entirety, offering a view that is more complete than anything available at ground level.

Perhaps the two best representations of these genres are Sam McKim's 1958 original "Fun Map" of Disneyland and the thirteenth-century Hereford map hanging today in England's Hereford Cathedral. In both, colorful, cartoonish illustrations and aerial presentations show stylized landscapes that are quite different from any views available on the ground or from any bird's-eye vantage point. These visualizations might best be called "carto-reality," a representation that pushes beyond the idealism and extreme simulation labeled "hyperreality" by theorists. Although both maps support agendas of perfection, they also draw attention to gaps that exist between perfection and reality. The same maps that tell us so insistently what to look at also generate a desire to peek at what is forbidden, out in the imperfect margins.

Subversion like this does not arise spontaneously, especially for visitors who have paid park admission or have entered a cathedral seeking spiritual truths. Most Americans find Disney parks enjoyable, even the most cynical visitors.[5] The moment of passing through the front turnstiles and claiming one's park map for the day cannot help but raise spirits. The brochure represents a treasure map, promising exploration and reward. Disney artists have long understood the excitement generated by colorful cartography and have capitalized on this by offering a wide range of whole-park and attraction-specific maps. Park maps must not only meet practical needs of visitors by marking bathrooms and first-aid centers, but they also generate excitement for new attractions. Maps of Tom Sawyer Island were offered after its opening in 1956, for example, and when It's a Small World moved to Disneyland after the 1964 New York World's Fair, a brochure map outlined a colorful route of "the happiest cruise that ever sailed!"[6] Like the full-park maps, attraction maps win over visitors with the promise of new, exciting worlds to explore.

At the heart of Disney's maps—as with all maps, some would argue—are stories. Louis Marin notes in *Utopics* that maps offer "potential narratives,"[7] a sentiment Peter Turchi echoes in arguing that "to ask for a map is to say, 'Tell me a story.'"[8] Like narratives, maps also offer boundaries—beginnings and ends—that create a more manageable world, and we find comfort in this. We also find it immensely useful. One need only navigate around a mountain to see the benefits of a cartographic representation over a single view from the ground. Despite this promise of expanded vision, maps are inherently limited: we know they cannot show everything. As Mark Monmonier explains, maps must "suppress truth to help the user see what needs to be seen."[9] In their necessarily flawed presentation, maps remind us that they can be both more and less than the real world, but are never the same thing as it. Philosopher Alfred Korzybski popularized the idea that "the map is not the territory," and in literature more than one author have proposed an absurdly large map with a 1:1 ratio, parodying humanity's desire (and inability) to represent the world fully.[10]

While deception is inherent to maps, most people unquestioningly accept cartographic images as authentic and natural—that is, the world itself. Just as visitors to the modern bastions of hyperreality happily buy into environments that are both like and unlike the real world—Las Vegas and Disneyland are perhaps the most famous examples[11]—users of maps tend to be complicit with the projects promoted by their makers. This is part of the ideological elegance of maps. Map users can believe that their maps both are and are not the territory, just as visitors to Disney World can, according to Jane Kuenz, "entertain contradictory and competing claims about the park and what they're doing in it."[12]

Keeping these fundamental features of maps in mind is crucial when examining guests' interactions with Disney maps. One seems to be offered a host of choices in them, when in fact the options are carefully scripted to ensure a feeling of being safely found. In his study of Disney simulacra, Stephen Fjellman reminds us that choice is almost always an illusion at Disney parks: "Walt Disney World's various cinematic designs determine, however gently, the range of decisions to be made at any one moment."[13] The project is successful, according to Millicent Hall, because Disney "creates the illusion of spontaneity."[14] Consequently, while the map for Tom Sawyer Island appears to invite free exploration, the wild terrain and wandering paths are ultimately planned, finite, and safe.

This balance between choice and control undergirds the most successful components of Disney's theme parks. A promotional map for It's a Small World promises the vastness of the globe, but one's boat route never deviates inside the attraction. Epcot's World Showcase similarly highlights access to the entire world, and its map dramatically reveals a guest's ability to circle the globe in an afternoon. As Richard Beard assures readers (and prospective visitors to the original Epcot Center) in a 1982 company-produced coffee-table book, one "can take a miniaturized trip around the world in three hours, pausing to snap a picture...[at] famous tourist sights.... In truth, after a tour of the World Showcase countries, you feel that you have really 'been there.'"[15] Wrapping representative countries around a single World Showcase Lagoon is a well-designed plan, but it is not, ultimately, the outside world. The map supports a fiction of the world being present not only in its entirety, but also in a state of harmony and equality. The park's geography and map together support a message of perfection: Beard muses that "possibly one of the reasons there is no international disharmony is that all the foreign countries have equal waterfront footage."[16] The message behind the park-wide and attraction-specific maps is ultimately conflicted, though. Glancing down at the paper reminds us of the absurdity of telling a single, all-encompassing narrative of the world, yet at the same moment the maps insist this is what lies before us.

Children who tack up Disneyland maps to their bedroom walls are not aware of how their maps have been manipulated to preserve an illusion of perfection. On them they find no markers of distance, maintenance buildings, storage facilities, queues for attractions, nor crowds. Some of these things they experienced in the park (queues and crowds, for example), and some are kept permanently away from guests' eyes (such as waste management centers). However, even the most oblivious vacationer is typically confronted, if only in momentary glimpses, with real-life employees keeping the park running: staff toiling in the kitchens, or employees slipping through cast-member-only doors to take breaks. When gazing at their maps back home, visitors can ignore such real-world intrusions. Break rooms and cast parking lots are simply absent. Similarly, maintenance takes place throughout the year in Disney parks, and visitors might even be confronted with renovation walls right before their eyes; on the map, however, one sees only pleasant groves of trees, the default symbol used to indicate off-limit spaces. In both the parks and on the maps, possibility is partnered with limits. As Mark Monmonier argues, the nature of maps is to reflect limitations; they tell us "where we can't go and what we can't (or must) do in specific places."[17]

At roughly 30,000 acres, the Walt Disney World complex in Florida places its borders as far from guests' eyes as possible, and in doing so offers a very different vacation experience from that offered at Anaheim's park.

The vastness of the property contributes powerfully to the project of making a guest feel both lost and found. Walt Disney World provides some practical road maps to help guests arrive at the park by car and to travel between the parks and hotels, but many more maps lay out just enough detail to help one access Disney's buses, boats, and monorails, the preferred transportation methods for maintaining control over visitors. Karen Klugman argues that traveling on the Disney World bus system minimizes any contemplation of the real world: "On the bus ride to the Magic Kingdom, I tried to follow along on [my road] map.... Not only do the circuitous routes, known as 'infinity roads,' confound one's sense of direction, but they also discourage any impulse to get there faster, when that is obviously not the point. The point is that you are no longer in control, so you might as well just sit back and enjoy the ride."[18]

The usefulness of a new term like carto-reality (from Latin *carta*, meaning document) is in distinguishing a map's representational project from hyperreality. Carto-reality relies on the inherently contemplative nature of a large, displayed page, coupled with a level of control and perfection not achievable by moving through a hands-on world, even through a simulation like Disneyland. The small brochure maps allow for a bit of contemplation as one walks, but they are meant to be discarded; their thin, paper construction guarantees their disposability. The large poster maps of Disneyland, however, demand fuller attention while hanging on a wall, and, like the Hereford map, pose themselves as worthy of respect.

Umberto Eco and Jean Baudrillard are quick to identify the capitalistic aspects of hyperreality, but carto-reality distinguishes itself on this front as well. A map can prove to be a purer tool not simply of simulation, but also of capitalism. At a Disney park, the souvenir map supports the crucial (and some would say primary) project of directing guests to shops and restaurants in which to spend money, but they also sell something far more valuable: a graphic, permanent version of the park's promise of perfection that will keep viewers returning as consumers throughout their lives. The artifact of the map contributes to the Walt Disney Company's general branding campaign, supporting the park's simulation more effectively than the park itself.

Disney maps and *mappaemundi* share not only a goal of depicting perfect worlds and the key features of maps, but also the problem of being largely overlooked by scholars. The ephemeral nature of Disney park maps has already been suggested; only a few artists, cartographers, or even Disney fans have devoted attention to them. Similarly, *mappaemundi* have long been overlooked by modern cartographers, who typically see these maps as products of a particularly uninformed period, displaying an almost willful refusal to be accurate. Most historical surveys pay them only a cursory glance before turning to the geographic strides of the Renaissance. The idea that geographical accuracy might not be the primary goal of a map appears to be unthinkable for modern cartographers. Denis Wood has found the inaccuracies and strange forms of early maps so formidable so as to claim "there were no maps before 1500," insisting that anything earlier should simply be called "a drawing of a landscape."[19] Even the Hereford map tends to be treated with condescension. John Wilford assures readers that it "must be judged as a work of art, not of information. No attempt was made to draw it to scale or to fix the latitude and longitude of important places."[20] However, the Disney theme park maps and *mappaemundi* certainly are maps of information; they simply ask viewers to consider truths about the world that surpass mere geography. This objective, their creators might argue, constitutes their truthfulness. James Akerman points out that in *mappaemundi* "the images make sense... as spatial illustrations of a scriptural cosmology."[21] They pose geography as their Church makers believed it should be, even when the world might not actually live up to the ideal.

Like the safe, enclosed shape of Disneyland, the medieval world possessed a form that, according to the Church, was perfect. This early permutation is most usefully understood through the T-O map. Isidore of Seville (c. 560–636) is believed to have introduced the distinctive shape,[22] and the Church fathers were chiefly responsible for producing them throughout the Middle Ages.[23] The maps employ "geometric symmetry, cardinal orientation, symbolic coloration, and locally focused geographic references,"[24] and their style is "symbolic, ornamental, and often beautiful; the geographic content, impoverished and usually misleading; the purposes, a representation of the mind more than of the earth."[25] T-O maps typically share several features, and although not all *mappaemundi* are of the T-O form, many retained these features as new genres developed (figure 2.1).

East tends to be oriented at the top in *mappaemundi*, where Eden's garden crowns the world. Jerusalem is located in the center, reflecting its place as the world's spiritual center. Three main continents made up the accessible world in the Middle Ages, and on the T-O maps they are depicted as perfectly shaped wedges, drawn with straight lines: Europe and Africa as quarter circles at the bottom (making up the west), and Asia as a half circle on the top. Each continent was believed to have been populated by one of Noah's sons after the flood, and the names of Ham, Shem, and Japheth are often labeled explicitly.[26] Perfectly situated bodies of water divide the continents on the T-O maps, constituting

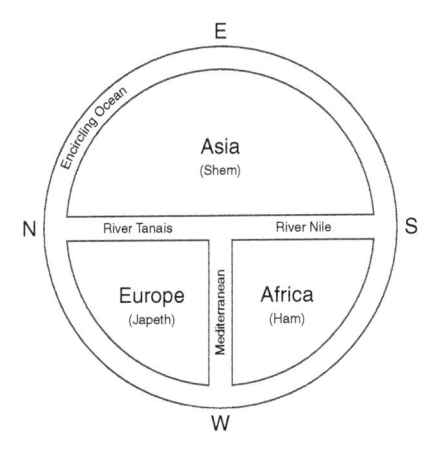

**Figure 2.1** Standard T-O map schematic, c. 700. Figure by Vanessa Sorensen.

the "T" shape. The Mediterranean divides Europe and Africa, and the division between Asia and the west consists of a series of bodies of water, most frequently identified as the River Tanais (today, the Don) and the Nile River. An encircling ocean, meanwhile, comprises the O shape. Contrary to popular belief, the world was generally understood by medievals to be a globe, but theories of climate zones hypothesized that the three continents were the only areas humans could reach.[27]

Of the thousand or so *mappaemundi* that exist today, the Hereford map is the largest, measuring roughly five feet by four-and-a-half feet. It was created circa 1290 CE on a single vellum page by, many believe, the same artist whose signature marks the bottom left-hand corner, "Richard of Haldingham and Lafford." The map appears to have been created originally for Hereford Cathedral, and while most extant *mappaemundi* survive as small illustrations in books, the Hereford map stands out most impressively as intended for public display. The original location of its display has been disputed,[28] but most scholars no longer think it was originally an altarpiece.[29] The Hereford map follows the rough T-O format of a round world, although it depicts coastlines with a little more geographical accuracy than the completely straight lines of the T-O maps. More than 500 illustrations of scenes fill up the map, taken from biblical, classical, historical, and mythical sources. Its overarching theme is Christ's apocalyptic return, signaled most prominently by Christ's appearance at the top, ruling triumphantly over the world.[30] Jerusalem is placed in the center of the map, with Eden's garden at the top, and the apocalyptic monsters of Gog and Magog in the far north (the left). John Wilford calls this work "the largest and finest of the circular maps to survive intact," and "a summary of medieval ideas and a landmark in medieval cartography."[31] By offering its users a chance to contemplate a perfect vision of the world, a mappamundi such as the Hereford map supports the Christian ideological project of its makers, reminding humanity of its double status in the world. The temptation and banishment of Adam and Eve remind us we are profoundly lost, for example, and our sinful state is reinforced by the depiction of Christ suffering in Jerusalem. In this redemptive act, humanity can acknowledge its guilt and salvation simultaneously: its state of being both lost and found (figure 2.2).

Although the Hereford map is wildly inaccurate in its geography, it is crucial that one understands this was not the norm for medieval maps.

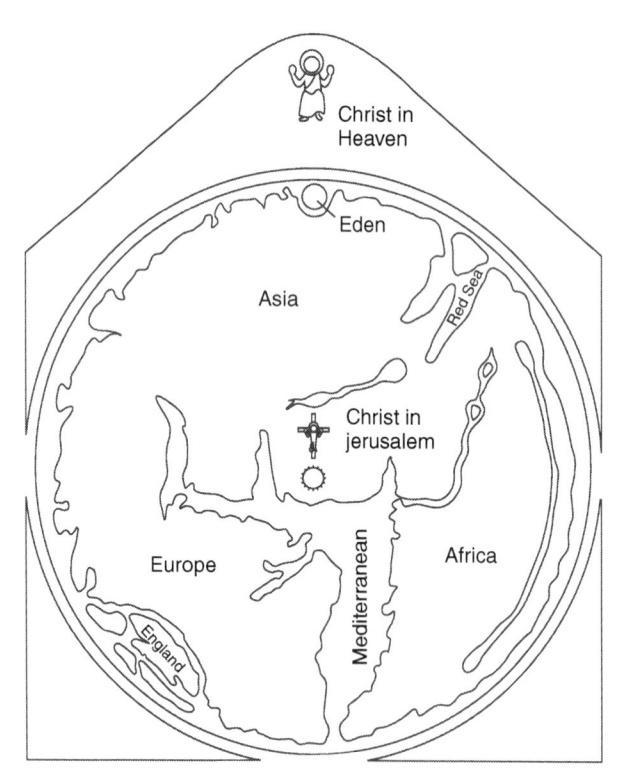

**Figure 2.2** Hereford mappamundi schematic, c. 1300. Figure by Vanessa Sorensen.

Seafaring maps produced in the Middle Ages almost always surpassed the *mappaemundi* in accuracy, offering the most up-to-date data available.[32] No medieval sailor would have used a mappamundi to navigate, for example, and no one believed that the nice, neat borders and clean straight lines of the coasts showed the real world. As C. S. Lewis points out, most viewers of the Hereford map would have understood that its perfection both represented and did not represent the world in which they lived: "For one thing the British Isles themselves are one of the most ludicrously erroneous parts of his map. Dozens, perhaps hundreds, of those who looked at it when it was new must at least have known that Scotland and England were not separate islands."[33]

In the mid-twentieth century, 650 years after the Hereford map was created, cartographic knowledge and geographic accuracy had certainly improved, but a man like Walt Disney was no less interested in posing a perfect version of the world. Like the medieval church artists, the Walt Disney Company was interested in using maps to present alternative views that challenged the images one saw around oneself. Walt Disney's motivations for making a theme park can be traced through a series of passions that consumed his attention as a young adult: a love of miniatures,[34] model trains,[35] and cartoon images as a mode of telling stories. All three were rooted in a desire to create idealized versions of a world that one could get one's hands around and control. Disney turned to simulation and models as a favorite retreat for the same reason we all do, according to Umberto Eco: "the pleasure of imitation... is one of the most innate in the human spirit."[36]

The relationship between maps and the Walt Disney Company goes back to the earliest days of Walt's storytelling. Maps played important roles in his films, as in the 1942 animated feature *Saludos Amigos*, set in South America,[37] and the Studio's first full live-action film *Treasure Island*.[38] Maps had to be made when Walt designed a miniature train layout for the backyard of his Holmby Hills home in Los Angeles,[39] and a series of maps was generated after Walt began toying with the idea of designing a theme park on Riverside Drive next to his studios.[40] As plans for the park grew, it became clear that a much larger plot would be required, as well as a larger number of maps tied to feasibility studies.

Martin Davis created the first known schematic diagrams of Disneyland, incorporating Disney's idea for a hub-and-spoke design that would allow guests to move in and out of the themed lands with maximum ease.[41] The radiating pathways to the various lands would also present a harmonious space like "the essence of the wheel."[42] However, there were two particularly important maps that followed, and both helped to establish the final design for the park, introducing many of the medieval aesthetic features that mark Sam McKim's 1958 map (figure 2.3).

This first of these maps was created by Disney Studio artist Herbert Ryman at the behest of Walt Disney. Over a September 1953 weekend, Ryman and Disney created the first illustrated, aerial-view map of Disneyland, based on Disney's need to present a more inspiring visual aid to potential investors—a map that would capture the grandeur of his vision. As Ryman recalls, he was shown a series of abstract, schematic maps that coldly showed potential layouts. Some of the maps "had a lot of preliminaries and groundwork on other parks that Walt had conceived of [for the Riverside Drive property]" and others "went to so much work figuring out sewers and electrical specifications, but they were unable to capture the vision that Walt was trying to achieve.... He explained to me that Disneyland was to be a world apart. Entering its portals was to leave behind the mundane hum-drum everyday world. This was my assignment."[43]

The resulting drawing shows the influence of Ryman's professional training coupled with Walt's visionary thinking. We have no evidence that either Ryman or Disney consulted medieval maps, but they certainly drew on popular understandings of *mappaemundi*. Ryman's artistic training spanned several continents and points to someone who almost assuredly would have been familiar with forms of the *mappaemundi*.[44] Because the theme-park map genre was new, one can also reasonably assume that when faced with the task, Ryman drew upon the most well-known models for mapping an entire world, those from the Middle Ages.

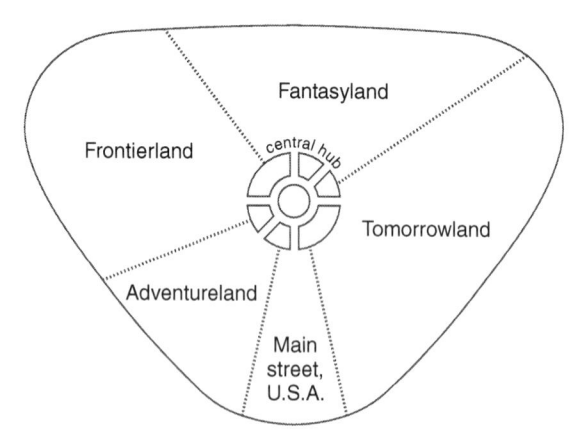

**Figure 2.3** Disneyland schematic with five original themed lands, c. 1955. Figure by Vanessa Sorensen.

The map that emerged after the long weekend looks very similar to *mappaemundi*, incorporating the same colorful illustrations of small vignettes, employing a bird's-eye, aerial perspective (that is both realistic and fantastic at the same time), and holding everything together in a clean, ordered boundary. Like the mappaemundi's encircling ocean, Ryman's map suggests a surrounding earthen berm that defines the world's outer edge; and, as on the Hereford map, guests' eyes are drawn to key locations through the use of eye-catching spectacles, referred to by the Imagineers as *wienies*.[45]

Not all of the features visualized by Ryman and Disney in their early map were included in the final park. Pathways were introduced between the separate lands to ease traffic flow, planted trees and the encircling train made an earthen berm unnecessary, and additional lands like Bear Country and Toontown later stretched the perfection of the initial boundary. However, Ryman's map highlights the importance of balance to the vision. Louis Marin describes the crucial role balance plays in maintaining Disneyland's perceived perfection: "Disneyland is a centered space. Main Street USA leads the visitors to the center ... [and] this semiotic function, the condition of possibility of all the messages, all the tours ... is taken into account structurally in ... the diagrammatic scheme of all the possible tours, an open and yet finite totality, the Disneyland map."[46]

A second key map of Disneyland is Peter Ellenshaw's 1954 oil and fluorescent paint creation, utilizing a glowing paint to produce a nighttime effect. Since Ryman's map had won over the bankers, Walt asked Ellenshaw for a map to win over the public. Ellenshaw's piece was famously presented by Walt Disney to a television audience on October 27, 1954; he beamed while debuting this effective preview of the park's harmonious, fantastic features: "That's it, right there. Disneyland, seen from about 2,000 feet in the air, and about ten months away."[47]

Sam McKim created in 1957 the third and most significant Disneyland map, the first "Fun Map" to be sold in the park. He benefited from the stylistic precedents set by Ryman and Ellenshaw, as well as from the park having been in operation for two years. This commercially produced poster matched the colorfulness, energy, and aerial perspective of the earlier maps; and as changes came to the park over subsequent years (new attractions and lands being added and removed), McKim adapted the map in seven versions, each of which ensured that guests buying the souvenir received a representation capturing the park's perfect, seemingly unchanging form.[48]

As we have seen in the *mappaemundi*, the perfection offered in McKim's map also came at the expense of geographical accuracy. This was true for maps of later Disney parks as well, many of which used

McKim's map as a model. When Florida's Walt Disney World was completed in 1971, it offered guests a poster-sized Fun Map. The first map was designed by Paul Hartley and introduced a number of geographical distortions to maximize the park's harmonious design. Jeff Kurtti warns viewers that "it might make both cartographers and historians apoplectic; he has purposefully distorted the locations of the landmarks and their relationships to each other for the sake of a more pleasing design."[49]

McKim's Disneyland map was replaced in 1966 with a new artist's view of the park, but together the corpus of Disneyland maps has played a crucial role in embedding images of the park in the world's subconscious. They do this in ways that actual visits to the park, with their intrusions of reality, can never accomplish. For decades, as the Walt Disney Company tells us, the maps have been "thumbtacked to bedroom walls across the country, preserving memories of trips to Disneyland and creating anticipation for future visits."[50] As *E-Ticket Magazine* explains, the introduction of the poster map marked a fundamental change in the ways Disneyland worked its magic on the public: "These were the best maps at the Park during a time of maps. Unlike 'throwaway' maps like those given out on Tom Sawyer Island, at Main Street USA's Bank of America, or in guides provided at the gate, these were designed to be used (and cherished) later. Kids have always taken them home and studied them to learn the Park, to retrace their recent visits, and to plan with enthusiasm their next trip to the Magic Kingdom."[51]

In addition to sharing a number of aspects of form, McKim's map and the Hereford map function in crucially similar ways. The overhead perspective casts viewers in a position that makes them both omniscient and humbled, which contributes once again to their lost-and-found status. While the bird's-eye view mimics a vantage point from which viewers can seemingly wield divine control, it simultaneously reminds them of the largeness of the world—one in which they can get lost. A utopic space benefits from the aerial perspective on such maps, according to Louis Marin; when paintings and maps blur their boundaries, as we see in the Disney maps and *mappaemundi*, a location is presented "as a whole, simultaneously. It is presented in its coexistence and co-presence.... The viewpoint is ... everywhere and nowhere, simultaneously."[52]

Additionally, by presenting audiences with scenes from history and fantasy, both maps display a kind of polytemporality. The world's perfection, we are reminded, transcends real time and space. All maps have an atemporal nature, of course, because they capture a fixed moment—a feature that makes them out-of-date at the moment of publication.[53] McKim's map and the Hereford map show themselves also to be polytemporal in their presentation of multiple pasts and futures simultaneously.

In the Hereford map, polytemporality is displayed most clearly in the Biblical scenes. Adam and Eve, for example, are shown being tempted inside the garden as they are simultaneously ejected outside the garden gates; chronological accuracy proves as fluid as geographical accuracy. Adrianne Wortzel explains this feature as a "fourth-dimensional narrative," whose illustrations are "layered over time."[54] For the medieval Christian, a true vision of the world is one in which Christ simultaneously saves humanity on the cross and reigns from above. On McKim's map, all of the Disney characters and narratives also exist simultaneously. A visitor to Disneyland sees this multiplicity of chronologies simply by walking from land to land; however, on the ground in Disneyland, one is never afforded the opportunity to take in the Old West and the world of tomorrow and the turn-of-the-century America simultaneously. In juxtaposing the layered narratives, maps reveal the patterns and relationships between the narratives more fully.

By folding their stories on top of one another, these maps also push viewers away from the present day, a goal embraced by Disneyland and the medieval Christian Church. Polytemporality directs a viewer's attention to the past and the future, zones in which reality can be more easily minimized. An early Disneyland brochure celebrates the park's ability to keep guests' attention away from current troubles: "In Disneyland you see yesterday, tomorrow, and fantasy—nothing of the present."[55] Similarly, Imagineer John Hench believes the harmony of Disneyland inspires people because "nobody worries about the past, and in a sense nobody worries about the future.... It's today where you have the problem."[56] Maps, to a greater extent than Disneyland or any medieval countryside, let viewers see the full breadth of perfection at once.

The doubleness of Christ in the Hereford mappamundi (appearing both at the top of the map and in the center) finds an intriguing analog in McKim's map. Jesus Christ is clearly the central iconic figure on the Hereford map, and the two appearances remind viewers of his dual nature: as God he looks over the world, and as a human he lives down among it; as Old Testament God he reigns, and as New Testament God he sacrifices himself. In much the same way, the head of Mickey Mouse appears twice on McKim's map. McKim was the first artist to add a border of Disney characters to the map's outer edge, and he placed the iconic Mickey head in the prominent top position, surrounded by thirty-nine figures from animated shorts and features. Exotic creatures populating the borders of the world are also found on the *mappaemundi*; in McKim's map, however, these are not dangerous creatures to be avoided (like sphinxes and mermaids), but familiar friends who reassure viewers of the safety of the world. Also like Christ, Mickey appears for a second time near the center of the map in the floral Mickey display that greets guests at the front gates. Mickey functions on the center of Disneyland's map much as he does in the park, welcoming guests and reminding the public that he exists down in the world among his fans. Rather than splitting God's role into Old Testament and New Testament forms (judge and redeemer) as we find in the Hereford map, the Disneyland map casts Mickey wholly in the role of a compassionate God. Disneyland replaces any hint of judgment with comfort, acceptance, and safety.

A final way in which the Hereford map and McKim map share similar functions is in their generation of subversion among users. Peter Turchi finds all maps to be inherently subversive simply by their raising questions: "Maps suggest explanations; and while explanations reassure us, they also inspire us to ask more questions, consider other possibilities."[57] Any project that promises perfection inevitably invites criticism. In *Team Rodent* Carl Hiassen derides Disney for being "so good at being good that it manifests an evil; so uniformly efficient and courteous, so dependably clean and conscientious… that it's unreal, and therefore is an agent of pure wickedness."[58]

The visualizations made available by carto-reality come with subversive risks likely not anticipated by those who commission them. The Hereford artist and Sam McKim might not have realized that, while their maps afford audiences contemplation of perfect worlds, they also allow users to become more aware of the gap that exists between the idealized world and the real one. In showing marginal areas, forbidden zones, and exotic creatures, the same maps generate desires to consider what is beyond the borders. In fact, the existence of the maps helps viewers to visualize forbidden elements more easily. The portrayal of Sodom and Gomorrah on the Hereford map, for example, depicts this well. The cities provide an ideal reminder to viewers of God's judgment, offering a titillating view of Lot's willful wife who turns back longingly to gaze on the sin she should be happily abandoning. Through the map, viewers are afforded a privileged position not merely to look at the exotic cities, reenacting the very crime for which Lot's wife is punished, but to gaze on them for as long as they desire. The Hereford map's display of other monstrous creatures also reminds viewers of the accursed world to which they are bound, and, like the sphinx and mermaid, these are often cast as temptresses. However, these are the same creatures that make the map interesting to viewers, possibly encouraging individuals to travel. They may, in fact, be the most effective tools for drawing people in to spend more time in the cathedral.

Subversion has similarly delighted many guests of Disney parks. Just as barriers separating the public from cast-only areas make guests want to look beyond them, so do drawings of innocuous clumps of trees on the maps invite the public to contemplate what imperfections are hidden beyond the margins. Experiencing a Disney park subversively has always been possible according to Karen Klugman, but the "alternative ride," as she labels it, can begin only after one has looked closely enough to acknowledge the gap between perfection and reality: "surmounting the subtle control of Disney's total environment begins with a recognition of it."[59] In the park, there are many ways to steal subversive glimpses. The Skyway once allowed guests to travel high above Disneyland and Walt Disney World's Magic Kingdom, but after decades of permitting subversive peeks at show buildings and forbidden areas, Imagineers closed the attraction. A primary benefit of this, in addition to ending numerous lawsuits, was in reclaiming the park's originally intended sightlines.[60] Park maps, however, have remained a way for the subversively inclined to imagine an over-the-park experience, even if only on Disney's terms.

Some guests of the Disney parks continue to look beyond the margins. Cast atlases of the parks can be purchased on eBay, for example, allowing glimpses into cast-only areas; and by paying a steep price, visitors can access certain backstage areas during guided tours. In both cases the Walt Disney Company maintains final control of the images. The corporation, however, cannot control all of the maps of their parks because numerous guidebooks generate their own, with varying degrees of subversiveness. However, in a particularly important case, Disney acted with a masterful stroke. The advent of high-resolution satellite imagery granted the public unprecedented access in the twenty-first century to forbidden Disney-park territory, and with it, new opportunities for subversive exploration. Acknowledging the inevitable growth of satellite images, Disney teamed up with Google Earth to create detailed three-dimensional imagery of specific park buildings they wanted guests to see.[61] In summer 2008, people looking at satellite imagery of Walt Disney World were suddenly rewarded with attractions and shops in full three-dimensional glory. Because any nonmagical buildings were left flat and untreated, they essentially disappeared from the public eye once again.

The presentation of a world that embodies perfection and allows one to be simultaneously lost and found was not new when Walt Disney began developing Disneyland. Sam McKim and other artists drew on many of the same features that worked so well for creators of the *mappaemundi*, and especially of the Hereford map. Built on the foundation of an imperfect world, the Christian Church and the Disney theme-park industry remain today two institutions that have not waned in their ability to offer the public a well-needed sense of order and orientation. Both succeed in offering a fundamentally optimistic view of the world that flies unabashedly in the face of reality; and both, through an offering of carto-reality, allow a level of contemplation that also challenges their same ideological projects. Few may have walked through Disneyland with images of medieval *mappaemundi* in their heads, but the juxtaposition is one that surely would appeal to Disney's mapmakers, as well as to a public eager to embrace the park both sincerely and subversively.

## Notes

1. Neal Gabler, *Walt Disney: The Triumph of the American Imagination* (New York: Knopf, 2006), 531–32; David Koenig, *Mouse Tales: A Behind-the-Ears Look at Disneyland* (Irvine: Bonaventure, 1995), 22–26.
2. Neal Gabler, *Walt Disney*, 499.
3. Karal Marling, ed., *Designing Disney's Theme Parks: The Architecture of Reassurance* (New York: Flammarion, 1998), 73.
4. Susan Veness, *The Hidden Magic of Walt Disney World* (Avon: Adamsmedia, 2009), 4.
5. Susan Willis, "The Family Vacation," *Inside the Mouse: Work and Play at Disney World* (Durham: Duke University Press, 1995), 34–53, at 40.
6. Dave Smith, *Disney A to Z: The Updated Official Encyclopedia* (New York: Hyperion, 1998), 562 and 291.
7. Louis Marin, *Utopics: Spatial Play*, trans. Robert Volrath (Atlantic Highlands, NJ: Humanities, 1984), 204.
8. Peter Turchi, *Maps of the Imagination: The Writer as Cartographer* (San Antonio: Trinity University Press, 2004), 11.
9. Mark Monmonier, *How to Lie with Maps*, 2nd ed. (Chicago: University of Chicago Press, 1996), 25.
10. Lewis Carroll, *Sylvie and Bruno Concluded* (New York: Gramercy, 1982), 655–824; and Jorge Luis Borges, "On Exactitude in Science," *A Universal History of Infamy* (New York: Dutton, 1972), 141.
11. Umberto Eco, *Travels in Hyperreality*, trans. William Weaver (New York: Harcourt Brace Jovanovich, 1986), 40.
12. Jane Kuenz, "Working at the Rat," *Inside the Mouse*, 110–62, at 110.
13. Stephen Fjellman, *Vinyl Leaves: Walt Disney World and America* (Boulder: Westview, 1992), 203.
14. Millicent Hall, "Theme Parks: Around the World in 80 Minutes," *Landscape* 21 (1976): 3–8, at 5.
15. Richard Beard, *Walt Disney's Epcot Center: Creating the New World of Tomorrow* (New York: Abrams, 1982), 134.
16. Richard Beard, *Walt Disney's Epcot Center*, 134.
17. Mark Monmonier, *No Dig, No Fly, No Go: How Maps Restrict and Control* (Chicago: University of Chicago Press, 2010), 1.
18. Karen Klugman, "Reality Revisited," *Inside the Mouse*, 12–33, at 17.

19. Denis Wood, *Rethinking the Power of Maps* (New York: Guilford, 2010), 22–23.
20. John Wilford, *The Mapmakers* (New York: Knopf, 1981), 47.
21. James Akerman and Robert Karrow, ed., *Maps: Finding Our Place in the World* (Chicago: University of Chicago Press, 2007), 78.
22. John Wilford, *Mapmakers*, 46.
23. Leo Bagrow and R. A. Skelton, *History of Cartography*, rev. ed. (London: Watts, 1964), 46.
24. James Akerman and Robert Karrow, *Maps*, 78.
25. John Wilford, *Mapmakers*, 45.
26. John Wilford, *Mapmakers*, 46.
27. Toby Lester, *The Fourth Part of the World: The Race to the Ends of the Earth, and the Epic Story of the Map That Gave America Its Name* (New York: Free Press, 2009), 76–77.
28. Martin Bailey, "The Discovery of the Lost Mappamundi Panel: Hereford's Map in a Medieval Altarpiece?" *The Hereford World Map*, ed. P. D. A. Harvey (London: British Library, 2006), 79–93, at 79.
29. Peter Barber and Tom Harper, *Magnificent Maps: Power, Propaganda, and Art* (London: British Library, 2010), 14.
30. Peter Barber and Tom Harper, *Magnificent Maps*, 25.
31. John Wilford, *Mapmakers*, 46.
32. Leo Bagrow and R. A. Skelton, *History of Cartography*, 50.
33. C. S. Lewis, *The Discarded Image* (Cambridge: University of Cambridge Press, 1987), 143.
34. Jim Korkis, *The Vault of Walt: Unofficial, Unauthorized, Uncensored Disney Stories Never Told* (Lexington: Ayefour, 2010), 13.
35. Michael Broggie, *Walt Disney's Railroad Story: The Small-Scale Fascination That Led to a Full-Scale Kingdom* (Virginia Beach: Donning, 2006), 95.
36. Umberto Eco, *Travels in Hyperreality*, 46.
37. Dave Smith, *Disney A to Z*, 482.
38. Dave Smith, *Disney A to Z*, 569.
39. Michael Broggie, *Walt Disney's Railroad Story*, 113.
40. Jeff Kurtti and Bruce Gordon, *The Art of Disneyland* (New York: Disney Editions, 2006), vii; Karal Marling, *Designing Disney's Theme Parks*, 38–39, 51.
41. Karal Marling, *Designing Disney's Theme Parks*, 62.
42. *Walt Disney Imagineering: A Behind-the-Dreams Look at Making More Magic Real* (New York: Disney Editions, 2010), 66.
43. Bruce Gordon and David Mumford, ed., *A Brush with Disney: An Artist's Journey Told through the Words and Works of Herbert Dickens Ryman*, 2nd edn. (Santa Clarita: Camphor Tree, 2002), 147.
44. Bruce Gordon and David Mumford, *A Brush with Disney*, 23–51.
45. The Imagineers, *The Imagineering Field Guide to Disneyland: An Imagineer's-Eye Tour* (New York: Disney Editions, 2008), 13.

46. Louis Marin, *Utopics*, 245–47.
47. Jeff Kurtti and Bruce Gordon, *The Art of Disneyland*, x.
48. Jack Janzen and Leon Janzen, "Disneyland Souvenir Maps, 1958–1965," *E-Ticket Magazine* 18 (1994): 4–7, at 6.
49. Jeff Kurtti and Bruce Gordon, *The Art of Walt Disney World* (New York: Disney Editions, 2009), 47.
50. Jeff Kurtti and Bruce Gordon, *The Art of Disneyland*, ii.
51. Jack Janzen and Leon Janzen, "Disneyland Souvenir Maps," 4–5.
52. Louis Marin, *Utopics*, 208.
53. Denis Wood, *The Power of Maps* (New York: Guilford, 1992), 125.
54. Adrianne Wortzel, "Sayonara Diorama: Acting Out the World as a Stage in Medieval Cartography and Cyberspace," *The Hereford World Map*, 415–21, at 419.
55. Neal Gabler, *Walt Disney*, 498.
56. Charlie Haas, "Disneyland Is Good for You," *New West* (December 4, 1978): 13–19, at 19.
57. Peter Turchi, *Maps of the Imagination*, 11.
58. Carl Hiaasen, *Team Rodent: How Disney Devours the World* (New York: Random House, 1998), 18.
59. Karen Klugman, "The Alternative Ride," *Inside the Mouse*, 163–79, at 166.
60. David Koenig, *Mouse Tales*, 184; *More Mouse Tales: A Closer Peek Backstage at Disneyland* (Irvine: Bonaventure, 2003), 41–42; and *Realityland: True-Life Adventures at Walt Disney World* (Irvine: Bonaventure, 2007), 146.
61. Kitty Bean Yancey, "It's a Small World, Thanks to Google Earth," USAToday.com (May 16, 2008); Web, accessed January 15, 2011.

CHAPTER 3

DISNEY'S CASTLES AND THE WORK OF THE MEDIEVAL IN THE MAGIC KINGDOM

Martha Bayless

> *Here you leave today and enter the world of yesterday, tomorrow, and fantasy.*
>
> Plaque at entrance to Disney parks

Since the construction of the original Disneyland Park in 1955, the castle—fancifully slender, extravagantly corbelled, strategically photogenic—has been the hub of Disneyland, the orienting beacon, the point to which all other points lead.[1] In addition to serving as a physical landmark, the castle, as well as amalgamated elements from other Disney castles, has been recruited as a logo for the Disney imaginarium as a whole. Thus, although the actual Disneyland castle is diminutive as far as castles go, the castle itself is central to Disney both geographically and conceptually: simultaneously spectacle and narrative, it serves as a nexus of transformation.

As castles are, in more than one sense, the strongholds of the Middle Ages, the centrality of the castle to the Disney enterprise suggests that the medieval is positioned as both portal and playground. But it is important to remember that what is on offer at the Disney parks is not, in the words of one critic, "history-flavored entertainment."[2] Although medieval castles were martial displays of power, their modern simulations are designed, like modern versions of fairy tales, to be inviting play spaces in which personal stories can be enacted. The castle-flavored entertainment of the Disney world is not set in the Middle Ages *qua* Middle Ages, but in a fairy tale that is set in the "Middle Ages," the abiding, prespecific, legendary time where fairy tales take place. It is a history-flavored Otherworld, a world with a location more conceptual than geographic or temporal. To enter the Disney fairy-tale narrative is to enter a dream vision, and the organizing principle of the vision is the castle. The narrative central to this vision is a child's narrative of self-realization: personal, family-focused, transformative. It is, moreover, a transformation increasingly gendered female, and thus culture-wide, both in Disneyland and elsewhere in American culture, the transformational castle has evolved as a particularly female domain, a domestic space for the enactment of American female transfiguration.

From its inception—and before—the Disneyland castle has embodied these elements of narrativity, fantasy, and transfiguration. At only seventy-five feet high, it is an animators' castle: edited highlights of castle essence, its turrets, battlements, and flying pennants multiplied to make it stirring rather than formidable. Constructed during the production of *Sleeping Beauty* (1959), the California castle was designed as a three-dimensional realization of the edifice in the movie, where the castle "is literally plucked from storybook pages as the film unfolds."[3] The filmic identity of the park castle is magnified by its strategic positioning: Walt Disney reportedly decreed that the California castle, like its reiteration in Orlando, should face south so that light would be optimum for visitors to pose for pictures in front of it.[4]

The castle will be familiar to visitors not merely in its role as Disney emblem, but also from its appearance in the animated sequence introducing Disney screen productions. In older productions, a flitting Tinkerbell sprinkles fairy dust from her wand over the castle; in more recent versions the castle is illuminated by shooting stars to the tune of "When You Wish upon a Star." The figure of Tinkerbell implies that the castle is an extension of Neverland, the place of eternal childhood where dreams come true; the wish-ready stars make the same promise. In the park, on screen, and in the imagination, the castle, approached through the heightened but more everyday realm of Main Street USA, rises above the realms of fantasy like an iceberg, a visual signifier of the depths of imaginative transformation.

Like their exemplars and antecedents, the Disney castles are derived from medieval constructions as imagined, restored, and reinterpreted as icons of romance in the nineteenth century. These are to authentic medieval castles what Grimms' fairy tales are to medieval popular tales: not the raw specimens but a collection of selected features, assembled from multiple sources and edited for maximum "authenticity" (rather, a kind of representational verisimilitude) and impact. As we shall see, all such castles resemble one another because each has selected and magnified the visual elements that spell "medieval" and "gothic." They do not constitute a castle as much as imply one.

The design of the castle is thus central to this displacement of reality. Medieval castles in their historical context were not palaces but fortifications, emblems of authority and intimidation. Walt Disney was alert to this fact: he is recalled as saying, "You know, tyrants in the past built these huge buildings—'look how big and powerful I am.' And they towered over people to impress people."[5] To avoid this intimidation, the California Disney castle is both large and small at the same time. At seventy-five feet, it is roughly one-third the height of a genuine turreted castle such as Neuschwanstein, which is estimated at 213 feet (figure 3.1). But the Disney version is designed with forced perspective, so that the "stone" blocks at the top are narrower than those nearer the spectator, tricking the eye into judging the upper levels to be farther away than they really are. The castle is hence simultaneously both dainty and towering. In this, it resembles the appealing miniaturized castle images in medieval manuscripts, where the lack of realistic perspective paints the knights or inhabitants of the castle nearly as tall as its towers.

**Figure 3.1**  Neuschwanstein Castle.

The Sleeping Beauty castle of California Disneyland and the Disney corporate logo derived from it fuse various elements several removes from any medieval prototype. Its immediate progenitor is the animated film of *Sleeping Beauty*, which in turn was modeled on other notable castles. One of the most emblematic of these was featured in the 1944 film of *Henry V*, starring and directed by Laurence Olivier.[6] The film begins on the stage of the Globe Theatre and gradually opens out to fifteenth-century England, transformed from a stage set to reality, before returning to stylized sets and folding back into the Globe. The words of the chorus, on the stage of the Globe, speak to this enterprise of using the imagination to enlarge the world:

> And let us, ciphers to this great account,
> On your imaginary forces work....
> Piece out our imperfections with your thoughts.[7]

*Henry V* in turn took its design from the pages of the Duc de Berry's *Très Riches Heures*, which similarly employs artistic images of castles rather than historic examples.

Thus a number of works of art mediate between the Disneyland castle and the actual edifices of the Middle Ages, and the same is true of the other inspirations for the Sleeping Beauty castle. Its most renowned model is the nineteenth-century fantasyland castle Neuschwanstein, the apotheosis of confected castles. Neuschwanstein is a forerunner of the Disney castles in concept as well as in design, its animating spirit King Ludwig II of Bavaria. Ludwig II (1845–1886), known as the *Märchenkönig* or "Fairy Tale King," was the Michael Jackson of his day.[8] Brought up in great wealth, separated from others by his status and position, Ludwig spent his childhood isolated and lonely, taking refuge in early Germanic tales and Wagner's re-creations of medieval narrative. Throughout his life he turned to legend and theater to escape the cares of his position. These impulses often took eccentric forms: he invited actors on excursions, but insisted they talk and act in character; made elaborate imaginary excursions entirely within the Royal Riding Pavilion; and when the politics of Bavaria became too overwhelming, he sent a government emissary in search of new realms to rule. Ludwig's castles were material emblems of his desire to take refuge in the carefree legendary era entered through theater, opera, and fairy stories.

Although his childhood was emotionally impoverished, Ludwig's cares escalated when he ascended the throne of Bavaria in 1864, at the age of eighteen. Court life in Munich proved overwhelming, and he soon began taking sanctuary in his country retreats. The strain of government increased as political complications escalated, and in 1866 the king was compelled to make complex navigations between the claims of Prussia and Austria as the Schleswig–Holstein crisis came to a head. Under crushing pressure, distraught, the king took refuge in his trinity of fantasy sanctuaries: castles, legends, and the playhouse, intertwined and commensurate. In the midst of the crisis he withdrew to the isolated Castle Berg, spent days riding on its lake in his steamer *Tristan*, and dashed to Switzerland to pay a desperate visit to Wagner, whose works had painted a more straightforward world of legends. The Schleswig–Holstein crisis culminated in the Seven Weeks' War, in which Ludwig's humiliation became complete. Bavaria was forced to acknowledge the supremacy of Prussia; Ludwig lost much of his sovereignty. The most potent symbol of this loss was even more personal: Ludwig was compelled to offer partial control of an important family stronghold, Hohenzollern Castle, to the king of Prussia.

Reeling under the loss of sovereignty, a blow emblematized by the loss of Hohenzollern, Ludwig began to make plans for a fantasy castle retreat, his own Neverland, in 1879. This was the castle later known as Neuschwanstein. Ludwig envisioned his castle as a place where the storied German past would come to life, illustrated by scenes from Wagner. The concept and the design of Neuschwanstein betray a debt to a number of other castles, chief among them the Château de Pierrefonds, north of Paris in Picardy. Ludwig visited the restorations of Pierrefonds in 1867 as a side excursion to his visit to the Exposition Universelle in Paris. The exposition, a sort of theme park without rides, featured exhibitions from all over the world. Its variety and theatrical qualities appealed to the stage-besotted king, and the Château de Pierrefonds formed a natural sideshow to the exposition. First built in the twelfth century and greatly enlarged in the early fifteenth, the greater part of the château had been demolished in a siege in 1617. By the nineteenth century it was a picturesque ruin of the type prized by the Romantics. In 1857, the emperor Napoleon III determined to "restore" the castle to a more habitable and even more picturesque state. For this enterprise, he chose the man who left a greater mark on the French Middle Ages than any other living in the nineteenth century: Viollet-le-Duc.

Eugène Viollet-le-Duc (1814–1879), a key figure in the French Gothic revival, remains best known for not only his restorations and "updatings" of Notre-Dame-de-Paris, but also for turning his attention to numbers of other medieval churches, castles, and miscellaneous buildings. "To restore an edifice," he wrote famously, "means neither to maintain it, nor to repair it, nor to rebuild it; it means to re-establish it in a finished state, which may in fact never have actually existed at any given time."[9] Viollet-le-Duc's re-imaginings might alter the appearance of an edifice considerably, as occurred in the southern French fortified town of Carcassonne. There his restoration imported medieval regionalisms from other areas, most notably in his treatment of the roofs on many of the fifty-three towers of the city fortifications. Traditionally these roofs had employed tiles and gentle slopes, but Viollet-le-Duc "restored" them using slate and steeply pointed cones, features of more northern climates where roofs must function under snowy conditions. These dark, steeply sloped roofs, many of them conical like those of Carcassonne, remain distinctive features of the Disney castles in both Anaheim and Orlando, two further climates in which roofs only very rarely see snow.

As Viollet-le-Duc restored Pierrefonds, the project expanded. Napoleon III envisioned the château as an imperial residence and called for extensive rebuilding both inside and out. Construction was still in progress at Viollet-le-Duc's death in 1879, and was finally halted, still not entirely complete, in 1885. The resulting château is distinctively akin to the Sleeping Beauty castle: both have an asymmetric arrangement of conical-roofed slender towers soaring above more substantial crenellated stone battlements. The Château de Pierrefonds, originally a foundation of a particular century, re-imagined in both the fifteenth and nineteenth centuries, emerges as imperial fantasy in stone, an alloy of castle features.

Impressed by Viollet-le-Duc's Pierrefonds, Ludwig II resolved to "restore" a castle for himself. From the beginning his castle was a theater rather than a fortification. To design it, Ludwig hired not an architect but theater set designer Christian Jank, who translated Ludwig's ideas into drawings for the benefit of architects. The courtyard was based on the stage set for the Munich production of *Lohengrin*. Walls and ceilings throughout the castle were adorned with scenes from Germanic legend and from Wagner's operas, involving the castle more closely in the world of myth and narrative. The whole provided Ludwig with a Neverland of story to which he could retreat. He wrote to Baroness Leonrod: "Oh, how necessary it is to create for oneself such poetic places of refuge, where one can forget for a little while the dreadful times in which we live."[10] As a distillation and amplification of the fanciful and the legendary, Neuschwanstein has earned its place as the progenitor of modern fairy-tale castles.

Ludwig made a second contribution to the Disney tradition in the form of designs for a Falkenstein castle, a project that never passed the planning stages. In 1883 Ludwig acquired a ruinous site at Falkenstein in Bavaria. He asked Christian Jank, the stage designer who formulated the plans for Neuschwanstein, to design a new fairy-tale castle for the site. The resulting sketches show an extravagantly romantic, slender, and towering reinterpretation of Gothic, like the fairy-tale godmother of the Sleeping Beauty castle. After interim architects were dismissed for lack of immoderation, the final commission went to the team of Julius Hofmann and Eugen Drollinger. Apparently suspecting that inadequate funding meant that the castle would never be built, they designed ever more extravagant features, until the plans were a towering fantasy of fairy-tale romanticism. When Ludwig was murdered by unknown assailants in 1886, at the age of forty, the castle remained unbuilt. Nonetheless, Falkenstein was just the kind of castle that someone looking to re-create a medieval fantasy world would construct. The original exists only in drawings and in a clay maquette, or model, dating from 1884. Since the 1920s, the maquette has been on display in the König-Ludwig-II Museum in Herrenchiensee, where Disney designers may have seen it in the widespread movement of American troops during and after World War II, and recalled it when first constructing the plans for Sleeping Beauty castle.

Falkenstein's romantic towers and fairy-tale design make it the apotheosis of the fantasy castle, as amply demonstrated by the fact that it was eventually built, more or less according to the original plans, in Burnet, Texas.[11] Texas "businessman and developer" Terry Young and his wife Kim were touring the exhibitions in Neuschwanstein when they first noted the drawings of Falkenstein.[12] They subsequently tracked down the original plans, which they used as the model for a limestone and granite "wedding castle" nearly ninety feet tall, called "Falkenstein Castle®." This Texas Falkenstein wedding castle, begun in 1995, is equipped with the now familiar crenellations, steeply roofed conical towers, and gargoyles much like those of Viollet-de-Duc on Notre-Dame. It has emerged with more symmetry and fewer towers than the original of Ludwig's vision, as well as a front entryway flanked by two thirty-foot pillars supporting a two-tiered balcony, giving the entry an appearance resembling an amalgamation of a Southern plantation and a lodge of the Pacific Northwest. The castle is available for royalty-themed "destination weddings": in 2011, the choices included the "Duchess Wedding Package" and the "Complete Royal Wedding Package." As the site says, "We wanted Brides to have an opportunity to be married in a Fairytale setting"—the capitalized words reflecting the two most important aspects of the feature, the bride and the fairy tale.[13] In this Texas descendent of Ludwig II's vision, as in the Disney castles, we can see the powerful idea of the castle as a transformative force, a step back into the fairy-tale land of dreams.

In the Middle Ages, the construction of castles typically signaled occupation of foreign territories. The same might be said for the incursion of the Disney Corporation into foreign lands: in each case, dominion is established by the iconic Disney castle. The first outpost of the Disney empire of parks from its California roots was the Disney World complex outside Orlando, Florida. Because the Orlando Disney properties include multiple parks, the one that reiterates the original Disneyland in California is identified by the Anaheim title "Magic Kingdom." This time named after Cinderella, the Florida castle once again occupies the central position in the park. At approximately 190 feet in height, it is more than twice the height of California's seventy-five foot Sleeping Beauty Castle. Constructed in 1971, the Florida castle takes its cues from the French Loire Valley châteaux of the Renaissance, particularly Chaumont, Chambord, Chenonceau, and the Château d'Ussé.[14] The Florida castle, however, boasts twenty-seven towers, an extravagance of towers much greater than any medieval castle of its size. Indeed, the castle consists almost entirely of fairy-tale towers.

Euro Disney (now Disneyland Paris) added its own challenges to the construction of castles, as described by one designer:

> Disneyland used Neuschwanstein, and Florida was an amalgam of many French castles. We needed to go to the realm of fairy tales and not tread on anybody's sense of integrity. I didn't want to do Gothic columns. I didn't want to do in Fiberglass what you could go into the city [Paris] and see. And right nearby were the finest castle examples in the world. So we created twisted tree forms that kind of grow out of rock as our columns. There's no way you're going to confuse that with the real thing. Likewise, having a fire-breathing dragon in the basement is not the sort of thing you're going to encounter at Chenonceaux.[15]

The castle pushes back further from reality to efface the reality surrounding, including the un-dreamlike fact that the last fifteen-year-old girl who married a prince and took possession of French castles, Marie Antoinette, ended her story beheaded. Like Ludwig II, Marie Antoinette discovered that the glory of fantasy far exceeds the reality of royal life.

In its position as one of the latest in a series of re-imagined fairy-tale castles, then, the Disney park castle provides a cue that the visitor is about to enter the filmic narrative of the park. It is the focus of the establishing shot, in film terms, that sets the scene for the story, the long shot down Main Street USA. In this sense, it produces a noteworthy parallel to the layout of the demi-fantastic film *Edward Scissorhands* (1990). In *Edward Scissorhands*, the amplified wholesomeness and pastel colors of a suburb of 1950s American ranch houses are contrasted with the dark and gothic castle/stone mansion at the end of the street, fittingly inhabited by a mad inventor played by Vincent Price. Director Tim Burton initially conceived the setting for *Edward Scissorhands* as Burbank, California, but the film was shot in the equally sunny and wholesome Tampa Bay area of Florida, both settings close in geography and character to the Disney castle settings of Anaheim and Orlando. Although the *Edward Scissorhands* castle appears more ominous than the pink-lit fairy-tale castle of Disneyland, the transformational effect is identical: ordinary America becomes most interesting when a castle looms at the end of Main Street. It is when the castle comes into view that stories begin.

The visitor approaching the park castle is hence walking into a Disney film, past the landmark that signals the beginning of the narrative. To draw the visitor into the narrative, the castle was designed as what early film producers called a "wienie" or "weenie," a concept much like Hitchcock's "MacGuffin": a motivating object that draws viewers into the narrative.[16] Ronald Davidson, a producer of serials for Republic, explains the meaning of the term: "The most important element of a serial plot is the weenie, that is the object of all the mayhem. The weenie can be a map, a document, a mine, an oriental scarab with mystical powers, an invention, or a Nazi plot to gain control of Middle Africa."[17] Another source characterizes Walt Disney's intention behind wienies:

> During the design phase, Walt told his designers, "What you need is a wienie, which says to people 'come this way.' People won't go down a long corridor unless there's something promising at the end. You have to have something that beckons to them." In Disneyland, Sleeping Beauty's Castle is the grandest wienie of them all—the most visible symbol of Disneyland.[18]

The castle was hence consciously designed as a visual and geographical wienie: a point toward which the narrative of a Disneyland visit is heading, as well as a point of orientation from all the Lands in the surrounding park. It serves most particularly as the gateway to Fantasyland and as its central orienting landmark. In that sense the castle is both a door and a compass. Moreover, like the medieval manuscripts depicting the castles of the Ducs de Berry from which it takes its inspiration, the castle is illuminated, and at night, lighting intensifies its dramatic impact. With the castle illuminated, and especially in the light of the nightly fireworks, the visitor becomes a character in a *son-et-lumière* spectacle, in which the castles beckons in its role as beacon.

In its first iteration, the California Sleeping Beauty castle, the interior is almost an afterthought; the principal appeal of the castle is simply its outward appearance. Nevertheless in 1957 a "Sleeping Beauty" walk-through opened in the castle: a series of miniature dioramas, punctuated by mock-illuminated manuscripts narrating the story, accompanied by music from the animated film. These dioramas retained the visual style of the Disney animated *Sleeping Beauty*, an amalgamation of the medieval, the late seventeenth-century vision of Charles Perrault (re-teller of *La Belle au bois dormant*), and the 1950s of the film's creation. The 1950s aspects are ultimately the responsibility of Eyvind Earle, the production designer of the *Sleeping Beauty* film. Over the years the walk-through was updated, but the dioramas were finally retired in 2001. A fairy-tale-like seven-year period of dormancy followed, and the current refurbished Sleeping Beauty walk-through was reopened in 2008. Thus the "new" California Sleeping Beauty walk-through is retroprogressive, returning to Eyvind Earle's medieval/seventeenth-century/1950s design, as the 1950s have hence joined the medieval period and later eras as a focus of second-hand nostalgia— "remembered" at a remove by its audience, and now employed as a generator of pleasing emotions and appealing stories.

Thus the interior of Sleeping Beauty's Castle is all story, a story in which the protagonist need only go to sleep to be transformed. Up to this point, the tale of Sleeping Beauty is much like the frame of so many medieval dream-vision narratives, such as *Pearl*, *Piers Plowman*, and Chaucer's *Book of the Duchess*, in which a protagonist with a problem sleeps and enters a transformative dream world. *Sleeping Beauty* as fairy tale and film is only a step away from this classic dream-vision narrative. Here, woken by the salvific kiss of the prince from a sleep (as the legend on the walk-through reads) "unto death," the sleeper is transformed into princess and bride, her transformation emblematized by the castle to which the prince and his bride head at the end of the narrative. The end of the ride shows the castle shining on a hill above the viewer, as happily-ever-after as an unreachable afterlife. In both the originating tale and the film, Sleeping Beauty's magical sleep is portrayed as literal, and she awakens at the end; but in another sense, the tale is tantamount to a dream vision. The protagonist is, after all, *Sleeping* Beauty, as if her sleep is in some way not past but defining and ongoing.[19] The world she enters upon waking—the world in which dreams have come true—is so fanciful that it is as imaginary as a dream.

In much the same way, Sleeping Beauty's Castle serves as a transformative nexus for the visitor to Disneyland. The grand entryway, the point to which Main Street USA and the promenade lead, would, in a historical castle, debouche onto the interior courtyard and the entrance to the castle building proper. But the Sleeping Beauty Castle entryway leads not to the rest of the castle—other than the Sleeping Beauty Walk-Through, there is no rest of the castle—but to Disneyland. No sooner do visitors enter the gateway than they are out the other side of the castle. Gertrude Stein's observation about California similarly applies to the Disneyland castle: "When you get there, there isn't any there there." But it would be misleading to say that the castle has no "contents": in another sense, the content of the castle is all of Disneyland. The castle entryway is a portal: on the one side, Main Street USA; on the other side, the realm of the imagination. The castle is the objective correlative of the transformative potential of Sleeping Beauty's dream; once entered, dreams come true.

The castle is hence the transformative point in a narrative. In the narrative of *Sleeping Beauty*, the protagonist must escape the curse of the evil fairy who has kept her stupefied and powerless, and Disneyland offers escape in a similar way. The situation of visitors to Disneyland brings to mind a drug-related graffito of the 1970s: "Acid soaks up 99 times its weight in excess reality."[20] Like those who consume the transformative potion, visitors to Disneyland are invited to shed the weight of excess reality. The park's objective—to relieve them of this weight—has been aptly described by John Hench, the iconic Disney designer renowned for his sixty-five-year tenure with the company, which included designing the castles for the Orlando and Tokyo Disney parks:

> "People come here loaded with good intentions," Mr. Hench said. "But like all humans, they've brought two things with them: last week's hurt or pain, which they can't forget yet, and next month's payment or God knows what. So we overwhelm them. Everywhere they go, we catch their attention; they have to take all this in. They say, 'Gee, we had a good time.' They don't know why. It's because they dropped those two things they'd been carrying. They forget tomorrow and they forget yesterday."[21]

Visitors' own yesterdays are supplanted by purified, fairy-tale yesterdays. The castle is their entryway to a land with the excess reality removed.

Thus, the Disney castles in these examples are all confected of other confections, staged and supplied with narratives to suggest that that the visitor is on the brink of transfiguration. The narrative of transformation has a long history in American child culture. Like the medieval romance, the narrative holds that the protagonist must undergo a decisive moment of transformation to vault her or him from obscurity to renown. The heroic identity is latent, obscure to everyone. To claim the new identity, the protagonist must only maintain, rather than develop, this hidden identity: the transfiguration is ineluctable.

Although this theme of latent heroism appeared in many guises, it often took the form of the ordinary person revealed to be royalty. The motif appears in novels such as Frances Hodgson Burnett's *A Little Princess* (1905) and *The Lost Prince* (1915) and through a long lines of books to more recent examples such as Meg Cabot's *The Princess Diaries* (2000; film released 2001). It is also the story of the young Arthur as written by Thomas Malory and filmed as the animated Disney feature *The Sword in the Stone* (1963). As realized in Disney's castles, however, the motif is quintessentially a story of female transformation, endorsed by the choice of Sleeping Beauty and Cinderella as animating forces.

These forces are most manifest in the Florida Cinderella Castle, which houses two fairy-tale-realizing enterprises. The more obscure of these is the Cinderella Castle Suite, an elaborate, virtually secret fairy-tale suite in the heart of the castle, based on the chateaux of seventeenth-century France. It is entered through a secret door in the castle, and its grandfather clock always shows one minute to midnight, as if time has slowed to the last moment before the transformation expires. A stay in the suite cannot be booked: it is available only as a prize. In the 2007 Disney World "Year of a Million Dreams" promotion, one visiting family per day was randomly chosen for a night in the suite, which features lavish furnishings, paneling, and stained glass, and even "magic mirrors" that turn into flat-screen TVs. Although the suite is ostensibly designed for Cinderella and her Prince Charming, with carved wooden initial C's on the eight-foot headboards, the suite is clearly designed for families, with side-by-side queen beds as well as a foldout seventeenth-century-style sofa, so that the suite sleeps a family of six. The Castle Suite is all about dreams coming true, as web comments make clear. One commenter remarks:

> to give my family the opportunity to stay in the castle ... well, that would just be priceless. Life gives us unexpected surprises whether good or bad and we have had our share of bad lately and to just get away from things at home for a while is good. But throw in all the magical moments Disney has to offer ... well, it just makes you forget troubles while you are gone.[22]

The more overt of the transformational possibilities housed in the Cinderella Castle is the emphatically pink Bibbidi Bobbidi Boutique, "a beauty salon where little girls are magically transformed into little princesses."[23] Thus girls can undergo a transformation within the very icon of transformation in the heart of Disney. The phrase "Bibbidi Bobbidi Boo" is derived from the Disney film of *Cinderella*, where it forms the transformative spell uttered by the Fairy Godmother as she changes Cinderella's rags into a glamorous gown and her helpers into an equipage ready for the royal ball.[24] The boutique offers three packages, the Coach Package (hair and shimmering makeup), the Crown Package (hair, shimmering makeup, and nails), and the Castle Package (hair, shimmering makeup, nails, purchase of dress, crown, wand, shoes, accessories such as ponytail hairpieces and barrettes, and photo package featuring a pumpkin carriage). The girls are princessed in name as well as in appearance; for instance, a girl named Emily will be called "Princess Emily" throughout the makeover. The beauticians, dressed as in the film, are termed "Fairy Godmothers in Training," and the reveal to the waiting family is accomplished theatrically, by lifting a curtain, waving a wand with a star on the end, and announcing "Bibbidi-Bobbidi-Boo!" Later in the park, employees (a.k.a. "cast members") greet the madeover girls as "Princess." The transformative experience is marketed heavily, as on one Disney website: "Another cast member recalls, 'Today when giving a Princess her big reveal, she was so happy that she shouted, "I guess dreams really can come true."[25] Thus clothes, like castles, are an outward and manifest marker of the fairy-tale realm. They are playhouses for make-believe. Just as the dictum proclaims, clothes teach women how to be female impersonators, and here clothes facilitate their transformation into princess impersonators. The great relief of the princess position is that princesses have to do no more than *be*—indeed, Sleeping Beauty hardly operates even on that level, but merely sleeps to achieve her destiny. No agency is required, and thus those who are clothed as princesses have done everything necessary to "make dreams come true" for the duration. The role is socially constructed; the construction is complete as park employees acknowledge the princesshood of their patrons.

But the craving for transformation—the dream of being celebrated—is not unique to small girls. Adult women can also be "princessed" at the Bibbidi Bobbidi Boutique. A woman identified as "Jeanie" describes her transformation on a website: "I got a princess makeover for my 33rd birthday. It helped make it one of my most memorable birthdays ever. The fairy Godmothers-in-training did a great job of making me a princess for the day! ☺"[26]

The ultimate adult fairy-tale princessing process, however, is bridal. In *Cinderella*, the Fairy Godmother transforms the drudge into a begowned damsel with an expiration date: if she hasn't attracted the prince by midnight, she will revert to her unprincessed, downtrodden state forever, and thus it is the prince who facilitates her final exaltation into a castled princess. One critic describes this process as it occurs in the film:

> The castle is visible from the tower room in which Cinderella, now grown, is reluctant to be wakened by her bird and mouse friends. As she wakes, she mock-scolds the animals for "spoiling people's best dreams," and sings "A dream is a wish your heart makes / When you're fast asleep." Although she refuses to tell the creatures the substance of her dreams—she follows the rules about telling—her gaze at the castle clues us to the direction of her dreams.[27]

In Cinderella's life, the castle, emblem of a carefree, romance-filled new life, is the wienie, as the identity of the bride and of the princess become intertwined. (In a related observation, it has been noted that the two Disney "girl heroines" most marginal to the princess-marketing trend, Pocahontas and Mulan, are the two who do not marry [and hence do not become brides] at the end of their tales, a point related to Ilan Mitchell-Smith's arguments in his essay in this volume.[28])

The wedding is the ultimate bibbidi-bobbidi-boo of the adult woman. As one critic has noted, their wedding day is the only day of their lives on which women are freed to be the unequivocally celebrated star of the show: "A groom knows that many future opportunities for attention and recognition lie before him .... His fiancée, on the other hand, will likely never again experience this level of attention."[29] To capitalize on this longing, Disney Fairy Tale Weddings and Honeymoons, founded in 1991, promotes the fairy-tale aspect of Disney as an inducement to conduct a "destination wedding" at a Disney property. Disney literature suggests: "To bring your fantasy wedding to life, host it near the enchanted Cinderella Castle inside the Magic Kingdom® Park. With romance and whimsy around every corner, you'll have all your guests believing in happily-ever-afters."[30] Even weddings performed elsewhere on Disney properties orient themselves in reference to the fairy-tale castle: "On its own island surrounded by the serene waters of the Seven Seas Lagoon, Disney's Wedding Pavilion provides a perfect indoor ceremony site with views of Cinderella Castle."[31] Disney takes this theme into further commercialization with its Fairy Tale Wedding line of wedding dresses, developed in 2007. "Every bride wants to be a princess on her wedding day," observes Pam Lifford, an executive vice president at Disney Consumer Products.[32]

As the reach of the Disney castle enterprise has expanded, it has also colonized the home, with outposts in girls' bedrooms. With more than 40,000 licensed items on the market, the Disney Princess line of products reached $3.4 billion in sales in 2006.[33] Among these products is an extensive range of Disney play castles, typically pink and explicitly princessy. But what constitutes a princess? One scholar reports the answer from her young daughter:

> "What's a princess?" I ask Abigail.
> "A rich girl," she answers promptly, "with a kingdom."
> She is a bit fuzzy on what exactly a kingdom is, however. "It's got lots of rooms," she explains tentatively.[34]

The realm of a princess is all interior, and the play castles bear out this hyperfeminine interiority. The Disney Princess Sparkle Transforming

Castle, for instance, is blue with a purple pastel roof and large pink doors, with handles forming a heart and surmounted by a crown. The castle unfolds to become a girl's bedroom, with a vanity and mirror (for beautifying), an armoire (for storing the princess's gowns), and a prominent but single-size pink bed with elaborate swirly headboard. The larger Disney Sleeping Beauty Castle Playset comes with character figures and is designed to reenact fairy-tale story lines, with a variety of domestic accessories such as a vanity mirror, banquet table, fireplace, and treasure box. Playing princess means playing house: a girl's castle is her home. By contrast, boys' castle playsets—not offered by Disney but widely available—are predictably martial, coming supplied with knights. They are typically all fortification, all exterior, with no inside rooms and no female characters. As in much of history, the domestic spaces of the building are gendered female, the outside male. The storybook imagination becomes a realm of gendered apartheid.

Thus the irony develops that although medieval castles were martial fortifications, built to intimidate and to consolidate power, their modern full-size simulations are gendered feminine, playful, and unthreatening. Associated with gowns with "Cinderella" skirts, tiaras, shimmer, pastel colors, and fairy-tale endings, the castles become a glorified domestic playspace in which, like Cinderella, no princess must do her own cleaning.

The promises of transformation have devolved, then, to child-sized dreams, no larger than the confines of a palace bedroom, a kingdom with a lot of rooms. The Middle Ages on view supplies a vehicle for these transformative fantasies. This fantasy element of the park has, however, met with some opprobrium. Michael Wallace lambastes the Disney parks' "history-flavored entertainment" for filtering out, as he says, "depressions, strikes on the railroads, warfare in the minefields, squalor in the immigrant communities, lynching, imperial wars, and the emergence of mass protests by populists and socialists. *This* history has been whited out, presumably because it would have distressed and repelled visitors."[35] The idea that theme park attractions featuring lynchings, minefield wars, immigrant squalor, depressions, and strikes would *presumably* repel visitors adds an unintentionally comic note to the critique. But Wallace has made several category errors here, failing to distinguish between amusement parks and museums, as well as between personal, child-centered narrative and adult histories of social forces. The key to Disney fantasy narrative is that the peril is personal and child-sized: not the oppression of thousands of disenfranchised workers, but, for instance, the sorrow of a single girl whose mother has died and who is reduced to an outcast in the family—a situation all too realistic in historical terms. The end of this and other essential Disney narratives is a child's happy ending: the protagonist is once more safe, cherished, celebrated, and in a family.

The fundamental disjunction between amusement and a full awareness of the horrors of the world has long occupied critics: to enjoy oneself requires precisely that horrors and oppressions be overcome and effaced. The fairy-tale world of Disney narrative is a dream vision in which all can end happily. It elides the fact that, outside the "Happiest Place on Earth," royalty is no guarantee against trouble and violence, weddings are no assurance of fairy-tale happiness, and ultimately all stories end the same: no one lives "ever after." These are the excess reality, the unspoken certainty after the end of the tale. The Disney narrative contends that within the smaller realm of the domestic, moments of play, transformation, and celebration are still possible. This is the promise of the castle.

## Notes

1. Images of Disney's various castles are readily available online; copyright issues prohibit their inclusion in this volume.
2. The phrase comes from Michael Wallace, "Mickey Mouse History: Portraying the Past at Disney World," *History Museums in the United States: A Critical Assessment*, ed. Warren Leon and Roy Rosenzweig (Champaign: University of Illinois Press, 1989), 158–82, at 159.
3. Beth Dunlop, *Building a Dream: The Art of Disney Architecture* (New York: Abrams, 1996), 99.
4. Beth Dunlop, *Building a Dream*, 103.
5. Disney's remark is recalled by Ken Anderson, as quoted by Beth Dunlop, *Building a Dream*, 99. I have added clarifying punctuation.
6. On this and other aspects of the background, see Robin Allan, *Walt Disney and Europe: European Influences on the Animated Feature Films of Walt Disney* (Bloomington: Indiana University Press, 1999).
7. William Shakespeare, *Henry V, The Riverside Shakespeare*, ed. Blakemore Evans, 2nd ed. (Boston: Houghton Mifflin, 1997), Prologue lines 17–18, 23 (with spellings modernized).
8. On Ludwig II, see Michael Petzet and Werner Neumeister, *Ludwig II. und seine Schlösser: Die Welt des Bayerischen Märchenkönigs* (Munich: Prestel Verlag, 1995); Georg Baumgartner, *Königliche Träume: Ludwig II. und seine Bauten* (Munich: Hugendubel, 1981); Werner Richter, *Ludwig II., König von Bayern* (Munich: Stiebner, 2001), abridged and translated as *The Mad Monarch: The Life and Times of Ludwig II of Bavaria* (Chicago: Regnery, 1954); Michael Kühler and Wrba Ernst, *The Castles of King Ludwig II.* (Wurzburg: Verlagshaus Würzburg, 2008). A more popular narrative biography is Greg King, *The Mad King: The Life and Times of Ludwig II of Bavaria* (London: Aurum, 1997). See also *Designs for the Dream King: The Castles and Palaces of Ludwig II of Bavaria*, ed. Diana Keith-Neil (London: Debretts Peerage, 1978).

9. Eugène-Emmanuel Viollet-le-Duc, *Dictionnaire raisonné de l'architecture française du XIe au XVIe siècle*, 10 vols. (Paris, 1854–1868), 8.14. Translation from Eugène-Emmanuel Viollet-le-Duc, *The Foundations of Architecture: Selections from the Dictionnaire Raisonné*, trans. Kenneth Whitehead (New York: Braziller, 1990), 195.
10. Desmond Chapman-Huston, *Bavarian Fantasy: The Story of Ludwig II* (London: Murray, 1955), 147.
11. Falkenstein is only one of a burgeoning American practice of castle-building. There are currently more than 300 castles in the United States, with varying degrees of medieval authenticity. The castles are listed with photos at dupontcastle.com; Web, accessed February 2, 2011.
12. "Our Castle Story," falkensteincastle.com; Web, accessed November 29, 2011.
13. "FAQ," falkensteincastle.com; Web, accessed November 29, 2011.
14. Having served as the inspiration for Charles Perrault's *La Belle au bois dormant*, the Château d'Ussé now styles itself the "Château de la Belle au bois dormant" (Sleeping Beauty's Castle) and features life-size wax figures of the fairy tale. Note that the name of the château is Chenonceau, the name of the village Chenonceaux. The other Disney parks also have castles as their central features: the Hong Kong park has a Sleeping Beauty castle modeled on the one in Disneyland, and the Tokyo park a Cinderella Castle modeled on Orlando's, with a popular fire-breathing dragon in the cellar.
15. Tony Baxter as quoted by Beth Dunlop, *Building a Dream*, 103–04.
16. The origin of the term is in dispute. Jesse Schell and Joe Shochet of Disney Imagineering write that "Weenie is a term coined by Walt Disney himself. It refers to the technique used on movie sets of guiding stage dogs by holding up part of a sausage. The classic 'weenie' is the castle at Disneyland. It draws the eye, and the eye draws the feet, and people walk to the castle at the center of the park" ("GDC 2001: Interactive Theme Park Rides," gamasutra.com; Web, accessed April 10, 2012).
17. goldenageofhollywood.co.uk/HistoryofFilm/BMovies.html; Web, accessed November 9, 2010.
18. Pat Williams with Jom Denney, *How to Be Like Walt: Capturing the Disney Magic Every Day of Your Life* (Deerfield Beach, FL: Health Communications, 2004), 203.
19. The fabulist R. A. Lafferty notes this possibility in his tale "The Story of Little Briar-Rose: A Scholarly Study" (available in *The Year's Best Fantasy and Horror: Fourth Annual Collection*, ed. Ellen Datlow and Terri Windling [New York: St. Martin's, 1991], 463–68), in which the entire universe is merely an ongoing dream of Sleeping Beauty.
20. Seen on a wall at Haverford College, Pennsylvania, 1977.
21. Quoted by Patricia Leigh Brown, "In Fairy Dust, Disney Finds New Realism," *The New York Times*, July 20, 1989.
22. "G. Rose," commenting on November 10, 2011, at "Cinderella Castle Suite," everythingmouse.com; Web, accessed November 29, 2011.

23. "Bibbidi Bobbidi Boutique," disneyworld.disney.go.com; Web, accessed December 12, 2010. The Bibbidi Bobbidi Boutique in California Disneyland is separate from the castle, as the castle is not large enough to house a sizable business.
24. "Bibbidi-Bobbidi-Boo" is also a song from the film, nominated for an Academy Award for best song in 1950, with music and lyrics by Mack David, Al Hoffman, and Jerry Livingston. The most popular recording, by Perry Como and the Fontane Sisters, dates from 1949 and reached number 14 on the Billboard charts.
25. "Bibbidi Bobbidi Boutique: One Year Later," disneyparks.disney.go.com; Web, accessed December 12, 2010.
26. "Bibbidi Bobbidi Boutique: One Year Later."
27. Naomi Wood, "Domesticating Dreams in Walt Disney's *Cinderella*," *The Lion and the Unicorn* 20 (1996): 25–49, at 35.
28. Marjorie Worthington, "The Motherless 'Disney Princess': Marketing Mothers Out of the Picture," *Mommy Angst: Motherhood in Popular Culture*, ed. Ann Hall and Mardia Bishop (Santa Barbara: ABC-CLIO, 2009), 29–46, at 39.
29. Anna Fels, *Necessary Dreams: Ambition in Women's Changing Lives* (New York: Anchor, 2005), 115.
30. "Magical Ceremony Locations," at "Disney's Fairy-Tale Weddings," disneyweddings.disney.go.com; Web, accessed December 12, 2010.
31. "Magical Ceremony Locations."
32. "Press Release: Alfred Angelo and Disney to Debut Their First Disney Princess-Inspired Bridal Gown Collection," disneyconsumerproducts.com (September 27, 2010); Web, accessed December 12, 2010.
33. Susan Linn, "A Royal Juggernaut: The Disney Princesses and Other Commercialized Threats to Creative Play," *The Sexualization of Childhood*, ed. Sharna Olfman (Westport: Praeger, 2009), 33–50, at 40.
34. Susan Linn, "A Royal Juggernaut," 40.
35. Michael Wallace, "Mickey Mouse History," 162.

# CHAPTER 4

# PILGRIMAGE AND MEDIEVAL NARRATIVE STRUCTURES IN DISNEY'S PARKS

Susan Aronstein

> *A trip to a Disney park is like going to heaven. A culmination of every dream and hope. A summation of the American life.*
>
> Karal Marling, "Imagineering the Disney Theme Parks"[1]
>
> *With Disney, the Pilgrim's Progress had become a family tour and Vanity Fair the Heavenly City.*
>
> Neil Harris, "Expository Expositions: Preparing for the Theme Parks"[2]

After the Super Bowl in 1987, the Walt Disney Company screened the first in a now-famous series of commercial spots. Featuring clips of New York Giants quarterback Phil Simms and an orchestral rendition of "When You Wish Upon a Star," the spot concludes with the campaign's tagline: in response to the query, "Phil Simms, you have just won the Super Bowl. What are you going to do next?," Simms replies, "I'm going to go to Disney World!"[3] Subsequent ads have featured a bevy of beaming star athletes and newly crowned beauty queens affirming that a trip to a Disney theme park marks the "culmination of every dream and hope."[4] And, indeed, in popular discourse, a trip to Disneyland or Walt Disney World is more than a trip; it is a pilgrimage, a journey that, as Karal Marling unironically asserts, "is like going to heaven."[5]

By designating the Disney theme parks as pilgrimage centers, academics and celebrities alike figure Disneyland and Disney World as the modern, secular heir to medieval religious sites such as Jerusalem, Rome, and Canterbury. Many agree with Neil Harris that this transition degrades a vision of the Heavenly City into Vanity Fair, in which pilgrimage is replaced by consumption.[6] However, Alexander Moore, in one of the earliest academic studies of Walt Disney World, presents a compelling anthropological analysis of the parks as functional pilgrimage centers.[7] Drawing on Victor Turner and Van Gennep, Moore demonstrates that a Disney theme park is "a bounded space apart from ordinary settlement" that provides "a place of congregation, some symbols on display, readily understood by the congregated pilgrims, common activities... and myths which the other elements (site, symbols, and activities) evoke."[8] As Moore argues, journeying into the parks requires visitors to cross a series of borders separating them from "ordinary settlement": the ticket booths, the berm that shields guests from the outside world, and finally, the two tunnels leading into the park, each marked by a plaque indicating, "Here you leave the world of today and enter the world of yesterday, tomorrow and fantasy."[9] Once inside, the parks provide guests with a place of congregation, The Magic Kingdom, in which the primary Disney symbols are on display: Mickey Mouse, Sleeping Beauty Castle, even Walt himself. Common activities—rides, parades, and shows—evoke the parks' central myths: Disney's version of fairy tales, America's history and destiny, and the technological utopia to come.

In the park, as Moore asserts, pilgrims undergo a rite of passage, an intensification through which they are renewed and affirmed; I would add that they also undergo a rite of transformation, from which they return "occupying a new status."[10] This new status, however, in a unique Disney twist, is presented as a return to a previous state: "induce(d)... to think and behave in the way that Disney [knows is] best for them," they become, as Walt Disney asserted about the guests who visited Disneyland in its early years, "more *like themselves*."[11] This chapter explores the ways in which Walt Disney's "*intended* shrine," California's Disneyland, originally affected this renewal and transformation, working to make visitors "more like" their Disney selves; in this manner, the park's techniques relied on similar structures and theories as medieval narrative and dramatic art.[12] I begin with Walt's vision of the park as a place of pilgrimage—where visitors could experience past, future, and fantasy as reality, where dreams would come true. Here, Disney's guests enacted an experiential American mystery cycle that placed them in the context of America's privileged history and destiny, while, in the park's narrative rides, they witnessed mini-morality plays chronicling a fall into "sin" and a return to "grace." From this examination of Disneyland as Walt himself envisioned it, I turn to a discussion of Disneyland post-Walt, focusing on the corporate additions and extensions that, lacking Walt's central vision and mythology, cloud the park's original drama, transforming it from a modern-medieval pilgrimage center into a postmodern consumption hub.

## Magical Memories of Disney: The Promise of Presence

As Moore argues, pilgrimage sites rely on collective memory, on their ability to "create links among widely scattered persons who share a common mytho-historical and cultural orientation."[13] Many scholars have demonstrated that Disneyland, in the words of Sharon Zukin, both "restores and invents collective memory."[14] Disneyland also invents and restores *personal* memory, and, indeed, its creation of collective memory depends on first instilling these "Disney memories" in the individual. To do so, the park urges us to discover our "inner-Disney." Its advertising campaign exhorts: "Open your eyes and you will find magical memories inside... the magical memories of Disney." These television spots both create and play upon our nostalgia for an ideal childhood, a simpler life, an America suffused in the golden light of an invented yesterday: "Do you remember a time?" As viewers do so, Disney holds out the hope of a return to that time: "come back to a time, back to a place." Here, the commercial's rapid sequence of events demonstrates, new memories will be made as families "celebrate the magic," becoming once more their lost selves—their true selves. These commercials constitute a call to pilgrimage; they urge viewers to leave the chaos of their everyday lives and to undertake a journey of renewal and transformation. At the end of this journey, Disneyland's celebratory parade and fireworks both confirm our transformation and send us back to the real world renewed, exhorting us to "always remember the Magic," "that dreams come true."[15]

But why journey to Disneyland to find Disney Magic? Pilgrimages were necessary in the Middle Ages, as Madeline Caviness reminds us, because works "did not circulate as commercial productions"; rather, "art was rooted in place and the only way to see famous works was to undertake a pilgrimage to the cathedrals and shrines that housed them."[16] Disney works, however, are ubiquitous, emblazoned on merchandise ranging from diapers to DVDs. How then, does Disney convince people to journey to its shrines? It does so by employing its iconic images in a way that harks back to the theories of medieval writers such as Gregory the Great. As Cynthia Hahn explains, Gregory believed that the "act of sight brings the exterior to the interior.... For Gregory... seeing never demands [an] effort of interpretation ... any necessary labor on the part of the viewer is conceived as the work of memory." These images "move the soul."[17] An eighth-century letter, spuriously attributed to Gregory, elaborates on the power of images: "When you see the picture, you are inflamed in your soul with love for him whose image you see."[18] While Gregory and his followers concern themselves with divine images—biblical tales, saints lives, Christian iconography, "enduring and revealing sign[s]"[19]—their theories about the function of images equally apply to modern marketing techniques, and The Walt Disney Company is well aware of the power of its signs to move viewers. "Celebrate the Magic" employs Cinderella Castle as its establishing shot, the parades showcase iconic Disney characters, and Mickey Mouse runs through both, exploiting these iconic images to trigger both personal and cultural memories and inflame viewers with desire, urging them to venture on a pilgrimage.

If the image in the Middle Ages pointed to "him whose image you see," a divine presence that transcends any earthly representation, the Disney images on film, backpacks, and play-sets point, ultimately, to their reified "real" presence in the Parks. Representation points to reality. As Walt Disney promised when unveiling his plans for Disneyland in the first episode of *Walt Disney's Disneyland*, "Disneyland the show and Disneyland the place are all part of the same."[20] Thus, Disneyland promised "reality," the show in the flesh. Commercials for the park still invoke this promise, cutting between scenes from the films to their actualization in the parks: the animated Cinderella becomes a real princess in a ball gown, Dumbo morphs from animation to one of "Dumbo's Flying Elephants," and smiling children "celebrate the magic."

### The Dreams and Hard Facts That Have Made America: Walt's American Mystery Cycle

Disneyland promises "presence," the seeing "face to face." It also purports to make "the past present," a process that Steven Nichols, in his discussion of medieval narrative, observes "show[s] that the present belong[s] to a coherent cosmogony, that it manifest[s] a divine plan for the universe."[21] Walt insisted, "I don't just want to entertain kids with pony rides and swings, I want them to learn something about their heritage,"[22] and, as his plans for a theme park developed from a relatively small attraction on the Burbank Studio lot to the full-scale Magic Kingdom in Anaheim, his pedagogical mission also expanded. Disney presented Disneyland as an American City on the Hill, "dedicated to the ideals, the dreams and the hard facts that have made America, with the hope that it will be a source of joy and inspiration to all the world."[23] Much of the unprecedented opening day live-television broadcast focused on Disney's literal re-membering of history to allow his visitors "to travel through the gates of time and into [their] very historic past": the Main Street just like the one from Grandma's childhood, the "frontier village that could have been carved out of the wilderness a hundred years ago by the pioneers themselves."[24]

In its presentation of America's heroic past and privileged future to the masses, a presentation that Mike Wallace argues has "taught more people history, in a more memorable way, than they ever learned in school," the park functions in the same way as did the medieval Corpus Christi cycle.[25] According to V. A. Kolve, these plays chronicled "the ways God has allowed himself to be known *in time* ... to the unlettered and un-Latined," "concentrate[ing] alike on the significant past and the significant future."[26] Both Disneyland and the medieval cycle plays omit the present while using the past and future to address their audiences in the present. Disney publicists explained to *Look* magazine in 1954, "In Disneyland clocks and watches lose all meaning, for there is no present. There are only yesterday, tomorrow, and the timeless land of fantasy,"[27] and the Corpus Christi plays present a typological presentation of Divine History, moving from type to antetype, from Adam to Christ, the Tree of Knowledge to the Cross, Creation to Doomsday, instructing their audiences to use the present as "a time for amendment and preparation," to "shape [their] actions" so as to secure their place in heaven."[28] Disneyland uses an equally typological presentation of American history to instruct its visitors and prepare them for the future, a Distory that functions "like a tonic, ... restoring ... faith in things to come, despite the threat of atom bombs and guided missiles," reminding visitors of a cosmic scheme, one that will lead to, as 1967's Carousel of Progress proclaimed, "a great big beautiful tomorrow."[29]

While the Corpus Christi plays move through the "seven ages of man" integral to the unfolding of God's plan on earth, Disneyland was designed to move its pilgrims through the historical "realms" key to the fulfillment of America's manifest destiny. On the opening-day broadcast, either Walt or one of the celebrity hosts (Art Linkletter, Ronald Reagan, and Bob Cummings) explained the park's historical narrative to the ninety-million Americans gathered around their television sets. As the first guests passed through the tunnels and onto Main Street USA, the announcer observed, "You find yourself in a bygone time, another world. The clock has turned back a half-a-century and you're in the main square of a small American town. The year: 1900." Here, the nation is at the crossroads of progress in a landscape "combining the color of Frontier days with the oncoming excitement of the twentieth-century."[30] From this moment of nostalgia and promise, Disneyland's historical narrative moves to Frontierland and America's creation myth. Reading from the plaque dedicating Frontierland, Disney intoned: "It is here that we experience the story of our country's past. The color, romance, and drama of Frontier America as it developed from wilderness trails to roads, riverboats, railroads and civilization. A tribute to the faith, courage and ingenuity of our hardy pioneers who blazed the trail and made this progress possible." Adventureland transports Disneyland's guests from the nineteenth-century American Wilderness to "a still unconquered and untamed region of our own world," in which they visit "a Tahitian village where [they] can experience a slice of life as it exists in the paradise of the Pacific; an African trading post, the spear-head of civilization in those primitive lands." Although the voice-over codes Adventureland as "now," its attraction is clearly its "then," its pristine and primitive state that, like the American West before it, waits for hardy pioneers to introduce "roads, riverboats, railways and civilization." The Disney pilgrim and pioneer moves from Adventureland to Tomorrowland, where America's destiny will be played out in "the fascinating world of the future," "offer[ing] new frontiers in science, adventures, ideals; the hope for a peaceful and unified world." Here, instead of Doomsday and Eternity, park patrons find American millennialism, the nation's realization of a utopia on earth. In all of these historical lands, we see the American character manifested in history: pioneer and inventor, adventurer and space-traveler.

### Sermons in Fiberglass: Disneyland's Dark Rides

If a journey to Disneyland is a pilgrimage to Walt's intended shrine for America's history and destiny, within the park itself the pilgrims undertake, as Moore notes, several other journeys, each in themselves "passage[s]," in which "the visitor is exposed to a marvelous array of symbols, evoking myths ... already known to the passenger-spectators."[31] While Disneyland's historical narrative reasserts the nation's, and, therefore, the individual's cosmic destiny, many of its attractions focus on constructing subjects worthy of that destiny: productive, docile, and properly gendered workers and consumers. Here, too, the park relies on medieval narrative techniques. At its most basic level, the Disneyland ride employs the structure of descent and ascent. In this structure, pilgrims leave the "real world" behind, journey down into darkness and chaos, and return to light and order. Like medieval morality plays, saints lives, and biblical tales, the stories (or myths) embedded in these journeys warn the riders about improper and dangerous behaviors and direct their desires toward the proper objects. In addition to echoing these medieval plays in plot and function, Disneyland's rides work on their audiences in the same way—and for the same reasons—that medieval narrative arts, such as stained glass windows and sequence paintings, did for their original viewers. While iconic images (such as the cross for medieval viewers and Sleeping Beauty Castle for Disney pilgrims) invoke a desire for presence, narrative images "stir and strengthen ... memories of edifying stories," "recall[ing] sacred history to the minds of the indoctrinated."[32] Although they translate the visual to the experiential, rather than the written to the pictorial, Disneyland's narrative rides also invoke edifying stories, recall "sacred" history to the minds of the Disney-indoctrinated, and lead the faithful toward the contemplation of, if not God, at least Disney doctrine.

These narrative rides distinguished Disneyland from other midways and amusement parks. From its inception, Walt Disney insisted that his park would have "no roller coaster or other rides in the cheap thrill category."[33] This insistence posed a challenge to his designers because the financial history of expositions clearly illustrated that fair-goers had a limited tolerance for pedagogy; what made money was "short and fast" rides.[34] In the end, they focused on what was uniquely Disney, the company's films, for a series of dark rides. While earlier dark rides, such as the Creation Ride that thrilled visitors to Coney Island at the turn of the century, had been mere spectacles, Disney designers marketed Disneyland's rides as a chance to enter into the adventure. The opening-day broadcast promised the television audience that, in Fantasyland, "we can fly with Peter Pan to Neverland; wander with Alice through Wonderland; ride Cinderella's pumpkin coach; in fact, anything your heart desires."[35]

At first, the designers envisioned these attractions as "walk-throughs," but they quickly decided that they needed to control the rate at which visitors moved through the attraction, and the Disney ride, which transports viewers in themed cars through the narrative, was born. The designers planned these rides as they would a storyboard for one of Disney's animated features, selecting the scenes from the films that would best carry the narrative. Realizing that the passengers would have "to grasp the meaning of a given setting in the blink of an eye," they kept their vignettes simple, eschewing extraneous detail for the essence of the scene. The fact that Disneyland's rides effectively convey their stories in this way speaks to their narratives' status as cultural myths and explains how these rides can rely, as did medieval narrative art, on its audience's ability to re-member—literally, to put the narrative back together—the films on which the rides are based. If, as Herbert Kessler argues, medieval audiences relied on intertextuality—liturgy and sermons—to reconstruct the stories portrayed in sequence paintings and stained-glass windows, Disney's riders rely on the company's films. Thus, the rides become one more step in the process, begun in their fairy-tale films' opening displacement of the "book," by which the corporation authorizes its version of the tale. Disney's rides, like medieval narrative images, "provide [their] audiences with] authorized versions of stories."[36]

On opening day, all of Disneyland's dark rides were located in Fantasyland, and these attractions support the park's pilgrimage ritual in their original cosmic mytho-historical narratives, particularly Snow White's Scary Adventures and Peter Pan's Flight. Walt dedicated Fantasyland to the "young and young at heart, to those who believe that, when you wish upon a star, your dreams do come true." "Here," he declared, "[is] a world of imagination, hopes and dreams. In this timeless land of enchantment, the ages of chivalry, make-believe, and magic are reborn and fairy tales come true."[37] As he had with America's past and future, Disney promised presence—chivalry, magic, and fairy tales reified, dreams becoming reality. As Fantasyland's rides (at least according to Disney marketers) fulfill this promise, they also teach the park's pilgrims both what to desire and what kinds of behavior will allow them to achieve these dreams. These rides, like the films that inspired them, are moral tales, mini-morality plays within the park's larger mystery cycle.

As with all of Disneyland's rides, pilgrims to Snow White's Scary Adventures begin their journey in its carefully themed line. The ride's façade combines the Queen's gothic castle with the Seven Dwarfs' cozy thatched cottage, invoking both the scene in which the jealous queen spies Snow White and the prince from her tower window and Snow White's first glimpse of her domestic refuge in the woods. A golden book sets the stage at the entrance to the line, which serves as the ride's equivalent to the film's framing book. It tells the tale of the poisoned apple and Snow White's falling victim to an "evil spell"; as riders wind further into the line, they peer into the Queen's dungeon/study, where they hear her plot "a special death" for Snow White. The next visual is a 3-D mural of the Dwarfs' thatched cottage; here riders board a minecart (each named after a dwarf) and enter into the world of the film. A series of vignettes, accompanied by clips from the film's soundtrack follows: the "dance" scene with the Dwarfs, with clean laundry hanging by the fire and Snow White on her way to bed ("The Dwarfs' Yodel Song"); a quick glimpse of the Queen, declaring "soon I'll be fairest of them all"; and the Dwarfs' glittering mine ("Heigh Ho!"). The music sounds an ominous note and the cart passes through a tunnel guarded by vultures and into the Queen's castle, where, in front of her mirror, the Queen intones "Magic Mirror on the Wall, with this disguise I will fool them all!" and turns to reveal the aged hag. The cart passes through the dungeon, which borrows images from the film—the book of spells, the hanging skeletons, the vultures—and the hag looms up twice more to offer the riders "apples" before passing into the "scary forest" scene, complete with crocodiles and ghastly trees. At the door of the cottage, the hag appears again, with a cackling laugh: "Just one bite!" The cart turns, the silhouetted Dwarfs spot the Queen attempting to dislodge a boulder, lightning flashes, and riders hear a scream. The music shifts from the discordant orchestral accompaniment to Snow White's flight through the forest to "With a Smile and a Song," and the cart exits. To the left, we see a book, with an illustration of Snow White and her Prince riding off to their castle in the sky, assuring us "they lived happily ever after." The ride takes one minute and fifty-one seconds to redact the animated film's eighty-four minute narrative. As the carts move past each vignette, passengers are able to "grasp the meaning of a given setting within the blink of an eye" because they already know the story.[38] Just as medieval viewers of sequence paintings could link isolated images from saints' lives and biblical tales, filling in the narrative and extrapolating the moral lesson, so Disney pilgrims can "read" Snow White's Scary Adventures: the film provides an intertextual frame for reading the ride, and the ride recalls the film to memory. Notice, as well, that it does so not through a linear rehearsal of the film's narrative; instead, the ride, as Suzanne Lewis argues of medieval sequence paintings, uses paratactic arrangements and montage to convey its meaning.[39] Rearranging the film to conform to the paradigmatic narrative of the Disneyland ride, Snow White's Scary Adventures descends from the domestic tranquility of the Dwarfs' cottage and the happy work place of the mine into the Evil Queen's dark dungeons and wild forests before returning to domestic bliss and happily-ever-after. Within this narrative, the ride employs both images from the film and melodies from its soundtrack to convey its message: girls are safest and happiest indoors, and men (even little men) protect and provide for them. Do the laundry, go to bed, and "someday [your] prince will come."

The narrative line in Snow White's Scary Adventures scrambles and truncates the film; even so, it still "tells" a story; Peter Pan's Flight, in contrast, relies more heavily on isolated vignettes from the film as passengers journey from the domestic space of the nursery, off to Neverland, and back again. This journey also begins in the liminal space of the line. The ride's façade combines a clock-tower (a medieval-ish Big Ben) with a half-timbered manor; as riders move into the line, the space around them recalls a pirate ship's hold with wooden arches and suspended "gas" lanterns. Murals on the outside wall depict scenes from a pirate's life on the left, and on the right, the rooftops of London gradually emerge from a flat surface to 3-D as patrons approach the nursery window that marks the beginning of the ride. The music, cheerfully and repetitively, reminds riders, "you can fly!" They board their pirate ship and swoop into the Darlings' nursery; Peter Pan and Tinker Bell provide the pixie dust and "here we go!" And, indeed, through swooshing drops, the use of lighting, and forced perspective, the ride invokes the feeling of flight. London dwindles; Neverland appears. As would a camera in a film, the riders zoom from a long, establishing shot, closer into the action, where they see, in quick succession, Tiger Lily awaiting rescue; Peter battling Captain Hook at Skull Rock; Wendy perched precariously at the edge of the plank while Peter, again, battles Hook; a distant glimpse of the Indian camp; Smee and Captain Hook fleeing the crocodile; and, finally, Tinkerbell and Peter steering the golden boat back to London, where the riders return to Fantasyland, "with a smile in [their] heart[s]."

In less than two-and-a-half minutes, these isolated scenes from the film, to paraphrase Gregory the Great, stir and strengthen the memory of edifying stories. And the edifying story told by Peter Pan is an interesting one, given the obvious comparisons to be made between Neverland and Fantasyland. Neverland is a stage on the way to adulthood: it is a space of adventures, but one that must be followed by a return to London. Furthermore, Neverland, as even the ride's few vignettes make clear, is a boy's space. Girls are in Neverland solely to tell stories, to compete with each other for male (Peter's) attention, and to be rescued. In the end, like Snow White's Scary Adventures, Peter Pan's Flight points its passengers home: girls to the domestic space of the nursery, and boys, ultimately, to the productive adventures of Frontierland and Adventureland, the real-world taming of the wilderness and civilizing of the jungle.

This same narrative of descent and return is repeated in the remainder of Fantasyland's dark rides: Alice moves from a nightmarish Wonderland back to the safety of home; Mr. Toad's Wild Ride chronicles the consequences of its protagonist's indulgences—in alcohol and fast cars—before emerging into the light; Pinocchio learns his lessons about the unbridled id on Pleasure Island and comes home to Gepetto's workshop "a real boy." In these rides, the "dark space" functions as a mini-sermon, showing its riders Disney's version of the seven deadly sins—vanity, curiosity, laziness, indulgence, license, disobedience, pessimism—all of which must be avoided if domestic bliss and American destiny are to be achieved. Fantasyland constructs proper American subjects, in the mold of their pioneer and colonial forefathers and foremothers, able to meet the challenges of the future and ensure the technological utopia Disney envisioned in Tomorrowland. And, indeed, on opening day, all of the Park's dark rides were located in Fantasyland; in the other lands, guests were expected to "do" rather than to observe; to be part of the adventure—to shoot a rifle in Davy Crockett's arcade, to travel the rivers of Africa, to drive the freeways of tomorrow, to take a rocket to the moon.

Fantasyland's dark rides depend on their use of Disney myth to convey their message effectively; they assume, in Moore's words, that "the symbols" (in this case, scenes), "on display [are] readily understood by the congregated pilgrims."[40] They are effective only because the Disney narratives on which they are based are omnipresent; without the intertextual interpretive context provided by the films, these rides would be meaningless—a series of disconnected images. However, two of Disneyland's most successful dark rides were not (at least originally) based on a Disney film: Pirates of the Caribbean and The Haunted Mansion. These rides succeed because, although they do not call to memory a specific Disney film, they invoke narrative templates that their riders already know—mostly from Hollywood films—and package them in the paradigmatic narrative of the Disneyland ride. Both rides are located in New Orleans Square, the first "themed" land not directly connected to Main Street USA's central hub, and the last addition to Disneyland supervised by Disney himself. Located between Frontierland and Adventureland, New Orleans Square houses the Disney abject—those elements of indulgence and license of every kind that must be eliminated from the park's narrative of domesticity, productivity, and expansion. Consumption and sexuality run amok. Like Neverland, New Orleans may be a fun place to visit, but it is not a place to call home, a fact that Disneyland reinforces in the land's two dark rides, which present more adult versions of Fantasyland's moral lessons.

Designed before Disney's death in 1966, the original Pirates of the Caribbean opened in 1967.[41] Since it cannot rely on the riders' instant recognition of images from Disney films, Pirates takes longer to tell its tale, to invoke its narrative template. At over ten minutes, it is one of the longest rides in Disneyland. Riders enter into a decaying New Orleans mansion to find themselves in a dank, perpetual twilight as they head toward the landing of a swampy lagoon. Boarding rickety boats, they pass through the last bastions of civilization, a bayou shanty town to the left and the elegant (or at least expensive) Blue Bayou restaurant on the right; crickets chirp and fireflies flit. The boat pauses before a tunnel marked by a skull and cross-bones, and the skull speaks: "Ya come seeking adventure and salty ol' pirates, eh? It be too late to alter course, mateys ... and mark well me words, mateys, dead men tell no tales." As this warning repeats, the boat plunges into underground caves, where it winds through dark passages to the merry strains of "Yo Ho Ho! A Pirate's Life for Me!" The boat plunges again and the echo "dead men tell no tales" displaces the music. Riders pass a series of vignettes providing an interpretive frame for the narrative to follow: two skeletons and a treasure chest on an island; a skeleton steering a ghost ship through the storm; more skeletons playing cards and drinking, surrounded by decaying luxuries; the skeleton captain lies in his bed; and a skeleton lies on an enormous pile of treasure. This is how pirates will end. Time flashes back, skeletons flesh out, and the ride enters into the pre-story, the seeking of the treasure, and sacking of the town. This is the adult version of *Pinocchio*'s Pleasure Island: consumption without production, and sexuality without marriage. Riders see the pirates plundering the town, teetering under towers of loot, procuring women. (A paunchy pirate proclaims, "I'd love to hoist me colors on that shy little wench," promising, "I be willing to share, I be.") In a fit of drunkenness, the marauding men burn the town to the ground, merrily singing:

> Yo ho, yo ho, a pirate's life for me.
> We pillage, we plunder, we rifle and loot.
> Drink up me 'earties, yo ho.
> We kidnap and ravage and don't give a hoot.
> Drink up me 'earties, yo ho.

Barely escaping conflagration themselves, the passengers ascend back to the landing and the sounds of civilized dining. The moral here is clear: piratical behavior—indulgence, license, sex, out-of-control consumption—leads to death. Like Dante, the passengers glimpse the behaviors that lead to the inferno, yet all in good fun: "a rollicking adventure with the boldest crew of swashbucklers ever to terrify the Spanish Main," as a 1967 radio spot affirms.[42] Good fun or not, New Orleans Square distracts patrons from the Disney pilgrimage. It harks back to a static and decaying European past, populated by pirates and ghosts. It lies off the path. As such, the Square functions as a dark ride writ large, embodying the behaviors that could derail America's forward march into the future, and the design of the Park urges patrons to return to the road, to progress, to the narratives of Frontierland and Adventureland.

### Where's Jack?: Corporate Abundance and Narrative Disintegration

Although New Orleans Square was added eleven years after Disneyland's opening, it reinforces Disney's original mythic vision, both as it contributes to the park's version of America's historical mission and privileged destiny and in its dark rides' construction of American subjects. In the years after Disney's death, however, corporate additions have blurred Disneyland's mytho-historical narrative. In 1972, Critter Country replaced the park's original Indian Village, disrupting Frontierland's central (and racist) tale of the march of civilization. Unlike the lands planned by Disney himself, Critter Country is only loosely, and rather cynically, themed: a place to market the animated features that have no room in Fantasyland. Brer Rabbit, Winnie the Pooh, and the remnants of the Country Bear

Jamboree live here, along with two major stores housing themed merchandise. Toontown, inspired by *Who Framed Roger Rabbit*, followed in 1993. Squeezed into a small space behind Fantasyland, Toontown breaks the barrier of the park's protective berm; furthermore, its reification of the world of Disney's early cartoons in Technicolor plastic shatters the Park's careful Disney realism. More Playschool than Fantasyland, Toontown is little more than an elaborate shopping mall as play space, its rides, and attractions a contemporary version of themed "pony rides and swings" for the kids. Neither Critter Country nor Toontown participate in Disneyland's narrative; they merely provide more attractions, more merchandise, more stuff.

This desire to sell merchandise also drives corporate remodelings of Disneyland's original space. Aladdin and Indiana Jones have moved to Adventureland, and Tomorrowland has become Retroland, a reified version of a 1950s' science-fiction future, hawking the products of today. It is also home to a series of characters who are neither entirely Disney (Buzz Lightyear is here, but so are R2-D2 and C-3PO) nor always thematically appropriate (Nemo and Dory). In addition, the rides added to the remodeled lands, from Indiana Jones Adventure to the Finding Nemo Submarine Voyage, function differently from those found in Fantasyland. Rather than calling existing stories to memory, Corporate Disney's dark rides provide sequels and spin-offs, new adventures rather than old memories: Indiana seeks another artifact; Nemo is lost again; Emperor Zurg must be defeated; the Rebel Alliance (still) fights the Empire. In spite of their incorporation of narratives of descent and ascent, departure and return, Disneyland's latest attractions do not teach. They entertain. More like a straight to DVD sequel than a stained-glass window, they satisfy a consuming audience's demand for more.

As the Walt Disney Company adds new lands and attractions, they also blur the borders between lands, again obscuring the park's original narrative; corporate creep breaks down the thematic unity of individual lands, as exemplified in the "pirate princess" merchandise available throughout the park. And, indeed, in the wake of the unexpected popularity of the *Pirates of the Caribbean* films, pirates are ubiquitous in Disneyland. They have invaded the Rivers of America and Tom Sawyer's Island, where Twain's narrative has been overwritten by Jerry Bruckheimer's film: the attraction is now essentially a "walk-through" based on *The Curse of the Black Pearl*. Nowhere, however, is the sacrifice of theme and message to merchandise as obvious as it is in the "re-imagineered" Pirates of the Caribbean, which opened in 2006. This version of the ride superimposes a thin "Where's Jack Sparrow?" tale on the original narrative, adding a few lurking animatronic Johnny Depp/Jack Sparrows into the existing vignettes. Neither a successful new tale nor a "calling to memory" of the film, the point here seems to be to exploit the success of the films, an excuse to stock Jack Sparrow action figures in The Pieces of Eight shop at the ride's exit.

The remodeled Pirates of the Caribbean makes no attempt to teach; it simply seeks to entertain. Riders want Jack Sparrow, and so it gives them Jack Sparrow, even at the expense of the ride's original moral message. In this Pirates, Jack extols the dubious virtues and ill-gotten rewards of his swashbuckling life. Another popular post-Walt attraction, Splash Mountain seeks to teach, but is not able to do so. This ride's failure to communicate effectively with its audience—in spite of its carefully constructed narrative based on a Disney film—demonstrates that, for dark rides to function as part of the Disneyland pilgrimage, they must tap into myths "already known to the passenger-spectators."[43] Splash Mountain, Critter Country's major attraction, opened in 1989; it provided Disneyland with a popular water flume ride, as well as an opportunity to market merchandise based on the Walt Disney Company's most problematic film, *The Song of the South*. This 1946 animated/live-action film, due to its controversial portrayals of race, has never been released on home-video in the United States. However, by removing Uncle Remus from the ride (as well as by replacing the film's tar-baby with a honey-laden beehive), Splash Mountain, as Jason Sperb observes, seeks to "take a frown, turn it upside down" and recuperate *Song of the South's* animated sequences for the Disney canon.[44] It strings together the film's Brer Rabbit tales, arranging them to reiterate Disneyland's central moral lesson: the virtues of a home and hearth well-earned. Brer Rabbit leaves his productive and idyllic small town in search of adventure; he runs afoul of Brer Fox and Brer Bear and almost lands in their soup pot; however, through wit and ingenuity, he finds his way home and the ride ends with Brer Rabbit, safe and cozy, extolling the virtues of home. This narrative should work: Disney's imagineers diligently created complex scenes, complete with song and dialogue, to carry the story. They also carefully crafted the line to place riders "in the story," with plaques along the way setting the scene: "This happened once upon a time ... when critters were closer to the folks and the folks were closer to the critters." However, although there are many "symbols on display," the majority of riders lack the intertextual context necessary to read those images, to provide the connections between them, and to extrapolate the lesson. Instead, Splash Mountain functions partly as spectacle, but mostly as an over-themed thrill ride. The point is the "daring five-story plunge down rustic Chick-A-Pin Hill."[45]

## Marketing the Magic: Disneyland's System of Objects

Walt Disney conceived Disneyland as a therapeutic pilgrimage center, one that would, John Findlay observes, "not simply ... entertain people but ... improve them."[46] He also saw it as a place to sell products. Like medieval pilgrimage centers such as Canterbury, Disneyland sold food, drink, and "pilgrim badges" to the wayfarers who passed through its gates. In the twenty-first century, however, the marketplace has obscured the pilgrimage center and the park has become more Vanity Fair than Heavenly City. While the "Disney Version" of American history informs much of our political rhetoric and the outline of Walt's American mystery cycle underlies the park's new corporate abundance, patrons' relationships to Disney's narratives have changed since the 1950s. Then, Uncle Walt both dominated the television airwaves and crept into schools with educational films and guides; he served as the spokesman for the American Way, and his productions provided a primer on subjects ranging from history to science. A generation trusted him with their children, and those children, in turn, grew up in the Church of Mickey Mouse.[47] Disney's version of America's history and destiny was firmly embedded in their collective memory and a trip to Disneyland evoked this version, reminding Americans of their "common mytho-historical and cultural orientation"; it provided "not only temporary escape from the outside world, but also a lasting sense of reassurance about the individual's ultimate fate in the world."[48] Now, however, we (mostly) recognize this version of history as rhetoric, as Distory, and maintain an ironic distance from the Disney past. We, theoretically, recognize we are engaged in play. We know it is Disneyland.

Our relationship to Disneyland's dark rides is more complex. The corporation's assiduous re-release of its films assures that Disney still supplies children with a set of tales, "known to all," that serve a pedagogical function.[49] And, as Laurie Finke and I argue, the rides based on these tales contribute to Disneyland's hidden curriculum: the teaching of "boys and girls to refashion themselves bodily to fit a 1950s version of bipolar gender that aims to produce not sexuality, love, romance, or mating—hetero or otherwise—but American citizens ready to take up their place as docile and productive workers and consuming subjects—properly gendered, raced, and American."[50] In today's Disneyland, however, the rides' pedagogical narratives take a backseat to the park's peddling of Disney icons. Becoming a princess, in spite of the lip service given to good manners and a kind heart, requires the consumption of objects: ball gowns and tiaras. Jedis need light sabers; knights need swords. Identity is constructed from the outside in.

Disney's Princess line provides a telling example of how Disneyland's function as a pilgrimage center has changed. Emblazoned on each dress, each tiara, each pair of shoes is the iconic image of a princess: Belle on the yellow gown, Cinderella on the blue, Sleeping Beauty on the pink. Disney's symbols and narratives no longer point to an outside referent; they point only to Disney and its products—to Jack Sparrow figures and Snow White dolls, Donald Duck sweatshirts and Goofy mugs, stuffed Mickeys and Disney Trading Pins. Rather than urging us to reconsider our place in a cosmic plan, they inspire us to consume—to purchase images, magical memories of Disney, images and memories that will "move the soul," stirring us to plan another pilgrimage, to return and "celebrate the magic."

### Notes

1. Karal Marling, "Imagineering the Disney Theme Parks," *Designing Disney's Theme Parks: The Architecture of Reassurance*, ed. Karal Marling (Paris: Flammarion, 1997), 29–177, at 169.
2. Neil Harris, "Expository Expositions: Preparing for the Theme Parks," *Designing Disney's Theme Parks*, 19–27, at 27.
3. "I'm Going to Disney World: First Ad, 1987," youtube.com; Web, accessed October 3, 2011.
4. Karal Marling, "Imagineering the Disney Theme Parks," 169.
5. Karal Marling, "Imagineering the Disney Theme Parks," 169. Other academics note this fact with considerably less approval. See Stephen Fjellman, *Vinyl Leaves: Walt Disney World and America* (Boulder: Westview, 1992), 10.
6. Neil Harris, "Expository Expositions," 27.
7. Alexander Moore, "Walt Disney World: Bounded Ritual Space and the Playful Pilgrimage Center," *Anthropological Quarterly* 53 (1980): 207–18.
8. Alexander Moore, "Walt Disney World," 209.
9. Fjellman and Moore are among those who discuss border-crossing at Walt Disney World; Louis Marin examines the "limits" at Disneyland in "Utopic Degeneration: Disneyland" (*Utopics: Spatial Play*, trans. Robert Volrath [Atlantic Highlands, NJ: Humanities, 1984], 239–57). Laurie Finke and I more fully examine crossing into Disneyland in "Discipline and Pleasure: The Pedagogical Work of Disneyland," *Educational Philosophy and Theory* forthcoming.
10. Alexander Moore, "Walt Disney World," 210.
11. Walt Disney, qtd. in John Findlay, *Magic Lands* (Berkeley: University of California Press, 1992), 67.
12. Stephen Fjellman, *Vinyl Leaves*, 22. Most academic studies on Disney's theme parks focus on Walt Disney World in Florida; however, Disneyland was conceived and supervised by Disney himself, who remained in control of the park's narrative until his death in 1966, and it thus remains closer to his original vision.
13. Alexander Moore, "Walt Disney World," 210.

14. Sharon Zukin, *Landscapes of Power: From Detroit to Disney World* (Berkeley: University of California Press, 1991), 223.
15. "Celebrate the Magic," "Remember Dreams Come True," and "Holiday Parade," youtube.com; Web, accessed October 3, 2011.
16. Madeline Caviness, "Reception of Images by Medieval Viewers," *A Companion to Medieval Art: Romanesque and Gothic in Northern Europe*, ed. Conrad Rudolph (Oxford: Blackwell, 2006), 65–85, at 65.
17. Cynthia Hahn, *Portrayed on the Heart: Narrative Effects in the Pictorial Lives of Saints from the Tenth through the Thirteenth Century* (Berkeley: University of California Press, 2001), 49.
18. Gregory the Great, qtd. in Cynthia Hahn, "Vision," *A Companion to Medieval Art*, 45–64, at 51.
19. Cynthia Hahn, "Vision," 51.
20. "The Disneyland Story," *Walt Disney Treasures: Disneyland U.S.A.*, DVD (Walt Disney Studios, 2001).
21. Stephen Nichols, *Romanesque Signs: Early Medieval Narrative and Iconography* (New Haven: Yale University Press, 1983), xi.
22. Walt Disney, qtd. in Karal Marling, "Imagineering the Disney Theme Parks," 52.
23. From Walt Disney's Disneyland dedication speech, aired live on national television, 17 Jul. 1955, from "Dateline Disneyland," *Walt Disney Treasures: Disneyland U.S.A.*
24. "Dateline Disneyland."
25. Mike Wallace, *Mickey Mouse History and Other Essays on American Memory* (Philadelphia: Temple University Press, 1996), 134.
26. V. A. Kolve, *The Play Called Corpus Christi* (Stanford: Stanford University Press, 1966), 3 and 103.
27. "Here's Your First View of Disneyland," *Look* 18 (2 Nov. 1954): 86, qtd. in John Findlay, *Magic Lands*, 54.
28. V. A. Kolve, *The Play Called Corpus Christi*, 102, 103.
29. *Daily Democrat*, 3 Sep. 1958, qtd. in John Findlay, *Magic Lands*, 91. Created for the 1964 World's Fair, the Carousel of Progress was an attraction in Disneyland's Tomorowland from 1967 to 1973; it moved to Walt Disney World in 1975 and was rewritten and restaged as "Walt Disney's Carousel of Progress" in 1994. "Carousel of Progress," youtube.com; Web, accessed October 3, 2011.
30. "The Disneyland Story"
31. Alexander Moore, "Walt Disney World," 213.
32. Cynthia Hahn, "Vision," 50; Herbert Kessler, "Gregory the Great and Image Theory in Northern Europe during the Twelfth and Thirteenth Century," *A Companion to Medieval Art*, 151–72, at 151.
33. Walt Disney, qtd. in Karal Marling, "Imagineering the Disney Theme Parks," 54.
34. Neil Harris, "Expository Exposition," 22.
35. "The Disneyland Story;" Marling discusses the design process for the original dark rides, "Imagineering the Disney Theme Parks," 62–75.

36. Herbert Kessler, "Gregory the Great," 163.
37. "Dateline Disneyland."
38. Karal Marling, "Imagineering the Disney Theme Parks," 124.
39. Suzanne Lewis, "Narrative," *A Companion to Medieval Art: Romanesque and Gothic in Northern Europe*, ed. Conrad Rudolph (Oxford: Blackwell, 2006), 86–105, at 91–92.
40. Alexander Moore, "Walt Disney World," 209.
41. "Pirates of the Caribbean Ride: Disneyland 2007" and "Disneyland: Pirates of the Caribbean: The Whole Ride (1990)," youtube.com; Web, accessed October 3, 2011.
42. "Pirate Radio Promotion," tellnotales.com/audio.php; Web, accessed October 3, 2011.
43. Alexander Moore, "Walt Disney World," 213.
44. Jason Sperb, "'Take a Frown, Turn It Upside Down': Splash Mountain, Walt Disney World, and the Cultural De-rac[e]-ination of Disney's *Song of the South* (1946)," *Journal of Popular Culture* 38.5 (2005): 924–38.
45. From the Disneyland site's official description of *Splash Mountain:* "Splash Mountain," disneyland.disney.go.com; Web, accessed October 3, 2011.
46. John Findlay, *Magic Lands*, 79.
47. Nicholas Sammond discusses Disney's influence on children in the 1950s in *Babes in Tomorrowland: Walt Disney and the Making of the American Child, 1930–1960* (Durham: Duke University Press, 2005).
48. Alexander Moore, "Walt Disney World," 210.
49. Henry Giroux, *The Mouse That Roared: Disney and the End of Innocence* (Lanham: Rowman & Littlefield, 1999), 4.
50. Susan Aronstein and Laurie Finke, "Discipline and Pleasure," forthcoming.

PART II

THE DISTORICAL MIDDLE AGES

CHAPTER 5

"YOU DON'T LEARN IT DELIBERATELY, BUT
YOU JUST KNOW IT FROM WHAT YOU'VE SEEN":
BRITISH UNDERSTANDINGS OF THE MEDIEVAL
PAST GLEANED FROM DISNEY'S FAIRY TALES

*Paul Sturtevant*

Scholars in this volume and elsewhere have argued that the films of Walt Disney present a unique vision of the Middle Ages,[1] and that, as a result, the Disney brand of medievalism influences legions of children introduced to Disney's animated films, theme parks, and merchandise each year. However, a question remains: to what degree is this true? It is well enough to state, based on theory, anecdote, or conjecture, that Disney films influence our cultural understandings of the Middle Ages. But without evidence confirming this influence and exploring its nuances, assertions about the effects of Disney's medievalisms are provisional at best.

The following chapter rectifies this shortcoming by reporting the results of a sociological study in which a group of young British people discussed their understandings of the Middle Ages and their memories of the sources of those understandings. Within this study, some participants discussed how Disney's animated films influenced their current perceptions of the Middle Ages, whether those films were self-evidently medieval in setting and provenance or not. This chapter begins by outlining the study's methodology and then discusses participants' perceptions of Disney's influence on their ideas. Based on these perceptions, it then explores the degree of Disney films' influence on understandings of the medieval in their audiences,[2] analyzing the participants' problematic perceived relationship between Disney's Princess fairy tales and the Middle Ages, as well as the degree to which *Aladdin* was regarded as an example—and counterexample—of the overriding sense that Disney's animated fairy tales are recognizably medieval. The chapter concludes by proposing some avenues for further research.

## The Study and Its Methodology

The analysis reported here is a portion of a larger sociological study conducted at the Institute for Medieval Studies at the University of Leeds between November 2008 and June 2009.[3] This study focused on the British public's understanding of the medieval past, and the influence of recent big-budget Hollywood films on those understandings. It comprised a series of ten focus group interviews with nineteen people, all between the ages of 18 and 26. None of these people had studied the Middle Ages academically beyond GCSE level (age 14–16), and all of them were educated in the United Kingdom.[4]

The interviews were designed with a constructivist methodology, similar to the ones developed by David Morrison in his audience-reception studies of the public's understanding of violence in the media, reported in his *Defining Violence: The Search for Understanding*. In this study of violence in the British media, Morrison set out to answer the question, "How do viewers define violence?" Fundamentally, Morrison's study attempted to "understand the factors at play when someone categorizes an act as violent," in order to "discover whether there is a single definition of violence."[5] Morrison and his team asked the participants in their focus groups to judge what in the media comprised "serious violence and what was, although violent, not serious violence."[6] They explicitly asked participants to judge violence subjectively, in their own words and defined according to their own metrics, rather than defining violence for them by a set of predetermined criteria; it is this subjective definition of terms and the ability of the participants to shape the discussion according to their own understandings that defines his study as "constructivist."

The present study treated "medievalness" similarly.[7] It set out to determine how individuals define "medieval" and "Middle Ages" in their own terms and according to their own understandings, and to consider the factors at play when someone categorizes something as "medieval" or from the "Middle Ages" (and furthermore what, if any, differences were evoked by these similar terms). Each interview began with two stream-of-consciousness exercises in which participants were asked to write down everything that they associated with the words "medieval" or "Middle Ages."[8] Participants were then asked to form small subgroups and discuss the commonalities and differences among their responses, and to present to the whole group a taxonomy of responses. They divided their responses into categories of their own devising (such as "war," "costume," or "disease") and ranked the importance of these categories as a part of the broader concept. This inspired, and was followed by, a group discussion in which the interview questions were similarly open-ended, such as "What does 'medieval' mean to you?" and "Where do you remember learning about this?" Follow-up questions were derived from participants' initial responses. In nine of the ten groups, this was followed by watching a recent medieval film and discussing how the film corresponded to or conflicted with their expectations.[9] The constructivist methodological philosophy caused the results of the study to range widely; responses touched on concepts of medieval geography, intellectual and material culture, iconic representations of the period, and the relationship between the Middle Ages and contemporary culture. As a result, in the instances when the participants turned the conversation to Disney as a source for their understandings, they did so spontaneously, without prompting from the moderator.

### Discussing a Disney Childhood

One question routinely asked by the moderator during the focus group interviews was "where do you feel you learned about the Middle Ages?" Most participants responded by recounting various experiences from their childhood: schooling, consuming popular culture, or taking trips to historical sites such as castles and abbeys. In their discussions of the popular culture that they consumed as children, they occasionally brought up Disney films as a major influence on their understandings of the Middle Ages. Of all the groups, the November focus group had the longest and most animated discussion of Disney films. This was possibly influenced by the composition of the group, as all five of the participants in this group were women; since many of Disney's films (especially the "Princess" fairy tales) have been marketed to girls, they may have had more familiarity with Disney's films than did some of the others. The November focus group felt that they learned from Disney films, but in a subtle way:[10]

> *Catherine*: I think by watching, like, when you're little, you get shown Disney films, so that's what sets an impression, and as you go through school you get taught more=
> *Emma*: =Yeah like you learn, like you see it all and then you put it together that it=

*Catherine*: =You learn a bit about that=
*Emma*: =Is with medieval and all that, but you already have seen, have got a like picture of it in your head. Then you come to, like, school and it's sort of, like, goes together.
*Elizabeth*: Yeah.
*Emma*: Like, you don't learn it deliberately, 's like, but you just like know it from what you seen and then what they tell ya.
*Jane*: I suppose you go to school and they say, they have knights in the medieval times, without being told you immediately see a, a guy on a horse with the sword and the shield and without them having to say, this is what they wore.

According to these participants, their expectations of the Middle Ages had been established by Disney popular culture and then reinforced and validated by primary school—or perhaps vice versa. In fact, it is difficult to identify an origin point because, especially to a child, any sense that school has more authority than a film may not yet have been established (and possibly remains problematic even in adulthood). Due to pervasive medieval imagery within children's popular culture, children are exposed to images of the Middle Ages at an age before they are able to differentiate readily between fantasy and reality. Adolescent cognitive psychologists George Scarlett and Dennie Wolf describe the "transition from the pretence of symbolic play to that of storytelling occurring between the ages of three and five." To them, before the age of five, children make little cognitive distinction between story and reality: "Between three and five, consciousness of the boundary [between fantastical pretence and practical action] develops, making possible a new and precise understanding of pretence which permits both the internal organization and social sharing of make-believe."[11] When children are exposed to the Middle Ages through children's popular culture, they become accustomed to seeing elements of the fantastical Middle Ages (like wizards and dragons) alongside elements of the historical Middle Ages (such as knights and castles). As children age, these fantastical elements eventually become understood as not existing in reality (or having existed in history), but the sense that these fantastical creatures are located within the context of the Middle Ages remains. In short, although they become understood not to be real, they remain understood to be medieval.

So, to the participants in the present study, Disney played a part in the formation of their ideas, but only a part; they routinely described the films as a part of a larger cycle of learning and validation also including education, popular culture, and familial and social interaction. In analyzing their discussion of Disney films as an influence on their understanding of the period as well, we are presented with a chicken–egg paradox: do these discussions indicate that the participants gained their understandings of the Middle Ages from Disney, or instead that their identification of these films as being medieval simply reflects their understanding of the period, independent of Disney's potential influence?

### Disney's "Traditional Old"/"Princess" Fairy-Tale Genre

The participants in the November focus group felt that many of the Disney animated fairy tales that they had viewed as children had a similar, recognizably medieval aesthetic. For example, Jane recognized that these films had a literary provenance, but one that was sanitized by the Walt Disney Company: "They've kind of taken the nice bits of the Grimm brothers' tales [...] what we know of them [the stories] is [sic] kinda had all the nasty bits taken out and it's mainly what Disney's done to aim them at children." The films that these participants discussed as being related to the Middle Ages are what they commonly called "traditional" Disney films. In their opinion, these included four films: *Snow White and the Seven Dwarfs*, *Sleeping Beauty*, *Cinderella*, and *Beauty and the Beast*. These four, they argued, were set in a similar fairy-tale version of the Middle Ages that Emma labeled "traditional old." Interestingly, these participants did not mention the three Disney films that are set in the Middle Ages: *Robin Hood*, *The Hunchback of Notre Dame*, and *The Sword in the Stone*.

It is possible to read too much into their omission of the three films set in the Middle Ages because a lack of evidence can only say so much. Due to the constructivist methodology used for this study—with follow-up questions derived exclusively from the participants' responses and with discussion centered on what the participants felt was important (rather than what the moderator found important)—this omission could not be interrogated fully. It is possible that these participants simply had not seen these films. Besides, by comparison with the four "traditional" Disney films mentioned, all of the overtly medieval films have male protagonists rather than female. Since this group was composed entirely of women, they may have been exposed by their parents to female-centric fairy tales more often as children and thus the more male-orientated medieval films may have sprung to mind less readily than those with female protagonists. With that said, the animated film discussed most by this group (although with some reservations about how "medieval" it is) was the 2001 fairy-tale parody *Shrek*.

*Shrek* satirically subverts numerous Disney conventions of gender and heroic masculinity, particularly with its protagonist male, a socially inept green ogre with a comedic Scots brogue (in contradistinction to the usual suave, conventionally attractive and American-accented characters typical of Disney's male protagonists). He is a rejection of the "ideal man" put forward by Disney in the 1930s to 1950s, and also a rejection of Disney's version of the 1990s "New Man,"[12] epitomized by the Beast as described by Susan Jeffords:

> the one who can transform himself from the hardened, muscle-bound, domineering man of the eighties into the considering, loving, self-sacrificing man of the nineties. His appearance is more than a horrific guise that repels pretty women; it is instead a burden, one that he must carry until he is set free, free to be the man he truly can be.[13]

*Shrek*, instead, rejects Disney's gender paradigms. As a result, the frequent references to *Shrek* alongside Disney's Princess fairy tales limit a strictly gendered interpretation of these participants' preference to discuss "Princess" fairy tales over Disney's explicitly medieval animated films.

However, the references to *Shrek* may reveal the participants' understanding of the intertextual relationship between fairy tale, legend, Disney, and the Middle Ages. While *Shrek* was not made by Disney (and thus is only tangentially related to the topic of this volume), it frequently parodies and pastiches many of the tropes established by earlier versions of fairy tales, particularly Disney films. When the November group was asked to devise categories for their responses to the word "medieval" and rank them based on their importance, they offered first "war," and next, of equal importance:

> *Elizabeth*: I think fairy tales for medieval cause there's loads of legends, and like King Arthur and Robin Hood … is that … medieval? […]
> *Moderator*: What do you think? (addressed generally) Catherine, do you think=
> *Catherine*: =Yeah!=
> *Moderator*: =the fairy tales and legends and stuff?
> *Catherine*: I don't know why, it reminds me of *Shrek*.
> *Elizabeth*: Yeah. knights and, dragons.

Later, the group enumerated the medieval legends and fairy tales they were referring to:

> *Jane*: […] King Arthur and Merlin, Chaucer, Heath Ledger … It's just that film [*A Knight's Tale*] was really cool, okay! […] Like dragons, and all that kind of thing. […]
> *Emma*: I don't have a clue where all the legends go they just mix up into one, like=
> *Eleanor*: =super-story.

*Elizabeth*: I just had Robin Hood as well as the other, you know, King Arthur and, u m...
*Moderator*: Are there any others, sort of legendary figures that pop out?
*Catherine*: Shrek=
*Elizabeth*: =We say Shrek.

Emma and Eleanor's idea that these tales blend together into one "superstory" is just the sort of postmodern cultural milieu of rampant deconstruction, parody, pastiche, and intertextuality of which *Shrek* and *A Knight's Tale* are a part. The fact that this group's list of legends includes three preeminent legendary figures of the Middle Ages (Robin Hood, Merlin, and King Arthur) and mythological creatures (dragons), alongside a beloved film actor (Heath Ledger) and his medieval author-cum-sidekick (Chaucer, from *A Knight's Tale*), and a fairy-tale parody ogre (Shrek), shows that their concepts of discrete divisions separating historical fantasy, legend, and reality, and modern medieval mash-ups of history, fantasy, and legend are slippery indeed. Additionally, as Elizabeth's initial statement demonstrates, there seems to be little distinction between fairy tale and legend at all. It is perhaps unsurprising, then, that Disney's Princesses can be de-contextualized for marketing purposes (as discussed below), or that their stories collectively were described as "medieval" in spite of a tenuous relationship with the period. All that is required to acquire the label "medieval" is a similar vocabulary of settings and icons that have come to denote the period.

*Snow White*, *Sleeping Beauty*, *Cinderella*, and *Beauty and the Beast* were singled out by the participants as "medieval" due to their similar setting. In addition, all present Emma's "traditional old" version of the past, which included a variety of similar, recognizably medieval visual tropes. To these participants, the primary link between Disney and the Middle Ages was through these iconic images. As we have seen above, Jane listed "knights," "horses," "swords," and "shield." Later, others in the group added to the list. Jane added "queens," women in "big dresses," and "peasants," while others added "castles," "long dresses," and "princesses." These icons seemed to be powerful indicators of "medievalness." Indeed, across the focus groups in this study, queens, knights, peasants, castles, horses, and swords were among the top responses to the stream-of-consciousness exercise (in which participants listed those things that they associated most with the words "medieval" or "Middle Ages"), and costume was mentioned frequently in the subsequent conversations.

While most participants in her group felt that Disney's animated fairy tales presented a homogeneous version of the medieval past, Jane volunteered an exception. She regarded the 1992 film *Aladdin*'s setting as exceptional among Disney films because it is not set in a forested, "English" setting. As a result, it was not medieval to her:

> *Jane*: I was just thinking, like you have exceptions like, like something like *Aladdin*. [...] obviously [some of the movies are] set in, been set in kind of like... England, forest and that sort of setting, [but *Aladdin*] it's been moved across to...
> *Moderator*: Oh, you mean it's not set in [England and forest
> *Jane*: Yeah it's] got a completely different setting=
> *Moderator*: =So are the other ones set in England and forests and stuff?
> *Jane*: Or France, I suppose, technically.

Wooded landscape is here identified both with the Middle Ages generally and with England specifically. France is mentioned but only hesitantly, as an aside and technicality (probably due to the setting of *Beauty and the Beast* in France). This ties into a broader sense, echoed across all the groups, that the Middle Ages were located primarily in England, the British Isles, or (at its broadest) Western Europe. For example, Justin and Stephen in the June group said:

> *Justin*: When I think of the Middle Ages it's probably set in Britain to be fair. I would say.
> *Stephen*: Or it involves Britain.

Chloe and Robert from the April group had a slightly more nuanced view. Chloe felt "the big one [difference] is that we thought 'medieval' was like Britain, like British and English whereas 'Middle Ages' was a bit more widespread." Later, she defined "a bit more widespread" as "Western Europe." Robert agreed, "When we'd said, like, medieval, we associate it with Britain." This is possibly, in part, a result of the English National Curriculum, which dictates that the medieval history taught in English schools is almost exclusively that of the British Isles.[14] Fundamentally, the British people who took part in this study seemed to project their own national identities onto the Middle Ages, viewing the period not just as history, but as *their* history.

This sense of "historical self" and "historical other" illuminates the November group's commentary on *Aladdin*. To the group as a whole, *Aladdin* is not a part of Disney's corpus of medieval fairy tales because "It's a different culture" (Elizabeth). Emma identified the Middle Ages, and Disney's medieval settings, as having an old "feel." *Aladdin*, while set in the past, does not have that same sense of age due to its setting:

> *Emma*: [...] the medieval kind of=
> *Elizabeth*: =yeah=

> *Emma:* =feel. That's like what I think of as like, <u>old</u>. But then, *Aladdin*'s not like that, but it's still old, I still think of it as in the, past [...]
> *Elizabeth:* It's not what you'd think of as Middle Ages or anything=
> *Emma:* =<u>no</u>=
> *Elizabeth:* =what you'd think but it's still in the past =
> *Emma:* =yeah
> *Elizabeth:* That's probably 'cause it's not set in England so you don't associate it with the Middle Ages.

Note Elizabeth's specific comment that she did not associate Aladdin with the Middle Ages because it was not set in England. Despite this, the group went on to recognize that *Aladdin*, different setting notwithstanding, maintained many of the tropes of the "traditional" Disney films they listed. These tropes are simply replaced with Arabian analogues:

> *Jane:* suppose they still have the same idea though 'cause they've still got like a [palace instead
> *Emma:* castle yeah]
> *Elizabeth:* castle yeah]
> *Jane:* of a castle, a princess and, princes and, an elephant instead of a...
> *Elizabeth:* (laugh) [Horse
> *Jane:* Horse]
> *Emma:* Horse] yeah, matching.
> *Jane:* It's the same idea, different culture.

So, although *Aladdin* was considered an exception to the stated rule due to its different setting, it was still recognizable to the group as one of Disney's fairy tales, even if it is not what they might have considered medieval.

## Similarities among the Films

It is possible to evaluate the four listed "traditional old" films (*Snow White and the Seven Dwarfs, Cinderella, Sleeping Beauty,* and *Beauty and the Beast*) as part of a discrete subgenre as a result of their similarities. In recent years, the Walt Disney Company has used these similarities to market the films collectively under the "Disney Princess" franchise, along with *The Little Mermaid, Aladdin, Pocahontas, Mulan, The Princess and the Frog,* and *Tangled.* This franchise is focused on the female protagonist of each film and is used to market a wide variety of aspirational merchandise to young girls and their parents, including DVDs, books, CDs, dolls, accessories, and video games. Peggy Orenstein describes the meteoric rise of the franchise in the *New York Times*:

> Sales at Disney Consumer Products, which started the craze six years ago by packaging nine of its female characters under one royal rubric,

have shot up to $3 billion, globally, this year, from $300 million in 2001. There are now more than 25,000 *Disney Princess* items. "Princess," as some Disney execs call it, is not only the fastest-growing brand the company has ever created; they say it is on its way to becoming the largest girls' franchise on the planet.[15]

Perhaps unsurprisingly, Disney has a website devoted to marketing this franchise, with sections aimed at children ("Games," "Activities," and naturally, "Products") and also for their parents ("Parenting a Princess").[16]

The relationship between this successful fairy-tale franchise and the Middle Ages is subtle. None of the four films listed by the participants depicts medieval narratives or history: they owe their narratives either to Charles Perrault's seventeenth-century folk tales, or in the case of *Snow White and the Seven Dwarfs*, to the nineteenth-century interpretations of these tales by the Brothers Grimm. That said, each of them calls upon the Middle Ages to a greater or lesser degree when creating their fairy-tale aesthetics and narratives. For example, three of them employ a parallel framing narrative. *Snow White*, *Cinderella*, and *Sleeping Beauty* open similarly (although each with differences in the details): a large tome is revealed that bears the film's title in gilt on the cover. The book opens, seemingly of its own accord, to reveal a manuscript page. The text is in an ornamental black letter hand and bears illuminated and colored capitals, and usually marginal ornamentation and illustrations. These openings announce the films as stories based on textual sources (and with the backing of textual authority) with a late-medieval provenance.

Each of these films also prominently features hypermedieval neogothic castles. Each is slightly different; but examined together, they form a recognizably similar corpus that has become representative of Disney itself through inclusion in its theme parks and on its logo (as discussed by Martha Bayless in this volume). Additionally, one of the reasons that the participants gave for labeling these films "medieval" seems to originate with the way that the characters are costumed. But the costumes in these films (and the identifiably "Disney" elements of these costumes) are not universally medieval; they are hybrids of different periods. For instance, the princes of *Sleeping Beauty* and *Snow White* wear simplified versions of late fourteenth- or fifteenth-century costumes, each with hose, cloak, and doublet. The costumes worn by the prince in *Sleeping Beauty* and by Snow White feature the puffed and slashed sleeve cap fashionable in early and mid-sixteenth-century Germany. This was a result of the filmmakers' use of illustrated versions of Grimm's tales as a visual and narrative source and the German descent of many of the filmmakers.[17] On the contrary, the clothing in *Cinderella* and *Beauty and the Beast* is recognizably not medieval. The aristocratic men of *Cinderella* wear late nineteenth-century military formal dress, complete with epaulettes and trouser stripes. The upper-class men of *Beauty and the Beast* wear the cutaway tailcoat, cravat, waistcoat, and breeches combination reminiscent of late eighteenth-century European formalwear.[18]

The most iconic costumes in three of these four films (and the one costume element specifically singled out for mention by the focus groups) are the similar ball gowns worn by the female protagonists. Many participants felt medieval costume was a central feature in what makes something seem "medieval" to them. Commonly, in these discussions, many participants across all the groups discussed the opulent dresses worn by aristocratic medieval women, assigning them an iconic status level with armor for men or muddy rags for peasants. But these dresses were not necessarily medieval ones; some conflated medieval aristocratic dresses with what Eleanor called "big bell skirts," a clear reference to Disney's typical female silhouette. *Cinderella* set the prototype: true to her time period, she wears a severely corseted gown bearing the crinolined bell shape popular during the mid-nineteenth century.[19] The silhouette of this gown is then transplanted onto subsequent Princesses. Aurora's dress bears medievalesque design details imposed on an off-the-shoulder version of Cinderella's silhouette, and Belle shares this silhouette in her gown. Interestingly, this has become such a representative shape for Disney Princesses that even though Snow White's dress does not conform to this shape in the film, many currently available dolls and toys have modified her dress to conform to this slim-waisted bell shape cited by participants.

In addition to squeezing each Princess into a similar dress, each of these "traditional old" films squeezes its women into similar conservative gender paradigms, described by Aida Pérez as "good natured, weak, and obedient princesses awaiting for a gentleman to give them life, who found in romance, marriage, and housekeeping the way to social validation."[20] These features are commonly projected onto the Middle Ages in popular culture due to the common association of "princesses," as members of a royal family, with the Middle Ages. This gender paradigm portrays females who, no matter how independent or able they may seem at the opening of a film, ultimately conform to heteronormative romantic relationships in which they passively accept their heroic aristocratic male. As Henry Giroux writes, "All of the female characters in the films are ultimately subordinate to males and define their power and desire almost exclusively in terms of dominant male narratives."[21] Although they may be judged positively based upon other traits, feminine beauty is regarded as the paramount signifier of virtue, as Elizabeth Bell describes: "Animated heroines were individuated in fair-skinned, fair-eyed, Anglo-Saxon features of Eurocentric loveliness, both conforming to and perfecting Hollywood's beauty boundaries."[22]

### Just How "Medieval" Are These "Traditional" Films?

In spite of some similarities in visual detail and ideology, when examined closely, these four films are recognizably set in very different time periods with varying relationship with the medieval. For example, *Cinderella* and *Sleeping Beauty* occupy opposite ends of the medieval spectrum. On the one hand, of the four films identified by the participants, *Cinderella* is the least overtly medieval. Its material culture is rooted firmly in the nineteenth century rather than the medieval. The introductory tome is illustrated not as a medieval manuscript, but in the line and watercolor illustration style similar to the editions of Jane Austen's novels illustrated by Hugh Thomson or C. E. Brock.[23] It is the only one of these four films that does not take place in a rural, forested setting, as identified by participants as belonging to England and the Middle Ages. The film retains elements of a Germanic or Scandinavian setting, but does not announce itself as medieval. Thus the primary reason the participants in the November focus group identified *Cinderella* as part of the Middle Ages seems to be either through its use of icons commonly associated with the Middle Ages, or, alternately, due to its common association with the other films in this set that present more obviously medieval tales. Iconically, it contains some of the elements presumed to be medieval by the focus groups—a castle, royalty, a big formal dress, and magic—but that seems to be the extent of it.

*Beauty and the Beast* is similar; its period setting seems to be the eighteenth century, and only bears tenuous links to the medieval. The anthropomorphic furniture that populates the Beast's castle is all of a Rococo eighteenth-century style; Gaston totes a blunderbuss. With that said, the film employs a framing narrative that tells the backstory of the Beast through the medium of stained glass in recognizably medieval fashion. The world shown in these stained glass windows is similar to Disney's previous fantastical renderings of the Middle Ages, but once the opening narrative concludes, the world revealed to be the present is that of the eighteenth century. It is difficult to know whether this limited link with the Middle Ages through this framing narrative was the reason for the participants' identification of the film with that period, or if it was more a result of its common association with the other Princess films.

By contrast with these less-medieval films, *Sleeping Beauty* is, of these four, the only film explicitly set during the Middle Ages. It employs the most consistently medieval aesthetic throughout, and takes much of its inspiration from Duc de Berry's early fifteenth-century *Très Riches Heures*. As designer for *Sleeping Beauty* Eyvind Earle pointed out: "I wanted stylized, simplified Gothic, a medieval tapestry out of the surface whenever possible."[24] In addition, uncommon among Disney's fairy tales until then, the film also provides a date for the setting within the dialogue. For example, Prince Phillip, when arguing against his arranged marriage in favor of marrying a peasant girl, uses the date to argue for his supposed modernity: "Now, father, you're living in the past. This is the fourteenth century!" Of course, this is ironic since a modern audience understands the fourteenth century to be not nearly as modern as Phillip wishes it to be. With that said, although it announces a date for itself (and thus seems to present itself as part of the real world, rather than in Bakhtinian "adventure-time"), it blends historical periods and fantastical elements freely.[25]

*Sleeping Beauty* uses the same framing narrative as its predecessors, opening with a gilded and heavily bejeweled codex that notably includes a number of medievalesque illuminations. The opening scene, when the birth of Aurora is announced to the kingdom, depicts many late-medieval elements: knights in plate armor and late-medieval jousting helms, warriors bearing pikes and swords, and heraldic banners flown from the rafters of the castle. The palace is replete with gothic detail, with white walls and impossibly high vaulted ceilings, creating a sense of space and medieval grandeur. By contrast, later in the film when Phillip is rescued from Maleficent's castle, viewers are shown the reverse side of medieval architectural fantasy. Maleficent occupies the mirror image of the palace, a crumbling castle of nineteenth-century gothic horror. The castle guards resemble animated gargoyles, with grotesque animalistic features. When the conflict between fairy-tale idyll and gothic horror comes to a head, Prince Phillip battles with Maleficent as she takes the form of the most iconic medieval monster: a fire-breathing dragon. While doing so, he bears a magical "sword of truth" and "shield of virtue"; the shield, blazoned with a cross, evokes imagery of St. George's battle with a dragon. It is difficult to tell whether Sleeping Beauty's clear "medievalness" and Earle's "simplified gothic" styling has caused the other two nonmedieval films to be grouped into that category, or whether, as implied previously, there is an overriding sense that fairy tale, when equated with legend, is considered medieval by default.

### *Aladdin* and Ideas about Medieval Islamic Culture

Like the November group, the June focus group discussed Disney films in relation to their understanding of the Middle Ages. This group, comprising three young men and one woman, focused their comments primarily on the film *Aladdin*. In a discussion about what medieval Muslims would have looked like during the Crusades, the June group explored how the film established a baseline for this aspect of their knowledge of medieval material culture:

> *Stephen*: I have to say if I had any idea of how the Muslims would be dressed, that has come from *Aladdin*. (laugh) That's, that's kind of basically my idea of, of what they'll be dressed like. So, I suppose that fairly matches up.
> *Moderator*: Does everyone sort of agree with that, that Aladdin is a, is a source for at least your understanding of Islamic dress?
> *Justin*: Yeah. Whether it's a good source or not [...] yeah.

These participants projected the dress they saw in *Aladdin*, which is not explicitly set in a specific country but in a generically Middle-Eastern setting that retains some of the region's architecture (onion-domed palaces), landscape (palm trees and vast deserts), and other cultural markers. Some specific references are given (notably the word "Arabian" in the song *Arabian Nights* and the depiction of the sphinx), but no explicit temporal references are made that would set the film in a place other than a vague time before guns and industrialization. As a result, *Aladdin* is set in a fairy-tale "adventure-time" and "adventure-space" similar to Disney's European fairy tales, except with different superficial cultural markers. Interestingly, no overt references are made to Islam in the film, which suggests that Stephen's and Justin's assertions that this film is a source for their idea of Muslim dress betrays the fact that they may see all Middle-Easterners as Muslim. Immediately after the discussion of Muslim dress in *Aladdin*, these participants continued their discussion of how surprised they were by what they termed the "sophisticated" depiction of the Muslims in the film *Kingdom of Heaven*, which their group viewed prior to the focus group interview:

> *Justin*: In a way, I didn't expect that, which is why I wasn't really sure about there being two big armies because I assumed that, um, I wasn't, I mean not knowing anything about, um, Jerusalem back then I didn't realise that, as a culture, you know, because Britain's always been very much, especially in the past has always been very much, you know, as an, advanced. I mean, I don't want to say advanced, do you know what I mean? It's been on the, on [the developed side of things.
> *Stephen*: E-e-even though,] even though I know in my head that around that period the Islamic world was the centre of learning pretty much, but you know a lot of mathematics and stuff comes from that period, for

some reason maybe it's, you know, some, some gut feeling some gut, um thing that's been instilled in me from somewhere from some book from some film from some TV program or whatever, I, I agree with you that you don't think of them as civilized.
*Justin*: I don't, I don't think it's un, I don't think that they're uncivilized they're just, I don't think of them as being
*Stephen*: =sop—sophisticated [is the word
*Justin*: Yeah,] sorry sophisticated.

Even though Stephen and Justin had learned that the Islamic world was, in many ways, more culturally and technologically advanced than Christendom during the Crusades, they held the contradictory perception that the medieval Islamic world was not "civilized" or "sophisticated." They had difficulty negotiating a compromise between these two conflicting ideas and did not come to a satisfactory reconciliation during the course of the focus group. They also held a nationalistic idea that, by contrast with the Middle East, Britain has always been an "advanced" or "developed" society. This is very arguably not the case, although it would be difficult to devise an objective datum by which to measure the relative advancement or development of a nation or culture.

Furthermore, the fact that this "gut reaction" that medieval Muslims were not sophisticated or civilized was brought up in a conversation about *Aladdin* does not necessarily imply that *Aladdin* is the only, or even the most significant source for this idea. The blame should not be placed on Disney alone. But a connection likely exists between these two points; otherwise this would arguably not have arisen spontaneously in a conversation about expectations generated, in part, by *Aladdin*.

This discussion between these two young British men gives some credence to those within the Arab community who take offense at the film's depiction of Middle-Eastern culture. For example, in 2007, the Islamic Human Rights Commission published a study arguing that the images of Arabs in *Aladdin* are offensive. They took issue with the use of the word "barbaric" in the lyrics of the opening song "Arabian Nights" that describes the film's setting: "Where they cut off your ear / If they don't like your face / It's barbaric, but hey, it's home!" Under pressure from the Arab community at the time of its release, Disney changed some of the lyrics for the home-video. But, as the Islamic Human Rights Commission reports, "It did however retain the line containing the word *barbaric*. The impression that this adjective leaves on the audience can be nothing but negative and derogatory."[26] Furthermore, "Arabian Nights" is the only introduction to a Disney animated film until that point portraying its location as a hostile place. The song concludes with, "A fool off his guard / Will fall and fall hard / Out there on the dunes." The Islamic Human Rights commission report also criticizes subtler negative images of Arabs:

> most of the Arab dwellers of *"Agrabah"* are shown as brutal, bumbling palace guards chasing Aladdin or maidens dressed in veils, street vendors or merchants selling their goods on market stalls. In contrast to the Arabs who are ruthless caricatures, Aladdin, Princess Jasmine and the Sultan are Anglicised (or Americanised to be precise) heroes of the film. They have American accents whilst the rest of the cast have exaggerated and ridiculous Arab accents. The genie even abbreviates Aladdin's name to "Al" creating a more likeable character that the audience can relate to. Rather than portray the Arab culture and Islamic religion in a positive or neutral light, the producers associate it with harsh punishments ... oppressive practices ... and, uncivilized or inferior cultural identifiers attributed to Islam.[27]

*Aladdin* was released to theaters in 1992. The participants in this study, between eighteen and twenty-three years old, would have been under seven years of age at the time of its release. This means, although it is unlikely that most would have seen it in the cinema, they likely were shown it on VHS or DVD at an early age. Additionally, with the infinite replayability of VHS and DVD, and with children's desire for repetition of the familiar, it is probable they saw it many times. As a result, it is entirely possible that many of the images criticized by the Islamic Human Rights Commission eventually helped to form the "gut reaction" against medieval Islam expressed by Stephen and Justin. This point requires further study, but it indicates that the portrayal of other cultures in popular culture aimed at children, of which Disney films are a major part, can set unconscious standards or prejudices that are hard to uproot even by cognitive dissonance. The most provocative point here is that the depiction of cultures and peoples in children's films, like the ones mentioned above, may not just have a temporary impact on the perceptions of the children who watch them that they ultimately "grow out of," but that they may establish expectations, "gut reactions," or cultural stereotypes that remain influential in their adult lives.

## Conclusion

Do the films of the Walt Disney Company influence individuals' understandings of the Middle Ages? At least for these participants, it appears that the answer is yes. Many of the participants recognized something medieval within these films. In the November group, Disney's "traditional" and Princess fairy tales evoked a similar image of the Middle Ages due to a number of common tropes and icons from the period, as well as a recognizably similar aesthetic and setting. With that said, not all of these films have a universally medieval aesthetic—*Cinderella*, for example, is notable in how little of it is drawn from the Middle Ages. Yet, it was grouped with three other films that were collectively labeled "medieval" by participants, possibly by preexisting association with these other three films, or due to the presence of a few icons (royalty, castles, big dresses) that they associated with the Middle Ages. Furthermore, the presence of "big dresses" on the list of medieval icons is peculiar since these bell-skirted ball gowns are a trope of Disney's fairy tales that had its origins in *Cinderella*, and thus the fashion of the nineteenth century, rather than the Middle Ages. This shows that often the participants' qualifications for "medievalness" were not necessarily related to the Middle Ages at all.

When considering comments of the June group, the connection participants made between Disney's fantasies and historical reality bears worrying implications. *Aladdin* seems to have contributed to an uncomfortable prejudice against Muslims which, even when faced with contradictory evidence provided by another film (*Kingdom of Heaven*), some struggled to overcome. This finding implies that popular culture aimed at children, particularly popular films like Disney's, plays a part in the formulation of prejudices that persist in later life. In this way, the study of Disney's medievalism is not necessarily an inconsequential intellectual exercise: if the children who watch Disney films gain their understandings of other cultures and history from the films that they consume, these perceptions can establish an unconscious precedent that affects how they see the world around them.

The study of the potential impact that Disney films may have on the public's understanding of the past is only at a beginning stage, and further research is warranted to explore the nuances of this topic. Important questions include: how do children who watch these films react to the medievalisms in them, and integrate that into their understandings of history? Where do children, or adults, draw the lines between historical fantasy and historical reality? Since *Sleeping Beauty* presents itself with a real date and real medieval material culture, but features fantastical elements such as fairies, magic, goblins, and a dragon, how do children distinguish fairy tale from history in this blended environment? All of these questions have yet to be explored in depth; only further sociologically based research can answer these provocative questions about the affect of Disney's medievalisms.

## Notes

1. See, for example, Robin Allan, *Walt Disney and Europe: European Influences on the Animated Feature Films of Walt Disney* (Bloomington: Indiana University Press, 1999), and Maria Sachiko Cecire, "Medievalism, Popular Culture, and National Identity in Children's Fantasy Literature," *Studies in Ethnicity and Nationalism* 9.3 (2009): 394–409.
2. This study does not examine Disney's target audience since adults, rather than children, were the study participants. With that said, these adults were children once; as a result, they were part of Disney's audience, although it must be acknowledged that the participants' primary interactions with Disney's films likely occurred a number of years ago during their childhood, and thus their interpretations of the films have been tempered by memory.
3. This study comprised a major portion of my PhD thesis, titled *Based on a True History? The Impact of Popular "Medieval Film" on the Public Understanding of the Middle Ages*. It is available at: www.etheses.whiterose.ac.uk/1117/. The thesis presents a more comprehensive description of the methodology, the theoretical context, and the results of this study than is possible here.
4. The General Certificate of Secondary Education (referred to by its acronym "GCSE") is a subject-area academic qualification in English, Welsh, and Northern Irish secondary schools (the Scottish equivalent is the "Standard Grade"). Students are required to take English, Science, and Mathematics exams, but a range of optional academic and vocational subjects are typically offered in secondary schools. "GCSE Level" is therefore, in England, Wales, and Northern Ireland, the common term used to refer to the academic level between ages 14 and 16.
5. David Morrison, *Defining Violence* (Luton: University of Luton Press, 1999), 1.
6. David Morrison, *Defining Violence*, vii.
7. Although not common in academic parlance, "medievalness" is the term I use to describe the subjective degree to which something is understood to be a part of the Middle Ages. A rigid thinker might be inclined to define something as either medieval or not medieval on a binary (since it would either be something from the Middle Ages or not), but it was far more common for participants in this study to describe "medievalness" as a relative quality, where something can be "more" or "less" medieval.
8. Half the group (chosen randomly) were asked to respond to "medieval" and half to "Middle Ages" first. They then repeated the exercise with the other term. Although participants typically wrote fewer words the second time they completed the exercise (as some said they felt reluctant to repeat themselves), the types of responses evoked did not change significantly dependent on which participants responded first.
9. The first group, conducted in November, was a pilot. This group did not watch a film and was only examined in regard to their understanding

of the Middle Ages. The films shown to the other groups were *Beowulf* (Zemeckis, 2007), *Kingdom of Heaven* (Scott, 2005), and *The Lord of the Rings: The Return of the King* (Jackson, 2003).

10. All participants' names have been replaced with pseudonyms to ensure anonymity. For reporting conventions, an equals sign (=) represents when a participant latched onto the statement of another participant or interrupted them. This usually occurred in moments of heated conversation. Underlined words indicate when special emphasis was placed on a word. Open square brackets indicate when conversation between two people overlapped. An ellipsis without brackets indicates when a speaker trailed off, and an ellipsis within square brackets (e.g., [...]) indicates where I have removed extraneous verbiage for clarity or brevity's sake, and words enclosed in square brackets indicate a clarifying comment. As much as possible and appropriate, I have retained the flow of conversation with minimal editing, and used punctuation to approximate their cadence of speech.
11. George Scarlett and Dennie Wolf, "When It's Only Make-believe: The Construction of a Boundary between Fantasy and Reality in Storytelling," *New Directions for Child and Adolescent Development* 6 (1979): 29–40, at 37.
12. Robyn McCallulm, "Identity Politics and Gender in Disney Animated Films," *Ways of Being Male*, ed. John Stephens (London: Routledge, 2002), 116–32, at 117.
13. Susan Jeffords, *Hard Bodies: Hollywood Masculinity in the Reagan Era* (New Brunswick: Rutgers University Press, 1994), 153.
14. For more on the English National Curriculum and its impact on the contemporary British public's understanding of the Middle Ages, see Paul Sturtevant, *Based on a True History?* 130, 132–36, 264–65.
15. Peggy Orenstein, "What's Wrong with Cinderella?" *New York Times* (24 Dec. 2006): n. pag.
16. "Disney Princess Home Page," www.disney.go.com; Web, accessed March 12, 2011.
17. Robin Allan, *Walt Disney and Europe*, 16–18, 37–50.
18. Mila Contini, *Fashion: From Ancient Egypt to the Present Day* (London: Hamlyn, 1965), 183–87.
19. Francois Boucher, *A History of Costume in the West*, trans. John Ross (London: Thames & Hudson, 1997), 372–77.
20. Aida Pérez, "*Shrek*: The Animated Fairy-Tale Princess Reinvented," *Fifty Years of English Studies in Spain*, ed. Ignacio Martinez, et al. (Santiago de Compostela: Universidade de Santiago de Compostela, 2003), 281–86, at 281.
21. Henry Giroux, *The Mouse That Roared: Disney and the End of Innocence* (Lanham: Rowman & Littlefield, 1999), 98–99.
22. Elizabeth Bell, Lynda Haas, and Laura Sells, ed., *From Mouse to Mermaid: The Politics of Film, Gender, and Culture* (Bloomington: Indiana University Press, 1995), 110.
23. B. C. Southam, ed. *Jane Austen: The Critical Heritage, 1870–1940* (London: Routledge, 1987), 59–60.

24. Robin Allan, *Walt Disney and Europe*, 233.
25. M. M. Bakhtin developed the theoretical concept of "adventure-time" and "adventure-space" as a part of what he calls the "chronotope": "the intrinsic connectedness of temporal and spatial relationships that are artistically expressed in literature" (*The Dialogic Imagination*, trans. Caryl Emerson and Michael Holquist [Austin: University of Texas Press, 1981], 85–158).
26. Saied Ameli, et al., *The British Media and Muslim Representation* (Wembley: Islamic Human Rights Commission, 2007), 47.
27. Saied Ameli, et al., *The British Media and Muslim Representation*, 47–48.

## CHAPTER 6

## THE SORCERER'S APPRENTICE: ANIMATION AND ALCHEMY IN DISNEY'S MEDIEVALISM

*Erin Felicia Labbie*

> Magic, like pure fantasy, was a short cut to knowledge and power.
>
> Lewis Mumford, *Technics and Civilization*[1]
>
> Any sufficiently advanced technology is indistinguishable from magic.
>
> Arthur C. Clarke, "Profiles of the Future"[2]
>
> Alchemy is, in fact, based on the difference between the visible and the readable. It likens esoteric signs (visible but illegible) to "carefully hidden" knowledge. Thus it separates a not-knowing from a knowing how to read.
>
> Michel de Certeau, *The Mystic Fable*[3]

Arthur C. Clarke's statement that "[a]ny sufficiently advanced technology is indistinguishable from magic" is a primary foundation of this chapter, which examines the medievalism of Disney's multiple incarnations of "The Sorcerer's Apprentice." The famous sequence "The Sorcerer's Apprentice" is first seen in *Fantasia* (1940), and it is then duplicated in *Fantasia 2000*. In both of these manifestations, the sequence stars Mickey Mouse as a usurper of power. Impatient to finish his manual labor, Mickey misuses the sorcerer's secrets to animate his tools so that they will finish his work for him. His desire for knowledge is inextricably bound to his desire to remove himself from the position of an apprentice. *Fantasia* (1940) and *Fantasia 2000* present the same animated sequence, but the significance of this sequence is altered by its context. In *Fantasia* (1940), the sequence is part of a larger story in which other companion pieces are narratively centered on genesis and creation; *Fantasia 2000* returns to that story of creation to place the sequence in a context of narratives focusing on environmental conservation and ecological awareness. This repetition with difference is due to the presence of what Tison Pugh, in his Introduction to this volume, calls retroprogression. The multiple iterations of "The Sorcerer's Apprentice" exhibit the ways that Disney's medievalism is manifested even in its most apparently modern or contemporary technological innovations and applications. The two animated *Fantasia* versions of "The Sorcerer's Apprentice" are modified narratively as well by the shift in format from animated film to digital image using live actors in the film *The Sorcerer's Apprentice* (2010); in this third incarnation of the tale, the sequence becomes a reminder that science, technology, and magic meet in everyday life, and that everyday life is always dependent on a certain degree of alchemy and a search for knowledge that is aware of its historical traces.

Although other short clips and longer films precede it in their chronological distribution, *Fantasia* (1940) is often perceived as the foundational film that established Disney's signature magic. In addition to the synchronicity of visual and acoustic symphonics that are achieved through the creative effects in *Fantasia*, the synthesis produces a narrative that illustrates the desire for the Middle Ages as a seat of magical origins. Connecting the power of creativity with a distinction between magic and sorcery, Sigmund Freud sought to define the two practices in *Totem and Taboo*.[4] Seeking a basic understanding of the process of animation—what gives life to objects—Freud argued that magic allows for the conflation of the ideal with the real in daily life, while sorcery focuses on spirits that do not participate in everyday life. Together, magic and sorcery bring life to inanimate objects. They also introduce vitality to the desire for happiness and hope for a future that recuperates the nostalgic wholeness of the past. Even when the past does not present such an illusory wholeness, the revisionary medievalism produced by Disney marks that past as a fantasy of potential. If, as Freud states, the basic form of magic is "mistaking an ideal connection for a real one," then the projection of desire onto the past offers a way of thinking about a happy place.[5]

Disney's projection of magic to provoke and promote happiness is dependent on its reflection of the Middle Ages through narrative forms that are alternately popular and esoteric. This tension is reflected in the sequence "The Sorcerer's Apprentice," as Mickey is at once a childlike figure with whom the viewer might identify and an animated, potentially monstrous shadow who realizes that he has put into motion bodies and images that he cannot control. For example, in the first of Disney's manifestations of "The Sorcerer's Apprentice" in *Fantasia* (1940), the narrator emphasizes the ancient content of the Faustian or Philopseudian tale. The extra-diegetic voice of the narrator introduces the sequence:

> And now we're going to hear a piece of music that tells a very definite story. It's a very old story, one that goes back 2000 years, a legend about a sorcerer who had an apprentice. He was a bright young lad, very anxious to learn the business. As a matter of fact, he was a little bit too bright, because he started practicing some of the boss's best magic tricks before learning how to control them.

In both *Fantasia* versions of "The Sorcerer's Apprentice," Mickey's impatience to become a sorcerer mirrors the multiple iterations and incarnations of the tale; it moves forward even as it reflects a long history that it carries into a debate about the limits or possibilities of knowledge, technology, and magic. In *The Sorcerer's Apprentice* (2010), Mickey is replaced with a human figure called Dave, who also struggles with these same issues, and who is genealogically related to the medieval figure of the magician Merlin.

In both *Fantasia* films, the medievalism indicated by the narrator's vague reference to a 2000-year-old legend about a sorcerer indicates not one but multiple sources, thereby complicating the search for medieval sources as a form of medievalism in the text. Disney's version of "The Sorcerer's Apprentice" is multiply intertextual; in addition to capturing its source history, the sequence illustrates the history of animation. These layers of representation indicate that the medievalism in "The Sorcerer's Apprentice" is at once literary and technological; the sequence brings medieval technologies into modernity through its narrative. By looking backward to the history of visual representation and its desire to achieve movement through drawing, Disney produces a model of animation that continues to grow through repetition and difference.

As a sequence that is repeated, "The Sorcerer's Apprentice" embodies a retroprogressive narrative that complicates the identification of sources, beginnings, and products or repetitions. Examining the history of Mickey Mouse's popularity, Bob Thomas asks, "What was that special alchemy that made audiences around the world respond to Mickey Mouse?"[6] An icon of Disney, Mickey Mouse—and specifically the Mickey Mouse who is the apprentice in "The Sorcerer's Apprentice"—mediates across time.[7] Mickey's childlike impatience demonstrates how a generational pull strives toward an ideal of "progress." Yet, as his actions reveal, the imagination is not linear; rather, it is nurtured by fantastic scenes of magic that reinvigorate a childlike impatience in adults.

Although "The Sorcerer's Apprentice" makes it clear that the Sorcerer (Yen-Sid—or Disney in reverse) represents the power of Disney, it is easy to conflate this power with Mickey's central role in "The Sorcerer's Apprentice." Mickey's dream of creating the world mirrors Disney's grand project, and Mickey reifies in animated form an ideal version of Walt Disney himself. Disney is seen in this conflux of the master sorcerer who controls creation and the young apprentice who seeks to attain the ability to create. In both cases, the sequence "The Sorcerer's Apprentice" is a microcosm for Disney films that are produced and then released to the public; once released, a production cannot be controlled by the producer or the sorcerer. As an apprentice toying with the idea of using magic or alchemy to animate an otherwise inanimate object (a broom), thereby eliminating his own physical labor (the carrying of water) so that he might shift his form of labor from the manual to the mental, cognitive, or mystical, Mickey's role in "The Sorcerer's Apprentice" replicates that of the artist and filmmaker seeking to use his power to produce new vision (figure 6.1). Yet, the necessity of mechanical reproduction of the broom (or of the film and its imagistic traces) always exceeds the purview of the creator. In this sense, Mickey becomes much like an animated version of Walt Disney, whose filmic and visual experiments often take on lives of their own as they work to achieve their goals of bringing magic to the masses.

**Figure 6.1** Mickey as the Sorcerer's Apprentice, magically relieving himself of undesired labor.

## Animation: Medieval or Modern?

Animation does not begin with the rise of modernity; rather, it begins with the first conceptions of visual representations of life, personification, and movement. Animation is not a peculiarly modern concept or product; instead, it employs both premodern and modern technologies to bring life to objects even while it calls attention to the practices of magic and alchemy. The attention to genesis and creation in "The Sorcerer's Apprentice" in the first manifestation in *Fantasia* (1940) recalls the origins of filmic animation, and the attention to prehistoric moments seen in, for instance, the dinosaur sequence reflects a long view of history.

Although it was first used in a cinematographic sense in 1912, the term *animation* was recorded in English in the 1590s. It is rooted in *animare*, meaning to give life to, or to create vitality, or the basis of life, *anima*. In Plato's *Timeaus*, the process of creation is linked to mathematical understandings of optics and forms of visual representation. The *Timeaus* connects practical understandings of perception to narrative or textual processes of creation. Medieval readers had access to the *Timeaus*, and this helped develop medieval understandings of optics and visual representations of the *anima*. Plato's allegory of the cave in the *Republic* presents another metaphor of animation by way of the light and shadows that conceal and reveal images, creating magical illusions that confuse the inhabitants of the cave. The Platonic understanding of optics as a perception and a return may be characterized by retroprogression: it is a nonlinear mode of perception that connects visual culture with narrative experience. This attention to optics is evident in *Fantasia* (1940) with the focus on movement, change, and metamorphosis of images. However, even classical philosophy is modern in the long history of recorded attempts to represent animation.

In "The Story of Animated Drawing," a history narrated by Walt Disney in an episode of his 1950s television series *Disneyland USA*, the viewer is introduced to the long history of visual animation that pre-dates its modern embodiments.[8] Historians of Disney and of animation agree that preclassical attempts to capture and represent movement are seen in such early images as that of an eight-legged boar, in which its many legs illustrate movement and the viewer thus interprets the image as a boar running.[9] Disney's awareness of the long history of attempts to represent bodies in motion suggests a care toward historicity and the pedagogical possibilities that its popularity might offer generations of viewers. Further, the attention to this premodern history of animation is mirrored in the movement of images throughout *Fantasia* (1940).

The process of developing technology that could create a visual experience of magic relies on historical awareness and evidence of premodern and medieval (as well as early modern) forms of representation.[10] In a more linear sense, the Bayeux Tapestry is often viewed as an example of medieval animation;[11] further, Leonardo Da Vinci's drawing of the human figure (c. 1492) represents animated arms and legs in the human form, thus projecting temporal and spatial dimensions in two-dimensional drawing.[12] Illuminated manuscripts juxtapose image and text to blend visual and dialogic animation. Medieval visual representation captures the spirit of animation in the wood cut; an early form of mechanical reproduction, the wood cut is also a parent to the cut-outs of early modern animation. The popularity of the wood cut in early medieval productions of books renders a visual art form that is not unlike the modernist interpretation of the cartoon. The use of the word *cartoon* to describe a visual image derives from the French *carton*, which became popular during the 1670s when drawings were rendered on "strong, heavy paper, pasteboard."[13] These tangible forms of art that are also mechanically reproducible assisted in the development of films like *Fantasia*.[14]

A modern history of animation records that technical reproduction became mechanized during the Industrial Revolution. In 1824, Peter Roget introduced the concept of the persistence of vision, which suggests that moving objects will be perceived as whole because visual perception seeks coherence. In 1872, the phenakistoscope was invented. Producing an illusion of movement through visual change, the phenakistoscope combined still images with their multiplicity, rendering a visual phenomenon in which a still image becomes a moving one. In this transition from still to life, the phenakistoscope illustrates the way that time is central to visual perception and the cognitive processing of images. The zoetrope or praxinoscope animates that connection between space and time by presenting movement within a three-dimensional sphere, rather than on the flat page.

In 1889, Thomas Edison invented the kinetoscope, an apparatus that projected a fifty-foot length of film in approximately thirteen seconds. In 1906, J. Stuart Blackton produced the first animated film titled *Humorous Phases of Funny Faces*. His process involved a photographic approach to film, in which he would draw a face on a blackboard, film it, stop the film, erase one face to draw another, and then film the newly drawn face. The process blends time with the visual desire to perceive wholeness. In 1910, Emile Cohl produced the first paper cut-out animation, and the beginnings of animated sequences followed. Between 1910 and 1915, artists produced short animated films that were composites of drawings or cut-outs of images. In 1915, Max Fleischer patented the rotoscope process, a version of film that recorded live-action footage, which would then be traced and rendered into pictorial images rather than into photographic ones. These modernist technological developments blossomed, and in 1923 Walt and Roy Disney opened their Disney Brothers Cartoon Studio.

Thus far, this history of animation is focused primarily on the visual techniques that support animation. However, the developments in sound and recording are equally significant in the production of the sound animated film. As J. P. Telotte reports, the emergence of Fantasound, which was used in *Fantasia*, allowed film to innovate the realism of animation as sound and image accompany each other.[15] Earlier sound animated films had been produced successfully, and as early as *Steamboat Willie* (1928), which is the first successful sound-animated film featuring Mickey Mouse. However, Disney relied on RCA and Cinephone to combine their creative visual image with a technical sound that would potentially replicate live symphonic music. Further, Telotte emphasizes the importance not only of finding new technological developments in sound, but also of having access to those technologies. Disney developed partnerships with sound production units that would allow them to mutually benefit. The film would become more realistic through the use of sound, and the technologies that produced sound found their voice in film.[16]

*Fantasia* foregrounds this love affair between visual representation and symphonic projection as it choreographs the images on the screen to the classical symphonic melodies that help music and cinema work together to become recognized as languages requiring no translation. The cliché that "cinema is the universal language" is likewise applied to music, and *Fantasia* functions on the level of perception that is directly linked to understanding and emotion. By animating figures on the screen, Disney ostensibly touches a part of each viewer and brings to life emotions. Further, as the conductor in *Fantasia*, Leopold Stokowski, states, "Music by its very nature is in constant motion, and this movement can suggest the mood of the picture it invokes."[17] Movement and change are vital to the production of visual animation; together, image and sound produce the alchemical world of *Fantasia*. The music in *Fantasia* is often compared to its narrative script, in which each musical score embodies a different story. As the film's screenwriter Joe Grant affirms, "*Fantasia* did have a book. The book was the music. We had to find a story in there. We were on a quest. Dick (Huemer) and I would listen to the music for months and months. Everything we found was in the music."[18] The narrative trajectory of the visual and acoustic elements of *Fantasia* synthesize, producing a narrative of the progress of technology and a myth of creation.

Industry's modern connections to technological developments offer one historical narrative of technics and science; it is also important to note how medieval and classical concepts of visuality and representation influence later forms of visual culture. The shift from medieval forms of technology to modern ones does not leave behind a different form of animation; rather, it maintains the artistic past through its own traces. In *Elemental Magic*, Joseph Gilland emphatically states, "We are not 'digital' artists, any of us. We are organic beings using digital tools."[19] The animated being who is an artist is also an alchemist and a scientist. In *Fantasia*, both in its 1940 and 2000 incarnations, this is presented both in the form of Mickey the apprentice and in the figure of the sorcerer. In *The Sorcerer's Apprentice* (2010), the contemporary figure of the apprentice is a budding scientist who also has genealogical ties to Merlin, the great magician. The impulse to find life within elements (like water, vapor, gas, oil, fire) combines with the art of visual drawing to produce a new world in each animated figure.

This brief history of modern animation considered in the wake of the slow reproduction of premodern art forms is replicated in the narrative urgency for magical progress in "The Sorcerer's Apprentice." As Mickey dismisses his slow manual labor in favor of the magical animation that is brought by alchemy and sorcery, he mimics the mechanical sciences that advanced visual animation during the Industrial Revolution and which continue, exponentially, to accelerate production throughout modernity and our contemporary digital age. The repetition of "The Sorcerer's Apprentice" in the two *Fantasia* films and in *The Sorcerer's Apprentice* also mimics and demonstrates the technological changes that alter the content of the narrative. The first *Fantasia* (1940) uses what were considered new modes of mechanical reproduction that combined sound and visual components to create unity, and the sequences produce a history of genesis; the second *Fantasia* (2000) employs contemporary digitalized animation to produce a synthetic version that recuperates the past while inserting up-to-date techniques and anthropomorphizing animals to comment on environmental change and responsibility; the third instance of the narrative in *The Sorcerer's Apprentice* (2010) shifts from visual animation to a digitalization of human forms that take on magical abilities, rendering humans into animated figures in a vast cosmic scheme of apocalyptic prevention.

By moving from the first instance of the cartoon animation of "The Sorcerer's Apprentice" in 1940, to the citation of it in 2000, and then to the revisionary citation of it in a film production using live figures (*The Sorcerer's Apprentice*), Disney not only illustrates how *Fantasia* is a living form that breathes through its multiple manifestations, as these shifting yet unified storylines also show how technology brings medievalism back to the present. Through technological shifts that allow a visual sequence in which the appearance of "real" brooms and mops come to life, the imitation of the cartoon sequence displaces linear temporality and replicates a medievalism that conjures a visual realism heretofore not produced in film. Indeed, a cinematic retroprogression, in which we move from cartoon animation to the digitization of real performers, captures a medievalist quality of spatial and temporal dislocation.

In contrast to a dream about the creation of the world, *The Sorcerer's Apprentice* presents a dream about preventing the apocalypse. The film's hero Dave (Jay Baruchel) finds the sorcerer Balthazar Blake in 2000 when he is nine years old, thereby replicating the youth of Mickey as the apprentice. Balthazar (Nicolas Cage) is engaged in an epic battle between good and evil with Morgan le Fay; Blake must protect the world from the apocalypse, but he can do so only with the help of Dave. In *The Sorcerer's Apprentice*, Blake is the good sorcerer who parallels Yen-Sid, and who teaches Dave to combine his knowledge of science with the magic that is in him due to his genealogical connections to Merlin. Immediately prior to meeting Balthazar, a young Dave impresses Becky, the object of his affections, by drawing on his school-bus window a picture of King Kong atop the Empire State Building surrounded by planes that are shooting at Kong. He is happy when, as the bus drives along, the picture lines up exactly with the "real" image of the Empire State Building, and Becky thinks this is "cool." Pre-9/11 New York could imagine and shoulder such coolness and openness of imagination. The imposition of the animated image of the clinging Kong onto the real image of the Empire State Building is a fantasy of openness and empire in this moment. However, as the film indicates, the prelapsarian, pre-9/11 city is ruptured by ten years of history. No longer a possible tale of creation, the film emerges as one of global destruction-prevention.

It would be simplistic to state that a pre-9/11 *Fantasia* in cartoon form is replaced by a post-9/11 limited imagination in the form of real digitally animated figures. Rather than seeing this as a replacement of an image, however, the digitalized pseudo-realist form of "The Sorcerer's Apprentice" furthers the medievalism of the sequence from the two *Fantasia* films and offers a different form of medievalism that also contributes to understandings of globalization. The apocalypse (and its perpetual threat) signifies destruction that opens possibilities of creation. *Fantasia* unites animation and alchemy in a manner that captures a view of the Middle Ages that is no longer peculiarly one of the generation of Disney films that produce romance of (or with) modernity. Rather, it seems to understand the way that citationality and repetition assert difference that is recognizable only to a knowledgeable reader.

By recuperating the medieval elements of mechanical reproduction and maintaining a sense of the connections between textual (or narrative) and visual forms of alchemy and magic, we retain a need for what Michel de Certeau means when he says that "Alchemy is, in fact, based on the difference between the visible and the readable. It likens esoteric signs (visible but illegible) to 'carefully hidden' knowledge. Thus it separates a not-knowing from a knowing how to read."[20] Indeed, one of the most productive measures of Disney's medievalism is its potential to return viewers to an impatience for knowledge and a desire to read.

## Mickey's Impatience and Medieval Alchemy

Mickey's impatience is at once an endearing characteristic that encourages the audience to identify with him, as well as a potentially dangerous impulse. Impatience is desire that is marked by temporality; it is a longing for the future enacted in the present. For children, impatience to acquire knowledge leads to a learning process that associates knowledge with power. In the context of an apprenticeship to a sorcerer, impatience is imbued with profound significance. The ambiguous length of time taken to master alchemy places the apprentice at the mercy of the sorcerer. The labor of the apprentice becomes a marker of time and knowledge, and it may produce impatience when juxtaposed with the desire for power. Such a medieval form of apprenticeship is illuminated in "The Sorcerer's Apprentice."

Mickey's impatience to learn and to practice the arts of alchemy (or magic) is well understood in light of the complaints of Geoffrey Chaucer's yeoman in the *Canon's Yeoman's Tale*. After his years of service to his teacher, the yeoman is still no closer to the ends of knowledge than he was on entering his apprenticeship. As Peggy Knapp says in "The Work of Alchemy," "The Yeoman blows on the fires, measures the ingredients, seals the vessels, conducts the calcinations, and so on, without quite grasping the 'slydyng science' he serves ... and of course without seeing its successes. Surely this is an image of alienated labor in the strongest sense."[21] Knapp's explication of the yeoman's servitude resembles Mickey's experience. In the presence of the power and knowledge promised in the figure of the sorcerer, the apprentice's manual labor appears hyperbolically alienated. Like the yeoman, Mickey's role as the apprentice is to perform the physical labor that allows the sorcerer to perform his alchemical magic. Carrying water on his shoulders and cleaning the studio becomes too tedious for Mickey, who seeks to practice the arts of alchemy and sorcery rather than to trudge on in his alienated labor.

Although a crucial difference exists between the yeoman and Mickey, in that the former learns to despise alchemy and Mickey remains enchanted by it, the yeoman who creates disaster by prematurely practicing the arts of his master is a prototype for Mickey's role as an impatient apprentice. Mickey attempts to control the animation of the brooms while he is awake, but he loses control of the broom because his conducting hands fail to perform their mathematical rhythm when he falls asleep in the arm chair/throne of Yen-Sid the Sorcerer. His decision to have the broom perform his labor places his role as an apprentice, as well as his master's studio, in jeopardy. Significantly, Mickey's conducting of the broom's labor (a performance that mimics the conductor of the symphony playing the music that drives his animation forward) does not become problematic until he falls asleep. In sleep, Mickey's body is unaware of the labor of the broom, and his conducting fails to be measured in time with the movement of the broom's labor. Mickey's dream of creation illustrates both the split between his mind and body and a displacement of space and time. In his goal of becoming a sorcerer, he is able to create the stars and an oceanic presence with the potential for life, and his dream reflects his own creation myth. However, the juxtaposition of this dream with the "reality" that his body is sitting in a chair sleeping while the broom brings water at an increasingly rapid pace, thus flooding the studio, calls attention to the mind–body split that is present in the dynamic of animation.

While sleep is the first mistake Mickey makes once he has used the sorcerer's power, it is not his most fateful error. Rather, on waking panic-stricken, Mickey enacts a Bluebeard scene in which viewers see Mickey's silhouette chopping at the broom with an ax. Not unlike Chaucer's yeoman, who sabotages the alchemical process by sharing its secrets in his prologue and tale, Mickey seeks to kill his own offspring. When he realizes that he has failed to control his powers, Mickey becomes enraged and attempts to mutilate and murder the workers (brooms) that he has conjured. The intertextual links between Mickey's role as an alchemist and his role as a Bluebeard character are buttressed by the attention they received by the composer Paul Dukas, who wrote both *L'Apprenti Sorcier*, which was a tonal poem known as an orchestral scherzo, and a symphony called *Ariane and Bluebeard*. Dukas's investment in music reflecting vague and romanticized medieval settings and moods projected both temporal dislocation and identification with the Middle Ages. The temporal dislocation of the music of *Ariane and Bluebeard* recuperates a fantasy of a medieval representation of barbaric murder. Although it is more clearly a commentary on the way that modernity renders mechanical reproduction uncontrollable, the Bluebeard sequence within "The Sorcerer's Apprentice" also references fantasies of medieval barbarism and violence. "The Sorcerer's Apprentice" mediates the violence and barbarism associated with medieval art forms, alchemy, and modern mechanical reproduction such that a commentary on the acceleration of production is evident in the placement of the Bluebeard scene within "The Sorcerer's Apprentice." Yet, Mickey is not defined by the Bluebeard scene; rather, he becomes disciplined by Yen-Sid, whose sorcery and proper use of alchemy return the scene to order.

Furthermore, Mickey's dream sequence in the two *Fantasia* films is replaced or rectified in *The Sorcerer's Apprentice*. In the cartoon representations in *Fantasia*, Mickey loses control of the brooms that he sets to work because he falls asleep, whereas in the 2010 film *The Sorcerer's Apprentice*, Dave, the apprentice, leaves the brooms to clean his studio while he showers in preparation for a date with the object of his affections, Becky. This shift from the fantastic realm of dreams to the mundane realm of daily hygiene enhances the realism of the 2010 film, and it places the alchemical and magical processes of sorcery within everyday life.

In both the animated versions of *Fantasia* and the digitized *The Sorcerer's Apprentice*, the scene is indicative of mechanical reproduction and its place in the retroprogression of the multiple films as they interact with medieval imagery. Once Mickey and then his parallel Dave have splintered the broom, the different fragments assume animated identities as they multiply and reproduce. As Knapp argues, multiplying is central to the alchemical procedure: "[a]lchemy, like capitalism, is intent on making things more plentiful, bigger, less measurable on a scale based on the worker growing his food. What might happen in the best case scenario for the alchemical studio is that more (in terms of exchange value) would be produced than came in."[22] Alchemy accelerates multiplication, just as mechanical reproduction enables faster duplication of art. Mickey's impatience to achieve a faster pace of labor results, however, in the uncontrollable mechanically reproduced fragments of brooms coming to life—being animated as it were—and becoming an army of laborers who ignore Mickey's attempts to control and organize them. By splintering the single broom, Mickey unwittingly creates multiple brooms that assume lives of their own and whose mechanical and automatic labor threatens the sanctity of the sorcerer's studio. Only through the return of the sorcerer to the studio and his accompanying Moses-like parting of the sea may the alchemical process that Mickey catalyzed be returned to its proper order. Mickey's childlike impatience to learn his master's art is extinguished by the sorcerer's scornful and disciplinary stare. The water that was dangerous is returned to its proper place, and the wood of the broom returns to its inanimate state. Indeed, this scene is mimicked in *The Sorcerer's Apprentice*, when Bathazar Blake must clean up after Dave's misguided use of sorcery.

In the animated sequence, Mickey's impatience distracted him from his studies; he veered from the source of the book to the premature practice of alchemy. In this mistake he departed from the discipline of narrative interpretation and illegitimately practiced alchemy without regard for its art or science. By returning him to the book (or the source), Mickey's master the Sorcerer Yen-Sid reminds Mickey and his viewers of the importance of the study of the history of alchemy and animation. Indeed, Yen-Sid reminds Mickey and us of the importance of reading.

## Sources and "The Sorcerer's Apprentice"

The multiple references within the Disney version invite a consideration of how the sources that comprise the fragment within *Fantasia* play with medievalism. As mentioned above, "The Sorcerer's Apprentice" is a tale told to the melody of Paul Dukas's *L'Apprenti Sorcier*. Dukas was inspired by Goethe's *Zauberlehrling*, a poetic account of an apprentice seeking the help of his master after he has abused the power of magic and alchemy; it also resembles another famous narrative by Goethe, *Faust*, in which the question of hubris is aligned with the limitations of science and magic. To the extent that these are also medieval questions, the famous line, "die geister, die ich rief" (the spirits that I called) is a common way of referring to a figure who has summoned powers that exceed their ability to control. Chaucer was aware of the danger of hubris, especially with regard to alchemical processes, as is evident in the *Canon Yeoman's Tale* when the character states, "For whan a man hath over-greet a wit, / Ful oft hym happeth to mysusen it."[23] The yeoman's detailed narrative of alchemical practices includes references to material found in both popular and philosophical classical and medieval treatises on alchemy. Indeed, hubris in the scene of alchemy is a theme that is dominant in the Middle Ages, and it is also evident as early as 150 CE where it is found in Lucian's *Philopseudes*. The Greek title meaning "Lovers of lies" establishes a contextual investigation into the realm of the supernatural and the difference between natural magic and artificially produced (or the sorcerer's) magic. In Lucian's text the sorcerer is an Egyptian mystic named Pancrates, and his companion Eucrates overhears him casting a spell. Included in the tools mentioned by Lucian are a broom, a pestle, and a wood bar used to close a door. Lucian's text inaugurates a long history of narrative investigations into the subjects of alchemy and animation. Yet, this classical origin is different enough from the retelling of the tale by Goethe to invite speculation that a more popularly read and known medieval tale might be a more central reference gestured toward by the narrator in *Fantasia*. A further difference between these tales and representations of the tale in "The Sorcerer's Apprentice" is the ultimate lesson learned: unlike Chaucer's yeoman, or the characters in Goethe's versions of the legend, both the animated figure of Mickey Mouse in "The Sorcerer's Apprentice" and the human figure of Dave in *The Sorcerer's Apprentice* learn the dangers of hubris, but they remain students of alchemy and sorcery. In fact, their lesson helps them to achieve a closer connection to magic and sorcery, uniting technologies and knowledge forms.

The centrality of Merlin's story in *The Sorcerer's Apprentice* suggests that the 2000-year-old text referred to in the voice-over introduction to the 1940 "The Sorcerer's Apprentice" is the legend of Merlin recorded circa 1135 in Geoffrey of Monmouth's *Vita Merlini* (*Life of Merlin*). In *The Sorcerer's Apprentice*, narrative is driven by the battle between Merlin's good, or natural magic, and Morgana's evil, or artificial, magic. The multiple narratives of Merlin catalyze a vast oeuvre of Arthuriana and support the lack of a singular source for the legend of "The Sorcerer's Apprentice." Because most of the traditional legends of Merlin, including those by Geoffrey of Monmouth, Thomas Malory, Wace, and Layamon, focus on Merlin's history and his relationship to Arthur, they establish a broad stage from which to launch Disney's grand animation of historical romance.

Identifiable medieval sources, however, do not necessitate medievalism. Even when a text is based on a source, or multiple sources, it might utilize a particular prior text to suggest differences rather than to perpetuate questions or ideas addressed therein. It is necessary then to address the precise ways in which the potential sources for "The Sorcerer's Apprentice" reflect a particular form of medievalism.[24] The question of the "source" also refers to a source of life. Source study is akin to the topic of animation in that it is at the source—the water well—for Mickey, the "2000 year old legend" for the narrator of *Fantasia*, that origins become muddled and mired in a fractal regression. What catalyzes, what powers, what motivates the production of change and the animation of objects? These are questions of animation and alchemy, as well as of the central configurations that help to define medievalism(s).

Events and technologies are identified as magic when their sources or their causes cannot be known or understood; in this way, intertextual and ambiguous references to a medieval past might be consumed as magical narratives. As the desire to understand a practical form of knowledge replaces nostalgia for a past that is idealized, the question of the source as a form of authority also shifts from textual origin to the possibility of daily practices. Seeing magic in practice condenses belief and introduces a moment of pleasurable shock. Because vision is so central to the perception of magic, visual pleasure as a form of knowledge is fundamental to the magical performance.

The magic of creation in "The Sorcerer's Apprentice" comments on the long history of sources conceived visually as the fractals of a drop of water that mutate into a flood. As is evident in the narrative of the creation myth retold in *Fantasia*, the world is created *ex nihilo* by each new narrative encounter, and it also carries with it the traces of all histories that have contributed to the present. In this way, *Fantasia* reflects a medieval scholastic approach to the concept of creation; even as it presents itself as a narrative of beginnings, *Fantasia* is self-reflective of its temporally complex (auto)citationality. Narrative differences are then evident in the repetition, not only of the same film viewed at different times and places, but also of the film (*Fantasia*) reproduced as a distinct film (*Fantasia 2000*), and then further revised in *The Sorcerer's Apprentice* (2010).

It may seem unlikely to speak of Disney's medievalism because in many ways Disney's endurance and success are predicated on the ability to persist in using contemporary technologies; however, the perpetual modernization of cinematic techniques foregrounds the medieval qualities of Disney's magic. Disney participates in cultural revolutions and change even as its production of new films comments on the ways that politics and art influence each other and cohabitate. During World War II and immediately prior to 9/11/2001, "The Sorcerer's Apprentice" and *Fantasia* offer narratives of potential revolution, and in 2010 that potential is transformed into *The Sorcerer's Apprentice*. Among its many aesthetic and political contributions, "The Sorcerer's Apprentice" illustrates Disney's unique magic that is known by way of its technological developments and its contributions to everyday life as well as to esoteric concepts such as alchemy; indeed, "The Sorcerer's Apprentice" demonstrates that what we often think is unseen or esoteric in daily life is a foundational part of a long history of knowledge that inscribes itself on literary and cinematic art and its participants.

In one sense, Disney relies largely on the history of technological developments that help animation become reified in film. In another sense, however, even the most apparently primitive technology allows a form of magical animation to capture the dreams, wishes, and imaginations of the viewers who are produced by the culture of Disney and the medievalism inherent in their oeuvre. Pugh's characterization of the retroprogression of Disney's medievalism is emphatically represented in the history of medieval alchemy and questions of animation within *Fantasia's* "The Sorcerer's Apprentice," in the repetition of it in *Fantasia 2000*, and in *The Sorcerer's Apprentice*. Through assertion and repetition, "The Sorcerer's Apprentice" demonstrates the nonlinear forms of history and time that capture the magic of Disney's medievalism.

## Notes

1. Lewis Mumford, *Technics and Civilization* (New York: Harcourt, Brace, 1963), 39.
2. Arthur C. Clark "Profiles of The Future," qtd. in Charles Solomon, *Enchanted Drawings: The History of Animation* (New York: Random House, 1994), 3.
3. Michel de Certeau, *The Mystic Fable*, trans. Michael B. Smith (Chicago: University of Chicago Press, 1992), 57.
4. Sigmund Freud, *Totem and Taboo* (New York: Norton, 1950), 98.
5. Sigmund Freud, *Totem and Taboo*, 98.
6. Bob Thomas, *Disney's Art of Animation: From Mickey Mouse to Beauty and the Beast* (New York: Hyperion, 1991), 17.
7. Bob Thomas follows John Hench to suggest that there is something ubiquitous about Mickey Mouse (*Disney's Art of Animation*, 17).
8. See also Frank Thomas and Ollie Johnston, "The Story of Animated Drawing," *The Illusion of Life: Disney Animation* (New York: Hyperion, 1981), esp. 15–29.
9. Bob Thomas, *Disney's Art of Animation*, 23. The image of the boar is available at "Introduction to Animation: History," animation.blogspot.com (March 19, 2006); Web, accessed May 7, 2012.
10. Other examples of early animation that inspired Disney are evident in Egyptian wall art from c. 2000 BCE where serial images create stories and movement. See esp. "The Wrestlers," at www.animationsource.org; Web, accessed August 5, 2011.
11. Donald Crafton, *Before Mickey: The Animated Film, 1898–1928* (Chicago: University of Chicago Press, 1993), 4.
12. Bob Thomas, *Disney's Art of Animation*, 23.
13. "Cartoon," www.etymoline.com; Web, accessed January 2, 2011.
14. *Pinocchio* (1940) also illustrates the potential for animation to bring life to inanimate objects. Historically, wood and water are central features of alchemical creation, and *Fantasia* and *Pinocchio* both focus on the way that wood comes to life (in the forms of brooms and of a boy, respectively). The medieval uses of wood and water to produce alchemical products are primary foundations for the transition of animation from the page to the screen.
15. J. P. Telotte, *The Mouse Machine: Disney and Technology* (Chicago: University of Illinois Press, 2008), 36–37.
16. J. P. Telotte, *The Mouse Machine*, 24–27.
17. Leopold Stokowski, qtd. in Bob Thomas, *Disney's Art of Animation*, 86.
18. Joe Grant, qtd. in David Koenig, *Mouse under Glass: Secrets of Disney Animation and Theme Parks* (Irvine, CA: Bonaventure Press, 1997), 42–43.
19. Although the spirit of this statement is captured in the print publication, Joseph Gilland, *Elemental Magic: The Art of Special Effects Animation*

(Massachusetts: Focal Press, 2009), 74–83, it is directly stated in his blog http://elementalmagic.blogspot.com
20. Michel de Certeau, *The Mystic Fable*, 57.
21. Peggy Knapp, "The Work of Alchemy," *Journal of Medieval and Early Modern Studies* 30.3 (2000): 575–99, at 582.
22. Peggy Knapp, "The Work of Alchemy," 583.
23. Geoffrey Chaucer, *The Riverside Chaucer*, ed. Larry Benson, 3rd ed. (Boston: Houghton Mifflin, 1987), 271, lines 648–49.
24. See Roger Dragonetti, *Le Mirage des Sources* (Paris: Seuil, 1987).

## CHAPTER 7

## THE SWORD IN THE STONE: AMERICAN TRANSLATIO AND DISNEY'S ANTIMEDIEVALISM

*Rob Gossedge*

Neither Walt Disney nor his chief animators were particularly interested in making *The Sword in the Stone*. Initial reviews were lukewarm, its performance at the box office was lackluster, and most critics, yesterday and today, are dismissive of the film. Keith Booker calls it "one of the most obscure in the Disney animated canon";[1] Alan Lupack and Barbara Tepa Lupack see it as consisting of a "predictable pattern of chases and transformations";[2] Jerome Reel terms the film's score as "workmanlike";[3] and Jerry Beck describes it as "one of Disney's most forgettable features, a mild entertainment that bears little relation to the studio's classic era."[4] As an adaptation of T. H. White's 1938 novel of the same title, discussion has been limited: Raymond Thompson states that the film "borrows little from the book beyond the basic situation of the young Arthur, or Wart as he is known, learning valuable lessons about life while magically transformed into various creatures by his tutor, Merlin the Magician,"[5] and Alice Grellner comments on how the film downplays or simply eliminates much of the novel's "multifaceted, ambivalent, misogynistic, often contradictory, and darkly pessimistic view of human nature."[6]

While this process of simplification and sanitization seems typical of Disney's adaptive process, *The Sword in the Stone* is something of an exception within the animated feature canon. As Jack Zipes notes, Disney has not only been a new teller of old tales, but it has also continually managed to erase—obliterate from cultural memory—earlier retellings by previous adaptors of myths and fairy tales, including Charles Perrault, the Brothers Grimm, and Hans Christian Anderson.[7] What makes *The Sword in the Stone* different from many of the studio's other adaptations is that even the cultural megalith that is Disney—and especially the Disney of the 1960s that had, by common contemporary consent, lost its commercial and artistic "magic"[8]—could not erase the massive corpus of Arthurian myth in favor of its own clean-cut, trivialized, and rigorously "innocent" narrative.

This chapter considers Disney's eighteenth animated feature in relation to its "source"—but not as a straight, uncomplicated adaptation of a single book to film. Rather, Disney's film is part of a cultural matrix of texts constituting the twentieth century's most important Arthuriad—a major retelling of the legend beginning with T. H. White's *The Sword in the Stone* but one that did not end with the book's publication in 1938, but continued to be developed, rewritten, and reinscribed as it was reworked into White's 1958 *Once and Future King*, adapted many times for radio, stage, and screen, and borrowed from, or referred to, in numerous contemporary and later Arthurian texts. Apart from taking its place within this complex textual history, Disney's *Sword* is also contextualized in terms of its relation to Disney's many other Arthurian productions, most of which are derived from explicitly American texts, as clearly demonstrated in the studio's recurring interest in Mark Twain's *A Connecticut Yankee in King Arthur's Court*.

Like those other major institutions of contemporary cultural and political American power—the Broadway stage, via Lerner and Loewe's enormously successful *Camelot* (1960), and the Kennedy Presidency, in the form of John F. Kennedy's Arthurian memorialization[9]—Disney, with *The Sword in the Stone*, undertook a large-scale act of American *translatio studii, translatio imperii*. Just as the medieval West translated the learning and power of the classical world to twelfth-century France—primarily, although not exclusively, through texts such as the *Roman d'Énéas* or the Alexander stories[10]—so the American redeployment of the European Arthurian story can be seen as a parallel phenomenon. Just as the reuse of classical stories by romance writers implied that medieval western Europe was a new center of power, as Greece and Rome had been, so the Americanization of the Arthurian legend—always a legend of and about power—was a similar act of *translatio*: the transference of learning (*studii*), realizing, and validating the transference of power (*imperii*). Whereas earlier American rewritings—by Twain and Howard Pyle—potently translated the legend into new cultural and national contexts, Disney's *Sword in the Stone* was far less effective in transferring its source material onto the screen and, thus, despite its consummate Americanization, largely failed to translate the power behind the myth.

## "That king was a cuckold. Who the hell cares about a cuckold?": Adapting White's *Once and Future King* for an American Audience

White's Arthuriad, like all major Arthurian cycles, has a complicated textual history. Large-scale retellings, including Geoffrey of Monmouth's *History of the Kings of Britain* (c. 1135), the French prose Vulgate cycle (c. 1215–1235), Malory's Arthuriad (completed 1469–1470), and Tennyson's *Idylls of the King* (1833–1892), are rarely produced in a straightforward fashion—whatever their authors, or later literary historians, may inform their readers. Although the HarperCollins edition of White's text, in print since 1996, claims to be the *Complete Once and Future King*, it is not. White published three novels under individual titles between 1938 and 1940 (*The Sword in the Stone*, *The Witch in the Wood*, and *The Ill-Made Knight*), and wrote two more by 1941: *The Candle in the Wind*, based on a play he had written in 1938, but which had been rejected by Noel Coward,[11] and *The Book of Merlyn*. White revised all five novels by 1958 and published them as one long book, in four parts, as the *Once and Future King*. In 1977, thirteen years after White's death, *The Book of Merlyn*, only parts of which had been incorporated into the 1958 version, was published separately, with the 1996 edition suffixing this volume to the end of the 1958 text, including the repeated episodes: this forms HarperCollins' "complete" edition, although it was never White's intention to publish *The Book of Merlyn* after completing the 1958 text.

The 1938 *Sword in the Stone* is largely a happy affair. It begins with the young Arthur, known as Wart, and his foster-brother Kay growing up in the castle of the Forest Sauvage under the guardianship of Sir Ector and the tutorship of Merlyn. The former is a benevolent patriarch of an idealized feudal society who provides the foundling Wart, secretly the son of Uther Pendragon, with a happy *familia*, while Merlyn directs the young Arthur in a series of adventures, many of which, though not all, are educational in purpose. There are encounters with a witch, a giant, and Robin Hood (known here as Robin Wood), as well as several episodes in which Wart is transformed into various animals: perch, hawk, snake, and badger. (Several of these scenes were omitted in the 1958 edition and replaced by more consciously political material from *Merlyn*.) Seven years pass in this near-blissful state, until it is announced that Uther has died. Following the traditional sword-in-the-stone motif, Wart—now renamed Arthur—is elevated from Kay's squire to King of England. He is told of his parentage, although Merlyn does not reveal his mother's identity to him, which precipitates the incestuous disaster in the following, and much darker, novel, *The Witch in the Wood*. This novel narrates the similarly inventive, yet much more disturbing, *enfances* of Gawain and his brothers at the hands of their mother, and Arthur's lover and half-sister, Morgause. *The Ill-Made Knight* begins with yet another childhood: that of Lancelot, whose pursuit of becoming the greatest knight in the world, "a sort of Bradman, top of the batting averages," is dynamized through erotic desire: first for Arthur, then his queen, usually called Jenny.[12] Time passes quickly in this text—no longer a children's novel—and the narrative is largely drawn from Malory, with White supplying additional psychological motivations for the traditional stories. *The Candle in the Wind* opens with Mordred plotting the destruction of Arthur's England, which is brought about by the novel's close. The novel ends with Arthur, on the eve of the battle of Camlan, "[l]ooking back on his life and despairing" (1996: 685). But then a page enters—a young Tom Malory of Newbold Revel—who is commanded to record the greatness of the Round Table and its mission to transform Might into the vessel of Right. And so the text ends with Arthur, now prepared for the destruction of Camlan, drawing himself up "to meet the future with a peaceful heart" (1996: 697). *The Book of Merlyn* momentarily takes Arthur away from Camlan and back to Merlyn and the animals of his youth with whom he continues, with a mixture of whimsy and forcefulness, to search for "an antidote to war."[13]

Enormously successful as individual titles and subsequent collected editions, White's Arthuriad was ripe for adaptation in both juvenile and adult modes. In Britain, Marianne Helwig turned *The Sword in the Stone* novel into a six-part serialization for BBC radio in the summer of 1939. Well received, it featured incidental music by Benjamin Britten, who had already completed a commission to score D. G. Bridson's dramatic rendering of Malory two years earlier, also for BBC radio.[14] Britten's second Arthurian score is a lively affair. Like the novel, it is full of playful quotation and stylistic imitation—Britten was an expert parodist—borrowing its sword-in-the-stone motif from that of Nothung, Siegfried's sword in Wagner's *Ring* cycle, while the music for Merlyn strongly echoes sections of *Das Rheingold*.[15] In 1952, Britten's score was utilized in another radio adaptation, again written by Hellwig and featuring a strong cast including Peter Ustinov as Merlyn. Six years later, following the publication of *The Once and Future King*, Collins, the novel's British publisher, recommended that the complete four-part novel would make an excellent serialization for Radio 4's *Woman's Hour*, although the BBC disagreed.[16] Nonetheless, further serializations of White's first novel were made in 1971 and 1978, another radio play was produced in 1981, while a lengthy reading from *The Book of Merlyn* was included in a 1986 radio biography of White, and an abridged reading of the 1958 text was broadcast in 1994.[17]

More famous, and more influential on Disney's adaptation, was the American stage musical *Camelot*, with words by Alan Jay Lerner and music by Frederick "Fritz" Loewe, first staged in 1960. As Walt Disney would not sell the rights to *The Sword in the Stone*, Lerner and Loewe's *Camelot* dealt only with the final two books of the 1958 sequence—that is, the material derived ultimately from Malory. (The darkly disturbing *enfances* of *The Witch in the Wood* remain unadapted for stage or screen.) The result is a much more "adult" version of *The Once and Future King* than other adaptations attempted. Immensely successful, the musical ran for two years on Broadway, and toured for two more, with Arthur played by a young Richard Burton and Guinevere by the relatively unknown Julie Andrews (the sort of woman, Lerner remarked, "that makes you wonder how Britain ever lost the Empire"[18]). It was turned into a similarly successful Warner Bros. film directed by Joshua Logan in 1967, with Richard Harris and Vanessa Redgrave replacing Burton and Andrews. A filmed version of the musical's 1980 revival, again starring Harris, was broadcast on HBO in 1982.

Despite the lasting popularity of their musical, Loewe had been reluctant to work on the Arthurian legend, saying to his partner: "That king was a cuckold. Who the hell cares about a cuckold?" When told that people had cared about the Arthurian legend for a thousand years, the Vienna-born Loewe replied: "Well, that's only because you Americans and English are such children."[19] Nonetheless, their musical entered American political folklore in 1963 when another T. H. White—Theodore H. White, a journalist for *Life* magazine—interviewed Jacqueline Kennedy a week after the president was assassinated. This interview began the posthumous mythologization of the Kennedy administration as America's Cold War Camelot:

> At night, before we'd go to sleep, Jack liked to play some records; and the song he loved most came at the very end of this record. The lines he loved to hear were: "Don't let it be forgot, That once there was a spot, For one brief shining moment that was known as Camelot." ... There'll be great Presidents again ... but there'll never be another Camelot again.[20]

The conception, production, and reception of Walt Disney's 1963 feature are intimately bound up with these adaptations of White's Arthuriad. It is palpably not a "straight" adaptation of White's 1938 novel. The film was released on Christmas Day, 1963—only a few weeks after *Life* magazine began remodeling Kennedy's White House as a new Camelot. The American Arthurian myth was in a rare tragic mode, and Disney's typically upbeat film, with its "narrative of democratic possibility accompanied by a faith in science and technology,"[21] seemed suddenly out of keeping with the national mood. Tragic ends are usually avoided in American Arthurian films (most obviously apparent in the many cheerful adaptations of Twain's *Connecticut Yankee*). On the rare occasions when they have produced tragic conclusions, as in *Excalibur* (1980) by the English director John Boorman, their commercial success has been limited. Jacqueline Kennedy's image of the boy-president-to-be was bathetic: "You must think of him as this little boy, sick so much of the time, reading in bed, reading history, reading the Knights of the Round Table."[22] Disney's boy-king would prove to be very different: unread, far from tragic, and wholly unelected. Out of sympathy with the American public, the film was poorly reviewed and fared even worse commercially.[23] Nonetheless, while the film suffered because of its context, it seemingly owed its very existence to the same musical J.F.K. would play at night: *Camelot*.

Although Disney bought the film rights to White's *Sword in the Stone* in 1940, there was little sustained effort to bring it to the screen before the studio witnessed the twin successes of White's more traditionally Arthurian 1958 novel and the derivative Lerner and Loewe musical of 1960. Walt himself remained uninterested in the Arthurian story and none of the studio's chief animators, known as the "nine old men," was keen on the film.[24] Only Bill Peet, story man and concept artist, fully supported the project and persuaded Walt to greenlight it after the studio boss saw a production of *Camelot*: its star, of course, would make her feature debut in Disney's other major, live-action, project of the early 1960s, *Mary Poppins* (1964). But even when it received the go-ahead, its budget was much smaller than that typical of Disney's animated features—*Sword* was budgeted at 40% less than the already-cheap *101 Dalmatians*, made two years earlier.[25] The film's theatrical re-releases would also draw on the larger exploitation of White's novel. Disney's *Sword* would reenter the theater much less frequently than other Disney features: the re-release of 1972 followed that of *Camelot* a few months earlier, and the 1983 re-release followed not only new performances and a film of the same Lerner and Loewe musical, but also coincided with the video release of John Boorman's *Excalibur*.

Thus the film's paratexts, rather than White's novel itself, seem to have dictated much of its cultural production and reception. Yet Disney's lack of interest in a *Sword in the Stone* project seems strange given the recurring interests and ideological positions White and the studio customarily shared: White's book was always, seemingly, ripe for Disneyfication. Both, as discussed in the next section, were typically concerned with the importance of pedagogy. Nature is another important shared value—and the works of both White and Disney have received recent eco-critical attention.[26] The ecological awareness of both can readily be seen in terms of a conservative elision of real political focus. Thus, for example, the tribal hierarchies of *The Lion King* quickly collapse into a "Circle of Life" sung by Elton John; the male fantasy of patriarchal dominance and total ownership of property of *Bambi*, also perhaps the studio's most feudal film, is displaced in the film's second half with the ecological message about the threat that Man poses to Nature.[27] While White believed from the 1940s on that the "central theme" of his Arthuriad was to "find an antidote to war," and while the political treatises of *Merlyn* are frequently flawed and contradictory (Merlyn, for instance, blames war on nationalism, economic competitiveness, and the ideal of communal property, and claims to be both "a staunch capitalist" and, several pages later, "like any other sensible person, an anarchist" [1996: 722, 801]), many of the text's most powerfully realized scenes— in particular, the juxtaposed episodes with the fascist ants and pacific geese—reveal Nature as a potent teacher of wisdom. Nonetheless, even the book's nature scenes are liable to descend into the same sentimental anthropomorphism in which Disney frequently indulges: a donnish Badger from a Cambridge tutorial,[28] a flea-ridden hedgehog singing Blake's "Jerusalem" in a thin Cockney accent (1996: 702). The second example is indicative of another shared tonal feature: enforced unseriousness. At this point in *Merlyn*, the aged, almost defeated Arthur is staring upon his ruined kingdom. As is frequent in the book, at the moments of its greatest complexity, White suddenly lurches into whimsy—a studied ideological defensiveness typical of the contemporary English upper-middle-class novel.[29] Disney's *Sword* replicates this unseriousness, although in less English tones. It was only natural that the tagline for the film's initial release—focused on Merlyn, rather than Wart—should read "Whiz-Bang Whizard of Whimsy."

Yet there is one major difference in the literary and Disney versions of *Sword in the Stone*. As both Alan Lupack and Heather Worthington explore, White's *Once and Future King* is "the book that grows up": just as Wart undergoes an idealized, natural education to become King Arthur at the close of *Sword*, before the rest of the narrative traces his journey to becoming the white-haired, cuckolded king of the final tragedy, so too does the book "grow up": tonally, generically, and thematically shifting from a juvenile novel to a pedagogical treatise to a full-blown adult romance.[30] Disney's version remains curiously static—and not just because its rights were only to the first volume. Although Wart is crowned as king at the novel's close, he remains a lost little boy throughout the film. Part of the problem is his education.

### "Books come first": Educating the Wart

In the 1958 text, Wart's schooling is concerned, almost exclusively, with justice, power, and kingship. From the carp he learns of autocracy; from the hawks, military order; from the ants, totalitarianism; from the geese, pacifism. And in his final dose of education with the badger, Wart receives a revision class, covering all he has previously learned in preparation for his final examination—kingship. The insistent "learning aim" in this strenuously, if still enjoyably, didactic text is that Might is not always Right. In comparison, the purposes of the education scenes in the 1938 text are much more varied. The episodes with the giant and Madam Mim, the black witch, are primarily comedic, but there are more important lessons: from Athene, Wart learns of the nature of trees and witnesses the creation of the earth, and from the grass snake, he is told of myths and legends of the past. The visits to the pike and hawks in the mews are largely the same in both versions, but the 1938 text's climactic visit to the badger is a much briefer affair, and does not contain any of the antiwar dialogue of the 1958 version. Although its rights belonged exclusively to the 1938 text, Disney borrowed from both versions, and the film's educational theme is, as a result, ambivalent. The theme of Might and Right is mentioned at several points, most clearly after Merlin's (here climactic) encounter with Madam Mim: "Righteousness and wisdom is the real power." Yet few of the actual lessons conform to this maxim in any meaningful way.

Curiously for a studio whose output has so persistently focused on the child, the first character Disney's *The Sword in the Stone* introduces is the teacher, Merlin. This was no accident: as discussed above, much of the advance publicity focused on the wizard rather than on the king-to-be, and Disney eschewed White's title in many non-English-speaking countries in favor of linguistic variations of *Merlin the Enchanter* (Spain, the Netherlands, and France) or *Merlin and Mim* (West Germany). The screenwriter Bill Peet based several incidental details of Merlin's character on Walt Disney, including apparently his nose.[31] This was no idle flattery. Disney—both the man and the studio—had been producing educational texts for decades. Of course, a strong didactic element runs throughout most Disney features, but the studio had been closely involved in government-sponsored education projects since World War II: the federal government underwrote Disney's production of military training films, granted the studio $2.6 million in subsidies,[32] and in the 1950s commissioned several films on the U.S. space program intended to improve educational standards in the face of Soviet Russia's dominant position in the space race. Such was the studio's commitment to education that the director of one early nature documentary thought little of rounding

**Figure 7.1** Wart's magical "education" at the hands of the film's co-star, Merlin.

up large numbers of brown lemmings and driving them over a cliff in a faked example of their suicidal tendencies.[33] With such pedagogical zeal for technology, science, and the natural world, it is no wonder that the studio seized and expanded upon White's reconfiguration of Merlyn as primarily an educator, rather than the medieval royal advisor. And "Walt the Wizard," Disney's familiar epithet, easily became Merlin the whimsical wizard (figure 7.1).

When Wart first meets the self-confessed "wizard ... sage [and] prognosticator," Merlin deplores the military basis of his present education. Instead, Merlin advocates the value of "a real education—mathematics, history, biology, natural science, English, Latin, French." Seeing Wart's blank expression, Merlin delivers the film's clearest point on the theme: "you can't grow up without a decent education, you know." Yet the lessons that follow do not require Wart to learn much. As in the books, Wart's first lesson is to be turned into a small fish. In White's novel, the purpose of Wart's encounter with the carp, "the King of the Moat," is to impress on him "what it is to be king":

> When [Wart] did see the old despot he started back in horror, for Mr. M. was four feet long, his weight incalculable. The great body, shadowy and

almost invisible among the stems, ended in a face which had been ravaged by all the passions of an absolute monarch, by cruelty, sorrow, age, pride, selfishness, loneliness and thoughts too strong for individual brains. There he hung or hoved, his vast ironic mouth permanently drawn downwards in a kind of melancholy, his lean clean-shaven chops giving him an American expression, like that of Uncle Sam. He was remorseless, disillusioned, logical, predatory, fierce, pitiless. (1938: 63)

This image of dreadful majesty—hardly to be captured in the relatively poor animation of Disney films in the 1960s—proves "hypnotic" to the young Wart, who is almost swallowed up (1938: 64–65). In the film, the lesson begins with Merlin teaching Wart how to swim, while singing of how "you must set your sights upon the heights / Don't be a mediocrity." The song, written by Robert and Richard Sherman, continues: "You see, my boy, it's nature's way— / Upon the weak, the strong ones prey," and then exhorts: "That is what you must expect, / Unless you use your intellect." The song reveals a different learning outcome to White's depiction of absolute kingship: the pursuit of intellectual power to defeat a bigger enemy. The "message" is most clearly demonstrated in Merlin's climactic, shape-shifting encounter with Madam Mim: the latter becomes a huge dragon, and the wizard defeats her by transforming himself into a series of dangerous microbes that incapacitate her—a parallel to contemporary American interest in biological warfare. In the early lesson, Merlin insists on the lesson's practical application: "Here's your chance to prove my point. He's the brawn and you're the brain. Use your head and outsmart the big brute." But the words, as so often in this film, do not match the action: Wart does not use his head and is saved from the carp's open jaws only by the intervention of Merlin and his talking owl, Archimedes. Nothing, it seems, has been learned: the lesson devolves into the first of the film's many structurally repetitive chase scenes.

In the next lesson, Wart is transformed into a squirrel, but the lesson on gravity is forgotten as he is pursued, in another chase scene, by an amorous female squirrel—"and a red-head at that," as Merlin remarks, before singing another Sherman brothers' tune and finding himself confronted with further bushy-tailed amour. Both refuse female advances in favor of continued homosocial companionship and Wart, if he learns anything, gathers that gravity is less powerful than love. In the next scene, Wart's foster-father Ector and his son Kay battle with magically animated kitchen utensils—*Fantasia* to big band swing. The cause of the mayhem is Merlin who, despite earlier having told Wart that "Now, don't you get any foolish ideas that magic will solve all your problems—because it won't," employed magic to spare him from manually completing his tasks. Indeed, despite Merlin's advice, magic frequently resolves Wart's problems, just as magic drives the plot forward whenever the narrative grinds to one of its many halts.

Toward the end of the film, with his teaching methods challenged by his talking owl, Merlin refuses to instruct Wart, and Archimedes briefly replaces him as tutor, pointing to a large stack of books and instructing the young Arthur to read. "All of them?" asks Wart, understandably unused to such pedagogical practice. "That, my boy, is a mountain of knowledge," Archimedes declares in response. Finally, Wart admits that he cannot read or write, and slowly Archimedes teaches the boy how to copy out his alphabet. But Merlin quickly disrupts the lesson and begins to toy with a model plane, and the scene shifts to the encounter with Madam Mim, which concludes with Merlin's final axiom—"knowledge and wisdom is the real power"—although little has been imparted to Wart, in his curiously content-free education.

Throughout this film about education, books remain the most visually apparent symbol. They fill Merlin's forest cottage, tower perilously in his ramshackle tower; he piles them up, they tumble down; Wart carries them and is instructed to read them. But they remain, throughout the film, unread, their pages never opened. The motif of the unread book is even evident in the film's opening. Like so many Disney features, *The Sword in the Stone* opens with a book—specifically a red-leather tome, with brass hinges and clasp, clearly embossed with the film's title. The cover turns to reveal two distinct texts. In large, multicolored script are clearly written, in mock-medieval hand, the words of the opening song that establish England's perilous state: "The good king had died / And no one could decide / Who was rightful heir to the throne." As each line is sung, a new leaf is turned, most accompanied with appropriate quasi-illuminations. But beneath each image is another text, in a smaller hand, beginning: "It befell in the days of Uther Pendragon when he was king of all England, and so reigned, there were great knights ..." Visible, but unspoken and unread, this close paraphrase of Malory's opening haunts the Disney film. While books contain "a mountain of knowledge," as Archimedes claims, this is a film that refuses to read, just as it refuses to engage in any meaningful sense with a medieval past.

### "These backward medieval times": Disney's Medievalism

Like Wart's content-free education, Disney stripped *The Sword in the Stone* of much of its Arthurian matter: while some of the characters remain, along with some of its iconography—the sword in the stone motif, the image of the perilous forest—they are textually isolated, devoid of their traditional significance. One of the most notable silences is Wart's kingship—particularly his right to rule.

As a predominant American cultural institution, Disney has surprisingly few ideological problems with kingship, and several of Disney's films can be seen as royal inheritance romances. *Bambi* and *The Lion King* each begin with the birth of a new prince; in both, the main narrative concerns the prince's education, simultaneous with the near-devastation of the land as it is beset by outside forces, following, in *The Lion King*'s case, the death of the legitimate king. Both features conclude with the restoration of the proper monarch, the birth of a new prince, and images of the land's and its inhabitants' fecundity. Like so many American authors of both high and popular culture (among them Eliot, Fitzgerald, Steinbeck, Hemingway, Coppola, and Gilliam), Disney overlays these narratives with allusions to the waste land myth, exploiting James Frazer's "magical connection" between the king and land, and transforming it into a male fantasy of patriarchal dominance. *The Sword in the Stone* opens in a similar fashion: following the bibliophobic introduction, the animation shifts to a dark, wolf-inhabited forest. Uther is dead and the kingdom has entered "a dark age," the narrator says, "without law, without order. Men lived in fear of one another, for the strong preyed upon the weak." Although this mostly light-hearted film does not focus on these images for long, the rest of the film follows the prince's "education" before he assumes the throne at the movie's end—except that Wart is not a prince, as Wart, explicitly, is not Uther's son.

The most obvious reason for this narrative silence is Arthur's potential illegitimacy, or "insecure filiation" as Elizabeth Edwards describes it.[34] For some medieval writers, "the stigma of illegitimacy" could be put to ideological use: producing parallels between Arthur and William, Duke of Normandy,[35] or the biblical David.[36] The *Suite de Merlin* reworks the narrative to make Uther "morally loathsome"; Malory rewrites Arthur's unsure right to the throne in terms of acute fifteenth-century anxieties over the issue of royal legitimacy.[37] Like Disney, some more recent Arthurian writers elide the issue of Arthur's parentage. Tennyson is ambivalent about Arthur's origins—multiple rumors of his birth are given in "The Coming of Arthur" (1869). Some hold him to be a "child of shamefulness"; some think him to be Uther's son; others, Anton's or Gorlois's; another story, told by Bellicent, tells of how Arthur was rumored to have been delivered to Merlin as a "naked babe" on a "dragon winged" ship at Tintagil on the night of Uther's death.[38] But Tennyson also bestows numerous images of legitimate authority upon him: he "is fair beyond the race of Britons and of men";[39] receives Excalibur from the Lady of the Lake; and finally, in Leodogran's dream, the image of "the phantom king" is divinely authorized:

> ... the solid earth became
> As nothing, but the King stood out in heaven,
> Crowned. And Leodogran awoke, and sent
> Ulfius, and Brastias and Bedivere,
> Back to the court of Arthur answering yea.[40]

Other authors, eschewing the rumors, mysteries, and divine dreams of Tennyson's verse, would, in the twentieth century, also expunge the details of Arthur's birth. Warwick Deeping's *Uther and Igraine* (1906), one of the earliest Arthurian novels, depicts Uther and Igraine as lovers before Gorlois forces marriage on her. Merlin, no longer the means of the deception, intervenes, putting Igraine into a trance after the wedding, after which Uther kills Gorlois. White's *Sword in the Stone* retains the traditional story, but delays the information for narrative purposes: Wart is told of his parentage at the end of the novel, although Merlyn does not inform him of his mother's identity, which precipitates the incestuous disaster in *The Witch in the Wood*.

Disney's film, however, is far from Deeping's romantic mode and avoids Tennyson's multiple images of divinely legitimized authority. The audience is left with only two causes for Wart's sudden elevation. The sword in the stone motif is the first: rarely has the former been so isolated, so loaded with dramatic and narrative importance. The Prose *Merlin* attributed to Robert de Boron (c. 1200) originates the device: appearing in an explicitly Christian context, it signifies that Arthur's reign will be the epitome of Christian history. Even for later authors, it remains a powerful symbol of Arthur's heroic "pre-eminence amongst his barons."[41] Although Disney describes the appearance of the sword in the stone as "a miracle" of "London-town," it retains none of its religious or heroic significance: it merely provides a neat conclusion to the film.

The other cause of Wart's elevation is his accent. Wart's American voice, supplied by three different actors, is emphatic: all other parts are spoken with a range of English approximations, from the Received Pronunciation of the "good" Merlin, to the working-class Cockney tones of the "bad" Kay. Throughout, Wart's accent marks him as separate from—and superior to—every other character in the film, in what is part of a U.S. cultural trend in cinematic medievalism beginning after World War II. While influential authors including Twain and Pyle Americanized Arthurian narratives in the nineteenth century, and while other medieval myths—above all, the Robin Hood tradition—would make early and potent transitions to Hollywood cinema, it seems that only in the 1950s did cinema audiences witness an aural *translatio* of medieval stories, wherein American heroes with American voices were superimposed on European narratives, otherwise played out in English accents: Tony Curtis's seemingly Brooklyn-born Myles in Universal's *The Black Shield of Falworth* (1954) or Robert Taylor's Ivanhoe or Lancelot in MGM's "iron jockstrap" movies of the early 1950s. Less heroic, yet still resolutely American, Wart's accent in *The Sword in the Stone* is the voice of American *translatio*. And, through his voice, Wart's rise from obscurity to king becomes not the troubled and troubling fantasy that so exercised the imaginations and codified the dynastic and imperial ambitions of countless medieval kings and barons but another fantasy—a particularly American fantasy that many other U.S. Arthuriads have chronicled—of meritocracy: anyone can become "king," especially if aided by the film's persistent, if underworked, theme of social rise via the acquisition of knowledge and technology.

But not everything in this movie is so easily maneuvered into a modern American context. Indeed, this is a film that frequently, and problematically, resists its own medievalism. In one of Wart's final lessons, Merlin shows the young squire two images of the world: the first is a two-dimensional image of a flat earth, at the corner of which is drawn an image of a storm blowing a ship off its edge. The second is a globe, with "The New World" clearly marked. Neither map is remarked upon. But Merlin does say that "we've got to get all these medieval ideas out of your head—clear the way for new ideas: knowledge of man's fabulous discoveries in the centuries ahead. That will be a great advantage." While Merlin, as already discussed, imparts little by way of knowledge—and less by way of wisdom—complaints about the medieval world run throughout the film. In the opening, Merlin grumbles about these "backward medieval times" as he struggles to pull up a pail of water: "no plumbing, no electricity, no nothing." Later, as Wart washes dishes by hand, he exclaims, "what a medieval muddle; we'll have to modernize it. Start an assembly-line system." Merlin's voice is indicative of the whole film: at no point is "medieval splendor," promised by Disney's 1940s poster, evident in the film. Everything here is "backwards"—even Merlin who literally experiences time in reverse.

Disney's Merlin is very different from his American predecessors. While Twain's Merlin was an enemy of modernity, Disney's is more like that other quintessential American Arthurian figure: the Yankee, Hank Morgan. Like Morgan he is historically displaced, living backwards in time, and brings with him a knowledge of the future—the "fabulous discoveries in the centuries ahead"—and remains a voice of criticism throughout the film. In some ways, then, *The Sword in the Stone* is not just part of White's Arthuriad, as it also belongs to the many cinematic adaptations of Twain's 1889 novel.

Indeed, Disney would go on to produce at least four variations on *A Connecticut Yankee*. The first was the live-action *Unidentified Flying Oddball* (1979), which borrows little from Twain except for the basic premise: an astronaut, Tom Trimble, with advanced technological skills travels back in time to the days of King Arthur. He is befriended by Clarence, makes an enemy of Merlin, and falls in love with Sandy, but most of the action centers on Mordred and Merlin's attempt to usurp Arthur. The devastating power of modern technology that destroys the chivalric flower of England in Twain's novel is here, instead, harnessed to support the king and the *ancien régime*, and it becomes a familiar structure in the films that followed. Next came an animated short, Sir Gyro de Gearloose" (1987), in which three talking ducks accompany a time-traveling inventor to Quackalot. In the 1995 film A *Kid in King Arthur's Court*, a gangly, unconfident Californian youth named Calvin is transported back to the Camelot of an aged Arthur after he falls through a crack in the ground caused by a sudden earthquake. He dazzles the court with rock music, rollerblades, and a Swiss Army Knife, falls in love with one of Arthur's daughters, and manages to save the kingdom before being transported back to modern-day California, where, for the first time, he manages to hit a home run. And in what is perhaps the most intelligent and scholarly of Disney's Arthurian films, *A Knight in Camelot* (1998), Hank Morgan has become Dr. Vivien Morgan, "a dreadlocked, fast-talking physicist from West Cornwall, Connecticut," played by Whoopi Goldberg.[42] With a 1990s' laptop replacing an 1880s' almanac, and late twentieth-century gender and racial politics replacing the post-bellum anxieties of Twain's novel, Disney's most recent *Yankee* film fully modernizes and Americanizes the Arthurian story.

Rooted in a native textual tradition and informed by a discernable ideological agenda, Disney's *A Knight in Camelot* is a far more successful example of American *translatio* than is *The Sword in the Stone*, which both appropriates and rejects an English Arthurian story in favor of a thinly worked idyll of a boy's unexpected, unwanted, and unexplained rise to kingship. At the end of the 1963 film, Merlyn reappears from his Bermuda vacation, dressed in rainbow-colored shirt and yellow and green shorts, complete with sunglasses, baseball cap, and red sneakers. He encourages the lonely, worried Wart that he will one day become a great king—"Boy, boy, boy, you'll become a legend. They'll be writing books about you for centuries to come. Why, they might even make a motion picture about you." Indeed "they" did—many. But Disney's *Sword in the Stone*, ultimately, was not really one of them.

## Notes

1. Keith Booker, *Disney, Pixar, and the Hidden Message of Children's Films* (Santa Barbara: Praeger, 2010), 38.
2. Alan Lupack and Barbara Tepa Lupack, *King Arthur in America* (Cambridge: Brewer, 1999), 321.
3. Jerome Reel, "Good King Arthur: Arthurian Music for Children," *Adapting the Athurian Legends for Children: Essays on Arthurian Juvenilia*, ed. Barbard Lupack (New York: Palgrave Macmillan, 2004), 217–42, at 230.
4. Jerry Beck, *The Animated Movie Guide* (Chicago: A Cappella, 2005), 272.
5. Raymond Thompson, "The Ironic Tradition in Four Arthurian Films," *Cinema Arthuriana: Twenty Essays*, rev. ed., ed. Kevin J. Harty (Jefferson, NC: McFarland, 2010), 110–17, at 111.
6. Alice Grellner, "Two Films That Sparkle: *The Sword in the Stone* and *Camelot*," *Cinema Arthuriana* 118–26, at 118.
7. Jack Zipes, "Breaking the Disney Spell," *From Mouse to Mermaid: The Politics of Film, Gender, and Culture*, ed. Elizabeth Bell, Lynda Haas, and Laura Sells (Bloomington: Indiana University Press, 1995), 21–41.
8. Elizabeth Bell, Lynda Haas, and Laura Sells, "Introduction: Walt's in the Movies," *From Mouse to Mermaid*, 1–17, at 5.
9. Pamela Morgan, "One Brief Shining Moment: Camelot in Washington D. C.," *Medievalism in North America*, ed. Kathleen Verduin (Cambridge: Brewer, 1994), 185–211.
10. For discussion of the *romans d'antiquité* and twelfth-century practices of *translatio studii, translatio imperii*, see Christopher Baswell, "Marvels of Translation and Crises of Transition in the Romances of Antiquity," *Cambridge Companion to Medieval Romance*, ed. Roberta Krueger (Cambridge: Cambridge University Press, 2000), 29–44.
11. Sylvia Townsend Warner, *T. H. White: A Biography* (London: Cape, 1967), 175.
12. T. H. White, *The Complete Once and Future King* (London: HarperCollins 1996), 342; hereafter cited parenthetically.
13. T. H. White, *Letters to a Friend: The Correspondence between T. H. White and L. J. Potts*, ed. François Gallix (Gloucester: Sutton, 1984), 115–16.
14. Alan Lupack, *The Oxford Guide to Arthurian Literature and Legend* (Oxford: Oxford University Press, 2005), 183.
15. Richard Barber, "Introduction," *King Arthur in Music*, ed. Richard Barber (Cambridge: Brewer, 2002), 1–8, at 6.
16. Roger Simpson, *Radio Camelot: Arthurian Legends on the BBC, 1922–2005* (Cambridge: Brewer, 2008), 35.
17. Roger Simpson, *Radio Camelot*, 67, 94–95.
18. Alan Jay Lerner, *The Street Where I Live* (London: Hodder and Stoughton, 1978), 217.
19. Loewe, qtd. in Alan Jay Lerner, *The Street Where I Live*, 172.
20. Theodore H. White, "For President Kennedy: An Epilogue," *Life* (6 Dec. 1963), 158–59, at 159.

21. Susan Aronstein and Nancy Coiner, "Twice Nightly: Democratizing the Middle Ages for Middle-Class America," *Medievalism in North America* 212–30, at 215.
22. Theodore H. White, "For President Kennedy," 159.
23. Kathy Jackson, *Walt Disney: A Bio-Bibliography* (Westport: Greenwood, 1993), 69.
24. Jerry Beck, *The Animated Movie Guide*, 272.
25. Neil Gabler, *Walt Disney: The Triumph of the American Imagination* (New York: Knopf, 2007), 620.
26. Gill Davies, "Nature Writing and Eco Criticism: Reading T. H. White in the Twenty-First Century," *Critical Essays on T. H. White* ed. Gill Davies, et al. (New York: Mellen, 2008), and David Whitley, *The Idea of Nature in Disney Animation* (Aldershot: Ashgate, 2008 157–77), as well as Kathleen Coyne Kelly's essay in this volume.
27. David Payne, "Bambi," *From Mouse to Mermaid*, 137–47; but cf. David Whitley, *The Idea of Nature in Disney Animation*, 61–77.
28. T. H. White, *The Sword in the Stone* (1938; London: HarperCollins, 1991), 265, 79.
29. Stephen Knight, *Arthurian Literature and Society* (London: Macmillan, 1983), 203–04.
30. Alan Lupack, "*The Once and Future King*: The Book That Grows Up," *Arthuriana* 11.3 (2001): 103–14; and Heather Worthington, "From Children's Story to Adult Fiction: T. H. White's *The Once and Future King*," *Arthuriana* 12.2 (2002): 97–119.
31. Rebecca Umland and Samuel Umland, *Arthurian Legend in Hollywood Film* (Westport: Greenwood, 1996), 122.
32. Elizabeth Bell, Lynda Haas, and Laura Sells, "Introduction: Walt's in the Movies," 5.
33. Greg Garrard, *Ecocriticism* (Abingdon: Routledge, 2004), 151.
34. Elizabeth Edwards, "The Place of Women in the *Morte Darthur*," *A Companion to Malory*, ed. Elizabeth Archibald, et al. (Cambridge: Brewer, 1996), 37–54, at 44.
35. Stephen Knight, *Arthurian Literature and Society*, 52.
36. Rosemary Morris, *The Character of King Arthur in Medieval Literature* (Cambridge: Brewer, 1982), 25.
37. Karen Cherewatuk, *Marriage, Adultery, and Inheritance in Malory's* Morte Darthur (Cambridge: Brewer, 2006), 111–16.
38. Alfred, Lord Tennyson, "The Coming of Arthur," *The Idylls of the King*, ed. J. M. Gray (Harmondsworth: Penguin, 1983), 21–35, lines 239, 359–424.
39. Alfred, Lord Tennyson, "The Coming of Arthur," lines 330–31.
40. Alfred, Lord Tennyson, "The Coming of Arthur," lines 430, 442–46.
41. Neil Thomas, *Diu Crône and the Medieval Arthurian Cycle* (Cambridge: Brewer, 2002), 116.
42. Barbara Lupack, "Camelot on Camera: The Arthurian Legends and Children's Film," *Adapting the Arthurian Legend for Children*, 263–93, at 271.

## CHAPTER 8

## WALT IN SHERWOOD, OR THE SHERIFF OF DISNEYLAND: DISNEY AND THE FILM LEGEND OF ROBIN HOOD

*Kevin J. Harty*

> For John Marshall and Stephen Knight,
> who "kan rymes of Robyn Hood,"
>
> with thanks.

No place would seem farther from the Hoodian greenwood than Sleeping Beauty Castle at Disneyland or Cinderella Castle in Walt Disney World. If anything, Disney's castles suggest the world of King Arthur and his Knights of the Round Table. Indeed, when Walt Disney died, the *Atlanta Journal* ran an editorial cartoon with the caption "Childhood's 'Camelot'" featuring a despondent young boy sitting cross-legged on a hill and looking off into the distance at a drawing of Disneyland labeled "The Legacy of Walt Disney."[1] While Disney enterprises produced an animated film version of *The Sword in the Stone* directed by Wolfgang Reitherman (1963) and a rather improbable made-for-television film version of Mark Twain's *A Connecticut Yankee in King Arthur's Court* entitled *A Knight in Camelot* directed by Roger Young (1998), with Whoopi Goldberg as a race- and gender-bending Hank Morgan, they also produced four very different examples of cinema robiniana with rather mixed agendas—and results: *The Story of Robin Hood and His Merrie Men* directed by Ken Annakin (1952),[2] the animated *Robin Hood* directed by Wolfgang Reitherman (1973), *The Rocketeer* directed by Joe Johnson (1991), and the made-for-television *Princess of Thieves* directed by Peter Hewitt (2001).

The following chapter examines each of these films as a "disneyfication" of the Robin Hood legend. In its Disney versions, Robin Hood is first and foremost a story about the "good guy"; Robin's (or his daughter's) thievery is carefully placed in the service of justice and his actions restore proper order to the kingdom. These films also all offer a version of Disney's "determined girl" narrative; their heroines display agency and spunk, even if, on the whole, they are relegated to traditional gender roles at the narratives' ends. In addition to these common transformations, each film also functions in its own political and social context: *The Story of Robin Hood and His Merrie Men* nods repeatedly in the direction of McCarthyism and its obsession with the "enemy within"; the animated *Robin Hood* advances a message of social responsibility; *The Rocketeer*, as do many action-hero films from the 1980s, returns America to its World War II glory days; and *Princess of Thieves* initially gestures towards a feminist rewriting of the legend only in its last scene to close down such a rewriting's radical possibilities.

Disney turned to the story of Robin Hood after the release of its first fully live-action feature, *Treasure Island* directed by Byron Haskin from Robert Louis Stevenson's short story (1950). But such a venture was risky. At the time, the standard for Hoodian films remained that set by Michael Curtiz's 1938 film *The Adventures of Robin Hood* starring Errol Flynn in the title role[3]—although the studio's first choice to play the role had been James Cagney! The film was among the most popular shown to troops during World War II, was subsequently rereleased in a new Technicolor print in 1948, and was sold to television in the mid-1950s.[4] In addition to the 1938 film's immense popularity and longevity, the fact that four other Hoodian films made after the war—*The Bandit of Sherwood Forest* directed by George Sherman and Henry Levin (1946), *The Prince of Thieves* directed by Howard Bretherton (1948), *Rogues of Sherwood Forest* directed by Gordon Douglas (1950), and *Tales of Robin Hood* directed by James Tiling (1952)—were neither commercial nor critical successes should have discouraged Disney and company from venturing into the greenwood.[5]

Furthermore, the production of a Disney Robin Hood film itself got off to a false start when the original idea for the film was scrapped. Hoping to build on the success of *Treasure Island*, Disney at first planned a Hoodian film that was almost a clone of the earlier pirate film. The film was to have focused on the adventures of a young boy who joins Robin's band, and also to have featured Robert Newton (Long John Silver in *Treasure Island*) as Friar Tuck. But child labor laws prevented the use of the young boy, and Newton had other commitments.[6] As a result, Disney changed the plot of the film to make it a romantic adventure starring Richard Todd, a competent enough actor but no match for Errol Flynn, as Robin, and Joan Rice as Marian, who, despite resembling a younger Olivia de Haviland, was, in fact, no de Haviland (figure 8.1).

Lacking both the hoped-for tie-in to *Treasure Island* and Flynn and de Haviland, the Disney studio attempted instead to authenticate the production. Publicity for the film noted the contributions of "Dr. Charles Beard, well-known authority on history and antiquities," and stressed the screenplay's debt to "the old 12th [sic] century ballads," to "Wyken [sic] de Worde's 1489 printed edition of 'The Lyttel Geste of Robyn Hood,'" and even to Robin's mention in "'The Vision of Piers Plowman,' written between 1355 and 1365."[7] Disney also released a novelization of the film's screenplay.[8] The film opens on a decidedly literary note with a shot of a book and turning pages—a standard Disney device for a film opening; a further literary chord is struck at the beginning of, and continues throughout, the film because of the centrality in the cinematic narrative of Allan-A-Dale (Elton Hayes), here characterized as a roving minstrel who advances the film's plot by singing ballads of Robin's exploits.[9]

In addition to these appeals to the film's literary heritage, a number of the narremes in the Disney film are familiar from the Hoodian legend's cinematic heritage. An archery contest pits Robert Fitzooth (Todd) and

**Figure 8.1** Marian (Joan Rice) tends to the wounded Robin Hood (Richard Todd). Still from the collection of the author.

his father Hugh (Reginald Tate) against archers in the pay of De Lacey (Peter Finch), whom Prince John (Hubert Gregg) has recently named Sheriff of Nottingham after the original Sheriff and his men successfully petition Richard I (Patrick Barr) to join him on his Crusade to the Holy Land. Also in the king's company is the Earl of Huntingdon (Clement McCallin), who entrusts his daughter Marian to the care of Eleanor of Aquitaine (Martita Hunt) until he returns. Hugh and Robert defeat the Sheriff's champion, Red Gill (Archie Duncan, who later played Little John in the long-running television series, *The Adventures of Robin Hood*, starring Richard Greene as the title character), with Robert's arrow landing closer to the center of the bull's eye and his father's splitting his. Hugh gives the golden arrow that is his prize for winning to Robert, who in turn bestows it upon Marian. Equally familiar are Robert/now Robin's first encounters with Little John (James Robertson Justice) and Friar Tuck (James Hayter). Robin first encounters the former crossing a narrow footbridge where they duel with quarter staffs to see who will cross first. John knocks Robin into the water, but is subsequently himself "baptized" by Robin's men to celebrate his joining their company. The worldly, jocund, and musical friar also has a watery encounter with Robin when they take turns ferrying each other across a stream on each other's back with the gentle inducement of the knife blades that they point at each other.

This version of the legend inflects the standard cinematic version of Robin Hood in two interesting and somewhat contradictory ways. Its empowering of women transcends the usual gender-based prescriptions of the 1950s, while its characterizations of its villains as enemies from within (who are often costumed in red) reflects the all-too-common red-baiting in the entertainment industry during the decade.

The film gives women real agency—a notable development in screen versions of the legend. Marian's aged nurse, Tyb, played by a befuddled Louise Hampton—in a not always successful nod to Marian's Bess (Una O'Connor) in the Flynn film—conforms to gender and class stereotypes. But Martita Hunt's Queen Eleanor is a force with which to be reckoned.[10] She thwarts John, and, with the assistance of the warrior-spiked club as well as crozier-bearing Archbishop of Canterbury (Anthony Eustrel), she directs the successful efforts to raise 100,000 marks to ransom her son Richard from an Austrian jail. Rice's Maid Marian also shows a remarkable amount of independence throughout most of the film. In the opening scenes, she woos Robert on her own terms; she later runs away, disguising herself as a page, to join Robin and his men, despite being ordered not to do so; and she delivers a much-needed contribution from the outlaws to the king's ransom, thereby setting in motion Robin's plot to rob the Sheriff of all his possessions as a final contribution to secure the full 100,000 mark ransom. In the film's last scene, she protests Richard's edict that she marry the Earl of Locksley, until she learns that Robin has been so ennobled.

The film's progressive portrayal of both Eleanor and Marian is countered by its more conservative construction of its villains. While there have been ongoing discoveries about the unacknowledged contributions of blacklisted Hollywood writers to the plots of any number of episodes from the long-running television series *The Adventures of Robin Hood*, which often hinge on the willingness or the refusal of characters to name names, the Disney film's politics are more in keeping with those of the studio's founder. Walt Disney himself was unapologetically and unabashedly anti-communist, as evidenced by his opposition to the writers' strike in the 1940s and by his subsequent support for the extension of the Hollywood black-list and the denial of work in front of and behind the camera to anyone whose patriotism or loyalty was suspect.[11]

The Disney film does not wear its politics on its sleeve, but the depiction of the villains in *The Story of Robin Hood and His Merrie Men* reflects Walt Disney's personal political sentiments. Alan Lupack notes connections between the politics of the McCarthy era and two other examples of cinema medievalia, especially in the use of villains as enemies from within and their attendant costuming in red.[12] In spite of the fact that King Richard's banner and his crusader's cross are red, red costumes in this Disney film are usually associated with the enemy. Indeed, while Todd's Robert first appears in red tights, he eventually changes to Lincoln green as he also changes his name to Robin Hood. But the Sheriff's men, in general, and *Red* Gill, in particular, also sport red tights, and whenever Finch's De Lacey as the Sheriff plans his evil machinations, his costume is red. This association between red clothes and villainy adds a layer to Prince John's wardrobe choice as he attempts to steal the ransom collected on his brother's behalf: he sheds his usual azure costume for one of scarlet.

The film's portrayal of its villains within the context of the McCarthy era extends to its unwillingness to grant them even a moment of glory. The Sheriff and Robin engage in a final sword fight, but no element of either derring-do or swashbuckling enlivens their duel, even if it does nod to the justifiably famous combat between Sir Guy (Basil Rathbone) and Robin in the Flynn film. The Disney Sheriff dies ignominiously when he is crushed by the mechanism of a closing drawbridge after he has broken his word not to alert the castle guards about Robin's attempt to escape.

While the story of Robin Hood has, especially since Howard Pyle's 1883 influential novel *The Merry Adventures of Robin Hood*, been considered a children's or, more properly, a boys' book, *The Story of Robin Hood and His Merrie Men*, with its foray into politics, is not totally child's fare. Disney would more consciously aim for a children's audience in its second outing into the greenwood, the feature-length animated *Robin Hood* directed by Wolfgang Reitherman, who ten years earlier had directed *The Sword in the Stone* for Disney (1963). *The Sword in the Stone* provided Reitherman with material that easily proved palatable for young audiences, the adulterous Arthur–Guinevere–Lancelot love triangle notwithstanding. Arthur is clearly an establishment figure, and as such late nineteenth- and early twentieth-century attempts in England and in the United States to solve the "boy problem" often included the suggestions that boys join groups with moral aims and read texts with moral messages, including the tales of Arthur and the Knights of the Round Table.[13] Any Hoodian tale, cinematic or otherwise, intended for younger audiences is, however, a project with some inherent problems. From the start, Robin Hood has always been an antiauthoritarian, antiestablishment figure. His primary claim to fame is that he is a thief, and the notion that his thievery was premised on a redistribution of wealth from the haves to the have-nots was a later permutation in the legend.[14] How then to present a story with such a central narreme—sanctioned theft—to a young audience?

Ironically, the narrative that provided the studio with an answer to this dilemma contained in itself many of the same problems. In the 1930s, as the studio was filming *Snow White and the Seven Dwarfs*, Walt Disney became intrigued with the idea of making an animated version of the twelfth-century tale of Reynard the Fox. The version of the tale that initially piqued Walt Disney's interest presented a kingdom of beasts ruled over by a mean-spirited, greedy Lion. When Reynard insults the royal leonine personage by failing to attend court, the Lion sends out a series of "hench-animals"—the Bear, the Cat, and finally the second Fox—to bring Reynard to heel and punish him. After the Bear is attacked by bees and the Cat loses an eye because of Reynard's trickery, the second Fox succeeds, and Reynard is sentenced to the scaffold, but his talk about a hidden treasure leads to a pardon on the condition that he turn over the treasure to the Lion. In the company of the Rabbit and the Ram, Reynard is sent to bring the treasure back to the Lion. Reynard tricks his escorts, decapitates the Rabbit, puts his head in a bag, and gives it to the Ram to return to the Lion as the treasure. Once again faced with execution, Reynard talks about yet another hidden treasure, which leads to yet another pardon. The Wolf, however, remembering the fate of previous leonine emissaries, challenges Reynard to a duel, which Reynard wins by cheating. As a reward for his cunning, Reynard is then appointed the Lion's advisor.[15]

Despite his initial enthusiasm for the animated Reynard project, Walt Disney clearly was also uneasy about the project: "The whole central character is a crook. That's what I'm afraid of."[16] The level of violence and the lack of an acceptable moral doubtless delayed action on realizing the film. So the project languished and underwent several treatments over the years, and Disney considered inserting three animated moral fables, including the story of Reynard the Fox, into *Treasure Island*, which were to be told at appropriate moments by Long John Silver.[17] That idea too was rejected once the pirate project was green-lighted as fully live-action. However, Ken Anderson, who had been a member of the original Disney creative team, persevered in his decades-long interest in scripting an animated tale of a fox, which finally morphed from the wily Reynard into Robin Hood.

In 1968, *The Aristocats* was still in production, and in accordance with Disney practice, the studio was keen to get to work on the next animated project. The brass at the studio wanted "a classic," and Anderson suggested "the story of the roguish outlaw Robin Hood, and they liked the idea. It was timely, and it would help people laugh at themselves just as they did during the Depression with *The Three Little Pigs*." The decision to turn familiar Hoodian characters into animals solved a number of problems, not the least of which was the morality (or amorality) at the root of a story aimed at young audiences of someone who robs, whatever the reason. As Anderson points out, "we decided to do what we [the folks at Disney] do best: use animals for characters."[18] Furthermore, turning Robin and company into animals establishes a degree of moral distance in the animated film. On the screen, younger audiences are not seeing the deeds of people, and the element of make-believe is thereby heightened to undercut any moral dilemmas that the film presents.

The film solves these dilemmas by departing from the standard Hoodian story and its expected narremes in some interesting ways. There is, for instance, no band of men, merry or otherwise; instead, there are simply Robin, a fox (voiced by Brian Bedford), and Little John, a bear (voiced by Phil Harris), who are eventually joined by Friar Tuck, a badger (voiced by Andy Devine). Robin's nemesis is Prince John, a thumb-sucking momma's boy lion *sans* mane (voiced by Peter Ustinov), who steals the crown from his more than fully maned brother Richard. The crown, in a humorous touch, literally does not fit John; his head is too small, and the crown continually falls down around his ears. The leonine John is avarice personified, and he is assisted in his efforts to rob from the common folk and give to himself by a sycophantic snake, Sir Hiss (voiced by Terry Thomas), his chief advisor; by the Sheriff, a wolf (voiced by Pat Buttram); and by two comically inept vultures, Trigger (voiced by

George Lindsey) and Nutsy (voiced by Ken Curtis). Robin's love interest, Maid Marian, is a comely vixen (voiced by Monica Evans) who is attended by Lady Kluck, a formidable chicken (voiced by Carole Shelley). Rounding out the cast of characters is the rooster balladeer Allan-a-Dale (voiced by Roger Miller), and a supporting menagerie including crocodiles, hippopotamuses, elephants, rhinoceroses, mice, cats, and dogs (figure 8.2).

As with the 1952 film, the animated feature opens with a shot of a book whose pages turn to detail the standard set-up for recounting the story of Robin Hood: Richard is away on Crusade, and his brother,

**Figure 8.2** Disney's animated vulpine Robin Hood. Still from the collection of the author.

acting as regent, taxes the starving populace to their last farthing. All seems familiar enough until Allan-a-Dale, here a crooning rooster, announces that the animal kingdom has its own version of the "story of what really happened in Sherwood Forest." Allan-a-Dale reappears throughout the film—just as his live-action counterpart did in the 1952 film—as his songs (and those of others) knit together a plot that is more a loosely strung-together series of episodes than a cohesive whole, and he reaffirms the veracity of the film's story with a last comment—"that's the way it really happened!"—as the final credits begin to roll. After Allan's first appearance, viewers meet Robin and Little John on a log bridge (in a nod to a standard Hoodian narreme), but they do not fight each other with quarter staffs to see who will pass over the bridge first; rather, they are simply enjoying each other's company and happily fall together into the water.

The passing by of Prince John's gold-laden entourage allows Robin to spring into action to separate the villain from his wealth. Little John wonders aloud whether in doing so they are "good or bad guys," and Robin immediately retorts: "We don't rob. We just borrow from those who can afford it." Little John's satisfied response is "Sweet, charity!" This exchange—in light of the subsequent continuing opposition in characterization between those aligned with Robin and those aligned with Prince John—is more than moral hair-splitting. Mark Pinsky pushes the envelope about how the film resolves any moral conundrum when he declares that, by suggesting it is justifiable to take up arms against unjust authority, "Robin Hood makes the Judean Zealots' case for revolt against Roman tyranny and oppression."[19] But the Disney animated film consistently advances an orthodox but nonsectarian (rather than identifiably Christian) moral agenda and takes great pains to make Robin's actions acceptable to younger audiences. At one point, Robin announces that his ultimate goal is to restore happiness to the people of Nottingham. Friar Tuck assures Robin that he is "no outlaw. Someday you'll be known as a great hero."

Prince John and company are all buffoons, but their clownish behavior does not mask their dastardly deeds—it enhances them. Friar Tuck may be portly, but his religious habit is threadbare. He is not the plump, almost gluttonous and lecherous Tuck from the 1952 film—or the quarrelsome friar from the more general Hoodian tradition. He responds to Robin's initial redistribution of wealth with the exclamation, "Praise the Lord, and pass the tax rebates!" When most of Nottingham's citizenry has been cruelly taxed by the Sheriff and then thrown into prison when they cannot pay a penny more, Tuck still tolls the bell in his empty church because the people need "some hope." When the sexton's wife—she and her husband are both church mice and poor, of course—puts her last farthing into the church's poor box in a nod to the biblical parable of the widow's mite (Mark 12.41–44), the Sheriff then robs the poor box. Tuck verbally and physically chastises him and is therefore sentenced to death, but he is hardly the friar warrior found in so many other examples of cinema robiniana. The church mouse's generosity finds parallel among other animals who are down on their heels in contrast to the rapacious greed of the Sheriff, Prince John, and Sir Hiss. When languishing and starving in jail, the poor literally share their last crumbs with one another. Prince John's decision to execute Tuck has a double purpose in that he hopes as well to lure Robin into a trap, since he rightly thinks Robin will attempt to rescue Tuck. This narreme is another Hoodian standard; all that varies is who needs Robin's rescuing from the gallows or pyre. The film also includes the expected archery contest, with Robin (disguised as a stork) splitting the arrow of his opponent, the Sheriff. The promised prize is a golden arrow and a kiss from Marian.

While the animated Disney *Robin Hood* advances an ethical agenda to counter the problems inherent in having a "crook" as its central character,[20] it also follows the lead of the 1952 film in allowing female characters agency. By donating the last farthing that she saved for a rainy day—the wisdom of the film is often proverbial—the church mouse wife acts when her husband seems not to know what to do. And in a key scene, Lady Kluck breaks out of the mold of simply serving as ditzy handmaid to Marian. Marian herself is more stereotypically portrayed in the film; she has literally been the object of Robin's more than lovesick gaze since they were both kits.

When Robin's true identity is revealed at the end of the archery contest, mayhem breaks out as Robin and company battle with Prince John's men. Of course, the battle itself is nothing more than a harmless and bloodless series of pratfalls—no one is killed, maimed, or injured. At one point, a herd of oversized rhinoceroses assumes an American football backline formation and rushes Robin and company. Kluck leaps into action to the accompaniment of a tune that vaguely sounds like the fight song "On, Wisconsin!" (whose flagship university's mascot is the badger) and bowls them over, routing their charge and helping to give victory to those opposed to John.

The film's liberality in such matters may stem from its somewhat arrested history. Vaguely conceived in the Depression era and finally realized in the late 1960s, the film not surprisingly can be read as advancing a message that advocates social responsibility and concern for the less fortunate (all of whom clearly have innate nobility no matter how lean their circumstances). The wealthy and greedy—not church and state—are the enemy. Indeed, both church and state in the person of Tuck and Richard, who makes only a brief appearance at the film's end, are the guarantors of the rights of the poor, the downtrodden, and the dispossessed. As Walt Disney wrote in the draft of a 1962 essay for a religious magazine: "The important thing is to teach a child that good can always triumph over evil, and that is what our pictures attempt to do."[21]

Disney's next cinematic foray into the greenwood would be more indirect: *The Rocketeer* invokes the cinematic history of the Robin Hood legend rather than offering a version of the legend itself. This film stemmed from the 1980s' nostalgia for the action heroes of the 1930s, when the *Indiana Jones* franchise and the later installments of the *Superman* franchise enjoyed great success; subsequently, *The Flash* ran on television for two seasons in 1990 and 1991, and Warren Beatty's *Dick Tracy* was released in 1990. At the end of the 1980s, Disney commissioned Joe Johnson to bring a version of the retro action saga, *The Rocketeer*, to the screen. Originally authored by Dave Stevens in the 1980s, the *Rocketeer* comics were a throwback to Depression-era pulp adventure stories. The comics version told the story of Cliff Secord, a down-on-his-luck assistant to an unsuccessful carney from Detroit who heads to California with Peevy, a Merlin-like mechanical genius, to compete in the All-American Flying Derby and to make money as a movie stunt pilot. On his first movie set, Cliff falls in love with an aspiring actress, but he proves as unlucky in love as he continues to be in launching any sort of sustained career until he is drafted into government service as the anonymous Rocketeer to thwart Nazi agents.[22]

The Disney film opens in Hollywood in 1938 with Cliff (Billy Campbell) and Peevy (Alan Arkin) already settled in California. Cliff's love interest, Jenny (Jennifer Connelly), is an extra on a swashbuckling action-adventure film starring screen heartthrob Neville Sinclair (Timothy Dalton), dubbed "the third-most popular star in Hollywood." The film also includes cameos by W. C. Fields and Clark Gable lookalikes. The conflict in the film centers on the retrieval of a rocket-backpack prototype that has been stolen by mobsters from Howard Hughes (Terry O'Quinn). The mobsters are unwittingly in the employ of Nazi agents, intent on stealing the prototype because of the failure of the Reich's scientists to develop a rocket backpack of their own. Hughes shows Secord a black-and-white animated Nazi short smuggled out of Germany detailing Hitler's plans to equip an army of rocketmen to overrun Europe and eventually the United States. As a Nazi zeppelin crosses the country headed for Los Angeles supposedly on a goodwill tour, Hughes and the government are desperate to recover the prototype and to discover the identity of a German spy who is directing efforts to put the prototype into Hitler's hands.

The spy, viewers soon enough learn, is Neville Sinclair, but only after we see him acting in a crucial scene in his latest film. This scene is a sword fight between Sinclair's character and his nemesis, down a massive spiral stone staircase, during which he stabs his opponent to death, and it is a clone of the signature scene in Errol Flynn's *The Adventures of Robin Hood*. In the earlier film, Flynn's Robin and his men have stormed Nottingham Castle, and Flynn finds himself in a one-on-one fencing battle with the film's dastardly villain, Basil Rathbone's Sir Guy of Gisbourne. (The film's Prince John, as played by Claude Rains, is a much more ineffectual villain.) As they battle back and forth—Sir Guy, of course, does not always fight fairly—their exchange involves both wordplay and swordplay.[23] Robin finally outmaneuvers Sir Guy and stabs him, after which he tumbles off the spiral staircase. A similar staircase appeared in the 1922 Fairbanks film, but it was not the site of a climactic battle. Flynn and Rathbone had "practiced" for this iconic scene in a final duel in an earlier film, *Captain Blood* (1935), which also starred Olivia de Haviland.

Sinclair's casting as an Errol Flynn-like actor is indebted to Charles Higham's scurrilous biography of the star, *Errol Flynn: The Untold Story*, in which Higham alleges that Flynn was a Nazi spy and Gestapo secret agent under the employ of Dr. H. F. Erben, a rabidly anti-Semitic Austrian medical researcher.[24] Flynn did indeed know Erben, but, if anything, Flynn's activities during the war would suggest that his sentiments were clearly anti-German and that he was hardly a Nazi spy or dupe. Any anti-Semitism on Flynn's part would have simply made him a fellow traveler with any number of people in the entertainment business at the time. Yet, as they admitted in an interview, screenwriters Danny Bilson and Paul De Meo freely accepted Higham's accusations about Flynn: "The bad guy is an actor who's really a Nazi agent. He's like Errol Flynn—we based the character on the rumours about Flynn being a Nazi agent (figure 8.3)."[25]

Given Disney's general philosophy behind family films—"Most things are good, and they are the strongest things; but there are evil things"[26]—the film's black-and-white depiction of good and bad guys works better if the film portrays the Flynn-like actor as a secret agent in the pay of the Nazis, intent on helping Hitler and his minions achieve world dominance. Furthering this clear delineation between right and wrong and good and evil is the shift in the film in the sentiments voiced by Eddie Valentine (Paul Sorvino). Initially, Valentine is a mafia capo straight out of central casting. He exists outside the law and is only concerned about earning money, no matter how he does so. Valentine and his "torpedoes" provide Sinclair with the muscle he needs to retrieve the rocket prototype. When Sinclair demands not only the rocket but also Valentine's loyalty—"I need the rocket, Eddie. *Now*. And I need

**Figure 8.3** Timothy Dalton as the Errol Flynn-like Hollywood heartthrob and Nazi agent. Still from the collection of the author.

your loyalty"—Valentine grins, "Loyalty's extra," and Sinclair doubles his price. But, at the film's end, when Valentine discovers that Sinclair is in cahoots with the Nazis, patriotism trumps greed, as he joins his former enemies, the G-men, in thwarting Sinclair's plan and in bringing down the zeppelin in a scene recalling the Hindenburg disaster. (Indiana Jones has a similar fight involving a zeppelin in *Indiana Jones and the Last Crusade*)

While *The Rocketeer* merely nods toward the Robin Hood legend, and the cinematic version of the legend at that, in its portrayal of the good guy's triumph over the enemy within, the made-for-television *Princess of Thieves* directed by Peter Hewitt marks the studio's fourth, and a more obviously Hoodian, foray into the greenwood. While a voice-over initially announces that the legend of Robin Hood is known to all, it also teases viewers by declaring that the legend has a postscript in the form of "a tale kept secret, then forgotten.... Robin and Marian had a child." This postscript locates *Princess of Thieves* within the cinematic tradition of Robin Hood sequels. As Kim Newman points out, the staying power of Errol Flynn's *The Adventures of Robin Hood* after World War II was such that several Hoodian films decided to tell stories that picked up "some years after the glory days, and [to] focus on new characters" including the offspring of Robin and Marian.[27] The 1946 *The Bandit of Sherwood*

*Forest*, directed by Henry Levin and George Sherman, introduced Robin and Marian's son. Sherman's 1958 *Son of Robin Hood* reveals that the son was really a daughter in disguise for fear that the merry men would not rally to the side of a woman in the continued fight against the tyranny of Prince (later King) John. Similarly, in *Princess of Thieves*, Gwen is a girl, but she cuts her long tresses and passes herself off as a teenaged boy, in part because, as a woman, she is relegated to second-class status or is patronized as weak and defenseless by friend and foe alike.

The year is 1184, and King Richard is crusading in the Holy Lands. Robin (Stuart Wilson) has a price on his head, as would his son. News comes to the Sheriff (Malcolm McDowell) of the child's birth, but his Herod-like rage melts when he learns that the child is a girl, who in the mind of the sexist Sheriff can offer no threat and does not merit his attention. As the credits roll, a young girl metamorphoses into a full-grown young woman, Gwen (Keira Knightley), the daughter of Robin and the now-dead Marian, who has been reared in a monastery by Friar Tuck (Crispin Letts) and whose constant companion has been a rather hapless lad, Froderick (Del Synnott), who seems destined for a life more studious than adventure-filled (figure 8.4).

Robin has been a mostly absent father, traveling with Richard in the Holy Land, and his daughter has an independent streak about her, inherited, we are told, from her mother. But Richard lies dying and has named as his heir an illegitimate son, Phillip (Stephen Moyer), who is on his way from France to England, where Robin and Will Scarlet (David Barrass), suddenly back home, are to protect him from Prince John (Jonathan Hyde), who wants the crown for himself. In this film version the band of usual Sherwood suspects consists of Will and Tuck. Aiding John are the Sheriff and his henchman Cardaggian (Peter Cellier) and assorted traitors in their pay. Mistaking Phillip's manservant Conrad (Adam Ryan) for his master, Cardaggian kills Conrad and thinks he has eliminated Prince John's rival for the throne. The real Phillip flees to the woods, teams up with Gwen and a band of rebels, and is eventually crowned king.

Throughout most of the film, Gwen goes to great lengths to break down any barriers imposed as a result of gender stereotyping. She openly complains about Richard's long absence: "the injustice is here, not in Jerusalem." She refuses to be her father's good little girl and to remain behind when he goes off to protect Phillip. She scolds her father, pointing out that she would be treated differently by him were she a son. Partially shorn, and clothed as a bow-and-arrow toting yeoman, she steals a horse from the monastery to join her father and Will in meeting up with Phillip in Harwich. The Marian character disguises herself as a boy in several film versions of the Robin Hood story, such as the 1952 Disney film

**Figure 8.4** Keira Knightley as Robin Hood's daughter Gwen. Still from the collection of the author.

when Joan Rice's Marian disguises herself as a page to join Robin in Sherwood. But Knightley's Gwen does not make a very convincing looking boy, even though she manages to fool the Sheriff and his henchmen.

When a greedy, gluttonous baron beats a child for stealing, Gwen intervenes on the boy's behalf, Robin-Hood-like, and redistributes a bit of wealth in Harwich to a group of children who exclaim in response to his/her gift, "Robin Hood! Robin Hood!" In the standard archery contest, Gwen's arrow splits the Sheriff's—McDowell's Sheriff is an accomplished archer—that previously landed dead center in the bull's eye:

> *Sheriff*: His [Gwen's] style with the bow. Does it remind you of anyone?
> *Attendant*: Robin Hood!

No one follows up on the remark or wonders if Wilfred of Lancaster, the name Gwen has adopted to pass for a man, might have any connection with Robin. After Gwen succeeds in rescuing her father from the Tower, she then takes the crown from John's head and gives it to Phillip, despite John's warning that "history will ignore" Phillip. Hyde's characterization of Prince John finds a parallel in that of Alan Rickman's Sheriff in Kevin Reynolds's film *Robin Hood, Prince of Thieves* (1991), although Rickman is decidedly more exaggerated in his characterization of the Sheriff, who, among other things, wants to cancel Christmas, than Hyde is here.

The basis for the plot of *Princess of Thieves*—that Richard was succeeded by his illegitimate son—is, of course, pure fiction, but then so is Gwen, and the whole Robin Hood legend, for that matter.[28] For purposes of the film's plot, however, Gwen falls in love with Phillip, and he with her, but marriage is out of the question because of their difference in rank. Robin finally recognizes his daughter's abilities, and father and daughter team up to defend Phillip and the realm, but this compromise is cold comfort to Gwen and Phillip. The voice-over returns to tell us, lest we be more than credulous about the events we have just seen on the screen, that history has forgotten these events: Prince John was indeed right, and Phillip does not even merit an historical footnote. Gwen and Phillip never married, the voice-over continues, but "it is known that Phillip pledged his heart to her, a common woman of uncommon valor!"

Unfortunately, the film does not have the courage of its convictions. Just minutes before, when all has been made right, thanks largely to Gwen's actions, she appears not in the garb of a yeoman, but in a dress with her now partially grown back tresses held in place on her head by a decidedly feminine head band. Her tomboy look is rejected; the (medieval) Barbie look is in. So much for protecting the heir to the throne when her father cannot, for rescuing him and Will from the Tower, and for again saving her father's life when she shoots an arrow to deflect an arrow sent flying at him from fifty paces by the Sheriff: Gwen is simply a woman in a dress, a blushing would-be bride not allowed to marry the man of her dreams. Likewise, Knightley's Guinevere in Antoine Fuqua's 2004 film *King Arthur* is condemned by her costume to gender stereotyping in its final scene. After having run around the frozen British landscape throughout the film acting more like Queen Boadicea than the queen from the tradition of medieval courtly romance and wearing nothing but war paint and an outfit more appropriate to Sheena, Queen of the Jungle, Knightley's Guinevere suddenly appears in a traditional white wedding gown complete with floral crown and veil to marry the title character. It seems that when it comes to Knightley, whether she is on the small or big screen, there are limits to how sexually transgressive she is allowed to be.

Each of the four Disney cinematic excursions into the greenwood is decidedly different than the other three. All adhere to Walt Disney's dictum that "we want to have a point of view in our stories, not an obvious moral, but a worthwhile theme."[29] Opposition to tyranny and oppression, concern for the downtrodden and disempowered, and a happy ending, all seem the hallmarks of films from the Sheriff of Disneyland. Politics of any kind is soft-pedaled. The heroes are outlaws, but they are outside the law because those who have wrongly seized power have put them there. There are strong women, but they are not too strong. There are devious, conniving enemies, but they are not so devious and conniving as to be undefeatable. Rather what seems to have led Walt and company into Sherwood was a simple recognition that the enduring legend of Robin Hood was a hook on which could be hung any number of themes, that the legend was, plain and simple, a very, very good story.[30]

## Notes

1. See the *Atlanta Journal* (December 19, 1966): 30.
2. In some sources and formats, the film is simply titled *The Story of Robin Hood*.
3. Certainly the case can be made that Allan Dwan's silent *Robin Hood* starring Douglas Fairbanks, Sr. (1922), the Flynn film, and Richard Lester's *Robin and Marian* (1976), although the last was not a commercial success, have set a standard for cinema robiniana still rarely approached by other examples of the genre. See Kevin J. Harty, "Robin Hood on Film: Moving beyond a Swashbuckling Stereotype," *Robin Hood in Popular Culture*, ed. Thomas Hahn (Cambridge: Brewer, 2000), 87–100.
4. Rudy Behmler, ed., *The Adventures of Robin Hood* (Madison: University of Wisconsin Press, 1979), 11, 38–39.
5. For details on each of these films, see the appropriate alphabetically arranged entries in Kevin J. Harty, *The Reel Middle Ages: American, Western and Eastern European, Middle Eastern, and Asian Films about Medieval Europe* (1999; Jefferson, NC: McFarland, 2006).
6. John West, *The Disney Live-Action Productions* (Milton, WA: Hawthorne & Peabody, 1994), 182.
7. See the film's press book issued by Walt Disney Productions Ltd., a copy of which can be found at the British Film Institute (BFI) Library.
8. *Walt Disney's Robin Hood and His Merrie Men: The Story of the Film Based upon the Screen Play by Lawrence Edward Watkin and Adapted by Edward Boyd* (London: Wm. Collins Sons, 1952).
9. The press book for the film on deposit in the BFI Library indicates that Disney also released a record album for the film containing the ballads and packaged with "a story-in-pictures brochure in FULL COLOUR."
10. The decision to include Eleanor in the cast of characters is notable; the Disney film is the first to do so. Eleanor makes passing appearances in

episodes of the 1950s' television series, *The Adventures of Robin Hood*, and she is also a character in the *The Zany Adventures of Robin Hood* (1984), in the BBC *Robin Hood* television series (2006–2009), and in Ridley Scott's *Robin Hood* (2010), where, as played by Eileen Atkins, she is once again an intimidating presence. The necessity of depicting women in film versions of the Hoodian legend has sometimes been debated; for instance, it was suggested that the character of Maid Marian be eliminated from the 1938 Flynn film (Rudy Behlmer, *Adventures of Robin Hood*, 17).

11. A discussion of Disney's personal politics, the writers' strike, and the red scare is beyond the scope of this essay; see Neal Gabler, *Walt Disney: The Biography* (New York: Knopf, 2007), 364–71. Interestingly, a number of black-listed writers penned episodes of the 1950s' long-running Robin Hood television series in which characters often refuse to name names. See Steve Neale, "Pseudonyms, Sapphire and Salt: 'Un-American' Contributions to Television Costume Adventure Series in the 1950s," *Historical Journal of Film, Radio and Television* 23.3 (2003): 245–57; and Rebecca Prime, "'The Old Bogey': The Hollywood Blacklist in Europe," *Film History* 20.2 (2008): 474–86.

12. See Alan Lupack, "An Enemy in Our Midst: *The Black Knight* and the American Dream," *Cinema Arthuriana: Twenty Essays*, rev. ed., ed. Kevin J. Harty (Jefferson, NC: McFarland, 2010) 64–70, and "Valiant and Villainous Vikings," *The Vikings on Film*, ed. Kevin J. Harty (Jefferson, NC: McFarland, 2011), 46–55. Kim Newman notes that, in yet another example of cinema robiniana, the *Rogues of Sherwood Forest* (1950), the Prince John character sounds "a lot like Senator [Joseph] McCarthy" ("The Robin Hood Collection," *Video Watchdog* 160 [January to February 2011]: 68).

13. Concern for the so-called "boy problem" most famously led to the formation of the Boy Scouts in England and then soon after in the United States. The leader of the American branch of scouting teamed up with Thomas Edison to produce an Arthurian film in 1917, which tells parallel stories of two groups of boys, one made up of n'er-do-wells and the other of scouts. Also in America, William Byron Forbush founded a rival group to scouting, the Knights of King Arthur, which, in the early twentieth century, was immensely popular across the country. For details about the Edison film, see Kevin J. Harty, "*The Knights of the Square Table*: The Boy Scouts and Thomas Edison Make an Arthurian Film," *Arthuriana* 4 (1994): 313–23. For a discussion of Forbush's Arthurian youth group, see Alan Lupack and Barbara Tepa Lupack, *King Arthur in America* (Cambridge: Brewer, 1999), 60–68.

14. Stephen Knight remains the most authoritative and comprehensive source for all things Hoodian. See his *Robin Hood: A Complete Study of the English Outlaw* (Oxford: Blackwell, 1994) and his *Robin Hood: A Mythic Biography* (Ithaca: Cornell University Press, 2003).

15. See John Grant, *Encyclopedia of Walt Disney's Animated Characters* (New York: Harper & Row, 1987), 269–70; and Ken Anderson, "Walt Disney

Productions' All Cartoon Feature *Robin Hood*," *Official Bulletin of IATSE* (Winter 1973–74): 24–26. Anderson was responsible for the film's story and character conception.
16. Walt Disney, qtd. in John Grant, *Encyclopedia of Walt Disney's Animated Characters*, 270.
17. John Grant, *Encyclopedia of Walt Disney's Animated Characters*, 270.
18. Ken Anderson, "Walt Disney Productions' All Cartoon Feature *Robin Hood*," 24.
19. Mark Pinsky, *The Gospel According to Disney: Faith, Trust, and Pixie Dust* (Louisville: Westminster John Knox Press, 2004), 94.
20. Mark Pinsky offers a reading of the film that sees it as more overtly religious than simply ethical (*Gospel According to Disney*, 94–98).
21. Walt Disney, qtd. in Mark Pinsky, *Gospel According to Disney*, 2.
22. For the complete text of the comic series, see Dave Stevens, *The Rocketeer: The Complete Adventures* (San Diego: IDW, 2009). For further details on the film version, which takes generous liberties with its source, see *The Rocketeer Official Movie Souvenir Magazine* (Brooklyn: Topps for Buena Vista Pictures/The Walt Disney Company, 1991).
23. For the scene's dialogue and stage directions, see Rudy Behlmer, *Adventures of Robin Hood*, 204–09.
24. Charles Higham, *Errol Flynn: The Untold Story* (Garden City, NJ: Doubleday, 1980), 32–89, 118–19. Higham's allegations were effectively refuted by Tony Thomas, *Errol Flynn: The Spy Who Never Was* (Secaucus: Carol Publishing, 1990).
25. Pat Jankiewicz, "The Two Rocketeers," *Starburst* 156 (August 1991): 12.
26. Mark Pinsky, *Gospel According to Disney*, 2.
27. Kim Newman, "The Robin Hood Collection," 66. The most recent example of cinema robiniana, Ridley Scott's 2011 *Robin Hood* starring Russell Crowe as the eponymous hero, is a prequel rather than a sequel. Scott's film tells the story of the feats that earned Robin legendary status.
28. Richard's legitimate heir was Arthur of Brittany, the posthumous son of his older brother Godfrey, and therefore Richard and John's nephew. But Arthur was denied the succession because he was only twelve years old and had never set foot in England. John succeeded to the throne upon the death of his brother Richard, but Arthur would later besiege his grandmother, Eleanor of Aquitaine, until his capture by John, who had him imprisoned. Arthur then disappears and is generally believed to have been executed by John. Shakespeare tells a literary version of Arthur's demise in his play *King John*. For an overview of John's life and contentious reign, see Bryce Lyon, "John, King of England (1167–1216)," *Dictionary of the Middle Ages*, ed. Joseph Strayer (New York: Scribner's, 1996), 129–30, at 7.
29. Mark Pinsky, *Gospel According to Disney*, 2. As Pinsky also points out, Walt Disney's views were not universally held in Hollywood. Sam Goldwyn

once barked that "pictures are for entertainment—messages should be sent by Western Union!" (2).

30. An earlier version of this essay was delivered as the keynote address at the 26th International Conference on Medievalism held at the University of New Mexico, October 21–22, 2011. I am grateful to Professors Anita Obermeier and Timothy C. Graham for their kind invitation to deliver the plenary, to Interim Dean of Arts and Sciences Mark Peceny for his warm words of introduction, and to the members of the audience for their helpful feedback.

CHAPTER 9

FUTURISTIC MEDIEVALISMS AND THE U.S. SPACE PROGRAM IN DISNEY'S *MAN IN SPACE* TRILOGY AND *UNIDENTIFIED FLYING ODDBALL*

Amy Foster

In 1955, Walt Disney Studios started production on three unique episodes of the newly launched *Disneyland* television show. These episodes, known as the *Man in Space* trilogy, reflected the essence of the Tomorrowland section of the newly opened Disneyland Park. They both portrayed the history of man's ideas about space and proposed some ideas about what was possible in space and how close Americans were to attaining these goals. Nearly a quarter century later, Walt Disney Pictures released the live-action motion picture *Unidentified Flying Oddball* (hereafter *UFO*), a Space-Age adaptation of Mark Twain's 1889 novel, *A Connecticut Yankee in King Arthur's Court*. The movie celebrates the ingenuity of an awkward NASA engineer named Tom Trimble, who finds himself accidentally transported, journeying back in time in an experimental spacecraft from Cape Canaveral in late twentieth-century Florida to England's Camelot in the early sixth century.

On the surface, these two Disney productions may seem unrelated: the first is clearly educational and promotional in content and by design, while the second is comical and fanciful. The former focuses on the future of spaceflight, whereas the latter glamorizes a centuries-old society and the antics of a techno-geek-turned-hero. Nonetheless, both productions exemplify the "Disneyfication" of the past and future. This chapter deconstructs the *Man in Space* trilogy and *UFO* from a historical perspective and understands them as reflections of Walt Disney's seemingly contradictory fascination with the medieval era and his technological enthusiasm, an enthusiasm that played out not only in the films and parks but also in Disney's support of America's burgeoning and continuing space agenda.

Walt Disney cherished the past and relished the future, perhaps too nostalgically for both. As historian Mike Wallace notes, "Walt's approach to the past was thus not to reproduce it, but to *improve* it."[1] He tried to capture his passion for the past and future in his television series, films, and theme parks. After his death in 1966, his brother Roy, his disciples such as Ward Kimball, and his successors maintained that trend. Scholars have criticized Disney's sterilization of history, labeling his reinterpretation of the past as "Distory."[2] In addition to its cleaning up of the past, Distory's glorification of technology and technological enthusiasm also downplays the complexities of our future. As anthropologist Stephen Fjellman notes, Disneyland and the Magic Kingdom do little with the present, and not much more with the future. Rides at Epcot like "Spaceship Earth" sponsored by Siemens and "Living with the Land" sponsored by Chiquita sterilize technological progress as much as other Disney parks, films, and shows sterilize the past. As historian Michael Smith argues, particularly about Epcot's Disneyfied interpretation of the history and future of technology:

> For the most part, historical moments are distilled into a succession of brief visual quotes, with only the most immediately recognizable figures and stereotypes warranting inclusion.... More troubling is the absence of agency and causality.... Decisions about design and function, social needs and social impact, are rarely glimpsed beneath the shiny, streamlined surface. When edited for display value, our view of technology achieves an autonomous, effortless quality only slightly more pronounced at Epcot than in the rest of American society.[3]

Smith identifies the problem perfectly: not Distory or Walt Disney's own technocratic populism, but Americans' myopic sense of superiority and technological elitism to which the Disneyfication of the past and future plays.

## *Man in Space* and Its Incarnation in Tomorrowland

No one was a more effective spokesperson for America's sense of itself as a privileged nation and its bright technological future than Walt Disney, as is apparent in his dedication of Disneyland, which opened in July 1955: "Disneyland is dedicated to the ideals, the dreams and the hard facts that have created America ... with the hope that it will be a source of joy and inspiration to all the world." His enthusiasm is apparent in the Disney parks as well as in his productions. The plaque on the archway of Main Street USA at Disneyland, which opened in July 1955, states "Here you leave today and enter the world of yesterday, tomorrow, and fantasy." Encapsulated in this pledge to his visitors, Walt Disney made a promise to adults—"here age relives memories of the past"—and to children: "here youth may savor the challenge and promise of the future."[4]

Disney designed core sections of his parks with such a futuristic vision in mind, especially Tomorrowland. On the park's opening day, Disney unveiled it as "a step into the future, with predictions of constructive things to come. Tomorrow offers new frontiers in science, adventure, and ideals, the atomic age, the challenge of outer space, and the hope for a peaceful and united world."[5] Most of the parks—including Disneyland in Anaheim, Walt Disney World's Magic Kingdom in Orlando, Tokyo Disneyland, and Hong Kong Disneyland—still host Tomorrowland.[6] There visitors can experience attractions such as Space Mountain and Astro Orbiter.[7] These rides were designed to mimic—or at least suggest—the feeling of spaceflight. In addition to Tomorrowland, Epcot in Walt Disney World, which opened in 1982, offers attractions that encourage its riders to experience either spaceflight or a futuristic Space Age lifestyle. Mission Space simulates a launch and travel to a colony on Mars while Spaceship Earth takes its passengers through a World's Fair-esque tour of human progress culminating in a look at the work, leisure, and the American household of the future.[8]

Through Tomorrowland, Disney gave visitors a chance to imagine a world in which space travel would be a routine part of the American experience (as NASA had hoped for the Shuttle), and television made it possible for him to bring that vision of the future into the American living room. Disney was a strong supporter of human spaceflight and America's space program, and he used the television show *Walt Disney's Disneyland* to promote spaceflight even before the U.S. government officially sponsored a federal space program.[9] In March 1955, the first episode of the *Man in Space* trilogy aired as a Tomorrowland feature on the program.[10] This series introduced American television audiences to what rocket engineers believed was possible in space. (A number of those predictions have come to fruition in NASA's already fifty-year history.) Director and co-author of the series Walt Kimball and his team of animators were determined to understand how rockets worked and to convey the science of spaceflight to an American public that, in 1955, still questioned whether space travel was possible. After all, the first episode in the series, *Man in Space*, premiered over two and a half years before the Soviet

Union launched *Sputnik*, the world's first artificial satellite, and six years before the first man flew in space.

The first two episodes in the *Man in Space* series—*Man in Space* and *Man and the Moon*—originally aired on March 9 and December 28, 1955, respectively. The third episode, *Mars and Beyond*, premiered two years later on December 4, 1957, just two days before the failed launch of *Vanguard*, which was intended to be America's first artificial satellite and just under two months before the successful launch of the U.S. satellite *Explorer 1*, which led to the discovery of the Earth's electromagnetic field.[11] Each of the three episodes begins with a historical treatment of their subject: rocketry, human interpretations of the moon, and speculation about Mars. These humorous historical segments exemplify Distory, presenting a sanitized version of technological history. They are followed by an equally Disneyfied vision of the future: depictions of how rocket engineers envisioned man's first voyages into space and the first missions to the moon and to Mars. Kimball's team asked some of the leaders of the American space effort not only to serve as the scientific advisors on the project and to teach the production crew the physics of spaceflight but also to appear on screen as content experts.

*Man in Space* featured Willy Ley, Dr. Wernher Von Braun, and Dr. Heinz Haber. Ley was a rocket enthusiast/historian and science writer who emigrated from Germany in 1935. Von Braun had served as the lead German rocket engineer responsible for the development of the V-2 rockets during World War II, and Haber was a German physicist and aerospace medicine specialist. Von Braun and Haber immigrated to the United States following the war, along with hundreds of scientists and their families under the auspices Project Paperclip, which endeavored in part to capture Nazi engineers and V-2s as a means to jumpstart an American rocket program and to prevent the Soviet Union from gaining this German expertise.[12] Von Braun and his team became the core of NASA's rocket design team during the height of the space race in the 1960s. Biographer Michael Neufeld notes that Von Braun's visit to California to meet with Kimball and discuss the two originally planned episodes—*Man in Space* and *Mars and Beyond*—resulted not only in the second episode to air in the trilogy, *Man and the Moon*, but was also the basis for the Rocket to the Moon ride at Disneyland, an attraction that was updated and renamed Mission to Mars in the mid-1970s after the 1969 Apollo moon landing made the original ride seem less cutting edge.[13]

The *Man in Space* series was not the first time that Ley, Von Braun, and Haber used a popular medium to promote spaceflight. Between 1952 and 1954, *Collier's* magazine published a series of articles on spaceflight, to which Ley, Von Braun, and Haber contributed. The articles presented similar themes as the *Man in Space* episodes: when will man conquer space? How will we get to the moon? What about life on Mars? At the time these articles appeared, Kimball was looking for ideas for the Tomorrowland series to pitch to Disney. Ley, Von Braun, and Haber were clearly not well-trained actors, but they were eager to promote spaceflight and saw television as an outstanding venue for dispersing the message that had been growing within the popular media—that the race into space was "a Promethean struggle for survival."[14]

Although eager to promote spaceflight, their complicated pasts, particularly those of Von Braun and Haber, presented Kimball's team with a unique challenge. During World War II, when both men were still in Germany, their privileged positions within the National Socialist system included membership in the Nazi party, and their work involved interactions with Jews and other prisoners of war. In 1944, Von Braun relocated V-2 rocket production to Nordhausen in Central Germany after his original laboratory and production site at Peenemünde on the Baltic Sea was destroyed by Allied air strikes. SS-General Hans Kammler had set up a concentration camp to provide workers for this underground rocket assembly facility.[15] Von Braun was fully aware of the use of slave labor to build the V-2, but he understood it—and his Nazi membership—as a Faustian bargain that he had to accept in exchange for the financial resources needed to fund his vision for spaceflight.[16]

Haber's past, however, was yet more ignoble. As a researcher in aerospace medicine, he worked directly with Dachau concentration camp inmates as experimental subjects. Neufeld noted that when Haber visited the *Collier's* headquarters in New York to work on the spaceflight series, a puckish staff member touched Haber's leather coat in the elevator and remarked, "Human skin, of course?"[17] Whatever his or Von Braun's complicity in the treatment of Jews and prisoners of war during World War II, both made a conscious effort once they moved to the United States never to discuss that part of their past.

Not only were Disney and Kimball content to wear blinders, thereby sidestepping the issue, they also employed the company's "distorical" techniques in presenting these scientists' histories. When introducing Von Braun in the second episode of the series, Kimball prepared a careful narrative that distanced Von Braun from the destructive history of the German V-2, saying simply that he was the Chief of Guided Missile Development at the Army's Redstone Arsenal and "also overall director of the original V-2 rocket."[18] For Kimball and Disney, the *Man in Space* episodes were about the hope of the future, not dwelling in the sordid details of the past.

The impact of the *Man in Space* trilogy could not have pleased Walt Disney more. In the weeks following the airing of the first episode in March 1955, President Dwight Eisenhower requested a copy of the film. Disney was happy to oblige, sending a copy to the Pentagon where top officials responsible for planning American space policy viewed it. By late July, Eisenhower had announced his plan for American participation in the International Geophysical Year,[19] which would include launching an orbiting scientific satellite sometime in 1957 or 1958.[20] Whether this episode of *Man in Space* was the inspiration for Eisenhower's decision is debatable, but Disney wanted to believe it was so. Von Braun was less inclined to make such a public announcement. What is nonetheless certain is that the public clamored for more. In the November 1955 issue of *Popular Science*, magazine editors previewed the *Man and the Moon* episode scheduled for premiere the following month and published an explanation of the science behind the show's content.[21] The series was ultimately so popular that the shows were rebroadcast on television and released in theaters in the late 1950s and later on video for private purchase.[22]

### NASA and the Space Program in the 1970s

When Walt Disney Studios was making *UFO* (also known by its original title, *The Spaceman and King Arthur*), the U.S. space program was undergoing a transformation of its own, and the film reflects some of these changes. The heyday of the Apollo lunar program had ended. Apollo 17, the sixth and final mission to land on the moon, was completed on December 19, 1972. In May 1973, NASA used the last remaining Saturn V moon rocket to launch *Skylab*, America's first space station. Over the next nine months, three three-man crews lived and worked on the space station, collecting medical data and making solar and earth atmospheric observations. In July 1975, NASA completed a joint mission with the Soviet Union's space program known as Apollo–Soyuz during which a three-man crew in an Apollo capsule docked with a two-man crew in a Soviet Soyuz capsule, marking a political end to the space race. This was also the last manned mission for six years. NASA needed a new mission and a new launch vehicle.

On January 5, 1972, President Richard Nixon announced his backing for the new Space Shuttle program. Designed as a replacement for the Apollo program, NASA promoted the Space Shuttle as a cost-effective vehicle for routinizing spaceflight. The Shuttle was very different than previous space vehicles. The orbiter and the solid rocket boosters were refurbished and used again for subsequent flights. Only the large external tank was expendable, burning up in the Earth's atmosphere after being jettisoned eight-and-a-half minutes after launch. The Space Shuttle remains the most technologically sophisticated spacecraft ever designed, a consequence of both its reusability and the plan to return the orbiter to Earth by landing like an airplane instead of splashing down in the ocean as with previous space vehicles. But the Space Shuttle never lived up to the expectations, becoming neither routine (NASA had hoped for up to fifty flights a year, but never exceeded twelve) nor cheaper to fly. Most recently, historians Kenneth Lipartito and Orville Butler have argued that the former was the critical factor behind the failure of the latter.[23]

The Shuttle's design took its form from the airplane. Brainstorming the cheapest way to deliver materials into space (based on the plan that this vehicle would be used to build the United States' first space station), NASA engineers settled on the idea of a reusable space plane. Since this vehicle was meant to land like an airplane, designers made it look like one (although more recent aerodynamic work conducted by NASA shows that flying bodies without wings can create enough lift to glide safely to the ground). This certainly made the pilot-astronauts happy. They had been complaining since the days of the Mercury program that being a test pilot in a capsule was embarrassing, describing the experience as being "a human cannonball" and "Spam in a can."[24] Rockwell International, the contractor for the orbiters, rolled the first Shuttle out of its production facility in September 1976. Slated to be named *Constitution* after the USS *Constitution*, one of the flagships built by the burgeoning U.S. Navy in 1797, NASA ultimately christened her *Enterprise* after fans of the television show *Star Trek* flooded the White House with letters demanding the name change.[25] Only a prototype and not capable of actual spaceflight, *Enterprise* served as the testing vehicle for the Approach and Landing tests flown in 1977 by astronauts Joseph Engle, Charles Fullerton, Fred Haise, and Richard Truly to determine the Shuttle's ability to land like an airplane.

In 1979, when Walt Disney Studios debuted *UFO*, NASA was forced to delay the Shuttle's maiden launch because of the difficulties engineers encountered with perfecting the tile system that would protect the orbiter from temperatures approaching 4300 degrees Fahrenheit during reentry into the Earth's atmosphere as well as reworking the design of the orbiter's three main engines to avoid overheating.[26] Despite continued delays that frustrated Congress, particularly the House Subcommittee for Space Science, NASA's administration understood that this vehicle was still very much a test vehicle, and one that would carry humans onboard.[27] NASA had never taken such a risk with astronauts' lives before. In the film, the budget committee chairman's consternation over putting a human crew in *Stardust* reflects similar anxieties over the Shuttle in the late 1970s.[28]

### Unidentified Flying Oddball

In the historical sense, the *Man in Space* trilogy was far removed from the story told in *UFO*. A span of more than two decades—as well as the entire space race with the Soviet Union—separated their release dates. What connects these two productions is Disney's fascination with and glorification of spaceflight and progress through technology. Throughout his life, Disney strongly believed in technological utopianism, the idea that contentment through technology was possible. He also believed that dominance came through expertise.[29] His willingness to highlight the work that Von Braun and his team were undertaking to conquer space as part of the *Disneyland* television series and the focus on the future encapsulated in many Disney parks confirms these values and the relevance of the space program in his mind. Even after Disney's death, the Walt Disney Company has kept this vision alive.

Walt Disney maintained a lifelong commitment to technocratic populism, the ideology that "sought to harness the creative, technological, and productive capacities of modern industry and use them for the benefit of ordinary people."[30] *UFO* projects this same attitude. The novel, on which the movie is based, serves as a satirical commentary on America's growing technological enthusiasm. In contrast, the movie celebrates Trimble's technological ingenuity and minimizes the intellectual capacity and creativity of sixth-century Anglo-Saxons. At the same time, the film paradoxically glamorizes life in this era.

In *UFO*, Tom Trimble is tasked with building a robot, named Hermes, to fly aboard the new Shuttle-like spacecraft *Stardust*. The vehicle's designer, Dr. Zimmerman—a character clearly intended to portray Walt Disney's personal friend, Wernher von Braun—pitches this new vehicle and its mission to the solar system's nearest neighboring star, Alpha Centauri, to Congress's Finance, Ways and Means Committee. When Zimmerman proposes a human crew for the untested vehicle in the film's opening scene, the senator chairing the committee promises to kill the program before he would risk the lives of "fine young American men." Zimmerman replies, "We have some women in the space program now."[31] The senator's response to that suggestion is even more apoplectic. So, Trimble builds Hermes, his robotic double, to fly aboard *Stardust*. But when Hermes grows fearful on launch day that he will not return from the thirty-year trip, Zimmerman sends Trimble to the launch pad to calm his animatronic doppelganger. While Trimble encourages Hermes, the rocket is struck by lightning (harking back to the ultimately harmless, but momentarily terrifying, lightning strikes to the Apollo 12 rocket just thirty-six seconds, then again fifty-two seconds after liftoff).[32]

The lightning causes *Stardust* to launch prematurely with Trimble inside. Because this new vehicle travels faster than the speed of light, it works as a time machine and takes Trimble and Hermes back in time to sixth-century England and the legendary King Arthur's Court, thereby setting the scene for Trimble's opportunity to marvel Camelot with twentieth-century technological wonders.

What Trimble finds in King Arthur's court, much like Twain's *Connecticut Yankee* protagonist Hank Morgan, is a medieval society saddled with ignorance, naïveté, and superstition. But the Disney interpretation also presents an ahistorical, quaint, and charming interpretation of medieval life: clean surroundings, images of health and prosperity for the medieval characters, bright colored clothing even for the peasants, and an indifference to the highly stratified class structure inherent within feudalism. These characteristics enable the film makers (director Russ Mayberry and screenwriter Don Tait, who wrote other Disney live-action films such as *The Apple Dumpling Gang* [1975] and the 1976 version of *The Shaggy D.A.*) to romanticize the early medieval period.

*UFO* embraces this romanticization that is characteristic of Disney's medievalism. One look at the costuming and set design alone captures these glorifying sentiments. As viewers might expect, King Arthur and the nobility in Camelot wear brightly colored clothing and are bedecked in jewels, which in itself is problematic because dyed clothes in the early Anglo-Saxon period were extremely valuable. Princely colors, like Tyrian Purple, were so expensive—in part because of the labor-intensive process of extracting the dye from thousands of Murex mollusks found only in the eastern Mediterranean Sea—that only the wealthiest would wear them.[33] Other dyes, like blues, reds, and yellows, required elaborate processes to obtain them from plants that limited their use to the noble class. As noted by Gale Owen-Crocker, "Although the Anglo-Saxons' enjoyment of bright colors is evident in their jewelry and their paintings, it is likely that the lower classes did not possess clothes which were dyed."[34] Their clothes—when new—would have been varying hues of brown, black, grey, and white, thanks to sheep with wool of those colors. But, similar to the visual necessity of changing Dorothy's silver shoes in L. Frank Baum's *The Wonderful Wizard of Oz* into ruby slippers in its 1939 film incarnation, so that the production could capitalize on the cinematic effects afforded by Technicolor, it was likewise necessary to embrace historical inaccuracy in *UFO* to create an appropriately Disney fantasy of the past.

What proves the greatest historical inaccuracy, but which helps to create the idealized medieval fantasy world that Disney desired for his guests and patrons, is the portrayal of the peasant class in *UFO*. Alisande, her father, and the page Clarence wear clothes with bright colors and of finer cloth than the peasants of the sixth century, or even the working class of Twain's nineteenth century, would have worn. In the twenty-first century, we take for granted the availability and variety of both ready-made fabrics and clothes. But until the 1810s for men and later for women, ready-made clothes were generally unavailable.[35] Until the First Industrial Revolution of the 1790s, people wove fabric using hand looms. Only when John Kay invented the flying shuttle and Richard Arkwright developed the water loom did it become possible to mechanize the weaving of cotton and wool fabrics. Given the fineness of silk fibers and the tendency of silk threads to snap under the tension of a powered loom, weaving silk cloth remained difficult to produce even in the nineteenth century.

Even the style of dress in *UFO* is problematic. Women of all classes in sixth-century England wore a cylindrical gown that would have been anchored over the shoulders with brooches or perhaps a simple button or toggle for the lower classes. In the colder climate of England, women would have also worn a "tight-sleeved bodice" underneath the gown for warmth.[36] But all women in this period would have worn clothes made from wool. Archeologists have found remnants of flaxen fabrics in the graves of the wealthy, but most would have likely chosen cloth made from a finer quality of wool with an elaborate diamond-pattern weave, and then embellished their gowns with embroidery (not jewels as depicted in *UFO*). The earliest discovery of silken fabrics, which would have been expensive and considered luxurious, is dated from the seventh century, at least a century after the intrepid Tom Trimble's visit to Camelot.[37] The clothes, the colors, and the styles of dress we see in *UFO* reflect less on Disney's desire to "relive memories of the past" and more on his desire that his patrons leave reality in the parking lot and enjoy the flights of futuristic fantasy enabled paradoxically through his medievalism.

As in the Disney parks and other Disney films, cleanliness and pristine conditions convey the fantasy of the past and the utopianism of the future. *UFO* follows the same formula—portraying King Arthur's Camelot as a healthy, if not sterile, environment—but life in sixth-century Europe was far from clean or healthy. Even in King Arthur's castle, while the walls would have been stone and the ceilings wooden, there would be no glass-in windows to keep out the elements, no running water to remove human waste, and only rushes or straw on the floors to provide some insulation and to collect the food and grease that dinner guests would toss aside. These castles also invited fleas and rats, harborers of some of the most deadly diseases of the era, including bubonic plague and typhus.[38]

Life outside the castle would have been far worse than Disney's version. Peasants like Alisande and her father lived in small cottages, often of wattle-and-daub (essentially sticks-and-mud) construction with thatched roofs and dirt floors. Peasants could rarely afford the luxury of a stone fireplace and chimney. Instead, they built a fire pit in the center of the one-room dwelling and left an opening in the roof for smoke and soot to escape, but this lack of ventilation could lead to respiratory conditions. If a family owned livestock, such as chickens, goats, or pigs, they would likely have kept their animals inside the hovel with them because livestock was too valuable to risk losing to exposure, disease, or theft. While the living conditions of Alisande and her father are by no means glamorous, the film illustrates a much more hospitable environment, a much more pleasant atmosphere than would have been the case for sixth-century peasants.

*UFO*'s Disneyfied Middle Ages provides a fitting backdrop for the film's glorification of the technological achievements of twentieth-century American culture, particularly human spaceflight. Unlike the Connecticut Yankee, whom Mark Twain used to challenge the American technological love affair, Disney's use of a NASA engineer as the protagonist in *UFO* instead promotes space-age technological achievement. Tom Trimble, while skilled as an engineer (although by his own admission he was never the smartest student), sees King Arthur's court as a charming but woefully backward society. When Trimble arrives in the sixth century, he first encounters Alisande (just as Hank Morgan did). Believing him a benign monster due to the strangeness of his spacesuit, Alisande escorts him to Camelot; upon meeting the legendary King Arthur, Trimble tries to explain who he is and where he comes from by presenting the king and his court with a compressed history of the United States, beginning with Christopher Columbus and continuing through the flight of *Stardust*. Not surprisingly, King Arthur finds Trimble's stories incredible and considers hiring the engineer as his court jester. Mordred encourages Arthur to burn Trimble at the stake instead. When Trimble uses his space suit, equipped with a heat-resistant outer layer and an internal cooling system (similar to the suits NASA developed for the Apollo program), to survive his immolation, Arthur believes Trimble must have great powers and engages the engineer from the future as his military advisor. Trimble impresses the king with his advanced technological gadgets from the twentieth century (including a laser gun that Hermes was supposed to use for collecting rock samples on foreign planets). Why do none of the people in Camelot fear or question Trimble and his technology? Because Americans—the primary audience for the film—see him and his gadgets as "good" and "progressive." It is the American way.

And just as in the Arthurian legend and *Connecticut Yankee*, in *UFO* Arthur's kingdom is threatened by Mordred. Trimble's familiarity with the legend of Camelot gives him the background to warn the king that Mordred is a direct threat to the security of the kingdom. Having won the king's trust, Trimble uses his futuristic resources to mastermind a plan to save the kingdom.

Tom Trimble represents the iconic protagonist in an American heroic quest: at NASA, his superiors see him as a quirky, nerdy engineer, and in his twentieth-century life, he admits to being average and never one to win the girl. But in Camelot, he is respected by King Arthur, he falls in love with a beautiful, young woman (Alisande), he is assisted by Clarence the page (to whom Tom gives the contraband pornographic magazine that Hermes has snuck onboard *Stardust* before the launch), and he saves the kingdom. But this is more than just the classic heroic quest; it is iconic Disney, in its twinned updating and re-medievalizing of the quest narrative.

As the classic protagonist of a heroic quest, it is Tom Trimble (not King Arthur) who assumes the leadership role, risking his life to save the kingdom of Camelot against the evils of Sir Mordred and a scheming Merlin. The character is self-effacing about his abilities, but his quick wit (along with some impressive technological advantages from the twentieth century) helps him to win the day, and Mark Twain depicted Hank Morgan similarly in *A Connecticut Yankee*. But as a marker of Disney's medievalism, there is more here to understand than simply a modern-day recreation of Twain's novel.

As with the clothing and living conditions, the interpersonal relationships scripted in the film stray from the historical realities of a medieval kingdom. In the 1920s, when Walt Disney began his animation career, his political views toward "sentimental populism" were well formed. Although culturally conservative, Disney believed in "glorifying ordinary Americans." He rejected elitist culture as "un-American" and "snobbish," and instead insisted that culture should be equally accessible to everyone. We can see this egalitarianism in Trimble's interaction with King Arthur and his court. Trimble refers to Arthur only as "King," never as "Your Majesty" as others in the film do (or as would be expected and demanded from the English Royal Court). He bounces between interpersonal relationships with a female peasant, a page, and the king as if those relationships were completely normal and acceptable. Trimble respects no boundaries, just as Disney would have his plucky hero. This blurring of the lines of acceptable social behavior not only fuels Disney's idealization and ahistoricism of the medieval past by furthering the nostalgic image of the period, but also provides a platform for Trimble to use his modern technology to become the hero, thereby emphasizing the futuristic medievalism that appears consistently throughout Disney films and theme parks.

We all would like the past—and the future—to live up to this lionized medievalist notion of kings and queens, of knights in shining armor, and of chivalry, as well as to an optimistic vision of a "great big beautiful (technological) tomorrow." We want the fantasy. Walt Disney attempted to capture that wishful dream of the past and the hope for the future in his television trilogy, *Man in Space*, in the film, *Unidentified Flying Oddball*, and throughout his parks. But in looking at these Disney creations through the lens of the history of the U.S. space program and the history of technology, we can see the cracks and the strain. Wernher von Braun's own troubled past marred the brilliance of American rocket technology. The politics of the Cold War and the space race forced the hands of presidents, such as Dwight Eisenhower, John F. Kennedy, and Richard Nixon, to funnel money into major space-related agendas, none of which—despite public appearances—were personal priorities for these men. And the lasting legacy of the Space Shuttle program may be that America's belief in technology's ability to meet our lofty expectations and our glorification of history are equally flawed. Disney's emphasis on futuristic medievalism in his creations reflects the blind faith that Americans have in technology and our sterilized interpretation of how we invented the twenty-first century.

## Notes

1. Mike Wallace, "Mickey Mouse History: Portraying the Past at Disney World," *Radical History Review* 32 (1985): 33–57, at 35; italics in original.
2. Stephen Fjellman, *Vinyl Leaves: Walt Disney World and America* (Boulder: Westview, 1992) 59.
3. Michael Smith, "Back to the Future: Epcot, Camelot, and the History of Technology," *New Perspectives on Technology and American Culture*, ed. Bruce Sinclair (Philadelphia: American Philosophical Society, 1986), 69–81, at 72–73.
4. Neal Gabler, *Walt Disney: The Triumph of the American Imagination* (New York: Knopf, 2006), 532.
5. From Walt Disney's Tomorrowland dedication speech, aired live on national television, July 17, 1955, included in "Dateline Disneyland," *Walt Disney Treasures: Disneyland U.S.A.* (Walt Disney Studios, 2001), DVD.
6. In Disneyland Paris (EuroDisney), this area of the park is called Discoveryland.

7. All the parks listed offer the roller-coaster attraction Space Mountain. Anaheim's Disneyland and the Magic Kingdom still offer Astro Orbiter. Disney engineers continue to modify the attractions to keep the spirit of Tomorrowland perpetually in the future.
8. Both attractions are located in a section of the park known as Future World. The layout of the park itself resembles that of the 1939 New York World's Fair (Smith, 70).
9. President Dwight Eisenhower did not sign the National Aeronautics and Space Act, creating the National Aeronautics and Space Administration (NASA), until July 1958.
10. "Man in Space," *Walt Disney Treasures*, dir. Walt Kimball (Walt Disney Studios), DVD.
11. Roger Launius, "American Spaceflight History's Master Narrative and the Meaning of Memory," *Remembering the Space Age*, ed. Steven Dick (Washington, D.C.: National Aeronautics and Space Administration, 2008), 353–85, at 355.
12. Clarence Lasby, *Project Paperclip: German Scientists and the Cold War* (New York: Atheneum, 1971), 252–57.
13. Michael Neufeld, *Von Braun: Dreamer of Space, Engineer of War* (New York: Knopf, 2007), 287; cf. Stephen Fjellman, *Vinyl Leaves* 351.
14. Brian Horrigan, "Popular Culture and Visions of the Future in Space, 1901–2001," *New Perspectives on Technology and American Culture*, ed. Bruce Sinclair (Philadelphia: American Philosophical Society, 1986), 49–67, at 58–59.
15. After the war, Kammler was tried for war crimes, both for his connection to the Nordhausen camp and for his larger role in the Holocaust, including supervising the construction of the Auschwitz gas chambers. Von Braun would eventually be interviewed as a defense witness for Georg Rickhey, the general director of the factory. Rickhey was ultimately acquitted, having been found to be simply a figurehead for Kammler. Von Braun was never prosecuted (Michael Neufeld, *Von Braun* 159, 235–36.)
16. Michael Neufeld, *Von Braun*, 473–77.
17. Michael Neufeld, *Von Braun*, 271.
18. Patrick Lucanio and Gary Coville, *Smokin' Rockets: The Romance of Technology in American Film, Radio, and Television, 1945–1962* (Jefferson, NC: McFarland, 2002), 144.
19. The International Geophysical Year (IGY) ran from July 1957 to December 1958. The International Council of Scientific Unions, formed in 1952, designed the IGY for nations around the world to sponsor events and activities focusing on studying geophysical phenomena. See "The International Geophysical Year," nationalacademies.org/history/igy; Web, accessed August 22, 2011.
20. Patrick Lucanio and Gary Coville, *Smokin' Rockets*, 146–47.
21. Patrick Lucanio and Gary Coville, *Smokin' Rockets*, 147.
22. Steven Watts, *The Magic Kingdom: Walt Disney and the American Way of Life* (Boston: Houghton Mifflin, 1997), 309.

23. Kenneth Lipartito and Orville Butler, *The History of the Kennedy Space Center* (Gainesville: University Press of Florida, 2007), 217–18.
24. Tom Wolfe, *The Right Stuff* (New York: Bantam, 1980), 57, 60.
25. T. A. Heppenheimer, *The Development of the Space Shuttle, 1972–1981* (Washington, D.C.: National Aeronautics and Space Administration, 2002), 100–01.
26. T. A. Heppenheimer, *Development*, 145–47, at 211, 355.
27. "Space Shuttle Is Ready to Be Moved to Its Pad after Two-Year Delay: More Delays Possible," *New York Times (1923-Current file)*: A17; ProQuest Historical Newspapers: The New York Times 1851–2007, for 1980; Web, accessed February 23, 2011.
28. It took until April 12, 1981, before the new orbiter was ready and NASA technicians achieved a level of technical competency to safely launch Commander John Young and Pilot Robert Crippen aboard the first Space Shuttle, *Columbia*.
29. Steven Watts, "Walt Disney: Art and Politics in the American Century," *Journal of American History* 82.1 (1995): 84–110, at 108.
30. Steven Watts, *Magic Kingdom*, 442.
31. NASA selected the first class of astronauts to include women in 1978.
32. Andrew Chaikin, *A Man on the Moon: The Voyages of the Apollo Astronauts* (New York: Penguin, 1998), 239.
33. Gale Owen-Crocker, *Dress in Anglo-Saxon England* (Manchester: Manchester University Press, 1986), 189.
34. Gale Owen-Crocker, *Dress in Anglo-Saxon England*, 191.
35. Michael Zakim, "A Ready-Made Business: The Birth of the Clothing Industry in America," *Business History Review* 82.1 (1999): 61–90, at 68.
36. Gale Owen-Crocker, *Dress in Anglo-Saxon England*, 39.
37. Gale Owen-Crocker, *Dress in Anglo-Saxon England*, 187.
38. William McNeill, *Plagues and Peoples* (New York: Anchor, 1998), 30–31.

# PART III

## DISNEY PRINCESS FANTASY FAIRE

CHAPTER 10

"WHERE HAPPILY EVER AFTER HAPPENS EVERY DAY": THE MEDIEVALISMS OF DISNEY'S PRINCESSES

*Clare Bradford*

When viewers access the Disney Princess website, they encounter the designated Princesses, who look directly out toward their audience, each in turn performing bodily movements that incorporate a curious mixture of stiffness and seductiveness as the Princesses flutter their eyelashes, smile or laugh beguilingly, drop into curtsey-like poses, adjust their hand positions or (in Belle's case) brush a strand of hair from their faces.[1] The Princesses are framed by "medieval" signifiers: the castle towers adorned with gold and surmounted by decorative finials and the spires and pennants that appear at the left and right of the website's front page. Located against a backdrop of pink and pastel colors and looped with the fairy dust swirling around the website, these towers are less clearly visible than the Princesses, who are attributed with a higher degree of modality.[2] The medieval is, then, hazily present, suggesting a misty, allusive relationship between the Middle Ages and the Princesses: a relationship whose value is vividly implied by the gold leaf and rich adornments embellishing the castle towers. The Princesses, on the other hand, are presented as "real" figures in what resembles a line-up rather than a group of associates; none of the them looks toward or refers to the others, signaling that each occupies a separate notional space. When viewers click on one or other of the Princesses, they are invited into a fantasy world signified by European-style castles (Snow White, Cinderella, Aurora, Ariel, Belle) and their "ethnic" equivalents: Jasmine's palace; Pocahontas's green headlands and river vistas; Mulan's pagoda and garden; and Tiana's dream restaurant in 1920s' New Orleans.

The castle towers on the front page of the Disney Princess website function in part to coalesce the disparate Princess figures under the rubric "Disney Princess," enforcing the conceit of a world to which visitors are welcomed with the greeting: "Welcome to the enchanting world of Disney Princess, where happily ever after happens every day."[3] This welcome, strikingly, extends to girl audiences far younger than the Princesses. Although the "Parenting a Princess" pages of the site offer advice to parents of children from babies to teenagers, the "Shopping for Princess Dreams" pages at the heart of the website feature images of the young girls (aged three to six) who comprise the website's principal demographic target. The "Little Princess" gallery to which parents upload photographs consists in the main of images of babies, toddlers, and very young girls (predominantly white) wearing clothing from the Princess product range. The website Princesses thus function quite differently from child protagonists in children's texts, with whom readers of roughly the same age are positioned to align themselves as reading subjects. Instead, they operate rather as aspirational figures positioning young girls as becoming-princesses, with the figures of Jasmine, Pocahontas, Mulan, and Tiana suggesting that Princesshood is not confined to figures from the European fairy-tale canon. The ten films associated with the Princesses range across seven decades, from *Snow White* (1937) to *Tangled* (2010), and draw, in the main, upon canonical retellings of European narratives.[4]

Writing on the "Constance group" of medieval romances, Geraldine Heng notes that women "constitute a figural presence through which the concerns, ideas, pressures, and values of a culture can be expressed, can signify."[5] The Princesses portrayed in the Disney Princess website and films are imbued with just such significations, which are intensified by the socializing imperatives that always inform children's texts. In *Gender Trouble*, Judith Butler poses the following questions: "What will and will not constitute an intelligible life, and how do presumptions about normative gender and sexuality determine in advance what will qualify as the 'human' and the 'livable'?"[6] Presumptions about normative gender and sexuality are central to Disney's depictions of girls and women, which are themselves riddled with tensions concerning notions of gender and sexuality, imbricated with the films' negotiations between medieval and modern. In general terms, the Disney Princess films produced from *The Little Mermaid* in 1989 seek to introduce agential girl protagonists consonant with post-1960s feminist discourses. However, these strong-minded girls, like their more conventional fairy-tale sisters, figure in storylines and representational modes whose metanarratives incorporate the patriarchal norms of the societies that produced traditional stories.

In this discussion I distinguish between the actual and implied audiences of the Princess website and films. Even very young children engaging with Princess toys negotiate their own meanings, improvise new sequences of play, and discard what does not suit them, and it may be that girls preoccupied with the Disney Princesses enter a phase that they move into and out of on their way to more wide-ranging possibilities. My focus is, rather, on the medievalist tropes, images, and stories deployed in Princess films and products, and the cultural work they perform by promoting values, offering subject positions, and encouraging their audiences to prefer and desire happy endings aligned with the outcomes of heterosexual romance. The medievalisms of Disney's Princesses operate in multifarious and often contradictory ways. They draw princess figures from disparate times and cultures into the hazy romanticism of the Disney Princess world, capitalizing on the symbolic capital associated with canonical retellings of traditional narratives. They naturalize and authorize traditional gender roles by deploying discourses of courtly love and narratives structured by the motif of the Fair Unknown. Their constructions of gender and sexuality imply that the success of Disney Princesses resides in their adherence to premodern patriarchal orders defined by marriage to a prince and the approval of fathers or father-substitutes. The Princess films and website treat the Middle Ages as simultaneously barbaric and romantic through a transtemporal medievalism that promotes the efficacy of tradition while celebrating modernity.

## The Mists of Time(lessness): Cultural Capital and Disney's Princesses

Concepts of cultural and symbolic capital are closely associated with the intertemporality of the Disney Princess films, which draw value from the narrative traditions to which they refer, and their claims to translate these traditions into wholesome entertainment for children: to deliver old stories to new audiences. Pierre Bourdieu identifies three "competing principles of legitimacy" that shape the hierarchies whereby cultural products are valued. The first comprises "the recognition granted by the set of producers who produce for other producers, their competitors"; the second, the "legitimacy corresponding to 'bourgeois' taste" and the affirmation of powerful groups, private and public; the third, the "consecration bestowed by the choice of ordinary consumers, the 'mass audience.'"[7] These are, as Bourdieu notes, competing principles, and their implications for the Disney Princess brand are often contradictory. Thus, Disney

Princess films and products comprise part of a global media conglomerate that competes with other such organizations, such as Time Warner and News Corporation; but within the field of animation for children the competition for supremacy is complicated by the fluidity of an industry characterized by the movement of animators, directors, and executives from one studio to another and by frequent corporate takeovers and mergers. The competition between Disney and DreamWorks is seen at its sharpest precisely in their rivalry over medievalisms: the success of DreamWorks's *Shrek*, which won the inaugural Oscar for feature-length animations, was widely viewed as a riposte to Disney, representing a contrast between Disney's reverential and nostalgic approach to fairy tales and the more brash skeptical style exemplified by *Shrek*.[8]

When we consider the Disney Princess films in the light of the second and third of Bourdieu's "principles of legitimacy," questions of judgment and taste are even more complex. Bourdieu treats capitalist society as a highly differentiated field whose gatekeepers protect their spheres of legitimacy, and within this field various constituencies view the Princess films differently. The films derive their claims of authority in part from the canonicity of the folkloric and literary texts with which most are associated, in part from the recognition they receive from prizes such as Academy Awards, and in part from their appeal to mass markets. As examples of "public, state-guaranteed" audiences, Bourdieu cites "academies, which sanction the inseparably ethical and aesthetic (and therefore political) taste of the dominant."[9] The diversification of disciplinary and interdisciplinary fields is such that scholars work within a wide range of theoretical and methodological paradigms. For instance, Henry Giroux analyzes gender constructions in some of the Princess films by examining plot elements, narrative outcomes, and questions of stereotyping, advocating an approach that combines pedagogical, economic, cultural, and textual critiques of Disney films and products.[10] Naomi Wood takes a narrower and more pragmatic view in her discussion of *Cinderella*:

> Disney's work ought to be treated with the same close attention that any other literary text receives—not simply to be dismissed as ideologically incorrect (after all, Perrault, the Grimms, and others are hardly "PC") or unfaithful to the original (since, in folklore, there is no original) or formulaic (what are fairy tales if not clichés?), but to be evaluated first as animated film and then as a version among other versions of American *märchen*.[11]

Investigating the Disney Princess play of young girls, Karen Wohlwend acknowledges that in some classrooms "popular culture media and toys are relegated to the unofficial space of the playground, deemed inappropriate topics for the serious business of learning to read and write."[12] Instead, Wohlwend's study tracks how a group of kindergarten children negotiate the "gendered tensions" that arise when they play with Disney Princess dolls and texts; for instance, the children bring their own dolls to school and insert them into narratives involving Princesses; or they invent relationships, such as stipulating that certain Princesses are sisters; or they change characters' genders, in one case "changing a dueling prince into a dueling princess."[13] Although Wohlwend and other scholars engage in critique of the texts, products, and practices associated with the Disney Princess brand, they exemplify the spread of approaches characteristic of scholarly work in this field. What unites Giroux, Wood, and Wohlwend (and forms a consistent theme across scholars writing on Disney-related topics) is a powerful sense of ambivalence. For scholarly research on Princess texts and products intersects with the personal histories of scholars, who bring to these texts their own lived experience as consumers, parents, and teachers; and, as Jessica Tiffin notes, the struggle between critique and engagement derives from "Disney's appeal, the pleasure it creates despite everything we can do to deny it."[14]

Not only do the Princess films derive value by drawing upon medieval narratives, but the films themselves, over time, accrete canonicity as the authorized versions of these narratives. Wood relates her experience of teaching elementary education students at a state university: "After dutifully reading the variants of 'Cinderella' by Perrault and the Grimms, my students will often politely tell me that these new versions are all very well, but that they prefer the 'original,' by which they mean Disney."[15] The canonization of Disney films evident in Wood's account relies on their domination of the market, which in turn relies on what Bourdieu describes as the capacity of "consecrated" texts to "become part of 'general culture' through a process of familiarization."[16]

This process of familiarization takes its hold over audiences not because of the innate potency of fairy-tale narratives but because of the strategies whereby Disney films reduce the distance between contemporary audiences and a fairy-tale "once upon a time." The Princess films frequently attribute names and identities to anonymous princes, princesses, witches, and other characters; for example, the seven dwarfs in *Snow White* and the three good fairies, Flora, Fauna, and Merryweather, in *Sleeping Beauty*. The invention of minor characters and subplots add density and energy to the skeletal narratives of traditional stories; thus, the servants Lumière, Mrs. Potts, Cogsworth, and Chip, who are transformed into household items in *Beauty and the Beast* and restored to their human forms when the Beast returns to life, create the illusion of a world filled with characters whose histories, relationships, and motivations shape their actions. Fairy-tale protagonists are humanized through sequences when they reveal their thoughts and feelings, and through exchanges with interpolated figures such as the appealing animals and birds with which they commune. Through these strategies the Princess films simultaneously invoke the authority of fairy tales and reinvent their narratives for mass audiences. It is significant that the Princess film most consciously modeled on medieval art and design, *Sleeping Beauty*, was the least commercially successful on its release, its poor returns resulting in Disney's deficit in the fiscal year 1959–1960. The film's designer, Eyvind Earle, researched medieval art and architecture, in particular, *Les Très Riches Heures du Duc de Berry*, to develop stylized backgrounds that fulfilled Walt Disney's brief for a film which, he stipulated, was to look like "a moving illustration."[17] These backgrounds, based on horizontal and vertical planes, flat expanses of bright color and an emphasis on details of vegetation, clothing, and architecture, are strikingly different from the more "modern" aesthetic of *Snow White* and *Cinderella*. In his authorized biography of Walt Disney, Bob Thomas attributes the box-office failure of *Sleeping Beauty* to the fact that during the film's production Disney was preoccupied with the development of Disneyland and other projects: "As a result, the characters lacked the human touches that Walt always endowed; they also lacked his humor." Earle's research into medieval art, in Thomas's view, produced an emphasis on "visual beauty and spectacular effects" that did not sufficiently humanize the Middle Ages;[18] and without Disney's guiding sensibility to confer human touches and humor, beauty was not enough. This view of Disney's medievalism treats the Middle Ages as somewhat like Aurora herself—beautiful but passive, requiring the kiss of a prince to be vivified.

## "Some day my prince will come": How to Be a Princess in Ten Easy Lessons

Discussing performativity and gender, Butler remarks that "acts and gestures, articulated and enacted desires create the illusion of an interior and organizing gender core, an illusion discursively maintained for the purposes of the regulation of sexuality within the obligatory frame of reproductive heterosexuality."[19] The Disney Princess films and products promote reproductive heterosexuality as a norm by investing it with the symbolic value of the medieval, thus attributing historical depth to the illusion of "an interior and organizing gender core." One of the principal strategies deployed by Disney is that of exceptionalism—that is, medieval figures are shown to be different from their peers, possessing desires and expectations that mark them out as proleptically modern. Belle, in *Beauty and the Beast*, is a bluestocking beauty; located in eighteenth-century France, the film's transtemporal setting slides between the Enlightenment and the Middle Ages. Belle and her father are treated as Enlightenment figures whose regard for science and learning distinguishes them from the superstitious, gullible villagers. In this binary opposition between the Middle Ages and the Enlightenment, the medieval stands for intellectual backwardness; however, the discourses of romance and innocence pervading the film's treatment of Belle and her relationship with the Beast make for a far more contradictory array of significances. The Middle Ages is, then, associated with barbarism and ignorance as well as with qualities of innocence and simplicity.

The opening scenes depict Belle visiting the village bookshop and then walking about the village "with her nose in a book," in the words of the song that accompanies her progress. Belle ignores the hypermasculine performances of Gaston, the local hunter, who wants to marry her. Through repeated cuts between scenes in which Belle expresses disdain for Gaston, and depictions of the Bimbettes, three village girls who pursue him, the film distances Belle from her provincial setting and constructs her as a modern-ish girl with aspirations to a life filled with artistic and intellectual pursuits; that is, it conducts a variety of retroprogressive fantasy in which viewers are positioned to recognize in the deficiencies of the past the virtues of modernity. Belle's dialogue calls on the identification of the medieval with the barbaric and uncivilized: she describes Gaston as "positively primeval." Like Belle, her father is an exceptional figure: whereas in de Beaumont's version he is a merchant, in Disney's he is an inventor, a shift that sustains a contrast between a polity characterized by ignorance and anti-intellectualism, and exceptional individuals who point to a utopian vision of modernity.

Books in *Beauty and the Beast* represent both tradition and imagination. The blue-covered book that Belle reads as she strolls around the village is a romance; she has borrowed it so many times from the local bookshop that the bookseller has given it to her. Her favorite part, she reveals, is "where [the female protagonist] meets Prince Charming, but she won't discover that it's him 'til Chapter Three." This detail establishes Belle as a desiring and desirable subject, aligned with the protagonist of the medievalist romance she reads and dreaming of her own Prince Charming. The book, which Gaston snatches from Belle and hurls into a puddle, later turns up on the parlor table in Belle's house when Gaston proposes to her. Seated at the table, he rests his feet on the book, so confirming his incapacity to rise above his "positively primeval" nature. In effect, Gaston and the Beast are two sides of the one figure: both are self-regarding, choleric, intemperate; and both desire Belle. The key difference between them is that whereas Gaston is incapable of becoming an Enlightenment man, the Beast is educable at the hands of Belle, his inner nobility actualized and his transformation assured when he allows her to leave the castle to save her father. The contrast between Gaston and the Beast is, then, one of temporality: Gaston represents a brutish (medieval) past, the Beast the promise of Enlightenment progress. The catalyst for Belle's recognition of the Beast's inner worth is the moment when he gives her a splendid library, symbolizing both the past and also a future the two will share, suggested in the subsequent scene in which they are shown seated on a rug before the fireplace, Belle reading to the Beast like a mother reading to her child.

This anticipation of Belle's role as mother is not new, having been introduced by Gaston during his proposal when he envisaged the following scene:

> *Gaston*: Here, picture this: A rustic hunting lodge, my latest kill roasting on the fire, and my little wife massaging my feet, while the little ones play on the floor with the dogs. We'll have six or seven.
> *Belle*: Dogs?
> *Gaston*: No, Belle! Strapping boys, like me!

Gaston's error in anticipating a future with Belle does not reside in the "obligatory frame of reproductive heterosexuality" that gives shape to his imagining,[20] but in the fact that he is irredeemably medieval. When she melts into the arms of the Beast at the end of the film, Belle is ushered into a future where "happily ever after" incorporates motherhood. The final snatch of dialogue is initiated by Chip, himself incorporated into a happy family vignette together with his mother and Belle's father: "Are they going to live happily ever after, mamma?," to which Mrs. Potts replies: "Of course, my dear, of course."[21]

The exceptionalism of Belle and other Disney Princesses is strikingly similar to a trope pervasive in historical fiction for children set in colonial times.[22] In many such texts, exceptional Indigenous characters are depicted as "more advanced" than other members of their clans or nations, more apt to befriend white protagonists and to value European culture and practices; Disney's Pocahontas is a conspicuous example.[23] This style of representation enforces a distinction between ancient cultures treated as rigid and static, and the orthodox imperial view of Western modernity identified with energetic progress. Exceptional Indigenous individuals expose "less-progressive" members of their cultures, vindicating imperialism by foregrounding the inferiority of colonized peoples. Both fields of narrative (historical fiction and Disney Princess films) manifest contradictory views of ancient pasts: non-Western cultures and the Middle Ages are both desirable and also abhorrent, valued for qualities such as mystery and simplicity and simultaneously derided for superstition and inflexibility.

The non-white Princesses, Jasmine, Pocahontas, Mulan, and Tiana, frequently cited as indicators of Disney's progressiveness, are doubly exceptional—first because of their specular and racialized difference. Richard Dyer argues: "As long as race is something only applied to non-white peoples, as long as white people are not racially seen and named, they/we function as a human norm. Other people are raced, we are just people."[24] Thus, Snow White, Cinderella, Aurora, Ariel, Belle, and Rapunzel are presented as unraced, simply beautiful girls who function as the norm against which all others are represented and interpreted. Second, the nonwhite Princesses are exceptional because they are shown to resist or discard "backward" elements of their cultures: Jasmine defies the requirement that she marry a prince; Pocahontas chooses to "walk in the footsteps of a stranger" through her romance with John Smith; Mulan transgresses rules of gendered behavior by dressing as a soldier to save her father; and Tiana overcomes the assumption that black women cannot be successful in business.

The precondition for the outcome of reproductive heterosexuality to which Disney Princesses aspire is a state of innocence, closely identified with the Disney brand, the medieval and romantic notions of childhood. Of all the Princesses, Snow White is the emblematic innocent, with her bobbed hair, simple headband, and high-pitched voice. She is also figured as domestic, overseeing the cleaning of the Seven Dwarfs' cottage and whipping up a wholesome meal; and as motherly, inspecting the dwarfs' hands before they eat and kissing them as they leave for the mine. Other Princesses similarly perform gendered expressions of innocence and motherliness through sequences in which they care for animals and birds: Cinderella's concern for the mouse, Gus; Aurora's for her timid friend Flounder; Jasmine's solicitude for her lovebirds. The innocence of the Princesses is also constructed through comparisons with more knowing and sexually available figures, such as the Bimbettes in *Beauty and the Beast*. Belle's high-necked blue and white dress, which Marina Warner compares with the "pseudo-medieval dresses of both Cinderella and Snow White," is set against the Bimbettes' plunging necklines, which evoke stereotypes of the saucy medieval wench;[25] and Belle's decorous behavior is compared with the Bimbettes' bodily performances, which are coded as promiscuous. The ultimate test regarding the values the films propose resides in their outcomes: Belle marries the prince, signaling that modesty and selflessness define the successful Princess.

The narrative shape that defines Disney Princess films and products is that of heterosexual romance, encapsulated in Snow White's song "Some Day My Prince Will Come." With their misty allusions to courtly love and chivalric romance, the Princess films incorporate a bundle of conventional components, including love at first sight; the propensity for lovers to daydream, sing romantic songs, and search for the beloved; sequences in which mistaken identity temporarily blinds one or other of the lovers; and obstacles that prevent or delay "love's first kiss." These elements map modern romance narratives onto Disney's versions of courtly love, focusing on the subjectivities of Princesses rather than those of their romantic partners. As Karin Martin and Emily Kazyak point out, Disney films typically incorporate visual cues such as "magical swirls of sparks, leaves, or fireworks" and swelling musical scores to underline the significance and inevitability of romantic outcomes.[26]

The films' set-piece finales comprise weddings, celebrations, and scenes in which newly married lovers depart for their new lives, with the sole exception of *Pocahontas*. At the end of this film, Pocahontas, having chosen to commit herself to her people rather than to John Smith, stands alone on a high rock, observing the sailing ship that carries Smith to England. This ending avoids an outcome in which Pocahontas and Smith become sexual partners, so bypassing the troublesome figure of the Indigenous person whose multiple affiliations disrupt boundaries between races and ethnicities. The closure of *Pocahontas* is a telling indication of the awkward fit between Disney's medievalism and the colonial history of the United States. Whereas films such as *Snow White*, *Cinderella*, *The Little Mermaid*, and *Beauty and the Beast* retroactively endow the medieval past with American virtues, the colonial setting of *Pocahontas* allows for no such relationship between past and present. Moreover, the mapping of the medieval onto modern America, and America onto the medieval, relies on homologies of racial purity: just as European medieval worlds in the Disney Princess films are populated entirely by Europeans, so the medieval settings of *Aladdin* and *Mulan* are racially homogeneous, and racial difference (exemplified by the barbarous Huns of *Mulan*) is depicted as a threat to good order.

The Disney Princess is either of aristocratic birth or, like Belle and Tiana, marries into nobility; in either case, her beauty is a manifestation of her interior qualities and/or her noble origins. She attains the goal of romantic heterosexual love through one of two narrative routes. The first and more straightforward of these is exemplified by the fairy-tale figures of Snow White, Cinderella, Aurora, Ariel, and Belle. In these narratives, young women are primed for heterosexual romance before they encounter their princes, manifesting desire through their imaginings of idealized partners, imaginings that they confide to animal or human confidants and that are fulfilled in the films' "happy ever after" endings. The second, ostensibly more modern, trajectory to romance (exemplified by Jasmine, Mulan, Tiana, and Rapunzel) incorporates episodes of conflict between partners, eventually resolved when the couple acknowledge their love for each other. The principal difference between the two narrative schemas is that in the first category external circumstances delay or complicate the path to romance, whereas in the second category protagonists' own insecurities or lack of insight thwart their progress. Writing about the Middle English romance *Octavian*, Jeffrey Cohen says that chivalric romances end with "the reinscription of family, the valorization of social hierarchy, and the reassertion of a world that, even if it has progressed in time, nevertheless has not significantly changed."[27] This formulation is strikingly close to the endings of Disney Princess films. As Cohen's discussion of *Octavian* demonstrates, the endings of chivalric romance frequently exclude their more dynamic, indeterminate, and promiscuous possibilities. The spectacular effects that surround the endings of Disney Princess films similarly obscure the anxieties that trouble them.

### "My heart belongs to Daddy": Fathers, Bad Boys, and Disney Princesses

Fatherhood is a powerful force in Disney Princess films. Fathers bequeath nobility to and exert influence over their daughters, whose marriages often effect the reproduction of economic capital. Even when the fathers of Princesses are absent, as in *Snow White*, *Cinderella*, and *The Princess and the Frog*, they instigate storylines: Snow White's and Cinderella's fathers marry cruel stepmothers, setting in train narratives in which the monstrous feminine is central. Angela Carter describes this schema in her story "Ashputtle or The Mother's Ghost," where she reflects that in "Aschenputtel," the Grimms' version of the Cinderella story, the father is "the unmoved mover, the unseen organizing principle, like God."[28] In *The Princess and the Frog*, Tiana's father has died by the time the story begins, but not before impressing upon Tiana the imperative of hard work, which, he promises, will enable her to "do anything you set your mind to." Disney's *Sleeping Beauty* features two fathers: Aurora's father King Stefan and his friend King Hubert, who arrange the betrothal of Aurora to Prince Phillip, Hubert's son. While the *Sleeping Beauty* scenario comprises the most explicit reference to practices of dynastic marriage in aristocratic families, all the Princess films strenuously advocate heterosexual romance and (with the exception of *Pocahontas*) marriage, so arguing for the maintenance of "traditional" social and economic orders, which are endowed with historical and cultural depth through allusions to fairy tales come true.

Giroux asserts that Princess films contradict Disney's "purported obsession with family values" through the absence of "strong mothers or fathers."[29] However, the power of fatherhood in the world of these films resides in narrative, discursive, and filmic features rather than in depictions of individual "strong" or "weak" fathers. Thus, Belle's father in *Beauty and the Beast* may, as Giroux says, be "an airhead,"[30] but airhead or not, his needs and problems impel Belle into action and shape her relations with the Beast. Belle's tender care for the wounded Beast is mapped onto her solicitude for her father; both the Beast and her father are misunderstood and rejected by their communities, and both are brought back to life through Belle's ministrations. When Belle utters the words "I love you," she sets in train a utopian outcome that reincorporates the Beast and her father into the aristocratic sociality represented by the Beast's transformed castle, epitomized by the final scene in which the happy couple dance in the grand ballroom to the acclamation of courtiers, servants, and Belle's father.

Narrative closure is always deeply ideological in texts that imply young audiences, since as John Stephens notes, "there is an idea that young children require ... certainties about life rather than indeterminacies or uncertainties or unfixed boundaries."[31] The "happily ever after" rubric in Princess films commonly incorporates a moment or image in which fathers hand Princesses on to romantic partners worthy of them, so authorizing the maintenance of patriarchal orders. In *Cinderella*, this moment occurs when the Grand Duke (the King's proxy) slides Cinderella's foot into the glass slipper, signifying that she is the ideal sexual partner for the prince.[32] One might expect that post-1960s' Princess films would incorporate outcomes that advocate an enhanced degree of female agency, but this is not the case. In *The Little Mermaid*, King Triton, Ariel's father, recognizes his daughter's love for Prince Eric and transforms her into a human so that she can live on earth; in *Aladdin*, Jasmine's father, the Sultan, similarly persuaded by his daughter's love for Aladdin, changes the law that formerly required her to marry a prince. For all Ariel's and Jasmine's spirited behavior, they are powerless in the face of entrenched practices, requiring their fathers' authority to achieve the goal of marriage to their princes.

While the narratives of Princess films are driven by the Princesses' desires for heterosexual romance and marriage, the most compelling figures in these films suggest far more ambiguous and fluid identities and desires: the dwarfs of *Snow White*, in whom childhood and adulthood are uncannily fused; the camp/drag performance of Ursula the sea witch in *The Little Mermaid*, who offers an alternative to heteronormativity; Mulan's guardian dragon-lizard Mushu, whose ambiguous racial identity pivots on his combination of Chinese-ness and Eddie Murphy's "inner-city black dialect."[33] In a shift from the cardboard cut-out princes of *Snow White*, *Cinderella*, *Sleeping Beauty*, and *The Little Mermaid*, three post-1960s' Princess films feature prince figures of questionable moral character and dubious motivation: Aladdin, Naveen in *The Princess and the Frog*, and Flynn Rider in *Tangled*. Aladdin and Flynn are petty thieves who happen upon Princesses in the course of their shady operations; and Naveen, disinherited by his father, the King of Maldonia, arrives in New Orleans in search of an heiress to marry. The back-story that features at the beginning of *Beauty and the Beast*, coded as medieval through its narration against the backdrop of a sequence of stained-glass windows, introduces the prince as another bad boy figure, "spoiled, selfish, and unkind"; but transformation into the Beast, at the hands of the beggar-woman/enchantress to whom he refuses shelter, converts him into the more complex shape, as Warner notes, of the untamed lover who affords Beauty the erotic pleasure of educating him into civility.

Aladdin, Naveen, and Flynn are tamer versions of the countercultural pirates discussed by Pugh in this volume's Introduction; and like pirates they are susceptible to incorporation into Disney's quasi-medieval order. Their characterization reflects changed perspectives of the masculine in popular and literary production for children and young people, from the tough, action-oriented figures who predominated in adventure narratives and *bildungsroman* during the nineteenth century and much of the twentieth, to boys and young men of wider emotional range, quick-witted and responsive, whose emergence in literature for the young has been intertwined with cultural shifts around concepts of gender and sexuality. Bad boys also offer the pleasures of fast-moving action: Aladdin and Flynn are introduced through energetic chase sequences during which they are pursued after stealing, respectively, a loaf of bread, and Rapunzel's tiara; and their adventures thereafter incorporate extravagant physical feats and rapid changes of fortune. Their characters are transparently intended to attract male audiences but must also serve as romantic partners worthy of Princesses.[34] Aladdin, Naveen, and Flynn allude to figures from a variety of multitemporal genres, including romance, swashbuckling film, and video games. Although the three films adopt different narrative strategies to redeem bad boys and render them worthy partners for Princesses, these transformations hinge upon humanist notions of a stable inner self, melded with Disney's invocations of the chivalric code and bolstered by the promise of economic success. If medieval romance assumes that a hero's corporeal beauty bespeaks his inner virtue, Aladdin, Naveen, and Flynn must access the nobility concealed under their bad-boy posturing, and realize it through selfless action.

Early in *Aladdin* the film begins to chip away at Aladdin's insouciant exterior to suggest the virtue lurking beneath: having escaped from the palace guards, Jafar (the Sultan's evil Grand Vizier), and hostile shopkeepers, Aladdin stops to savor the loaf of bread he has stolen, only to notice two starving children watching him. He gives them the bread, thus establishing himself as more generous, more sensitive than he pretends. Even before this scene, the peddler who introduces the story of Aladdin describes how the magic lamp "once changed the course of a young man's life. A young man who like this lamp was more than what he seemed. A diamond in the rough." These broad hints, and references to Aladdin's vulnerable position as a penniless orphan, mark him as the combination of Cinderlad and Horatio Alger so common in Disney's medieval world. The film's repeated allusions to Aladdin's inner worth as a "diamond in the rough" imply a teleology of personal progress during which his potential is to be fulfilled, his roughness smoothed away.

This narrative of progress is, of course, plotted against Aladdin's romance with Jasmine, complicated by his disguise as "Prince Ali," a disguise that encodes his princely potential. Jasmine is in dire need of rescue, trapped in a Muslim culture described as "barbaric," imprisoned in her father's palace, and forced to marry Jafar. As Aladdin discards his bad-boy persona (which is, after all, the consequence of his poverty and lack of status), he becomes more and more American: he shows no allegiance to Muslim custom or tradition, and presents as a young entrepreneur, always eager to recognize a market advantage. Jasmine is the kind of Muslim woman whom Western commentators most desire to rescue from her abjectness, so often represented as medieval; and the newly polished Aladdin is ideally situated to achieve this feat, freeing her, as Erin Addison notes, from "Arab men, Arab (Islamic) law, and Arab culture."[35] His identity is made clear at the end of the film:

> *Sultan*: Well, am I sultan or am I sultan? From this day forth, the Princess shall marry whomever she deems worthy.
> *Jasmine*: I choose ... I choose you, Aladdin.
> *Aladdin*: Call me Al.

Like Fair Unknowns in Arthurian romance (whose identities are often disguised), Aladdin's induction into aristocratic society is marked by marriage to a princess, and the acquisition of wealth.

Charged by Tiana with being a "spoiled little rich boy," Naveen's transformation from bad boy to prince is contingent upon his conversion from profligacy to hard work and thrift under Tiana's tutelage. While the trajectory of Naveen's progress is colored by the implication that self-made is morally superior to inherited wealth, Tiana's single-minded preoccupation with the establishment of her restaurant represents her rejection of love and romance. By making Naveen over as a hardworking family man, the narrative reinstates Disney's vision of a natural order in which princes enable Princesses' dreams to come true. Ray the Firefly discloses Naveen's intentions, telling Tiana: "Soon as he [Naveen] get himself kissed, and you both turn human, he go find a job, get you that restaurant." The film's surface messages about female success are, then, obscured by its narratives of patriarchal succession, as Tiana's ambition, the restaurant that constituted her father's dream, is realized only through Naveen's intervention; and she learns that to become a Princess she must desire a prince.

The figure of Flynn Rider in *Tangled* amalgamates the comedy-action hero with the swashbuckling and romantic associations of Errol Flynn, layering them over a fairy-tale hero attributed with comedic lines that undermine the romantic nostalgia of the film's setting, such as his initial exchange with Rapunzel:

*Rapunzel:* Who are you, and how did you find me?
*Flynn Rider:* I know not who you are, nor how I came to find you, but may I just say ... Hi. How you doin'?

Flynn is introduced in a sequence during which he steals Rapunzel's tiara from her parents' castle before cheating the twin thugs who are his companions, absconding with the tiara, and seeking refuge in Rapunzel's tower. His bad-boy behavior is ameliorated because the thugs are patently criminals and Flynn is handsome and witty. He is also an orphan and, in the film's most startling play with the "Fair Unknown" motif, of aristocratic ancestry: in one of several episodes when he and Rapunzel face mortal danger, Flynn confesses that his name is really Eugene Fitzherbert. By the end of the film Flynn/Eugene is the very model of a modern-medieval prince, possessing true nobility and good looks coupled with a twist of modern/postmodern irony: a Princess, incorporation into her family, and the promise of wealth. When Flynn/Eugene restores Rapunzel to her parents at the end of the film, mother, father, and daughter sink to their knees in an embrace; then Rapunzel's mother gestures to Flynn/Eugene, who is ushered into the circle of aristocratic wealth and entitlement. All three bad boys are readily assimilated into hereditary orders based on the maintenance of masculine authority.

While the Princess films are directed toward preteen to teen audiences, the Disney Princess website positions very young girls as young princesses and inducts them into the world of Disney's modern medievalism. Participants are invited to assist in preparations for celebrations: on Snow White's page, the Forest Friends festival, Bashful's dinner party, Dopey's birthday; on Tiana's page, Naveen's birthday party, Big Daddy's Masquerade Ball, and the Bayou Romantic Cruise. Having completed these activities, participants receive a certificate to print for their "book of charms." A striking aspect of the Princesses' language is its emphasis on notions of gendered work. When they seek help from their "friends" (that is, implied website audiences), the Princesses often do so with a nod and a wink toward the neediness of boys and men. Snow White confides that she has no time to choose a dress to wear because she needs to help Dopey pick flowers; Tiana says that Louis the trumpet-playing alligator has promised to help her but is nowhere to be found. A tone of amused resignation attaches to such utterances, enforcing the idea that "we"—the Princesses and their girl audiences—must make allowances for "them," the boys and men whose fecklessness, forgetfulness, or stupidity is as natural as the Princesses' selflessness. In more general terms, the Princesses are shown to perform duties centered on pleasing men. Snow White makes gooseberry pies for Grumpy, because, she says, he is not fond of cake. Similarly, Tiana's skill at cooking is almost always framed in relation to what boys and men will like; during the activity based on the romantic bayou cruise, she reminds her audience that "the quickest way to a man's heart is through his stomach."

With its misty evocations of a transtemporal medievalism, the Disney Princess website positions young girls to regard traditional forms of femininity as preferred modes of being female. This positioning is associated with the consumerism at the center of the website, which promises its audiences the pleasures of watching and performing Princess narratives, wearing Princess clothing, and snuggling up in personalized *Tangled* Rapunzel fleece blankets. The babies and young children whose photographs adorn the Princess website comprise a demographic of young girls who will become the primary viewers of Princess films. Both the website and the films disclose cultural anxieties around gender and sexuality, anxieties that manifest in the contradictory discourses that swirl about them. Nowhere are these contradictions more apparent than in the ideological functions performed by Disney's medievalisms.

**Notes**

1. The ten Disney Princesses are: Snow White (*Snow White and the Seven Dwarfs*, 1937), Cinderella (*Cinderella*, 1950), Aurora (*Sleeping Beauty*, 1959), Ariel (*The Little Mermaid*, 1989), Belle (*Beauty and the Beast*, 1991),

Jasmine (*Aladdin*, 1992), Pocahontas (*Pocahontas*, 1995), Mulan (*Mulan*, 1998), Tiana (*The Princess and the Frog*, 2009), and Rapunzel (*Tangled*, 2010). As of December 2011, Rapunzel has been incorporated into the Disney Princess website.
2. The term *modality*, when used of visual images, refers to the various ways in which they seek to persuade viewers of their accuracy and reliability; for example, degrees of naturalism expressed through color, the absence or presence of background details, and the use of light and shade. See Kress and van Leeuwen, *Reading Images* (London: Routledge, 1996), 159–80.
3. *Disney Princess: The Official Princess Website*, Disney.go.com; Web, accessed November 30, 2010.
4. Several of the Disney Princess films are based on fairy-tale narratives filtered through retellings by Perrault (*Cinderella, Sleeping Beauty*), the Brothers Grimm (*Snow White, The Princess and the Frog, Tangled*), and Jeanne-Marie Le Prince de Beaumont (*Beauty and the Beast*). Aladdin derives from a story from *A Thousand and One Nights*; *The Little Mermaid* from Hans Christian Andersen's literary fairy-tale of the same name; and *Mulan* from Chinese folk narratives. *Pocahontas* is the only Disney Princess film based on an historical figure, presenting a fictionalized account of Pocahontas's relationship with the Englishman John Smith early in the seventeenth century.
5. Geraldine Heng, *Empire of Magic: Medieval Romance and the Politics of Cultural Fantasy* (New York: Columbia University Press, 2003), 192.
6. Judith Butler, *Gender Trouble* (1990; New York: Routledge, 1999), xxi.
7. Pierre Bourdieu, *The Field of Cultural Production* (Cambridge: Polity, 1993), 50–51.
8. As Maria Takolander and David McCooey argue, gender representations in *Shrek* are no more progressive than those in the Disney Princess films: "*Shrek*, rather than celebrating any liberation from patriarchal traditions, is in fact a response to the colloquial 'crisis in masculinity' and a defense of the primordial ogre of patriarchy" ("'You Can't Say No to the Beauty and the Beast': *Shrek* and Ideology," *Papers: Explorations into Children's Literature* 15.1 [2005]: 5–14, at 5).
9. Pierre Bourdieu, *Cultural Production*, 51.
10. Henry Giroux, *The Mouse That Roared: Disney and the End of Innocence* (Lanham: Rowman & Littlefield, 1999), 98–114.
11. Naomi Wood, "Domesticating Dreams in Walt Disney's *Cinderella*," *The Lion and the Unicorn* 20.1 (1996): 25–49, at 25.
12. Karen Wohlwend, "Damsels in Discourse: Girls Consuming and Producing Identity Texts through Disney Princess Play," *Reading Research Quarterly* 44.1 (2009): 57–83, at 58.
13. Karen Wohlwend, "Damsels in Discourse," 63–70.
14. Jessica Tiffin, "Review: *The Emperor's Old Groove*," *Marvels & Tales* 18.2 (2004): 329–31, at 330.
15. Naomi Wood, "Domesticating Dreams," 25.
16. Pierre Bourdieu, *Cultural Production*, 108.

17. "The Making of Sleeping Beauty," *Sleeping Beauty* Special Edition DVD (Walt Disney Video, 2003).
18. Bob Thomas, *Walt Disney: An American Original* (New York: Walt Disney Company, 1976), 295.
19. Judith Butler, *Gender Trouble*, 173.
20. Judith Butler, *Gender Trouble*, 173.
21. Similar "happy family" homologies appear throughout the Princess films, from the "contented family units" (Knapp 125) of the birds and woodland creatures in *Snow White* to Rapunzel's ersatz family in *Tangled*, comprising Rapunzel, Flynn Rider, the chameleon Pascal, and the courser Maximilian, who together embark on the quest to restore Rapunzel to her position as princess.
22. Clare Bradford, *Unsettling Narratives: Postcolonial Readings of Children's Literature* (Waterloo: Wilfrid Laurier University Press, 2007), 10–11; 73–77.
23. This trope appears across settler society children's literatures from the United States, Canada, Australia, and New Zealand, typically in fiction by non-Indigenous producers.
24. Richard Dyer, *White* (London: Routledge, 1997), 1.
25. Marina Warner, *From the Beast to the Blonde: On Fairy Tales and Their Tellers* (New York: Farrar, Straus, & Giroux, 1994), 314.
26. Karin Martin and Emily Kazyak, "Hetero-Romantic Love and Heterosexiness in Children's G-Rated Films," *Gender & Society* 23.3 (2009): 315–36, at 325.
27. Jeffrey Cohen, *Medieval Identity Machines* (Minneapolis: University of Minnesota Press, 2003), 68.
28. Angela Carter, *Burning Your Boats: The Collected Short Stories* (New York: Penguin, 1995), 392.
29. Henry Giroux, *The Mouse That Roared*, 103.
30. Henry Giroux, *The Mouse That Roared*, 103.
31. John Stephens, *Language and Ideology in Children's Fiction* (London: Longman, 1992), 41.
32. Bruno Bettelheim, *The Uses of Enchantment: The Meaning and Importance of Fairy Tales* (1976; New York: Random House, 2010), 269–76.
33. Sheng-mei Ma, "Mulan Disney, It's Like, Re-Orients: Consuming China and Animating Teen Dreams," *The Emperor's Old Groove: Decolonizing Disney's Magic Kingdom*, ed. Brenda Ayres (New York: Peter Lang, 2003), 149–64, at 152.
34. The change of title from *Rapunzel* to *Tangled* was reportedly prompted by the Walt Disney Company's belief that *Tangled* was more likely to attract male audiences, since "Disney can ill afford a moniker that alienates half the potential audience, young boys, who are needed to make an expensive family film a success" (Dawn Chmielewski and Claudia Eller, "Disney Restyles 'Rapunzel' to Appeal to Boys," *Los Angeles Times* [9 Mar. 2010], articles.latimes.com; Web, accessed 30 Nov. 2010).
35. Erin Addison, "Saving Other Women from Other Men: Disney's *Aladdin*," *Camera Obscura* 31 (1993): 5–25, at 6.

## CHAPTER 11

## DISNEY'S MEDIEVALIZED ECOLOGIES IN *SNOW WHITE AND THE SEVEN DWARFS* AND *SLEEPING BEAUTY*

*Kathleen Coyne Kelly*

> On the one hand, there is nothing more biophilic than the work of animating nature, which requires not simply filming animal movement, for instance, but being able to reproduce it realistically by hand. By necessity, Disney artists became naturalists. On the other hand, in representing nature, Disney transformed it into something else.
>
> Matthew Roth, "Man Is in the Forest"[1]
>
> ... the grace and infinity of nature's foliage, with every vista a cathedral ...
>
> John Ruskin, "The True and the Beautiful in Nature, Art, Morals and Religion"[2]

The history of animation and its precursors (including the praxinoscope, the zoetrope, and the flip book) is one in which technology and aesthetics continually influence each other, and in which the available technology produces the aesthetics, the signature look, of a given era. The earliest animations, for example, were driven by a desire to simulate the motions of the human form, but such animations could only do so in limited ways. In the first animated projection, Charles-Émile Reynaud's *Pauvre Pierrot* (1892), the focus is on the movements of Pierrot, Arlequin, and Colombine: that these figures moved at all was a wonder for late nineteenth-century audiences. In the first photographed animated projection, Stuart Blackton's *Humorous Phases of Funny Faces*

(1906), Blackton's extradiegetic hand animates various people on a blackboard. Despite the caricatured nature of the images, the focus is once again on the human face and body in motion.[3]

At a time when animated pictures employed no sound, animators developed character through exaggerated motion, and such hyperbole came to dominate the look of early cartoons. *Gertie the Dinosaur* (1914) is the first significant example of what has come to be known as character animation, which establishes the personality, thinking processes, and emotions of a character through physical appearance and movement alone. Gertie is a winning creature indeed. After Gertie, mere motion was no longer sufficient to entertain audiences. Walt Disney understood this both aesthetically and commercially, when he created the character of Mickey Mouse. As his early directions to the animators at his young company reveal, Disney focused almost entirely on character animation even as he innovated in the realm of sound, and, later, speech.[4]

Advances in technology shaped the look and function of backgrounds as well. In *Pauvre Pierrot*, Pierrot moves jerkily against a static, prettily painted watercolor background. This is the backdrop of the traditional stage—a two-dimensional flat—that exemplifies how the features of one medium are often imported into a newer, more attractive medium. In *Steamboat Willie* (1928), as Mickey pilots his steamboat down the river, the theatrical flat is replaced by the traveling matte of live-action film in which the background unwinds like a ribbon behind the boat. Motion is an illusion conveyed by the relationship between the boat and the shore. In these early animated shorts, the background and foreground are often painted in different styles, resulting in a disconnection between the two. However, in most contemporary cartoons (those produced after the early 1960s), whether drawn by hand or digitized, backgrounds are fully integrated with the characters in the foreground.[5]

In this essay, I look past the bodies in motion in *Snow White and the Seven Dwarfs* (1937) and *Sleeping Beauty* (1959) to focus on Disney's backgrounds. The natural settings, or ecologies, of *Snow White* and *Sleeping Beauty* evoke the medieval spaces of fairy tale, illuminated manuscript, and tapestry; in both films, the backgrounds are animated paintings that possess an aesthetic integrity all their own. The medieval worlds in *Snow White* and *Sleeping Beauty* come to life through extensive quotation and allusion to other, earlier pictorial representations of the Middle Ages as well as through a number of technological innovations in animation. Disney's new technologies not only create the medievalized look (imagined differently in the two films) but also render the medieval as "real," and this process raises interesting questions about realism in representations of nature as an aesthetic value—"truth of nature," as John Ruskin puts it in *Modern Painters*. Ruskin argues that the highest art reveals nature as it is—as it truly is, not through imitation, but by "convey[ing] ... the greatest number of the greatest ideas."[6] Ruskin declares that it is an "error" among "the thoughtless and unreflecting, that they know either what nature is, or what is like her."[7] The gendering of nature as feminine is, of course, not unique to Ruskin; neither is the language suggesting that the full appreciation of nature (by itself and as a functional equivalent to art) is reserved for an elite few. I am more interested in the process (again, not unique to Ruskin) by which nature is abstracted as an *idea*—thus able to be medievalized—and the consequences of such an abstraction. We can, in fact, trace a crooked line from Ruskin and the pre-Raphaelites (themselves invested in medievalism) to Disney through the American realist painter Robert Henri (1865–1929). Disney, in speaking of his animators, many of whom were painters in their own right, approvingly quotes Henri's dictum that "the great painter has something to say. He does not paint men, landscapes or furniture, but an idea."[8]

We usually think of nature in its geographical, spatial, localizable aspect. Too often, nature becomes abstracted as an idea when it is imagined as being distant from us: not here, but elsewhere, a place that entails traveling *to*. But we also are quite capable of constituting nature as temporal, as existing not now, but in the past (the vanished wilderness) or the future (the restored wetland). As a thing of the past, nature regresses, is forever lost. As a thing of the future, nature progresses on an infinite arc ahead of us. Tison Pugh, in this volume's Introduction, describes Disney's world as a space best understood temporally: "where yesterday is tomorrow today, where fantasies of the past serve as templates of possible futures." In *Snow White* and *Sleeping Beauty*, nature is indeed "yesterday," located in a Middle Ages accessed only through fantasy. At the same time, Disney's medievalized ecologies are offered as something that we might achieve in the future: perhaps someday we might actually stumble upon those magical forests and serene glades seen on screen. Another fantasy that *Snow White* and *Sleeping Beauty* offers is the idea of a pristine, unspoiled nature to be used and enjoyed by all. Such a vision is central to conservationism, a set of beliefs that informs Disney's construction of medievalized nature in these two films. In what follows, as I explore how Disney medievalized nature, I also explore how *Snow White* and *Sleeping Beauty*, in a small but significant way, participated in mid-twentieth-century discourses on the environment.[9]

### *Snow White and the Seven Dwarfs*

*Snow White* opens with a familiar image (and now a cliché of movie medievalism): a bound manuscript on a table, lavishly embellished with gold and laid on royal blue velvet and accompanied by a golden chalice.

As the parchment pages turn magically by themselves (the real-life book—a Disney-designed prop—was filmed using stop-action animation), viewers read a pseudo-Gothic script adorned with blue, red, and gold capitals: "Once upon a time ... " The screen fades to black, and then slowly brightens to reveal the animated scene, a many-turreted castle on a high cliff, framed in the foreground by green woods.

This establishing shot depends upon the effects of the multiplane camera. As Roger Ebert describes it, the multiplane camera creates "the illusion of three dimensions by placing several levels of drawing one behind another and moving them separately—the ones in front faster than the ones behind, so that the background seemed to actually move."[10] While versions of the multiplane camera existed before *Snow White*, the Walt Disney Company's innovation was a camera that could film as many as seven layers of artwork at once, adding depth and dimension not seen before in animation. The effects of the camera are most striking when animating nature scenes. In the opening scene in *Snow White*, the camera seems to move into the space, drawing us after it, past the trees, closer and closer to the castle, until the scene dissolves to a window. The camera continues to draw viewers in as the window grows larger and dissolves to an interior. Once inside, we are again drawn in closer as we watch the Queen, filmed from behind, approaching her magic mirror. Viewers are drawn out of our world into a painted space that we experience as "real," even though what we see is the result of a camera filming layers of painted paper moving at different speeds. Moreover, the illuminated manuscript and the crenellated castle framed by the green woods serve as authenticating signs of the medieval. Form (cinematic technique) and content (manuscript and castle) combine to create the illusion that we have landed in the Middle Ages.

In addition to the multiplane camera, another innovation that distinguishes *Snow White* from previous animated films is the use of three-strip Technicolor, which results in rich, suffused colors—not, as Disney says, the "cheap" or "poster-like" colors of other animated shorts. Disney told his animators: "We are not going after comic supplement coloring. We have to strive for a certain depth and realism through the use of colors."[11] Although the hyperreal colors of Technicolor exist only as a cinematic effect, Technicolor registered as "real" in the evolving aesthetics of the animated film—that is, "real" as an *illusion* of the real. As one reviewer wrote in 1938: "Visually, the film is one of the finest examples of Technicolor. Disney is said to have perfected certain processes of photography which create illusions of depth in some of the scenes. Whether this is accomplished by the perspectives of draughtsmanship or by the lensing is not material."[12] The reviewer is describing the effects of the multiplane camera as well as those of Technicolor; to the contrary, technology does matter.

The magic of the opening scene inheres in its detail, depth, and color—a result of new technologies that Disney used to create a medievalized *mise-en-scène*. In addition, the backgrounds for *Snow White* were painted with transparent watercolors that contribute to its dreamy, ethereal quality, a look that Disney borrowed from European storybook illustrations. Gustaf Adolf Tenggren (1896–1970), a Swedish illustrator who worked for Disney in the late 1930s, was the immediate influence on *Snow White*; Tenggren in turn was influenced by English illustrator Arthur Rackham.[13] Early twentieth-century American lithographs and prints by painters and book and calendar illustrators such as Atkinson Fox (1860–1935) and Maxfield Parrish (1870–1966), who, influenced by the pre-Raphaelites, painted romanticized, otherworldly landscapes, provided another source for the backgrounds of *Snow White*. While audiences may not be able to name Tenggren or Rackham or Parrish, their styles were as recognizable in the 1930s as they are today.

In the opening scene, as the camera pulls us in past wild nature (the framing woods), we leave the forest "behind" us, curious to know what is happening on the other side of the window. The woods that we seem to pass through are peaceful and benign, but the castle in which we find ourselves is an evil place controlled by a jealous Queen (Lucille La Verne). The castle, while aesthetically pleasing, is sterile, oppressive, and forbidding—as is the Queen herself. It is a relief to turn to the figure of Snow White (Adriana Caselotti), whom we first see cheerfully scrubbing the lower cobblestone steps of the castle. Attended by adoring white doves, Snow White sings as she draws water from a well covered with wisteria and clematis. She takes pleasure in the simple task of splashing water on the stones. Enclosed in a courtyard planted with blossoming cherry trees, Snow White mediates between the imposing, barren stone of the castle that is the Queen's province and an abundant, domesticated nature.

Disney encouraged his animators to, as he says, "picture on the screen things that have run through the imagination of the audience, to bring to life dream fantasies."[14] What is so striking about his instructions is that Disney did not see himself as creating a fantasy *ex nihilo*, but as accessing desires already in circulation. Disney was a man who had a shrewd grasp of the workings of ideology. Steven Watts argues that while Disney espoused no particular political agenda, he practiced an "instinctive populism," a stance that privileges the values of ordinary, mostly rural, citizens.[15] The studio's rise, as Watts notes, coincided with the Depression; it is no accident that Disney shorts and features during the 1930s, while offering escape, simultaneously celebrate the value of honest, hard work and of simple pleasures.[16] And so *Snow White*, the best of all possible animated worlds, is (like all fantasies) not a politically neutral space. The dwarfs in *Snow White* can be read as representing the populist ideal of honest labor, indeed, of unalienated labor by which one works the land for one's own sustenance. Such a philosophy is consonant with the prevailing conservationist ideology of the day. Dedicated to the protection of natural resources for human use in a sustainable way, American conservationists during the first third of the twentieth century established fisheries and forest preserves (to be replenished and managed for harvesting), and, more importantly, state and national parks and conservation areas—not necessarily because these places had intrinsic ecological value, but because Americans enjoyed them for hunting, fishing, and camping as well as for their beauty.[17]

Disney explicitly promoted conservationist views in his *True-Life Adventures Series*, nature documentaries that included films such as *Seal Island* (1948) and *The Living Desert* (1953). A conservationist aesthetic is also apparent in many of Disney's animated films, particularly *Bambi*. *Snow White* and *Sleeping Beauty*, like *Bambi*, offer a manufactured nature that is controlled by every stroke of the pencil; their ecologies parallel the meticulously designed spaces of Disneyland and Walt Disney World, where every inch of space is appropriated for human use. In this context, the dwarfs' cottage can be viewed as a model of managed resources. Its gables and thatched roof seem to grow out of the forest floor, and the interior is as organic as the exterior. Much of the interior decoration consists of stylized animal heads and designs, suggesting a harmonious continuity between inside and outside. While it evokes an Old World dwelling in a fairy-tale Black Forest, the cottage also owes much to the popular American Craftsman-style bungalow of the 1930s—ubiquitous in southern California, home to Disney and his animators. The cottage thus combines a medievalism once removed with the era's dominant conservationist ideology (figure 11.1).

Theodore Roosevelt and Gifford Pinchot, whom Roosevelt appointed as the first Chief of the United States Forest Service (1905–1910), would have admired the dwarfs for their old-style conservationism. Pinchot described forest conservationism as "the art of producing from the forest whatever it can yield for the service of man."[18] Disney's dwarfs delve into the earth for its riches, not out of greed, but for their modest profit. In a deleted scene, the dwarfs build a bed for Snow White, selecting four living trees that stand *in situ* in rectangular symmetry and carve the trees into bedposts. The dwarfs, with the tacit consent of the forest animals who observe, and sometimes aid, the dwarfs' building of the bed, embody Pinchot's declaration that "forestry is the knowledge of

**Figure 11.1** The dwarfs' "medieval-Craftsman" cottage.

the forest. In particular, it is the art of handling the forest so that it will render whatever service is required of it without being impoverished or destroyed."[19] In a famous scene, Snow White enlists the animals' help in tidying the cottage.[20] This cleaning scene can also be viewed as a conservationist moment: chaotic nature is tamed and made to submit to culture. Nature in *Snow White* is made legible in conservationist terms as a collection of resources to be managed for human good.

The forests in *Snow White* and, as we shall see, in *Sleeping Beauty*, do not, of course, look like any forest one might be able to visit or hike through, either now or in the Middle Ages. They do not remind the viewer of Yosemite or of the remains of the New Forest in England (created as a hunting preserve in 1079 by William the Conqueror), or even the Białowieża Puszcza in Poland (often described as the last forest in Europe, and which contains oaks dating to the Middle Ages). Still, Disney's forests are capable of generating a strong desire to be transported to them, if only in fantasy: they exist—not some *where*, but some *time*. *Snow White* and *Sleeping Beauty* offer a fantasy Middle Ages—to borrow from Winston Churchill, who famously said of the legend of King Arthur: "It is all true, or it ought to be; and more and better besides."[21]

### Sleeping Beauty

As much as we might take pleasure in *Snow White* today, we cannot experience the wonder that the film aroused in 1937 because we live in an age of digitized cartoons such as DreamWorks's *Shrek* films (2001–2010) and the computer-generated imagery of films such as James Cameron's *Avatar* (2009). It is difficult to comprehend *Snow White*'s impact on its first audience. Roger Ebert is one of many who remind us that the Russian director Sergei Eisenstein called *Snow White* the greatest movie ever made.[22] *Sleeping Beauty* is a different sort of technological and aesthetic achievement than that of *Snow White*, particularly with respect to its mixture of the medieval and the modern. Based on Charles Perrault's fairy tale (1696), which was the inspiration for Tchaikovsky's ballet *The Sleeping Beauty* (1890), which in turn furnished the Disney film score, *Sleeping Beauty* was the last fairy tale produced by Disney himself.

While *Snow White* invokes the Middle Ages indirectly through its echoing of European storybooks, *Sleeping Beauty* explicitly quotes the art of the Middle Ages. Chief color stylist Eyvind Earle, following stylist Mary Blair's initial conceptual paintings, was responsible for the overall look of the film and described it as intentionally Gothic.[23] He cites the *Très Riches Heures* (c. 1410), made by the Brothers Limbourg for the Duc de Berry, as one medieval source; indeed, Sleeping Beauty's castle looks very much like the Château de Saumur and the Louvre as depicted in the *Très Riches Heures* calendar for September and October, respectively. Chief layout artist John Hinch also visited the Unicorn Tapestries (c. 1500) at The Cloisters in New York City for inspiration. Disney often hired artists as animators, and such is the case with *Sleeping Beauty*. For example, Earle and Joshua Meador were Disney animators who also produced their own critically acclaimed work. In *Sleeping Beauty*, both interpreted the landscapes of medieval tapestries and manuscripts through their respective modernist sensibilities. Earle describes his own style as "designed realism ... There's much of the Oriental, the Gothic, the Persian in it, as well as the color of moderns like Van Gogh."[24] While the arching boughs of the trees in the middle and far distance in *Sleeping Beauty* recall Ruskin's organic cathedrals, they are painted in a modernist style reminiscent of Charles Burchfield's "Winter Sun through the Poplars" (1916). The thicket of thorns with which Maleficent surrounds Sleeping Beauty's castle descends from Burchfield's "An April Mood" (1946–1955). The film is, as animation historian Charles Solomon says, "curiously Gothic but also very contemporary in design."[25]

*Sleeping Beauty*, like *Snow White*, opens with a real (but equally ersatz), extravagantly gilded, and bejeweled manuscript; it rests on a lectern in front of what looks like the Unicorn Tapestries. As in *Snow White*, one is drawn into the book as the camera moves up the page to a painting of a castle in the far distance. The camera moves over the landscape, closer to the castle, and then cuts to a parade of people. The illustrations are highly graphic, stylized versions of the medieval illuminated page. The castle backgrounds in close-up are solid, textured layers of stone. The forest is equally, greenly substantial in close-up as the tree trunks dominate the foreground. On the other hand, the main characters are drawn with a light, graphic hand and painted in gouache, resulting in opaque, one-dimensional colors. Recognizable and now signature Disney cartoon characters, all are obvious overlays.

*Sleeping Beauty* reprises the binaries of castle and culture versus cottage and nature of *Snow White*: the fairies' home, growing out of a towering tree, is as organic as the dwarfs' cottage. Both the bustling, happy castle of Sleeping Beauty and the gloomy castle of Maleficent are offered as counterpoints to nature. In addition, the differences between the two castles might be read as contributing to a more complicated view of conservationism than found in *Snow White* (and produced after *Bambi*), suggesting that there are both good and bad conservationist practices. In this reading, the good fairies' magic also figures as a complicating commentary on conservationism. The fairies must give up their magic if they are going to live in disguise in the forest; that is, they must dwell in harmony with nature's own laws. However, they are hopelessly incompetent without their magic, as we see in the scene when they try to make a birthday cake and a ball gown for Aurora. When the fairies use their wands (to reassert their control over nature), they unknowingly betray themselves to Maleficent (Eleanor Audley), the antithesis of benign nature. Additionally, Maleficent's biggest transgression may well be that she wastes resources: her castle is a gloomy heap of stones; she rules over creatures who are perversions of the good animals of the forest; and, most damningly, she uses magic for evil, creating, for example, that thicket of thorns—wild nature out of control—that surrounds Sleeping Beauty's castle.

The relations among gender, nature, and conservationism are also in play here (and in *Snow White*): the heroic Prince—masculine, civilized power—is pitted against Maleficent—feminine, wild power.[26] The power of the masculine over nature figures in the famous scene when Aurora sings "Once upon a Dream." The forest animals adore Aurora, and unwittingly move the love plot forward when they steal the Prince's cloak and boots and disguise themselves as Aurora's pretend suitor. Aurora happily dances with a precariously balanced semblance of her dream Prince, but, at one point, after a spin away, Aurora returns to the arms of Prince Phillip himself as he takes the place of his animal imitators, who, startled, scatter back to their places in the forest. This scene signifies on many levels: Aurora's spin away keeps her in her dream, in innocence; her spin "back"—her first face-to-face meeting with Prince Phillip—tips her from fantasy into reality, from childhood into womanhood. Aurora and her animal companions rearrange themselves in a hierarchy that authorizes the Prince as sovereign. The animals in *Snow White* and *Sleeping Beauty* enhance Disney's medievalized ecologies. Surely in some previous golden age (we are never far from the pastoral in this medievalized landscape), we might have been able to talk to the animals? And they mutely loved us back?

### The Cinematic Frame and the Aesthetics of the Medieval

If national parks were established for the enjoyment of natural beauty, among other things, it should not be overlooked that enjoyment and appreciation are not natural processes, but are, to some extent, learned. Alison Byerly writes persuasively about the influence that the picturesque had on the policies that shaped the American park system. Nature was made to fit an aesthetic in which the tableau was privileged: "many parks and gardens needed tasteful 'improvements' in order to conform. This aestheticization of landscape removed it from the realm of nature and designated it as a legitimate object of artistic consumption." Byerly argues that nineteenth-century responses to the wild nature of the American West were influenced by the philosophical/aesthetic idea of the sublime; that is, the experience of a landscape as awe-inspiring, immense, and seemingly infinite. However, the sublime soon gave way to the picturesque through, Byerly argues, the "conscious aesthetic framing of the landscape."[27]

Disney animator Marc Davis, who worked on both *Snow White* and *Sleeping Beauty* as well as on *Bambi*, is also invested in the tableau and the frame: he describes his art as taking "what nature has put before me and organiz[ing] it into its most decorative aspect."[28] In this respect, the cinematic frame not only circumscribes medievalized nature in *Snow White* and *Sleeping Beauty*, but also confirms nature's status as an aestheticized object. When one compares the two films, *Snow White* looks boxed-in, a pretty sylvan scene in a frame; in contrast, *Sleeping Beauty* offers the illusion of a vast wild nature extending outside of the camera's frame of reference. The difference is largely the result of an innovation in technology: *Sleeping Beauty*, like *Snow White*, was shot in Technicolor, but Disney combined it with a process called Technirama, which creates a sweeping panoramic view. Because Technirama requires a wider screen, the animators worked with unusually large sheets of paper as they produced their drawings. *Snow White* maintains an intimacy of scene (as in the picturesque), while the backgrounds in *Sleeping Beauty* suggest depth and distance (as if the animators were striving for the sublime).

The framing of nature in these two films is made legible through Disney's use of already-available discursive systems: in general, landscape painting and nature photography, and in particular, pictorial representations of the medieval landscape. What registers as real is not nature, or even a representation of nature or an allusion to nature, but the feeling that the two films are "just like" the green world of the illuminated manuscript or tapestry—whether produced in the Middle Ages or imitated by later artists such as the pre-Raphaelites. In contrast to the increasingly suburbanized and urbanized mid-twentieth-century landscape, the medievalized and magical *then* of *Snow White and the Seven Dwarfs* and *Sleeping Beauty* is vastly preferable, capable of arousing strong feelings for a nature that never was, a nature that only exists representationally—in other words, following Derrida, only tautologically real.

### Remediation and Realism

Realism as a value in animated films may seem counterintuitive; that such an ideal evolved can be explained in part through Jay Bolter and Richard Grusin's formulation of *remediation*, which they define as "the representation of one medium in another."[29] The pointing hand on the computer screen, for example, has its antecedent in the pointing finger in the margins of the medieval manuscript; photography imitated painting; film borrowed from photography; the digital now quotes the analog. Cartoons, of course, are not new media surpassing older forms; cartoons developed alongside live-action film. Still, both cinematic forms remediatize textual narrative, photography, and painting; animation also remediatizes the comic strip.

Bolter and Grusin argue that remediation is driven by a "double logic" of "immediacy" and "hypermediacy." Immediacy is the fantasy that there is no medium, but simply the experience. Hypermediacy is the continual awareness of media as media. The cartoon or animated film is by definition hypermediate, which has not prevented critics and film-goers from experiencing animation as immediate—as real, which is perhaps best explained by Jean Baudrillard's idea of the simulacrum, in which the real has "no origin" and "substitute[s] the signs of the real for the real."[30] Odd as it may seem, advances in animation, an art form that lends itself to infinite representations of fantasy, have often been driven by a desire for realistic representation.[31] Both the limits of technology and an interest in privileging an indexical relation between characters and the real world help to explain why the first cartoon characters were caricatures: animators, happily creating imaginary worlds, were not quite willing to ask their audiences to suspend their disbelief by attempting to deliver "real" human figures.

But there is a logic to the privileging of realism in animation. We can see it in Disney's development of *Snow White* and *Sleeping Beauty*. While Disney would never have expressed it this way, his choice to remediatize the fairy tale succeeds brilliantly because his audience already knows, if not the details of a given fairy tale, how fairy tales work generally and generically. As Tison Pugh phrases it in the Introduction, the fairy tale is "medieval-ish." Moreover, in these films, Disney does not turn to the "real world" for his animations of nature—Yosemite, the New Forest, or the Białowieża Puszcza, say—rather, Disney turns to other discursive systems for his forests and animals: storybook illustrations, medieval tapestries, and illuminated manuscripts. Disney chose to remediatize medieval, medievalized, and "medieval-ish" representations of nature, not nature itself. Already familiar with such representations, viewers are disposed to experience nature in *Snow White* and *Sleeping Beauty* as "real." In fact, nature is not present in these two films. Instead, we see pictures of a nature located elsewhere and else*time*, a *mise en abîme* of images that never references the real world at all, but only the "plausibl[y] ... familiar," as Catherine Besley would say.[32]

While Disney would be aghast to think that he had anything in common with Jean Cocteau, what Cocteau calls the *réalisme irréel* (unreal realism) of cinema applies here, for film, as he says, "makes it possible to show irreality with a realism that impels the spectator to believe in it."[33] Disney's fantasy and Cocteau's *irréel* is made "intelligible as realism" because of a "conventional and therefore familiar, 'recognizable' articulation and distribution of concepts. It is intelligible as 'realistic' because it reproduces what we already seem to know."[34] I am tempted to read Disney's exploitation of already-known representations of the Middle Ages as a brilliant (and punning) application of the "natural" law of conservation: textuality—or perhaps cinematextuality—is a closed system, and is made up of a limited set of figures/images (in spite of their seeming infinitude) that cannot be created or destroyed, but only transformed—here, from one medium to another.

### Medievalized Nature, Melancholy, and Yasgur's Farm

The imagined, medievalized ecologies of *Snow White* and *Sleeping Beauty* have a place in early twentieth-century conservationist discourse. In many respects, conservationism is simply good business, for government, for companies dependent on natural resources (timber, fossil fuels)—and for Disney. Today, the Disney Worldwide Conservation Fund (established on Earth Day in 1995) is described on the Walt Disney website as a "global awards program for the study and protection of the world's wildlife and ecosystems." Disney's Animal Kingdom, which opened in Orlando in 1998 (also on Earth Day), is a conservationist effort built on a paradox that Michael Eisner describes with what ecologists would view as misplaced irony: "Thirty years ago, all you could find on our Orlando property were vast herds of grazing animals and some rather intimidating reptiles. Today, after billions of dollars of investment, we have unveiled our most original theme park concept yet: vast herds of grazing animals and some rather intimidating reptiles."[35] The destruction of the central Florida habitat in order to build another habitat for exotic animals designed for the viewing pleasure of human visitors is, for many environmental activists, conservationism at its worst, and the Walt Disney Company has been thoroughly criticized for it. This displacement of an indigenous nature with an exotic nature (however endangered) puts into unhappy relief the degree to which nature, when transformed into a conservationist "idea," becomes something to be manipulated for human purposes—and economic gain.

Hoping to pursue this point further, I emailed the Walt Disney World Resort in search of a document that was on their website when I began this project: a charter signed by then-governor Jeb Bush in which the Walt Disney Company declares its commitment to conservationism, explaining that the use and enjoyment of Florida's natural resources brings billions of dollars into the state. The letter that I received in response stated that the charter was "unavailable" and continued: "Since the company's earliest days, conservation and the environment have been recurring themes in Disney offerings, from motion pictures and television programming to our parks and resorts." This is absolutely true, but perhaps not always in the firmly positive way intended by the authors of Disney form letters. Continuing to promote old-style conservationism today may actually hobble the growth of responsible environmental consciousness.

Disney's location of nature in *Snow White* and *Sleeping Beauty* in the Middle Ages represents nature as past, as always already not here, not now, not us, which surely contributes to creating conditions for exploitation, out of calculated risk for profit, or ignorance, or even despair: "Nature is gone. It was gone before you were born, before your parents were born, before the pilgrims arrived, before the pyramids were built. You are living on a used planet."[36] To say so, even for rhetorical effect as Erle Ellis does here, dramatizes the danger of constructing a largely nostalgic, even melancholic, relation with nature. And melancholy is a state with which many medievalists are quite familiar. A longing for the past is, as Louise Fradenburg describes it, the hallmark of medievalism in the academy: "So much medievalism has kept itself inspired—kept itself desiring—through an extremely romantic equation of modernity with deprivation and of the past as a fullness which must be recovered."[37] *Snow White* and *Sleeping Beauty* can be read as locating this "fullness" in images that refer to an imaginary (though, paradoxically, recognizable) preindustrial past; however, what is recovered is a remediatized image of nature, not nature itself. Nature, like the past, ultimately resists recovery. Instead of experiencing ourselves as "enmeshed" in nature, a "radical intimacy, coexistence with other beings, sentient or otherwise" as Tim Morton argues for, we instead may find ourselves enmeshed in an endless discursive loop.[38]

The idea of nature-as-past is not unique to the films under discussion. Nature writing, which includes quasi-fictional accounts (such as Farley Mowat's *Never Cry Wolf* [1963], made into a film by Disney in 1983), creative nonfiction, and personal memoir (often mixed with scientific observation), is often elegiac in tone. Sometimes utopian and dystopian speculative fictions depend upon contrasting a polluted, urbanized setting with an idealized landscape that exists in time either before or after the "now" of the novel. In H. G. Wells' *The Time Machine* (1895), the Time Traveler at first thinks he has discovered a peaceful, pastoral setting (and problematically, as it turns out, which is typical in much utopian/dystopian fiction). In Margaret Atwood's *The Year of the Flood* (2009), people remember, or have heard stories about, or find remnants of, a lost, pristine planet Earth. In memoir, a familiar trope involves dwelling upon the lost, special places of youth. (Verlyn Klinkenborg's *The Last Fine Time* [1991] is a good example.) More generally and more relevant here is the nineteenth-century aesthetic resistance to industrialization known as medievalism as it was expressed in literature and in the arts. The pre-Raphaelites, in their reinvention of a Quattrocento aesthetic, strove to represent a perfected nature that they extrapolated from their imaginary vision/version of the Middle Ages. Moreover, one might productively argue that this sort of medievalism is co-incident with, if not complicit in, the modern construction of "nature" as a place and an idea separate from us.[39]

I had initially hoped to make a case for Disney as a generally positive influence on the post-World War II generation that is largely responsible for today's environmental (versus conservationist) movement. Thus when I came across Douglas Brode's *From Walt to Woodstock: How Disney Created the Counterculture*, I feared that I had been scooped. Brode's book is blurbed in this way:

Disney films preached pacifism, introduced a generation to the notion of feminism, offered the screen's first drug-trip imagery, encouraged young people to become runaways, insisted on the need for integration, advanced the notion of a sexual revolution, created the concept of multiculturalism, called for a return to nature, nourished the cult of the righteous outlaw, justified violent radicalism in defense of individual rights, argued in favor of communal living, and encouraged antiauthoritarian attitudes.[40]

*From Walt to Woodstock* is, to paraphrase Graham Chapman, a silly book. It is full of errors and extravagant claims. For example, Brode posits that Disney—a man who testified as a friendly witness before the House Un-American Activities Committee—"would have been thrilled" if he had lived to see Woodstock. Brode shares this anecdote: "One longhair, passing a toke to a companion, studiously observes the sex, drugs, and rock and roll around him. Smiling wryly, he sarcastically comments, 'Can you believe these kids were raised on *Disney* films?' His friend, while attempting to inhale, chokes on his own laughter."[41] The informed reader may detect one error already: one cannot pass a "toke." Possibly Brode invented the tale himself. However, it is true that the original Woodstock Nation (of which I am a member) grew up on Disney films. Children got back to the garden as they suspended their disbelief and entered into the worlds that Disney made. And while I cannot trace a direct line from Walt to Woodstock any more than Brode can, it scarcely needs arguing that Disney profoundly influenced those American baby boomers who went to the movies, watched television, read the children's books based on Disney films, or went to Disneyland (which opened in 1955). However, while some boomers grew up to renounce city life and form communes and small farms, others went to work for companies that manufactured chlorofluorocarbons. Mindful of my own boomer status, I must confess that I (medievalist, gardener, animal companion, kayaker) connected quite deeply with the little furry creatures and the magical forests of the films of Disney's Golden Age in just the way that most ecocritics scorn.

There is no easy answer to the question of whether Disney's idealized and medievalized representations of nature have done harm or good. Twentieth-century conservationism has evolved into many different, mostly more productive, positions on the environment. A case in point is the Deep Ecology movement, which stresses the interconnectedness of the Earth's ecosystem—a fully interdependent system in which humanity has a place, not at the top (below God and the angels in a Great Chain of Being), but simply a place. Deep Ecology in turn is interrogated by many who insist that we must deal with nature, not as a pristine something (which never existed) to be restored, but as it is now. Erle Ellis calls this position *postnaturalism*; Tim Morton, *the ecological thought*. Out of old-style conservationism ideas more thoughtful and viable have grown. The Walt Disney Company cannot now undo the exotic ecosystem that it has grafted onto the native Florida ecosystem, we cannot find or even make Snow White's forest in the real world, and we cannot return to a Woodstockian utopia held again at Max Yasgur's farm—a desire for such is rooted in melancholy. Instead, we can work through melancholy to grief—in Freud's formulation, grief entails acceptance—and recognize and even undo the ideologies that construct nature as other to us. There is a there there—it just happens to be here.[42]

### Notes

1. Matthew Roth, "Man Is in the Forest," *In-Visible Culture* 9.9 (2005); Web, accessed August 19, 2011.
2. John Ruskin, "The True and the Beautiful in Nature, Art, Morals and Religion," *Modern Painters, Vol. 1: Of General Principles and Truth* (Boston: Estes & Lauriat, 1894), 142.
3. Compare *Humorous Phases of Funny Faces* to the first animated projection on film, *Fantasmagorie* (Émile Cohl, 1908), shot on negative film in which a stick figure is the main character. The film's entire focus is on motion.
4. "Disney" in this essay is both the man and a monumental and rather complicated metonymy for first the company, then the studio, and, finally, the corporation. Disney generates strong feelings across the spectrum, from respect and admiration to contempt and hostility. As one might expect, the Disney website and the documentaries that are packaged with Disney's animated films on DVD and Blu-Ray are quite hagiographical (although there is the occasional crack in the façade). The scholarly reception of Disney is mostly antagonistic (e.g., Regina Cornwell, "Emperor of Animation," *Art in America* 69.10 [1981]: 113–20). It is a rare scholar who does *not* criticize Disney for sexist, racist, and classist representations. In agreement with such critiques, I find *The Little Mermaid* to be egregiously racist, speciesist, and obesist, and consider *Tangled* to be a facile, bourgeois exploitation of girl power.
5. See the "limited animation" cartoons made by United Productions of America (UPA) from the 1940s through the 1960s. Many contemporary cartoons eschew what we would call "background" altogether.
6. John Ruskin, *Modern Painters*, ed. Lawrence Woof (1846; Electronic Edition lancs.ac.uk/fass/ruskin/empi/index.htm), I.1.2.11.
7. John Ruskin, *Modern Painters*, II.1.1.49.
8. "Four Painters Paint One Tree," *Sleeping Beauty* Platinum Edition DVD (Walt Disney Home Entertainment, 2008).

9. Many ecocritics characterize Disney's depiction of nature as reductive and sentimentalizing. Patrick Murphy is particularly harsh: "Disney consistently attempts to reflect a sense of 'virginal' innocence promoting the 'magic' of childhood often through characters' friendships or ability to communicate with animals, while at the same time reflecting the cultural drive toward the conquest of nature through promoting a capitalist work ethic among dwarfs, princes, mice, servants, and heavily anthropomorphized animals" ("'The Whole Wide World Was Scrubbed Clean': The Androcentric Animation of Denatured Disney," *From Mouse to Mermaid: The Politics of Film, Gender, and Culture*, ed. Elizabeth Bell, Lynda Haas, and Laura Sells [Bloomington: Indiana University Press, 1995]: 125–36, at 126). But David Whitley, in *The Idea of Nature in Disney Animation* (Aldershot, Hampshire: Ashgate, 2008), asks us to consider that many of Disney's films both reflect and shape the various (and sometimes conflicting) ideologies that frame our understanding of the natural world. Whitley is not arguing that such Disneyfied understandings are correct, but instead focuses on the powerful emotional impact of Disney's representations of nature. Whitley argues from *pathos* in the best sense of the word (2).

10. Robert Ebert, "Snow White and the Seven Dwarfs (1937)," *Chicago Sun-Times* (October 14, 2001), rogerebert.suntimes.com; Web, accessed April 14, 2012.

11. "Still the Fairest of Them All: The Making of *Snow White*," *Snow White and the Seven Dwarfs Platinum Edition* DVD (Walt Disney Video, 2001).

12. John Flinn, "Snow White and the Seven Dwarfs," *Variety* (December 28, 1937), variety.com; Web, accessed April 14, 2012.

13. See Mary Swanson, *From Swedish Fairy Tales to American Fantasy: Gustaf Tenggren's Illustrations, 1920–1970* (Minneapolis: University of Minnesota Press, 1986).

14. Walt Disney, qtd. in Steven Watts, *The Magic Kingdom: Walt Disney and the American Way of Life* (Boston: Houghton Mifflin, 1997), 108.

15. Steven Watts, *The Magic Kingdom*, 70; 83–85.

16. Sergei Eisenstein, having in mind the grimness of the Depression, describes the world outside of the movie theater as comprising "grey squares of city blocks. Grey prison cells of city streets." He then goes on to say: "Disney's films are a revolt against partitioning and legislation, against spiritual stagnation and greyness. But the revolt is lyrical. The revolt is a daydream" (Jay Leyda, ed., *Eisenstein on Disney*, trans. Alan Upchurch [London: Methuen, 1988], 3–4). Disney, according to Eisenstein, offers a way out, but it is only a fantasy.

17. A fundamental debate that fragments the current ecological movement focuses on the terms *conservationism* and *environmentalism*—terms that, in the minds of most Americans, overlap, to the point of being nearly synonymous. Among contemporary ecological activists, however, the terms are clearly distinguished one from the other. Conservationism is

seen as being founded upon the notion of the use and management of the environment, a stance that presupposes that natural resources ought to be conserved for human use. Environmentalism, on the contrary, takes as its premise the idea that nature has an intrinsic value that is entirely independent of human use and participation; nature, for environmentalists, is not a consumable product. Traditional conservationism constructs nature as something to be controlled and shaped; contemporary environmentalism tends to recognize "nature" as the product of a culturally constructed discursive system and may, in some cases, seek to undo this system.

18. Gifford Pinchot, *The Training of a Forester* (Philadelphia: Lippincott, 1914).
19. Gifford Pinchot, *The Training of a Forester*, 13. Pinchot did not have the dwarfs' imagination: "For example, a forest may be handled so as to produce saw logs, telegraph poles, barrel hoops, firewood, tan bark, or turpentine" (13).
20. As Patrick Murphy sees it, Snow White exploits their unpaid labor ("'The Whole Wide World Was Scrubbed Clean,'" 126).
21. Winston Churchill, *Birth of Britain, Vol. 1. 1956–58* (London: Weidenfeld & Nicolson, 2002), 60.
22. Roger Ebert; John Culhane, "Snow White at 50: Undimmed Magic," *New York Times* (12 Jul. 1987), articles.nytimes.com; Web, accessed April 14, 2012.
23. "Picture Perfect: The Making of *Sleeping Beauty*," *Sleeping Beauty Platinum Edition* DVD.
24. April Daien. "A Chat with Eyvind Earle," eyvindearle.com, Web, accessed August 19, 2011.
25. "Picture Perfect: The Making of *Sleeping Beauty*."
26. See Elizabeth Bell, *From Mouse to Mermaid*, 107–24, for one of many feminist readings of Maleficent.
27. Alison Byerly, "The Uses of Landscape," *The Ecocriticism Reader*, ed. Cheryl Glotfelty and Harold Fromm (Athens: University of Georgia Press, 1996), 52–68, at 53.
28. "Four Painters Paint One Tree."
29. Jay Bolter and Richard Grusin, *Remediation: Understanding New Media* (Cambridge: MIT Press, 2000), 45.
30. Jean Baudrillard, "The Precession of Simulacra," *Simulacra and Simulation*, trans. Sheila Glaser (1981; Ann Arbor: University of Michigan Press, 1994), 1–42, at 1–2.
31. To say so is not to discount the many fine animated films generated in reaction to realism; see Lev Manovich, "'Reality' Effects in Computer Animation," *A Reader in Animation Studies*, ed. Jayne Pilling (London: Libbey, 1997), 5–15, at 6–7, and Paul Wells, *Animation and America* (New Brunswick: Rutgers University Press, 2002), 44–49.
32. Catherine Belsey, *Critical Practice* (London: Routledge, 1980), 47. When Aurora pricks her finger in *Sleeping Beauty*, we see the scene indirectly, as a shadow on the wall. Perhaps we can read this *mise en abîme* as a moment in which the film recognizes its status as simulacra.

33. Jean Cocteau, *Entretiens sur le cinématographe*, ed. A. Bernard and C. Gauteur (Paris: Pierre Belfond, 1973), 138.
34. Catherine Belsey, *Critical Practice*, 47.
35. Michael Eisner, *Work in Progress* (New York: Random House, 1998), 404.
36. Erle Ellis, "Stop Trying to Save the Planet," *Wired Science* (May 6, 2009); Web, accessed May 6, 2012.
37. Louise Fradenburg, "'Voice Memorial': Loss and Reparation in Chaucer's Poetry," *Exemplaria* 2.1 (1990): 169–202, at 177.
38. Tim Morton, *The Ecological Thought* (Cambridge: Harvard University Press, 2010), 8.
39. See Raymond Williams, "The Idea of Nature," *Problems in Materialism and Culture* (London: Verso, 1997), 67–85.
40. Douglas Brode, *From Walt to Woodstock: How Disney Created the Counterculture* (Austin: University of Texas Press, 2004), back cover.
41. Douglas Brode, *From Walt to Woodstock*, x and ix.
42. Susan Wall read a draft of this essay at a crucial time; as always, I am happy to express my thanks to her, as well as to Barry Hoberman, editor par excellence.

CHAPTER 12

# THE UNITED PRINCESSES OF AMERICA: ETHNIC DIVERSITY AND CULTURAL PURITY IN DISNEY'S MEDIEVAL PAST

*Ilan Mitchell-Smith*

The moment for complaining about Disney's ignorance of ethnic diversity seems to have passed when the release of *Aladdin* in 1992 proved to mainstream America that Disney's protagonists are not always white. In the years since, Disney films and television have continued to disavow themselves of their reputation for presenting racially selective characters and culturally exclusive subjects. The question of Disney's racial politics is especially pertinent to the Disney Princesses, who (since 1992) stand shoulder to shoulder on Disney advertising materials like a mixed-race sorority whose philanthropy consists of cheerfully role-modeling a racially diverse America. Disney's nonwhite Princess movies—*Aladdin*, *Pocahontas*, *Mulan*, and *The Princess and the Frog*—have yielded a variety of critical responses, from arguments that Disney represents nonwhite people and non-Western cultures only in pursuit of an economic bottom line to more critical assessments that find an abiding racism in Disney's representation of minority cultures and races. In considering Disney's presentation of young female protagonists and their racial and cultural identities, it is important to note that all Princesses come from their own specific fantasy pasts that are symbolically "medieval" in the sense that, for all of them, the modern world has not yet arrived. Even *The Princess and the Frog*, the most "modern" of the Disney Princess movies, is set in a fantasy version of New Orleans-of-the-past: an American medieval fantasy where a prince, an evil wizard, and a mystical shaman are as likely to appear as a jazz band or a steam boat. While some scholars address Disney's use of the past in its depiction of race, the tendency has been to see Disney's use of history as a mechanism by which the company furthers its American and Eurocentric agendas.[1]

Proceeding from these more sweeping arguments regarding the imperialist and racist project of Disney's treatment of ethnicity and the past, this chapter traces a consistent trend in which the hopes and desires of nonwhite Princesses are presented in conflicting and contradictory ways. Early in their films, nonwhite Princesses model stereotypical postfeminist American values, which are presented in contrast to the traditional and medieval(ish) cultures where these heroines live. The Princesses' ethnicities, represented not only by somatic characteristics of facial features and skin and hair color but also through clothing and jewelry, are separated from their cultures, which become the forces against which they must strive. Jasmine, for example, rejects the marital rules that the film *Aladdin* presents as culturally ancient and Middle Eastern; Pocahontas also acts against the cultural mores of her tribe; Mulan breaks with the laws forbidding female military service that are a part of her ancient Chinese custom; and Tiana frees herself from the poverty of the fantasy/old time African-American New Orleans ghetto, where the people are too complacent for her entrepreneurial aspirations. These protagonists, despite their varying sociotemporal settings, are modern American girls who find themselves in conflict with ancient and repressive regimes, and so they together symbolize an inevitable mixed-race American culture that is emerging for all people, in all places, and at all times of the past.

Towards the end of each Princess's story, this initial separation from traditional culture is compromised or even undone, and the Princesses often inhabit the very roles that they rejected earlier in their films. Despite voicing harsh criticism for their traditional cultures and the expectations of stereotypical femininity at the outset of their stories, these Princesses embrace and embody these expectations by the close of their narratives. Academic treatments of Disney Princess movies tend to approach this mixed message as a failure on the part of Disney to create Princesses with real agency or empowered voices. The success of these movies and their associated merchandise, though, suggests that the audience does not see this failure. Instead, the popular response to Disney's Princesses implies that audiences find in them positive and useful (if not empowered) role models. It is worth noting that the American popular imagination often depicts the medieval and/or fantasy past in conflicting ways, especially in presenting female identity. Medieval and medieval-fantasy films, for example, often indulge in idealized presentations of princesses side by side with round criticisms for how antifeminist the premodern past was.[2]

Disney follows this tradition in its presentation of nonwhite princess protagonists, essentially giving the audience two distinct Middle Ages: one embodying the negative stereotypes of traditional cultures and the other embodying the escapism of stereotypical princessdom. The conflicted messages at the ends of these films need not be viewed as weaknesses in script writing, but instead as a presentation of contradicting gendered identities, both of which audiences experience as true. These Princesses embrace a fantasy Old World embodied by traditional cultures at the same time that they are criticizing them for their failure to meet modern concerns. Disney's Middle Ages is, for these Princesses, a place where this free-form integration of seemingly exclusionary roles and ideas can take place, where businesswomen, soldiers, and activists can also be damsels in distress and decorated brides.

Academic treatments of Disney's films have responded to its conflicting depictions of Princess identity largely with sweeping criticism. While critics tend to agree that the nonwhite and non-Western Princesses are problematic in the way that they treat marginalized groups and female protagonists, they generally argue this point in two specific ways. One line of criticism proposes that these films advance American and Eurocentric agendas and that Disney's Princess movies reproduce marginal peoples in a way that benefits corporate and national ideologies. Scott Schaffer, for example, describes Disney's appropriation of other cultures' stories as a process of separating traditional narratives from their contexts in order to rewrite them in a way that props up American identity;[3] Erin Addison makes a similar argument in her reading of *Aladdin*'s Jasmine, arguing that her depiction is more American than Middle Eastern, while the antagonists of the film are heavily marked as Arabic and foreign.[4] In a similar vein, Henry Giroux and Janet Wasko outline the ways in which Disney writes America into the cultures that it reproduces for its films.[5] Another line of critique argues that Disney Princesses, initially presented as empowered and feisty, unravel their own empowerment by stepping into traditional and culturally appropriate roles at the end of their stories.[6] These two areas of criticism leave the question of diversity and multiculturalism in a tricky spot: if Princesses model modern and American values, they are open to the criticism that they are not truly representing members of their culture, but instead are thinly veiled Americans. On the other hand, if Princesses behave in ways that are traditional and culturally sanctioned, they are open to the criticism that they have ceded their voices or their agency and are submitting to conservative, outdated, and ultimately antifeminist value systems.

The issue of diversity is further complicated because academic treatments of multiculturalism in these films often rely on a loose bundle of identity-making categories such as culture, ethnicity, and geographical areas of origin. The idea of "origin" is especially pertinent here, as perceptions of race and identity tend to rely on assumed relationships between present identities and premodern geographies and cultures. All races, cultures, and ethnicities are often imagined to have come from a kind of medieval "before time," in which this bundle of identity markers was more tightly bound and ethnicity and culture were neatly placed within well-defined geographical spaces. Disney relies heavily on this image of history and overtly represents the past as a time in which these categories of identity coincide such that ethnicity, culture, and geography are completely and simply synonymous.

Disney's preference for this version of the past, one in which races and cultures are segregated to their own originary areas, crystallizes an initial observation about Princess movies: not one of these movies is "diverse" or "multicultural." There is no representation of the world as a place in which different kinds of people coexist casually and unremarkably. The Eurocentric and exclusively Caucasian fantasies of *Snow White and the Seven Dwarfs*, *Sleeping Beauty*, and *Cinderella* are never integrated by nonwhites and non-Westerners. Instead, the worlds of the Disney Princesses are segregated ones, in which the racially marked geographies of different peoples are presented as "separate but equal." The justification for this depiction is, as mentioned above, the period of the setting as a kind of originary medieval before time—when the complications of racial and cultural difference can be neatly ignored because, presumably, no one had gone anywhere yet. If the medieval functions symbolically as a place and time before the complications of technology and urbanity, for Disney it is also a time before racial mixing. Instead of a multicultural or diverse worldview, Disney's representation of different peoples consists of changes in focus from its medieval and Eurocentric concern with female protagonism—primarily in the first five Disney Princess movies (*Snow White*, *Cinderella*, *Sleeping Beauty*, *The Little Mermaid*, and *Beauty and the Beast*)—to concentrate on "other" racially and culturally distinct geographies that are still, nevertheless, medieval in their settings.

*Aladdin*, for example, is set in an Arabia whose intentionally vague historical and geographical location allows for a unified and uncomplicated combination of ethnicity, culture, and nation in the sense that all characters are uniformly "ancient Arabians" (contrary to the ethnic and cultural difference that informed the Middle East even in the earliest periods). Similarly, *Pocahontas* distills all Native Americans into one totalizing representation of "natives of the time before white people" who are neatly located in a discrete geographical, cultural, and racial area. Historical accounts of Pocahontas's life reveal complicated interactions of different people and cross-racial and cross-cultural marriages, but the film avoids these complications in favor of a simple depiction in which white people and Indians are two distinct peoples with their own "home areas," even to the point of rewriting colonization and conquest into a peaceful parting of the two groups. *Mulan* relegates its players to a China of the ancient past wherein Chinese is a simple category that at once indicates ethnicity, culture, and nationality. Tiana in *The Princess and the Frog* could be the exception to these earlier Princesses, but the setting for her story is also heavily marked as a kind of before-time when ethnicity, culture, and geography are inseparable. Her fantasy New Orleans is represented not as a part of the larger America, but instead as its own self-contained culture and area. While the film contains white characters, these characters are presented as culturally separate; they are employers of African-Americans and consumers of African-American culture (in the form of music and food), but they are not of the culture, and their wealth keeps them separate from the *real* New Orleans.

A depiction of the past as a place where cultural, ethnic, and national categories completely overlap is presented in these films as natural and self-evident, but historical treatments of race and history tend to paint a more complicated picture. Furthermore, filmic representations of the past often vary from this model, and the results demonstrate that ethnicity and culture can easily be considered as separate categories, even in films set in the past. For example, *The Emperor's New Clothes* (2001) is set in Napoleon's France, but the actors and extras who inhabit the Paris of this film represent various races. The film does not overtly mention this representation, but instead quietly represents differently looking people as wholly French (nationally, culturally), yet racially mixed. Disney films do the opposite: the Disney Princesses, while racially varied since 1992, are all located in their own culturally specific geographies. The criticisms that most academics make against *Aladdin*—namely that it is a profoundly racist film that assigns negative racial stereotypes to antagonistic characters—is well founded and bears repeating. Under this criticism, the protagonists are read as modern and American, which is, again, an accurate assessment. They are not often read, however, as white. In fact, Dorothy Hurley, while finding the film (as others do) to contain an abundance of negative racial stereotypes, finds Aladdin's and Jasmine's hair to be significant in that it signals a nonwhite ethnicity. "Aside from indicating their Arab identity," she asserts, "blackness in this instance is also associated with the exotic (non-European-ness)."[7] Jasmine, then, reads as American in culture, as she also remains foreign and exotic in her ethnicity and geography (figure 12.1).

**Figure 12.1** Jasmine as Arabian princess.

This characterization of Jasmine as ethnically Arabian while culturally American is important because it reveals a similarity in the way that Disney depicts all of the nonwhite Princesses. They share characteristics that separate them from their cultures and associate them with modern America so that they present a unified and familiar notion of "Princess" to the consumer. This separation also effectively redefines the very idea of "Princess," such that the term has less to do with the class concerns of their originating culture and more to do with inner worth; the Princesses form a cohesive group regardless of their differing class backgrounds. The idea of the "Disney Princess" as a solid category is made unstable, however, because the Princesses themselves are kept irrevocably apart by their ethnicities and their specific and individual geographical settings. The subtle tension of this arrangement, in which they represent a uniform notion of "American princess" while their ethnicities and settings are profoundly different, is most apparent when the Princesses are displayed as a single cohesive group. As Clare Bradford discusses in chapter 10, the official Disney Princess website encourages this tension and further develops "Princessness" according to a kind of double identity, in which each Princess is both a modern and American role model and a representative of her culturally distinct and chronologically distant background. The official Princesses appear on the website arrayed in the center of the screen as a united group, and they take turns laughing and smiling as if they are all part of a single choreography of demure femininity. The group of Princesses is overtly diverse and integrated, and arranged such that the different skin colors and/or ethnicities are evenly distributed. The arrangement of the skin colors seems to be the only concern in the positioning of the Princesses, in fact, as no regard is given to the cultures, places, or historical periods from which each might have come. This presentation obscures the backgrounds and histories of each Princess in favor of an emphasis on appearance, and so ethnicity is pulled away from culture. Both Gabriel Gutiérrez and Lee Artz argue that Disney's diversity is ultimately based on a need to fit the demographics of consumer groups,[8] and this presentation of Princesses accomplishes this goal by representing the variety of skin colors that might make up an American audience. In considering the appearance of these Princesses, it is important to keep in mind that their production is sometimes driven by racist assumptions about body differences and body type. Pocahontas, for example, was created from a pastiche of female models, some Native American, some Filipino, and some African American.[9] The creators of Pocahontas describe this choice as an attempt to use a variety of "ethnic features" to depict a range of ethnicities in the single form of the native American Princess, such that girls from a range of ethnic groups might associate with her. The creators' frank description of their creative process is a bit shocking, but all of the Disney Princesses function in this way, especially on the website. When Disney makes another Princess movie featuring a nonwhite protagonist, in all likelihood we will not see a Japanese princess, nor will we see a subcontinental Indian one, because those skin colors and roughly defined racial categories are already represented by current members of the Princess pantheon. Because the Princesses on this website each stand for a range of physical appearances within America, they are all functioning as pastiches meant to evoke connection with a range of viewers.

Initially, the voice on the opening website welcomes the viewer to "the magical world of the Disney Princesses." Once on the initial page (described above), the voice then continually invites the viewer to "choose a princess, and experience her magical world." A difference emerges at this point between the singular world that all of the Princesses share (the world of the Princesses as represented by the initial page) versus the individual and discrete world of each Princess (*her* world). This difference is admittedly subtle in terms of the word choice of the narration, but the difference is more pronounced when the viewer clicks on a Princess and is transported to her specific and culturally marked world. While the initial page obscures cultural markers in favor of skin color and ethnicity, cultural differences are foregrounded when the viewer travels to a particular world.

On these individual Princess web pages, each Princess is pictured against a background featuring culturally and nationally specific images that locate her and the viewer in a particular culture and place in the past. The viewer is no longer in a shared world in which all of the Princesses speak with one voice, but instead the viewer finds herself in ancient and mythical China, or in the Arabia of *Aladdin*, or on the uncolonized cliffs of Pocahontas's early America. In the game that the viewer is encouraged to play on these pages (under the Princess is a bright button labeled "Play"), the selected Princess appears in her bedroom, which is also culturally and nationally coded. Each Princess's game is almost identical to the others: there is going to be some kind of celebration or tea party or parade, the Princess tells the viewer, and the Princess needs help choosing clothing and accessories for the event. The selection process for choosing these items is also exactly the same, but the clothing and accessories reflect the stereotyped aesthetic of each Princess's specific setting: Mulan's dresses are clearly Asian, Jasmine's are stereotypically Middle Eastern, and Pocahontas's accessories feature earth tones and foliage. The experience in navigating from one Princess page to the others is overwhelmingly "the same but different." They are all Princesses and the same on the initial page, but they live in the specific geographies of their own individual pasts. This experience leaves the viewer with a kind of double association with each Princess—on the one hand, each Princess must live in her own culture and geography, and on the other hand, each Princess inhabits, and represents, the unified Princess world that they all share.

This communal world that they all inhabit, which is pictured on the initial page, uses the spires of a medieval castle as the background for the groups of Princesses. It is significant that a medieval backdrop would serve as the background for this page, because it suggests that the medieval iconicity of a "princess" informs even the least medieval of these women. Pocahontas, after all, does not come from any kind of real Middle Ages, and Tiana is even more divorced from the Middle Ages in the literal or historical sense. When this initial web page presents viewers with the united image of these Princesses, though, they are all unmistakably medieval. This castle is also significant because, in addition to presenting as medieval, it also evokes the spires of the logo castle of the Walt Disney Company. As such, it represents not so much the historical Middle Ages, but instead the medieval fantasy of the Walt Disney Company in our contemporary world. In other words, the world that all of the Princesses share is contemporary America writ medieval by the fantasy of Disneyland.

The tension between the unified (modern American) world of the Princesses and each one's foreign and culturally specific world is not disruptive on the website. These worlds coexist seamlessly, and the Princesses flit back and forth easily between the homogenized/contemporary Disney world that they all share and their culturally specific temporalities and geographies. Nevertheless, the potential for incongruities is present here because these women not only are all American Princesses, but they are also anchored to their culturally specific origins in a kind of double consciousness that arises not between race and nation, as W. E. B. DuBois would use the term, but instead between past and present, between cultural background and contemporary identity.

This mild tension that informs the double consciousness of the website can be seen as emblematic of larger conflicts between the nonwhite Princesses and the cultural backgrounds that drive the plotlines and thematic development of these movies. This conflict is most evident in a similarity between the nonwhite Princesses: they are all, in one way or another, unhappy with the cultures that threaten to confine or limit them, and they all work to modernize their cultures. Rebecca-Anne Do Rozario identifies this discord in the later Disney Princess movies and sees it as a conflict between fathers and daughters.[10] Fathers and daughters are certainly a part of the equation, but the nonwhite Princesses are unhappy for a wider range of reasons: Jasmine feels confined and is kept from experiencing the larger world; Pocahontas is displeased with tribal warmongering and ecological ignorance and directs this displeasure at both the British/white explorers and the patriarchal rulership of her own people; Mulan is frustrated that the outdated and traditional proscription against female military service prevents her from saving her family's honor; and Tiana is unhappy with her poverty and the complacency of New Orleans as she hopes to start her own business. These Princesses are also urged or even pushed towards marriages that they reject, and so the idea of love and marriages in these later movies is complicated and folded into a larger question of choice and freedom in the face of constraining traditional cultures. Instead of singing about "some day" when a "prince will come" (as Snow White does), these Princesses sing songs in which their desires to free themselves from their constraining cultures are made clear. Jasmine sings of "A Whole New World" where people will not tell her what to do; Pocahontas lectures John Smith and the audience on their misperceptions of the wilderness; Mulan sings that she is "not meant to play this part" (of a traditional bride and a good daughter); and Tiana (in "Almost There") rejects "this old town" and its people, who "always take the easy way."

The rejected ancient and outdated codes of behavior are also depicted in these films as culturally foreign and temporally distant. The message is that these customs and cultural values have not yet caught up with the Princesses' ideas regarding gender and class, which are presented as common-sense reactions to stultifying ideologies and also read as contemporary and American. This trope is most obvious in the character of Mulan, who begins her story trying to wear an elaborate and traditional Chinese dress to attend an equally elaborate and traditional matchmaking ceremony, which should result in a wedding that will follow the same expectations for tradition, formality, and ridiculous and constricting clothing. When Mulan proves incompetent in performing traditional femininity, the audience is positioned to sympathize with her instead of viewing her as inept. The comedy of this scene arises in the tension between Mulan's contemporary worldview/personality and the outdated traditions of her foreign and weird culture. Similar expositions appear in the other films: Jasmine is not allowed to choose her husband, nor is she allowed to leave the castle, which echoes stereotypes of Middle Eastern female enclosure and control. While Pocahontas's worldview models the positive and new-age stereotypes of Native American culture—click a picture of Pocahontas on the website to learn how to construct a dream catcher—her father and tribe are depicted in terms of less positive stereotypes of Native Americans, including tribal warfare and, similar to both Jasmine and Mulan, arranged marriages. Tiana's depiction is more complicated because *The Princess and the Frog* accentuates positive portrayals of New Orleans, but the film nevertheless associates abject poverty with the African-American communities of New Orleans, and as her song suggests, the lazy nature of the town and the people are something she must avoid. The film is careful not to depict Tiana as desiring privileged white culture, but in Tiana's "planning-the-restaurant" song sequences, the old and dilapidated mill of Old New Orleans is replaced by a modern and urban night club, depicted in the northeastern artistic style of the Harlem Renaissance artist Aaron Douglas. Tiana's dreams of upward mobility remain in African-American culture, but they are switched to a northern and urban culture that stands in contrast to the poverty of southern, Old World New Orleans. The choice to make Voodoo (not the religion here, but the stereotypical medieval/fantasy magic associated with charlatans and the occult) the source of villainous power in the film accomplishes essentially the same goal: traditional African-American New Orleans culture is seen as culturally foreign, and it conflicts with the upwardly mobile, Horatio-Alger-style dreams of the protagonist.

A further separation is made between protagonists and their cultural backgrounds through accents and dialects that indicate otherness, whereas American accents read as natural and protagonistic in these films. Radha Jhappan and Daiva Stasiulis find that the presence of accents, especially British accents in Disney films, indicate authority and intelligence. Even in antagonistic characters such as Jafar, they argue, accents are associated with intelligence.[11] This is certainly the case in the Disney films—Jhappan's and Stasiulis's study is inclusive—but in the movies under discussion here the authority and intelligence that these accents represent are often undermined and represented as false. In focusing on the British accent, Jhappan and Stasiulis do not address the contrast between British and American accents, which, in Disney's Princess movies, are universally assigned to the female protagonists. The American audience is meant to identify with the protagonists, and so their accents resemble those of the audience, which renders them uncoded and therefore invisible. The American accent is the point of connection, then, between the audience and the Princess, but it is a point of difference between the audience/Princess and the other characters of the film, especially those of the older generation, who represent the culture and time in which the film is set. Whether they are in the form of overly traditional but loving parents (all of the parents in these films have accents heavier than their children, especially the fathers), well-meaning but comically ignorant sidekicks (such as the alligator and the dragonfly in *The Princess and the Frog*, who have pronounced accents associated with New Orleans and the "Bayou"), or dastardly villains, such as *Aladdin*'s Jafar, accents are assigned to those characters who represent the Old World and are, in most cases, laughable or antagonistic, and wielders of false or confused authority. The female protagonists, who speak in American accents, are presented in contrast to these characters and their associations with the outdated and foreign values of their cultures. For example, the fathers in all four of the nonwhite Princess movies speak with pronounced accents relating to their culture and geography. These are the same fathers who represent some of the constraining elements of these cultures, and so their patriarchal authority, represented by their accents, is meant to be doubted.[12]

The Princesses are therefore marked as American, but just as in their roles on the Princess web page, they maintain a definite and inescapable rooting in the Old World cultures from which they come. Jasmine, Pocahontas, Mulan, and Tiana are not modern Americans, after all, and placement within their own culturally discrete pasts and strong ethnic identifications maintains a continual tension for the audience. Under this tension, each Princess speaks in an American voice in a foreign time and place. While they all unanimously speak the values and culture of contemporary America, they remain Arabian, Native American, Chinese, and pre-civil-rights African American. Their voices, therefore, sound as an always-already emerging American culture that is depicted as an obvious truth, but one nevertheless to which only young women—only Princesses—have access.

Through their desires, their accents, and their ethnicities, these Princesses are positioned to criticize foreign and past cultures for being too medieval and for failing to be America. In this sense, the Princesses act as agents for American and corporate imperial agendas, as a number of scholars have argued.[13] What is interesting about the role that these Princesses play, however, is that their criticism, and their positions as contrary to their cultures, is often abandoned at the end of their narratives, or at least it is compromised. In *Aladdin*, for example, Jasmine begins the narrative as a modern and American voice who argues for marriage rights, desires to move around freely, and rejects the confined life of a Princess. Her dressing in commoner's clothing and her desire to see the world as it truly is suggests even more insurrections against the traditional values of her culture. By the end of the film, however, she marries a man her father approves of, and her engagement to Aladdin establishes her firmly as an entitled and protected Princess who is a solid representation of her culture. Mulan strives throughout her film to be taken seriously as a soldier and as an honor-bearing member of her family, but instead of remaining in the military, in the position she has won for herself, she gives up military life and marries the general's son. This is an especially important moment for our discussion, because Mulan's initial inability to act in a properly gendered way informs the exposition of her story and empowers her voice as a force for change against gender-based discrimination. What, then, are viewers to make of her rejecting her military career for a traditional marriage in which her gender role seems to be completely normative? Certainly, critics read the end of *Mulan* in ways that criticize Disney for not following through with a depiction of a strong woman, and to some extent Disney should be held to these charges. Giroux, for example, notes that, while Mulan "is presented as a bold female warrior who challenges traditional stereotypes of young women," at the end of the movie "the ultimate payoff for her bravery comes in the form of catching the handsome son of a general."[14] Artz affirms this reading of Mulan, and, like Giroux, assumes that the film's end cancels out any previous moments in which Mulan was empowered or displayed agency. Artz sees Disney films in general (including Princess films) as establishing or maintaining hierarchies that reinforce a strict social order, and he points out that these endings, in which the Princesses act in accordance with the values of their cultures, reinforce hierarchized social orders. In his reading of *Mulan*, Artz lists the accomplishments that Mulan achieves at length, but concludes abruptly that the marriage at the end of the narrative returns Mulan to her "proper place." "Ultimately," he argues, "traditional romance and Chinese feudalism survive."[15]

These criticisms reveal important ways that Disney films are invested in affirming dominant ideologies, but the preference that Giroux and Artz give to the final scenes misses the way that these Princesses continue to speak to their audiences not just from the end of their movies, but from all parts and from various popular depictions. Mulan, for example, appears on a variety of toys and posters and in a variety of books and sequels that continue after the initial film. A survey of the merchandise associated with Mulan reveals that Mulan-the-warrior cannot be dismissed as easily as her critics would assume. While she is often depicted in fancy Chinese dresses similar to the one that was so ridiculous at her film's beginning, she spends equal or more time wearing armor and carrying a sword, rejecting the "married-Mulan" image that she, in other clothing and accessories, affirms. Furthermore, the sequel to *Mulan* sees her back in action, and the plot of the story involves Mulan stopping three arranged marriages and saving three princesses, against whose passivity Mulan is constantly measured. To be fair, *Mulan II* was released after Giroux and Artz wrote their analyses, but this movie demonstrates that the character of Mulan, and all of the Princesses, have a pervading presence that emerges from all points of their narratives and products, and that the roles that they model do not come solely from the end of their narratives. Any discussion of Mulan as a role model would have to account for her dual identity: she is a soldier in armor saving China, and she is at the same time a beautiful and stereotypical Chinese princess married to a general's son, despite how much these roles might contradict each other.

Similar dual roles emerge towards the end of the other movies as well. Pocahontas, who voices modern ecological and political concerns and criticizes colonial exploitation, ends her movie with a simple expression of enduring love for a romantic male lead (who is also a white colonizer). She disappears back into her native land and people at the end of her film, becoming once again a fully embedded member of her culture and geography. In *The Princess and the Frog* as well, Tiana achieves her dreams of saving enough money to open her restaurant, but her success at saving pennies is paired with her marriage to the prince who, now that he has settled down, will presumably have access to the wealth of his parents. The film does not completely undercut Tiana's success at achieving her dreams, but her role as a young entrepreneur is overlaid with her role as a romantic Princess, and both identities operate separately but simultaneously at the end of the movie. While the critical response to such moments identifies the ways in which these scenes make the earlier empowerment of the Princesses untrue, the popular audience responds differently: consumers of Mulan, for example, will continue to think of her as the fighting Princess, and efforts to convince them otherwise would end up perpetuating the very reading they are purporting to prove. Furthermore, Irene Bedard, the actress who voiced Pocahontas, publicly spoke about her reaction, as a Native American, to the film. While she did not praise the movie for portraying its subjects accurately or correctly, she describes it as an important step towards a more true Native American presence in cinema.[16]

It is tempting, and to some degree important, to see Disney's presentation of ethnic identities as part of Disney's corporate and financial agenda that spits out damaging role models. We might also, though, see Disney's depictions as descriptive rather than prescriptive, in the sense that Disney is representing conflicted identities that already exist. Criticisms of Disney, and popular media in general, tend to proceed from the assumption that media influences our lives and our perceptions of ourselves. Mia Towbin and her colleagues, for example, state that "media are powerful sources of learning" for children, and these researchers assess Disney's full-length features to list both the positive and negative portrayals of issues such as race, gender, and sexual orientation before they conclude with suggestions for clinical applications.[17] Overreliance on the effect that narratives have on young female consumers can sometimes have the effect of painting children (especially female children) as completely passive and open to emotional and social control. We need to allow that children are often able to negotiate and manage their intake of ideas, and that consumption of culture might not be purely imitative. The very success of these films invites us to look beyond any negative impact that they pose to young consumers. Doing so reveals that Disney Princess movies use racially and culturally specific medieval pasts to offer a fantasy in which irresolvable tensions in contemporary American female identity can somehow coexist.

A final example from the Disney Princess website demonstrates this function of Disney's presentation of Princess identities. On this website, young girls are the most obvious audience, as most of the activities (e.g., the dress-up game and clips from the Princess movies) are geared towards their demographic. A secondary audience of the Princess franchise is also the parents who ultimately make the participation of the girls possible. For these parents (mothers are marketed to in particular), there is a section of the website entitled "Parenting a Princess" that features a blog entitled "Confessions from the Castle." This blog is interesting because it is not at all what the cynical viewer would expect: the posts are not overly pro-Disney, nor do they sell or even mention Disney products. Instead, these blogs become a place where mothers present and discuss the unresolvable and conflicting identities that they, and their girls, are trying to reconcile. In "An Eco-Princess Mani-Pedi," for example, Sabrina Weill blogs about her choice between the chemical-laden nail polish to which her daughter is drawn and the eco-friendly alternative that she has found.

What is interesting about this short piece is that there is no conclusion, no lesson, nor any didactic message. Instead, the mother and the daughter try together to reconcile their ecological and healthy choices against the very real draw of a "glittery top coat with floating pink sparkles and shiny floating pink hearts."[18] The resulting blog discussion reveals conflicting identities that both mother and daughter negotiate. Similarly, another entry deals with parental rules regarding makeup, and the author faces a similar negotiation: stereotypical female-gendered consumption is both desired and rejected, and the mothers and daughters explore ways in which ecological and feminist concerns share space with more stereotypical and traditional feminine behaviors and products. Like these blogs, the Disney Princesses Jasmine, Pocahontas, Mulan, and Tiana present a fantasy in which a non-Western cultural heritage can be claimed for its Princess-making potential while at the same time rejected for its failure to embody contemporary American sensibilities.

## Notes

1. For example, Scott Schaffer, "Disney and the Imagineering of Histories," *Postmodern Culture* 6.3 (1996): 1–34.
2. For example, in *Braveheart* (1995), the audience is invited to enjoy the "princessness" of Edward II's French wife while at the same time marveling at the medieval practice of "Prima Nocta." In *King Arthur* (2004), Keira Knightly's Guinevere not only is imprisoned and almost killed by a darkly "medieval" and antifeminist Roman Catholic religious cult, but is also depicted as a spirited and empowered fighting princess (alternating between fighting costumes and flowing dresses). These depictions are part of a larger trend in American popular depictions of the Middle Ages in which the period is both a savage time of barbarity and also a fantasized period of romance and heroism.
3. Scott Schaffer, "Disney and the Imagineering of Histories," 4–5.
4. Erin Addison, "Saving Other Women from Other Men: Disney's *Aladdin*," *Camera Obscura* 31 (1994): 5–26.
5. Henry Giroux, *The Mouse That Roared: Disney and the End of Innocence* (Lanham: Rowman & Littlefield, 1999), and Janet Wasko, *Understanding Disney: The Manufacture of Fantasy* (Williston, VT: Blackwell, 2001).
6. Lee Artz, "Monarchs, Monsters, and Multiculturalism: Disney's Menu for Global Hierarchy," *Rethinking Disney: Private Control, Public Dimensions*, ed. Mike Budd and Max Kirsch (Middletown: Wesleyan University Press, 2005), 75–98, is a good example of this kind of criticism.
7. Dorothy Hurley, "Seeing White: Children of Color and the Disney Fairy-Tale Princess," *Journal of Negro Education* 74.3 (2005): 221–32, at 226.
8. Gabriel Gutiérrez, "Deconstructing Disney: Chicano/a Children and Critical Race Theory," *Aztlán* 25.1 (2000): 7–46, at 19–21; and Lee Artz, "Monarchs, Monsters, and Multiculturalism," 80.

9. Leigh Edwards, "The United Colors of *Pocahontas*: Synthetic Miscegenation and Disney's Multiculturalism," *Narrative* 7.2 (1999): 147–68, at 151–52; and Gary Edgerton and Kathy Jackson, "Redesigning Pocahontas: Disney, the 'White Man's Indian,' and the Marketing of Dreams," *Journal of Popular Film and Television* 24.2 (1996): 90–98, at 94–95.
10. Rebecca-Anne Do Rozario, "The Princess and the Magic Kingdom: Beyond Nostalgia, the Function of the Disney Princess," *Women's Studies in Communication* 27.1 (2004): 34–59, at 53.
11. Radha Jhappan and Daiva Stasiulis, "Anglophilia and the Discreet Charm of the English Voice in Disney's *Pocahontas* Films," *Rethinking Disney: Private Control, Public Dimensions*, 151–80, at 153.
12. This argument applies least to Tiana's father. While he represents the poverty against which Tiana struggles, he wields little authority and Tiana is positioned to carry on his cooking ability as opposed to fighting against him. It is worth noting that Tiana's father has the least pronounced accent of all of the fathers in the nonwhite Princess films.
13. For example, see Scott Schaffer, "Disney and the Imagineering of Histories"; Henry Giroux, *The Mouse That Roared*; Wasko, *Understanding Disney*; and Heather Neff, "Strange Faces in the Mirror: The Ethics of Diversity in Children's Films," *The Lion and the Unicorn* 20.1 (1996): 50–65.
14. Henry Giroux, *The Mouse That Roared*, 102.
15. Lee Artz, "Monarchs, Monsters, and Multiculturalism," 84, 86.
16. Gary Edgerton and Kathy Jackson, "Redesigning Pocahontas," 95.
17. Mia Towbin, et al., "Images of Gender, Race, Age, and Sexual Orientation in Disney Feature-Length Animated Films," *Journal of Feminist Family Therapy* 15.4 (2003): 19–44, at 40.
18. Sabrina Weill, "An Eco-Princess Mani-Pedi" and "Little Princess, All Made Up," Confessions from the Castle, Disney.go.com; Web, accessed December 15, 2010.

CHAPTER 13

ESMERALDA OF NOTRE-DAME: THE GYPSY IN MEDIEVAL VIEW FROM HUGO TO DISNEY

*Allison Craven*

> "Truly ... it's a salamander, a nymph, a goddess, a bacchante from Mount Menelaus!" At that moment, one of the "salamander's" plaits of hair came down and a yellow copper coin ... rolled to the ground. "Ha! No it's not," he said, "it's a gypsy girl!" All illusion had vanished.
>
> Victor Hugo, *Notre-Dame of Paris* [1]

On the Feast of Fools, 1482, at the Palais de Justice, in Victor Hugo's *Notre-Dame de Paris* (1831), the eye of Pierre Gringoire is fixed upon La Esmeralda, whose dancing has captured the restive audience for his mystery play, *The Right Judgement of the Virgin Mary*. The vision of the dancer closes a prefigurative cycle of supernatural femininities from sainted Virgin to gypsy girl. Later, in a gypsy ritual overseen by Clopin at the Court of Miracles—the countersphere where the gypsies are enumerated as a violent tribe—Esmeralda saves Gringoire's life by marrying him. But she has also attracted the vengeful lust of Frollo, a witch-hunting priest and alchemist, who directs his servant Quasimodo, the hunch-backed bellringer, to abduct her. Phoebus, the knight, rescues her, and Quasimodo is severely punished on the pillory. During an assignation with Esmeralda, Phoebus is stabbed by Frollo and Esmeralda is arrested, tortured, and wrongly convicted for murder and witchcraft. Quasimodo rescues her from the gallows and takes her to asylum in the cathedral of Notre-Dame, but Frollo pursues her again until she is hanged. The story concludes with Quasimodo's disappearance from Notre-Dame and the discovery long after of two skeletons in an embrace, in the vault where Esmeralda's corpse was laid.

Disney's Esmeralda, in the 1996 animated *Hunchback of Notre Dame*, is transformed from Hugo's: she is no longer in terror of Frollo, nor naively trusting of Phoebus, or as grotesquely twinned with Quasimodo in the monstrous spectacle of their shared alterity. Disney's Esmeralda is a burlesque dancer, swinging around a pole and perching teasingly in Frollo's lap, confronting strangers in her housecoat. She is a woman for a profeminist cinema, brazenly defying Frollo, standing up for "her people," and showing thoroughly that "identity as constructed through the past cannot escape the charge of presentism."[2] The passage of this transformation, and the ways in which the faux Disney Middle Ages crystallizes from the framed temporalities of Hugo's historical novel, are canvassed in this chapter. Disney's medieval productions are mediated by what Kathleen Coyne Kelly and Tison Pugh characterize as "the oscillating effect between past and present" in screen medievalism,[3] and what Mikhail Bakhtin calls the chronotope of adventure time.[4] The rhetoric of oscillation is even more pronounced as Disney jauntily co-opts the "then" of the historical subjects as a quirk of their belonging now.

The retroprogressive spectacle of the makeover of Quasi, Esmeralda, and Phoebus as heroes to contemporary children, tweens, and teenagers was approximately five years in the making and began with the dispatch of an animation team to the precinct of Notre-Dame in Paris, expressly to honor Hugo's source novel. Disney's version retrieves characters and scenarios, temporally inflected in the upbeat parodic codes of classic feature animation, and in dialogue with earlier treatments in Hollywood films, notably Wallace Worsely's 1923 silent film and William Dieterle's 1939 version of *The Hunchback of Notre Dame*. Like these films, Disney's film upholds the iconic visual presence of Notre-Dame cathedral and maintains the narrative focus on the hunchback rather than on Esmeralda, a tweaking of the story that occurred in the earliest adaptations of Hugo's novel in the 1830s. Whereas a more deadpan pretence of the past is maintained in the Hollywood films, the Disney-animated Middle Ages is constantly bounced into the rhetoric of presentism through reflexive comedy and by the reinterpretation of Quasi as a troubled youth to appeal to the target audience. Esmeralda is incorporated as a sympathetic and sexy action heroine who supports Quasi's coming of age. Camp medievalism and Disney's burlesque temporalities are intrinsic to this rendition of the story as time and place are knowingly incorporated into the jokes, rendering the Disney medieval as a pastiche of (cinematic) modernity. Esmeralda's role is formed in a lineage of fictional gypsies that stems from the Orientalism of Hugo's own time: she is iconic of this Orientalism and of its retroactive adaptation by Disney. As animated identities, she and her companions are also subject to the renewability of current technologies, and as their appearance coincided with the onset of the era of digital animation, cartoon medievalism makes Esmeralda emblematic of the classic Disney medium: not obsolete but as exotic as the gypsy girl in Hugo's Paris.

## Hugo's Medievalism: Retrotemporality and the Spectacle of Notre-Dame

Hugo's *Notre-Dame de Paris* is an historical novel, a retro fantasy of the tail end of the medieval past celebrated in the post-Revolutionary Paris of Hugo's own era, during the period of the transformation of France from monarchy to social democracy. The drama of the novel depends, in part, on a view of the medieval as "barbaric other" to modernity.[5] Yet because it is an historical novel, John Sturrock argues that it is "more easily assimilated to contemporary historiography" in conveying a sense of "what daily life might have been like for various classes of Parisians" in 1482.[6] Hugo also incorporates a polemic about the preservation of Notre-Dame, detailing the architecture of the cathedral and inscribing a vantage point, from which the narrator-historian tells, in the chapter "A Bird's Eye View of Paris," "what view of the whole presented itself from on top of the towers of Notre-Dame in 1482" (136). The view is described in an extraordinarily detailed prose map of Paris in the fifteenth century— the old Cité, the University, and the Town—incorporating a history of the place in the preceding 350 years and embedding Hugo's wry criticisms of the contemporary administration. Hugo's novel is reputed to have generated a revival and restoration of the medieval cathedral of Notre-Dame that had been deconsecrated during the Revolution and incorporated into revolutionary practices.[7]

Hugo's interests in the cathedral are secular, and his comments on Notre-Dame concern social and architectural values, detailing variations between Gothic and Roman cathedrals, of which, he says, Notre-Dame is neither one nor the other (127). He praises it as a monumental "building of the transition" (128), combining both "the pointed, upward aspects" of the Gothic signifying "populism" and "licence and dissent from authority," and the Romanesque "rounded arch" signifying hierarchy and dogmatism, and it thus figures a societal transition "from one outlook to the other."[8] The grotesque body of the bellringer, Quasimodo, who dwells in the cathedral because of his deformity, is deeply associated with the social role of the building.[9] However, it was an English translation, *The Hunchback of Notre-Dame* (hereafter *The Hunchback*), that gave the work the title by which it continues to be known, with the effect of "switch[ing]… attention from the cathedral to its weird inhabitant," and thus subordinating the ideas to its plot.[10] This switch also displaces the gaze from a feminine spectacle (Cathedral of Our Lady) to the grotesque masculinity of Quasimodo.

Of the prominent versions of *The Hunchback* that contribute to the medieval archive of Hollywood film and influence Disney's, this emphasis on the spectacle of the hunchback has persisted, with male leads outranking the performance of Esmeralda, although her fate occupies most of Hugo's overarching plot and multiple subplots. Worseley's silent film was a vehicle for Lon Chaney's repertoire of monstrous masculinities,[11] and Patsy Ruth Miller in the role of Esmeralda undergoes a Cinderella narrative.[12] Dieterle's version featured Charles Laughton and Maureen O'Hara in the key roles and attempted to realize the "complexity of the [Hugo] original" above Worsley's.[13] The cathedral fills the opening shot, framed in a window before a zoom out reveals King Louis XI, who proclaims a newfangled printing press as a herald to a new order of progress against the "old writing" symbolized by the cathedral. Frollo demurs, vowing to protect France from "books" as well as from "witches, sorcerers, and gypsies." Esmeralda survives and the gypsies are liberated in this version, so that the gypsy is associated with the ascendant modern order, victorious and free. But her marriage to Gringoire leaves Quasimodo wishing he was "made of stone like" the gargoyles (a reference to Hugo). He is intricately part of the cathedral and its passing era, merging with its receding spectacle in a concluding distant shot.

A later French production directed by Jean Delannoy in 1956, starring Anthony Quinn and Gina Lollobrigida, is deeply loyal to Hugo's novel, and the *mise-en-scène* includes actual exteriors of Notre-Dame. Medieval time in these reenactments is—as it were—both fictive and "real," layered simulacra consisting of studio settings based on sites and scenarios drawn from Hugo's historiographic fiction, and condensing Hugo's elaborate descriptions of the cathedral into a monolithic symbol of time and place. Whereas in Hugo the cathedral is an expansively detailed environment that conjoins history and fiction, cinema in its capacity to visually depict and objectify the cathedral in a single depth shot has adapted its spectacle as a monstrous Gulliver, towering above the ville, that indexes the freakish human spectacles.

In all of the films, the towering height of the cathedral and belltower justifies an aesthetic of elevation, whereby the gaze of the hunchback is imposed as a dominant perspective. Hugo's Quasimodo is deformed, lame, deaf, and electively mute, and his disabilities have made him "vicious" (166). But he is not without desires and Hugo's portrait of Quasimodo details his intimate relationship with the cathedral, his "maternal edifice" (166): "crawling like a lizard" over its towers (164), "leaping from projection to projection," and "rummaging about in the belly of some sculpted gorgon" (169). This acrobatic spectacle of Quasimodo is adapted in all film versions, with Chaney scampering over the cathedral facade like a human fly, and Laughton and Quinn stepping more daintily but no less daringly, and Disney's animated Quasi more in flight around the cathedral than upon it. In the films, these scenes give rise to an emotive point of view attributed to the hunchback on high in the cathedral, a down-gaze that imputes Quasimodo's isolated confinement, and, perversely, his power. From on high he peers downwards, making the medieval seem as modern as a skyscraper. It is not the scrutinizing historiographic gaze of Hugo's over Paris, but a concentrated peering down on the populace in the square below, a plotting gaze, which is both poignant and disorienting in its contradiction of the base social rank of the monster. It is a gaze that, with his rescue of her to sanctuary, Esmeralda comes, briefly, to share.

Disney takes up these tropes, imposing the views of cartoon Paris with the cathedral central. Disney's publicity for *The Hunchback of Notre Dame* also incorporated the mystique and historical aura of the cathedral. *Disney Adventures* featured a special Hunchback comic, an article on Renaissance gargoyles, the history of Notre-Dame Cathedral, and a mini feature, "Cool Cathedrals Around the World."[14] Disney's dialogue with earlier film versions is most apparent in the way Disney modeled its hero, Quasi, on Laughton's hunchback, with a boulder-sized hunch, protruding eye, and red hair (a Hugo trait), and in verbal allusions, such as Laverne the gargoyle's observation that Quasi is "not made of stone like us." But the story of the gypsy and the hunchback is rewritten as a melodrama of a young man's insecurities and coming of age. Whereas Laughton's "unsightly" deformity (or this, at least, is how it is posed cinematically) in 1939 signified the alterity of medieval humanity, subject to nature's punishments for sin, Quasi's hunch is more emotional, his misshapen face and body suggestive of unformed adolescent physique. His world and self-perception are transformed by his encounters with Esmeralda. The medieval setting lingers obviously and decorously as a backdrop to his youthful qualms, which are expressed in a playful contemporary patter scripted from sitcom and Broadway.

## Disney's Medievalism: The Retroprogressive Playground

"I could use a drink ... ugh ... it's like a 1470 burgundy, not a good year."

Phoebus, voiced by Kevin Kline

Of all the lame gags in the burlesque book, Phoebus's lament on the state of medieval alcohol crystallizes the bouncing two-way mirror effect—"we're then but we're now"—of the medieval temporality in Disney's *Hunchback*. This sense of bounce is also iterated through an aesthetic of elevation—rising and falling—that is imposed throughout and initiated as the first titles roll. The towering cathedral of Notre-Dame is seen in the sky from above the clouds before the view drops to street level, with an animated "track" through medieval Paris, a place of banal national realism with a boulangerie and baker. It is a typical Disney winking appropriation of the establishing conventions of narrative cinema, and a nodding assertion that whether fairy tale or history, "what it might be, or have been, is like now," barring costume, the discontinuous quirks of animated montage, and the codes of Broadway. The effect is patently clear in the Gargoyle trio's—Victor, Hugo, and Laverne—show-stopping number, "She's Gotta Love a Guy Like You," complete with accordion riffs for Left-Bank atmosphere, and Hugo singing of "Paris, the city of lovers," way ahead of its twentieth-century time in 1482.

Some descendants of Hugo are said to have taken exception to the production, on the grounds of "omission of Hugo's name from the movie publicity" in France, and digression from the original plot, and the commercialization of the merchandise or "spinoffs."[15] But Kathryn Grossman argues compellingly that Disney's musical of *Notre-Dame* [sic] represents and commodifies Hugo's novel, "recreat[ing] the *mélange des genres*, strong visual effects, evocation of medieval Paris, and central role of the cathedral in the original."[16] She also finds comparison in the forms of merchandising that accompanied the novel in the 1830s—rag dolls of Quasimodo and Esmeralda—and argues that, since Hugo himself contributed to and authorized radical adaptations of *Notre-Dame* (and his other works), that "modern redactions ... merely extend this tradition," which Hugo "endorsed and encouraged."[17] Moreover, she suggests, in the 1990s, Disney's *Hunchback* "had become the pre-text to the text, itself a pre-text to reading Hugo's world," a reality honored in the seven-month-long exhibitions at the Victor Hugo Museum in Paris on the release of the film in France.[18] Hugo's world, of course, was in the nineteenth century, not the Middle Ages.

Even so, the capacity for medievalist cinema to, in Stephanie Trigg's words, "interrogate both the historical and ontological status of cinema itself"—explicit in "marginal parataxes" like the historiated lettering of titles[19]—is a quality that is both invoked and quietly lampooned in Disney's *Hunchback*.

It is a Disney style well established in earlier works of medievalism, like *Sword in the Stone* and *Beauty and the Beast*, in which a mythic moral discourse is heroically elevated and burlesque performance subverts the spectacle of anything other than the pastiche marvel of animation art, with the stone cathedral gargoyles coming to life and quipping of the medieval setting, "we're just part of the architecture." Thus Disney's *Hunchback* and its various musical, medieval settings seem hyperparodic of what Adrian Martin describes as the "intermedial effect" in "progressive" medievalist cinema since the 1970s that results, he argues, from the "layering of *different regimes of representation:* cinema, literature, theatre, musical performance."[20] Martin's examples are *Perceval le Gallois* and *Amor de Perdicao*, in which "the appeal ... to a medieval aesthetic provides a way of inventing a cinematic modernity," whereby the "literary weight of recited text is insisted upon; the action stops for a song or dance or intermedial demonstration of some sort ... creating all manner of deliberate anachronisms within the conventions of historical depiction." Martin argues that these films, both a long way from Disney, "seek to exaggerate, rather than to eliminate, the *strangeness* of the past, its alien-ness and unreadability—its *alterity*—in relation to our present day codes and mores," resulting in a mode that he coins as the "archaic innovative," a "tool" for dealing with the cultural present and the future.[21]

In cartoon medievalism, especially Disney's *Hunchback*, the parodic intermedial effect predominates, rendering the depicted temporality with excess and carnivalizing its historicity. Hugo's text, however, unlike *Perceval le Gallois*, is not medieval but a faux nineteenth-century imagining of the medieval. The Disney parody may operate intermedially, using similar kinds of devices to the archaic innovative "progressive" medievalism, but the effect produced by parody makes the past seem overly familiar, even indistinguishable from the present, warding off the potential uncanniness of the past, and with the same goal of devising a means of dealing with the present. There is a further layer of parody because it comments not only upon the historical past but also on earlier cinematic recitations of Hugo's text, all of which configure the competing forces of piety, tyranny, monstrousness, and carnival that evoke Hugo's fictive medievalism. In the context of Disney's address to children, animation also intermediates as a form of illustration, a picture-book aesthetic, and corresponds to the mid-Victorian practice of adapting classic tales for children, which were typified by elaborate illustration.[22] Less concerned with historicity than action and adventure, Disney's cartoon imposes modernity on the historical setting through its playful rendering of the medieval as a kind of playground, both industrial and performative. Adventure time, which is "primitive and anachronistic when compared to modern time," is foregrounded over the historical setting precisely because "adventure tropes are crucial" and "self-legitimating" to modernity.[23]

Disney's *Hunchback* playfully takes up the exiled, elevated gaze of the hunchback of earlier films, establishing it from the pre-title sequence, in which Clopin's shadow puppet of the hunched hero scurries up the belfry stairs, initiating an ascendant visual trope that draws the gaze and action upwards, and translating the meaning of this elevation for a younger audience. The elevation of the hunchback's adapted down-gaze is accordingly transformed: initially expressing a horror gaze of enslavement to superstition and then metamorphosing into the modern anxiety of a repressed adolescent. Disney's Quasi (mellifluously voiced by Tom Hulce) yearns to attend the Festival of Fools and thus seems to represent a teenager banned from a school sports team. His first solo set piece, "Out There," expresses his wish to join the world below, to be "not above them but part of them," while zipping acrobatically around the cathedral heights. The sequence concludes with a deliberate falling "pan" down to the street, where dancing Esmeralda first encounters Phoebus, the drop to street level reestablishing Quasi's distance and dominant down-gaze. Quasi's shy desire for the more mature Esmeralda brings about momentary inversions of the hunchback's down-gaze as he looks *up* to her not only because—unlike earlier hunchbacks—he is shorter (even if the tumescence of Disney animation creates variances in their heights). In this method of adaptation to a target audience of children and teenagers, the historical "then" of the setting is co-opted to sympathize with the youthful subjects and their acceptance as belonging now.

### Disney's Children of Notre-Dame

Disney's re-creation of the tale was not the first for children, as it was preceded by Tim Brooke-Hunt's Australian animated feature in 1986. But Disney's is undoubtedly the better known, and it targets an ambiguous age range. Amy Davis observes that in the 1990s, "darker themes" entered Disney animation in *Hunchback*, *Mulan*, *Tarzan*, and *Atlantis*, reflecting an address more to adolescents and adults.[24] Disney's *Hunchback* is a coming-of-age story but, as typical with addresses to multiple age groups, the main strategy is the reinvention of Quasimodo as "Quasi," the adolescent child (albeit of twenty years old). He is a maker of toys and subject to childish obedience to Frollo, who tutors him in the alphabet. Esmeralda's role is of a big-sisterly friend. The colorful carnival elements address young children: the color, masks, and dancing of the Feast of Fools; its Harlequin-like narrator, Clopin; and Djali, Esmeralda's goat, usually female, becomes male with comic orality (eating, burping, vocalizing, and smoking a pipe). Disney also erases most horror elements, notably the torture of Esmeralda, and burning is substituted for hanging as the threatened means of execution. By contriving a plot about Quasi desiring to attend the Festival against Frollo's wishes, Disney circumvents elements of Hugo's story that would threaten his innocence, such as his arrest and whipping. They stage his humiliation on the pillory, a brutal set piece from Hugo that is covered in all the films, in which Quasimodo languishes shirtless and tethered until Esmeralda, in an act of kindness, brings him water, for which he later repays her with rescue and sanctuary. In Disney's version, Frollo's goon soldiers bully Quasi at the Festival, enabling the intertextual set piece to unfold, with Esmeralda going a step further and freeing him from the wheel. Nor, in the film's resolution, does Quasi kill Frollo but rather watches from a perilous vantage as Frollo brings about his own demise. The preservation of the innocence of the hero is a Disney convention that the honoring of Hugo does not alter.

Through both Esmeralda and Quasi, Disney assimilates the staple figures of teenage fiction, the outsider and the underdog. Quasi's challenge is "self-actualization," and, if a good education is needed for success in *Sword in the Stone* and *Beauty and the Beast*,[25] in *The Hunchback*, the message concerns putting aside your differences to work together, as with Phoebus and Quasi. The risk in this for Quasi is less Frollo's ire than Esmeralda's attraction to Phoebus. Disney was criticized for "promoting a negative image of the handicapped, who are portrayed as objects unworthy of romantic love" in the sense that Quasi does not "get the girl" but hands her to Phoebus,[26] although in no version does the hunchback win the gypsy, and the hunchback's sexuality has always been delicately handled through the code of his ugliness. In an infantile gesture derived from Hugo, Laughton's Quasimodo covers his unsightly face in the close presence of O'Hara's Esmeralda; Chaney's id-beast flaunts his repugnance by flicking his tongue at onlookers but smiles and sighs benignly, if disgustingly, at Miller. Both O'Hara and Miller are girlish, unthreatening Esmeraldas. Disney's Esmeralda is more in the style of Delannoy's, played by Gina Lollobrigida, a glamorous earth-mother, saucy, intelligent, and witty, whose sexuality, in a French production of more desensitized times, is of less concern than in Hayes code-compliant Hollywood. Her opposite, Anthony Quinn (some years pre-*Alexis Zorbas*) is virile, tall, and athletic, and has a less pronounced hunch.

Disney's hunchback is regressed to Laughton's pre-Oedipal child; thus, the sexual threat to Esmeralda that is usually shared in the story between Frollo and Quasimodo is thoroughly attributed by Disney to Frollo. This is one of several gestures that impute Quasi's juvenescence and emphasize Esmeralda's sexual maturity and self-possession. Davis observes that these qualities in Esmeralda are more characteristic of Disney villainesses, whereas the heroine is more usually "young, naive and innocent,"[27] but these qualities are Quasi's in Disney's *Hunchback*. Accordingly, Disney circumspectly adapts the hunchback's love of the cathedral bells. Hugo's Quasimodo "loved [the bells] above all else"; he "caressed them" and "spoke to them" (166), and only his desire for Esmeralda distracts him from his "harem" (167). The various film hunchbacks perform this passion with gusto (even tragedy as Chaney tolls his own death knell) and the thundering bells distress the Esmeraldas—all except for Disney's. As the bells stand for something coyly felt by Quasi—his manhood—their potency is subsumed in Disney's theme song of the production, "The Bells of Notre Dame," which is rousingly imposed over the title sequences. The manly Phoebus, who was always a rival to the hunchback, is permitted by Disney to preempt Quasi in claiming "sanctuary" for Esmeralda in the cathedral well in advance of Quasi's heroic rescue of her from the pyre. Esmeralda's swooning and ill-fated attraction to Phoebus is adapted by Disney as a lively chemistry, and as Davis points out, they are initially on opposite sides until Phoebus rebels and joins Esmeralda's quest, and is then rescued several times by Esmeralda and owes his life to her.[28]

As medieval masculinities, adolescent and adult, were subject to a premodern worldview, Quasi's anxieties and Phoebus's dependence are temporally disoriented. As Vern Bullough explains, in medieval life male sexual performance was "key to being male" and male fragility was a threat to society, with witchcraft regarded as a main source of impotence and hence threat to maleness.[29] But as Kelly and Pugh argue, movie medievalisms "show the historical and representational implausibility of transhistorical sexuality."[30] Quasi's hunch, rather than a preternatural sign of disorder, is his burden of budding modern masculinity. Esmeralda offers him friendship, and the heroism with which he responds is a release from his burden. More befitting his era, Quasi does his man-thing for Esmeralda, not with bells, but when he shows her a secret route out of the belltower—down the outside. They escape safely after a near crash. Nervously, Quasi says, "I hope I didn't scare you"; Esmeralda replies, "Not for an instant." Djali—the first male goat in *Hunchback* history—utters a raspy chortle that appears to be cartoon goat-speak for an ironic, "Sure." Indeed, courtly love prevails, and, although Quasi's efforts outstrip the knight's, Phoebus (still in armor but modernized to a distinguished "soldier" and "Captain of the Guard") wins Esmeralda—or rather she wins him, rescuing him three times over, after he saves her just once (figure 13.1).

Their bond exceeds the narrative, expanding into a sequel, *The Hunchback of Notre Dame II: The Secret of the Bell*, in which Phoebus and Esmeralda have borne a child, Zephyr, a rare instance in Disney or any children's media in which principal characters reproduce. This sequel is aimed at young children, and Esmeralda and Phoebus are marginal in

**Figure 13.1** Quasi, Djali, and Esmeralda escape from Notre Dame.

the story, which concerns Quasi's childish romance with his new friend, Madellaine, and their adventure of rescuing Zephyr from the evil sorcerer, Sarousch, with a moral lesson for Quasi about learning to trust others. Esmeralda's sexuality evolves to motherhood in the series, but Quasi remains an adolescent child, subject to moral learning and emotional growth. Even in the retrotemporalities of postmodern medievalism, they will never be together.

## Gypsy Magic: Esmeralda and the Exotic Art of Animation

> The two of them remained for a few moments without moving, in silent consideration, he of so much grace, she of so much ugliness.
> 
> Victor Hugo, *Notre-Dame of Paris* (367)

The most amazing spectacle of Hugo's gypsy is her supernatural beauty. Juxtaposed with Quasimodo in a mutual gaze, there is a sense in which Esmeralda, too, is some kind of monster. This fictive tableau, high in the belltower, is unseen by any fictional audience, only the reader. It freezes the joint spectacle of their extreme marginality and frames for a moment the alterity of the medieval past as a spectacle of human grotesquerie—as curious as the baroque gargoyles that adorn Notre-Dame—literalized in the transfixed pair, gazing upon each other. But the medieval subject does not look back to the modern, and the tableau is not re-created in Disney's version. Instead, Quasi is overawed by Esmeralda when she visits his belfry, and she is charmed by him and the relative luxury of his apartments ("you've got so much room," she coos). A bedazzled youth, he responds by making a doll, a replica of Esmeralda, to add to his toy city. It is a reflexive gesture, the doll becoming an inner model of the film's animated heroine.

Gypsies were not uncommon in nineteenth-century literature and theater. The orientalism and glamour—in that medieval sense of bewitching—of Hugo's *femme fatale* Esmeralda eclipsed the fortune-telling gypsies constellated in rustic dramas and edged into the margins of major novels. By the early twentieth century, after numerous adaptations, Esmeralda had gained iconic status, appearing among the carnival costumes of the 1906 Butterick annual *Masquerades, Tableaux, and Drills*, along with the Goddess of Liberty, Josephine, Rosalind, Butterfly, and Mother Goose.[31] Her revival in the playful temporalities of Disney animation goes both to the history of gypsies in medieval Europe and to the atemporal aura of carnival gypsy girls. Disney's Esmeralda, a composite of the speaking voice of Demi Moore (and the singing voice of Heidi Mollenhauer), with Elizabeth Taylor eyes and bushy Lollobrigida hair and packaged in a gypsy costume, also bears a corporate aesthetic. Her good looks are normalized, her narrative role is dutifully subordinated to Quasi's coming of age, and her romance with Phoebus short-circuits the possibilities of Quasi's desires. All the features that Esmeralda shares with her antecedents—her dress, her dance, her religion, her desires—are temporally bounced: she is a gypsy "then," but an action heroine "now."

Esmeralda's appearance in the 1990s—the so-called Disney Decade, the period of its expansion into the largest media company in the world for a time[32]—was accompanied by the ethnically diverse heroines Jasmine, Pocahontas, and Mulan all performing contemporary femininities in historical or oriental settings. These characters apparently represented Disney's efforts to create more culturally inclusive fairy tales. They attracted critique, although sensitivity about Disney's treatment of race did not begin with the oriental girls of the 1990s: such concerns date back as far as *Song of the South* of 1946 and its "racially charged adaptation of ... Uncle Remus tales."[33] The critiques charged Disney with cynical inclusiveness, such as in Anne Ducille's observation that the "instant global gratification" afforded to children by fantasy toys from "Disney's Princess Jasmine to Mattel's Jamaican Barbie" presented merely "dye-dipped versions of archetypal white American beauty."[34] But the oriental heroines seem to exhibit more active physical presence and sexuality than their counterparts in earlier eras. Esmeralda is described as a new kind of Disney "tough gal" by Davis, who compares her to Meg (*Hercules*), Audrey (*Atlantis*), and Captain Amelia (*Treasure Planet*), extolling that they have a "voice" and can "take care of themselves."[35] Yet there is deep nostalgia in the construction of the retroprogressive oriental girls and the way the films, like *Aladdin* and *The Hunchback*, exhibit the influences of nineteenth-century Orientalism,[36] and this is emblematic in the gypsy, Esmeralda.

The carnival gypsy is comparable to the harem girl of Arabian tales as a generic oriental figure, what Aravamudan calls a "xenotrope," a term he coined to mean a "stereotype of the foreigner" or figure of the other that "produces exoticism alongside the dissertative [or moral] function" in oriental narratives.[37] But Orientalism is not singular, as a variety of Orientalisms flourished in French culture before and after the Revolution. The court of Madame de Pompadour favored various motifs,[38] and Moore explains that "Egyptomania hit Paris, courtesy of Napoleon's expedition; [and] the Turkish ambassador's arrival there in 1797 stimulated a craze for all things oriental."[39] Literature of the nineteenth century was filled with oriental tales based on the *Arabian Nights*.[40] Hugo himself, in a preface to *Les Orientales* in 1829, observed these influences in Europe and in his involuntary preoccupations as "Oriental colours came … to imprint themselves on all his thoughts, all his dreams; … in turn … Hebraic, Turkish, Greek, Persian, Arab, even Spanish, because Spain … is half African, Africa is half Asiatic."[41] This extraordinary confluence of cultures is embodied by Hugo's Esmeralda. The sixteen-year-old "Bohemian" is dark and her color is fetishized as having the "lovely golden sheen of Roman or Andalusian women" (82). Nomadic Esmeralda is thought to have come to France "via Hungary" and she has journeyed through "Spain … Catalonia … Sicily … the kingdom of Algiers," from whence she "brought … weird dialects, songs, and alien notions, which had turned her language into something as motley as her half-Parisian, half-African costume" (263). Her name is ridiculed as "Egyptiac" (75), and she is numerously referred to as "Egyptian," although her characterization is not wholly of Egyptianate Orientalism but rather combines fantasy elements with the activities of historical gypsies in Europe.

Historical Orientals in French society, according to Susan McLary, included both gypsies and Jews, and both groups were feared, she says, more than actual Middle Easterners because of their multilingual ability to "pass" as indigenous in the host culture. Gypsies performed exotic songs and dances "for … popular audiences in Paris," meaning a bohemian subculture, posing both class and sexual threats.[42] Hugo's Esmeralda is such a gypsy and is also comparable to Bizet's Carmen as she sings like a bird and speaks in a cobbled Spanish (86). The goat, Djali, who accompanies her everywhere, spells witchcraft to Frollo, and acts as a sign of Esmeralda's abject hybridity and social liminality and, by assimilating the animal, also pairs her with the beastly Quasimodo (whom Hugo likens to a variety of animals).

The dance of the gypsy girl is a spectacle in all versions of *The Hunchback*. Hugo's descriptions vary in their eroticism but nonetheless detail her "golden ... bodice, ... billowing ... dress, her bare shoulders, her slender legs, uncovered now and again by her skirt" (82). In the 1923 film, Patsy Ruth Miller's lithe Esmeralda prances and twirls, balletic but modest, busking in a bodice trimmed with coins, her tambourine aloft. Maureen O'Hara in 1939 is similar in style, but her dance is framed within a show as "the flower of Egypt," the dancing "wonder," in which she performs in a gypsy costume, swapping her pinafore for gypsy skirt, peasant blouse, belt, scarf, and tambourine. The subversive lewdness of Frollo's desires are emblematic in Dieterle's film, when, in search of Esmeralda, he summons an "inspection" of all the "gypsy girls," and they appear in a line up, all dressed like Esmeralda, a chorus-line of white women in costume. Lollabrigida's raunchier Esmeralda, the first in color, appears in red, sings a la *Carmen*, and dances sensuously like a belly dancer with slow, serpentine gestures erupting to a tarantella sans tambourine but accompanied by the body music of coin bracelets and finger symbols, and a diegetic lute player. She is more obviously presented as an exotic oriental of ambiguous ethnicity (notwithstanding Lollabrigida's Italian accent in French or dubbed in English).

Disney's Esmeralda is a similar exotic dancer (and preproduction stills indicate that early drawings of Esmeralda were of an even leggier, harem-girl pole dancer).[43] Her first appearance suggests the trace of Egypt as she dances to an Eastern horn. Her costume is carnival gypsy: purple skirt, midriff cummerbund, coin-trimmed scarf, (off-shoulder) white peasant blouse, and hoop earring, bangles, and anklet. Her Festival performance gown is more Salome or Jezebel, red and diaphanous, and she wears an exotic tiara, not earrings. But this second costume is less seen in merchandise because Esmeralda more usually appears in spin-offs in her gypsy uniform. She is, after all, a warrior for a cause. Her fighting rivals her dancing as spectacle, and Phoebus says that she "fights almost as well as a man"; when she foils the guards with kicks and thwacks, he exclaims, "what a woman!" The cultural hybridity of Disney's dark heroine thus becomes a faint gender masquerade as well.

Her use of violence might suggest, as Narelle Campbell says of live-action medieval heroines in children's television, that there is a "dual message that female agency ... is not quite sufficient of itself—that a girl can attain her dreams if she has the support of masculine brute force."[44] Accordingly, Esmeralda's use of violence is presented as just, partly through her alliance with Phoebus, who joins her cause and who survives because of her courage. Her exploits are also harmonized and justified through the scene of her prayer to the Virgin for her "people," her much-vaunted song "God Help the Outcasts," in which her indeterminate cultural background is interpreted as latently or innately Christian. The prayer of Disney's Esmeralda, however, has no source in Hugo, where not only are invocations to the Virgin uttered by those who wish the gypsy dead but, more subversively, chaste, heathen Esmeralda is venerated by her gypsy tribe "like a Virgin Mary" (263). The prayer song in Disney, instead, appears adapted from Dieterle's film, even to the juxtaposition with the greedy prayers of other female worshippers for material blessings. In both films, the gypsy is Christianized, magically aligning Esmeralda with Disney ideology, and resetting gypsy time for Hugo's faux-medieval Oriental.

In the telescoping time of postmodern media, the spectacle of the oriental girl, Esmeralda and her sisters, also now marks what was less apparent in the mid-1990s, the decline of the analog era of animation. Disney's distinct "pneumatic" style of photo-realist animation,[45] which had evolved with the ascendency of feature-length animation, its appeal grounded in the orthodoxy of realist form derived from live-action cinema, was undergoing a digital transformation.[46] In Disney's *Hunchback* the crowd scenes were computer generated,[47] as were some of the wild acrobatic antics of Quasimodo and Esmeralda.[48] This digitally influenced style of classic animation was bracketed with the established Disney brand as the first *Toy Story* had appeared in 1995 and the Disney/Pixar alliance in digital animated productions was gaining ascendancy. Arguably a more realist style, if posthuman likeness is preferred, digital animation has always targeted nonchild audiences. The style is accompanied by original plots rather than adaptations, or at least less transparent retellings. The illustrative aesthetic of conventional animation is eschewed both discursively and in the sense that hand-drawn images are obsolete in the form.

So, rather than a tool of the new, the animated medievalism of Disney's *Hunchback* becomes an emblem of a passing era and acquires a nostalgic aura of the exotic: an historic, illustrative medium, threatened by extinction. The dancing gypsy girl is thus closer to the spectacle of the first animated feature films in the 1930s, more reminiscent of the dancing heroine of *Snow White and the Seven Dwarfs* than iconic of the digital era. Whereas the discourse of femininity in mass media has long been invested in texts, arguably since the mid-1990s, it has been more invested in medium, making Disney's Esmeralda, like Hugo's Notre-Dame, a monumental image of this transition, and one whose medieval framing disguises her nineteenth-century character. The vibrancy of the gypsy is turned to nostalgia, at least in Disney's medieval playground where—to twist Gringoire—if not "vanished," the "illusion" is revealed. The Disney oeuvre has expanded dramatically since *The Hunchback*, the corporate expansion of the 1990s resulting in entertainment franchises well beyond the digital or classic series of animated feature films, the latter now the babysitters' choice for youngsters. The expansion has reinvigorated the market for adventure, transforming the view of Disney audiences as exclusively children yet adapting the same values of playful action-adventure spectacle to adult audiences, notably in a series of quasi-historical fantasy films, including recently *Prince of Persia: Sands of Time* (2010). Orientalism persists in these productions, and the live-action performance mode addresses adult audiences as it is less illustrative or parodic, and more flamboyantly mythic-realist, and minus the playful comic reflexivity and musical formats of classic animation. In either mode, bouncing burlesque or epic ancient, the illusion of historical temporalities supplements Disney's mediation of modernity via medievalism.

### Notes

1. Victor Hugo, *Notre-Dame de Paris*, trans. and ed. John Sturrock (1831; London: Penguin, 2004), 82; hereafter cited parenthetically. The quoted words are Gringoire's.
2. Kathleen Coyne Kelly and Tison Pugh, "Introduction: Queer History, Cinematic Medievalism, and the Impossibility of Sexuality," *Queer Movie Medievalisms*, ed. Kathleen Coyne Kelly and Tison Pugh (Surrey: Ashgate, 2009), 1–17, at 5.
3. Kathleen Coyne Kelly and Tison Pugh, "Introduction," 5.
4. Mikhail Bakhtin, *The Dialogic Imagination*, ed. Michael Holquist trans. Caryl Emerson and Michael Holquist (Austin: University of Texas Press, 1981).
5. To adapt Susan Aronstein, *Hollywood Knights: Arthurian Cinema and the Politics of Nostalgia* (New York: Palgrave Macmillan, 2005), 4.
6. John Sturrock, "Introduction," *Notre-Dame de Paris*, 7–24, at 13.
7. Lucy Moore, *Liberty: The Lives and Times of Six Women in Revolutionary France* (London: Harper Perennial, 2007).
8. John Sturrock, "Introduction," 17.
9. John Sturrock, "Introduction," 18.
10. John Sturrock, "Introduction," 11.
11. David Magill, "Spectacular Male Bodies and Jazz Age Celebrity Culture," *Framing Celebrity*, ed. Su Holmes and Sean Redmond (London: Routledge, 2006), 129–43.
12. Several versions of *Notre-Dame* made for film and television are not mentioned here, and at least two preceded Worseley's, including

*Notre-Dame de Paris* (dir. Albert Capellani, 1911) and *Esmeralda* (also known as *The Hunchback of Notre Dame*, dir. Edwin Collis, 1922, starring Sybil Thorndike and Booth Conway). There have been many other adaptations as plays, ballets, and other forms.
13. Kathryn Grossman, "From Classic to Pop Icon: Popularizing Hugo," *French Review* 74.3 (2001): 482–95, at 488.
14. These articles are found in *Disney Adventures* (October 1996), and include Liz Smith, "Great Gargoyles," 10–11; Chris Larson, "Quasimodo's Home: Take a Look Inside the Real Notre Dame," 27–29; and Chris Larson, "Cool Cathedrals Around the World," 41.
15. Kathryn Grossman, "From Classic to Pop Icon," 482. For comment on French audiences' reception of Disney's *Hunchback*, see Jacques Guyot, "France: Disney in the Land of Cultural Exception," *Dazzled by Disney? The Global Disney Audiences Project*, ed. Janet Wasko, Mark Phillips, and Eileen Meehan (London: Leicester University Press, 2001), 121–34.
16. Kathryn Grossman, "From Classic to Pop Icon," 488.
17. Kathryn Grossman, "From Classic to Pop Icon," 490, 486.
18. Kathryn Grossman, "From Classic to Pop Icon," 492.
19. Stephanie Trigg, "Transparent Walls: Stained Glass and Cinematic Medievalism," *Screening the Past* 26 (2009): n.p., latrobe.edu/au/screeningthepast; Web, accessed August 22, 2011.
20. Adrian Martin, "The Long Path Back: Medievalism and Film," *Screening the Past* 26 (2009): 7, latrobe.edu/au/screeningthepast; Web, accessed August 22, 2011.
21. Adrian Martin, "The Long Path Back," 7, 2.
22. For example, see Robert Mack, "Cultivating the Garden: Antoine Galland's *Arabian Nights* in the Traditions of English Literature," *The Arabian Nights in Historical Context*, ed. Saree Makdisi and Felicity Nussbaum (Oxford: Oxford University Press, 2008), 51–81.
23. Srinivas Aravamudan, "The Adventure Chronotope and the Oriental Xenotrope," *The Arabian Nights in Historical Context*, 235–63, at 242–43.
24. Amy Davis, *Good Girls and Wicked Witches: Women in Disney's Feature Animation* (Eastleigh: Libby, 2006), 219.
25. Adapting Susan Aronstein, *Hollywood Knights*, 85–88.
26. Kathryn Grossman, "From Classic to Pop Icon," 489.
27. Amy Davis, *Good Girls and Wicked Witches*, 208.
28. Amy Davis, *Good Girls and Wicked Witches*, 208.
29. Vern Bullough, "On Being a Male in the Middle Ages," *Medieval Masculinities*, ed. Clare Lees (Minneapolis: University of Minnesota Press, 1994), 31–46, at 41–42.
30. Kathleen Coyne Kelly and Tison Pugh, "Introduction," 9.
31. *Masquerades, Tableaux, and Drills* (New York: Butterick Publishing, 1906).
32. Janet Wasko, *Understanding Disney: The Manufacture of Fantasy* (Malden, MA: Blackwell, 2001).
33. J. P. Telotte, "The Changing Space of Animation: Disney's Hybrid Films of the 1940s," *Animation* 2 (2007): 245–58, at 252.

34. Anne Ducille, "Dyes and Dolls: Multicultural Barbie and the Merchandising of Difference," *Differences* 6.1 (1994): 48–68, at 49.
35. Amy Davis, *Good Girls and Wicked Witches*, 207.
36. See Alan Nadel, "A Whole New (Disney) World Order: *Aladdin*, Atomic Power, and the Muslim Middle East," *Visions of the East: Orientalism in Film*, ed. Matthew Bernstein and Gaylyn Studlar (New Jersey: Rutgers University Press, 1997), 184–203.
37. Srinivas Aravamudan, "The Adventure Chronotope," 247.
38. Christine Algrant, *Madame Pompadour: Mistress of France* (London: HarperCollins, 2003).
39. Lucy Moore, *Liberty*, 366.
40. Robert Mack, "Cultivating the Garden."
41. Victor Hugo, qtd. in Susan McClary, *Georges Bizet: Carmen* (Cambridge: Cambridge University Press, 1992), 30.
42. Susan McClary, *Georges Bizet*, 34.
43. "Early Production Reel," *The Hunchback of Notre Dame*, DVD (Walt Disney Pictures, 1996).
44. Narelle Campbell, "Medieval Reimaginings: Female Knights in Children's Television," *Screening the Past* 26 (2009): 4, latrobe.edu/au/screeningthepast; Web, accessed August 22, 2011.
45. Marina Warner, *From the Beast to the Blonde: On Fairy Tales and Their Tellers* (London: Chatto & Windus, 1994).
46. Paul Wells, "'Thou Art Translated': Analysing Animated Adaptation," *Visions of the East*, 199–213.
47. Eric Faden, "Crowd Control: Early Cinema, Sound, and Digital Images," *Journal of Film and Video* 53.2/3 (2001): 93–106.
48. "CGI Demo," *Hunchback of Notre Dame* DVD.

CHAPTER 14

REALITY REMIXED: NEOMEDIEVAL PRINCESS CULTURE IN DISNEY'S *ENCHANTED*

Maria Sachiko Cecire

"The real world and the animated world collide." This tagline, used to market the 2007 Disney film *Enchanted*, assumes an audience that knows what is meant by "real world" and "animated world." In particular, the animated world implied by the tagline is one defined by a history of Disney fairy-tale tropes, which invites potential viewers to enjoy its "collision" with reality. The slogan for this mixed animated and live-action Princess narrative suggests a subversive approach to the Disney canon, one that promises to grapple with the disjuncture between the medievalisms of its fairy-tale realms and the trappings of modern life. The result, however, is a film that refuses any historical anchor for Disney's fairy-tale ethos, fashioning instead what Carol Robinson and Pamela Clements call "neomedievalism," in order to insist upon the pervasive relevance of that ethos in the contemporary world.[1]

*Enchanted* was Disney's first return to the musical Princess film since the 1998 feature *Mulan*, and its first attempt at this mode of storytelling in the twenty-first century. At the time of *Enchanted*'s release, Disney had not produced an animated feature based on a European fairy tale since *Beauty and the Beast* (1991). The Disney brand nonetheless remained evocative of the medievalized fairy tale into the twenty-first century, as reflected in the Walt Disney Pictures logo—a turreted pseudomedieval castle—and in the continued popularity of its Princess merchandise. *Enchanted* marked a return to the European fairy tale, but rather than drawing upon a traditional story or legend, its plot derives from the tropes of canonical Disney films and is filled with references to the studio's animated features.

In *Enchanted*, characters from the medievalized realm of Andalasia appear in live-action New York City, transformed into "real" people and animals.[2] The film thus begins as an animated parody of Disney's formulaic fairy-tale narratives, but ends as an homage that rehabilitates the Disney brand and celebrates its apparent ability to turn reality into a fairy tale. This structure of transformation relies on the techniques of what Henry Jenkins has called "convergence culture," techniques, moreover, that are gendered.[3] In transforming masculine parody into feminine homage, *Enchanted* formally renegotiates the medievalist ideologies of gender that continually trouble the Princess genre, not only within the neomedieval Manhattan that it creates, but also, potentially, for individual viewers.

*Enchanted* comes well after the two major periods in Princess animation at Disney: the first being under Walt Disney's personal direction (producing *Snow White and the Seven Dwarfs*, *Cinderella*, and *Sleeping Beauty*) and the second under "Team Disney," led by Michael Eisner (yielding *The Little Mermaid*, *Beauty and the Beast*, *Aladdin*, *Pocahontas*, and *Mulan*).[4] *Enchanted* is thus distinguished by a retrospective and metatextual position relative to the medievalism of preceding Disney Princess films—a neomedievalism—that it realizes through the techniques of convergence culture. Jenkins defines convergence culture as "the flow of content across multiple media platforms, the cooperation between multiple media industries, and the migratory behavior of media audiences who will go almost anywhere in search of the kinds of entertainment experiences they want." It is highly participatory, in that consumers "seek out new information and make connections among dispersed media content," drawing upon the collective intelligence that a hyperconnected media environment enables.[5] *Enchanted* engages the same forms by manipulating Disney's own extensive media archive, making new connections as it maps "medieval" fairy-tale tropes onto modern-day New York City. This narrative strategy enables what Robinson and Clements call "neomedievalism," which is "further independent, further detached" from the Middle Ages than is medievalism; it "consciously, purposefully, and perhaps even laughingly reshap[es] itself into an alternate universe of medievalisms, a fantasy of medievalisms, a meta-medievalism."[6] *Enchanted's* play on the medievalisms of previous Disney fairy-tale films yields neomedievalisms that are self-aware and even further abstracted from the Middle Ages than their sources. Robinson and Clements suggest that such "[n]eomedieval constructs of the medieval lack the medieval sense of solidarity and finiteness—all is fragmentary, fluid, either susceptible or conducive (depending upon one's values) to constant change. In this way, neomedieval constructs participate in the postmodern techniques of fragmentation: anachronism, pastiche, bricolage."[7] Disney's appropriation of these techniques may be read as a tribute to its fans and an embracing of the new media landscape, but it is also an intervention in the consumer's participatory role: an attempt to provide company-approved guidelines for how viewers should create meaning from Disney films and products.

*Enchanted* opens with a reminder of the Walt Disney Company's multimediated neomedieval empire: the current iteration of the castle logo, introduced in 2006, appears as part of a sequence of sweeping aerial animation in the computer-animated style of Disney's Pixar films. This mash-up of the Cinderella/Sleeping Beauty castle dominates a pastoral landscape dotted with lights; a ship that recalls those of *The Pirates of the Caribbean* films (2003, 2006, 2007, 2011) and of the Disney theme-park rides sails down a river. A historically incongruous train emerges in a cloud of steam, evoking the American steam locomotives of the Walt Disney World Railroad. As the "camera" pulls back, the castle fills the screen in a confection of pastel spires and turrets. Fireworks erupt behind it, just as they do daily behind the castles of the Disney theme parks. The opening sequence confirms Jean Baudrillard's contention that Disney "seeks to erase time by synchronizing all the periods, all the cultures, in a single traveling motion, by juxtaposing them in a single scenario."[8] Indeed, this animated sequence resolves into the static Disney Pictures logo, asserting that this imagery of synchronous anachronisms and cultures is not merely branded by Disney; it *is* Disney.

*Enchanted* proclaims its place in the Disney canon, and in the canon of medievalized Princess narratives in particular, by placing its opening sequence inside the castle logo itself. A long zoom brings the viewer from the static logo shot through one of the castle's central windows and into an interior chamber, where a manuscript titled *Enchanted* lies on a flower-strewn podium. After the titles and music fade, the book opens, and then a voice-over narration begins, as if reading from the book's pages. This device pays homage to Disney's *Snow White and the Seven Dwarfs*, *Cinderella*, *Sleeping Beauty*, and *The Sword in the Stone*, each of which begins with narration from a richly illuminated manuscript. The *Enchanted* volume, however, opens to reveal a colorful pop-up book: at once a mass-produced commodity, storybook, and children's toy. Here the animators embrace Disney's status as the producer of beloved commodities and identify the brand's core consumers as children, or else former children who grew up with the Disney legacy. The first pop-up page unfolds into the Andalasian royal castle, and its turrets and towers recall the Disney Pictures logo that houses the book itself. This circularity implies the continuities between the idea of fairy-tale romance, Disney's animated films, and other Disney products that link the corporation to its consumers. And yet the three-dimensional quality of the pop-up book also suggests difference from the earlier films that use the manuscript device, signaling *Enchanted*'s roots in the modern rather than the medieval era, and a commitment to a form of representation that is at once more "realistic" (three-dimensional) and more self-consciously artifice. In this revamping of the traditional Disney codex, the opening sequence both welcomes its viewers into a "once upon a time world" and announces the film's neomedievalist framework.

The narration that accompanies the pop-up book establishes the premise for a typical Disney Princess narrative: the power-hungry queen of Andalasia fears that her stepson Edward will marry and take her throne. "And so," the narration concludes, "she did all in her power to prevent the prince from ever meeting the one special maiden with whom he would share true love's kiss." The book's computer-animated pages fade into Disney's traditional cel animation, which reveals the heroine Giselle flitting past the window of her woodland cottage—a copy of Aurora's in *Sleeping Beauty*—simultaneously with the words "the one special maiden." This shift in animation style implies a move backwards into the realm of fairy-tale films from Disney's hand-animated past, inviting the viewer to compare the plot to Disney's previous fairy-tale films. Edward meets Giselle within a few minutes of the animation's start, following first the sound of her singing voice and then a troll bent on capturing her. Giselle falls from a tree in her escape and lands in Edward's arms; upon learning her name, he cries, "We'll be married in the morning!" The two ride into the sunset, completing Giselle's song about true love's kiss as a duet. The succeeding scene depicts Giselle arriving at the palace the next morning, dressed in a wedding gown and accompanied by her absurdly large retinue of animal friends. Edward's stepmother Queen Narissa disguises herself as a crone and intercepts Giselle, pushing her into an enchanted wishing well that will take her to "a place where there are no happily ever afters." Giselle (now played by Amy Adams) emerges as a live-action character in Times Square, marking the start of the second part of the film. Giselle is sure that Edward (James Marsden) will rescue her, and waits for him with divorce lawyer and single father Robert (Patrick Dempsey) and his young daughter Morgan (Rachel Covey), whom she befriends. Alerted and then accompanied by Giselle's chipmunk friend Pip, Edward follows Giselle to New York, where Pip loses his power of speech. Narissa sends her henchman Nathaniel (Timothy Spall) after Edward to prevent him from finding Giselle, providing Nathaniel with three poisonous apples with which to kill the princess-to-be. The rest of the film chronicles Giselle and Robert's growing romance as Giselle influences Robert's practical view with her fairy-tale sensibilities, and as she begins to question her own "medieval" assumptions about love.

Carolyn Dinshaw has shown that, in contrast to Disney's fairy-tale medievalisms, the vernacular usage of the word "medieval" can come to stand for that which is backwards and illiberal, even violent and feudal. She describes how the sodomitical violence in *Pulp Fiction* (dir. Quentin Tarantino, 1992) "must be met by a personal vengeance that is itself ritualized, torturous, dark, and perverse." She asserts that "[t]his is the realm of the medieval in *Pulp Fiction*: it isn't exactly another *time*, in this movie in which time is peculiarly flattened out both by the manipulations of narrative and by the drenching of everything in postwar cinematic and pop culture references ... The medieval, rather, is the space of the rejects—really, the abjects—of this world."[9] *Enchanted* asks to what extent Disney's medievalisms are "medieval" in this way, the "rejects" of contemporary society. Like *Pulp Fiction*, *Enchanted* uses pop culture (here, Disney) references to distance the idea of the medieval from any specific history. By the film's conclusion, Disney recuperates its fairy-tale approach by broadening the definition of the medieval to include neomedievalisms, thereby claiming the flexibility of its previous medievalisms. This narrative strategy relies in part upon the viewer's affective relationship to Disney's medievalisms, allowing positive associations with the brand to rewrite their meanings. Giselle concludes, for instance, that it is better to go on "a date" before agreeing to marry, but it takes just two days for Robert to become the "prince" who resuscitates her from an enchanted sleep with "true love's kiss." (Edward gallantly stands aside when his own attempt fails, and instead finds a bride in Nancy [Idina Menzel], Robert's fashion designer girlfriend.)

Disney's shift from self-parody at the film's beginning to self-promotion at its end takes place through Giselle's translation of reality into a hybrid fairy-tale space. Giselle views Manhattan as an amalgam of medievalisms and fragments of previous Disney classics, recombined in the contemporary landscape to form an anachronistic but interconnected web of romantic neomedievalisms. In that sense, she is an expert at interpreting reality and models for viewers how to collect and arrange fragments from Disney sources to reinvent their worlds: to convert their mundane lives into neomedieval Princess narratives. Disney thus broadcasts its awareness of postmodern culture and its desire to engage with it, but uses the fragmentary approach of intertextuality to reconcile contemporary life with patriarchal and "medieval" (that is, medievalist) romance narrative.

*Enchanted*'s relentless citation of extant material echoes the picking and choosing that Jenkins describes in *Textual Poachers*, his work on television fan culture. These techniques position Disney as a fan as well as a producer, in what reads as an attempt to confer grassroots credibility upon the film. Jenkins calls fans' reuse of corporate material to create new products such as fan fiction and fan art "textual poaching"; drawing on Michel de Certeau's arguments about readerly "poaching," Jenkins contends that fans "poach" fragments from their favorite shows and reinterpret them to fabricate their own experiences and meanings. This concept relies upon the unequal power relationship between the fan and the producer of the original material, and Jenkins argues that "[f]ans construct their cultural and social identity through borrowing and inflecting mass culture images, articulating concerns which often go unvoiced within the dominant media."[10] In this view, fans consciously or unconsciously piece together source material, forcing it to conform to their interests and desires. Jenkins extends this approach to the individual identity and narrative of all media consumers: "Each of us constructs our own personal mythology from bits and fragments of information extracted from the media flow and transformed into resources through which we make sense of our everyday lives."[11] Disney constructs a new mythology from the "bits and fragments" of its diverse media output in *Enchanted*, especially drawing on its Princess films. Jason Sperb notes that Disney "mastered 'convergence' long before the advent of new media," citing the reappearances of elements from the mixed animated/live-action film *Song of the South* (1946) in television shows, records, books, games, theme park rides, and other media.[12] In *Enchanted*, Disney employs fannish recombinatory techniques to "make sense" of Disney's legacy in a contemporary context.

Director Kevin Lima admits that there are so many Disney references in *Enchanted* that he "doesn't know if there's a number," but states that "you could watch this movie a hundred times and still find things."[13] References include reused plot devices and characters, live-action restagings of iconic moments from previous Disney films, and allusions to Disney's film production history. Chuck Tryon likens such "sampling" (to borrow a musical term) in mashed-up online videos to the social practice of quoting lines from films with friends. He suggests that by taking movie lines out of context and reusing them in life, individuals display their own cleverness while also paying affectionate homage to the original. Translated to video-making, "the recycling of the original is certainly connected to a desire for building community while also providing the video maker a venue for illustrating his or her skill in manipulating a familiar text."[14] *Enchanted* similarly encourages the audience to imagine itself as such a community, joined by their shared memories and fondness for previous Disney films. It gives those with even the most cursory familiarity with Disney Princess films the sense of belonging to a club that understands its playful quotations, and rewards serious devotees with numerous obscure references. Lima reveals, for instance, that Robert's law firm Churchill, Harline, and Smith is named for the three songwriters of *Snow White and the Seven Dwarfs*.[15]

*Enchanted*'s references also allow Disney to demonstrate its savvy in a media landscape that has been transformed in the past decade by user-made videos that have been uploaded to video-sharing sites like YouTube. Part of this involves Disney's assumption of a critical distance from its own products, using the references to parody its own narrative and aesthetic tendencies. Tryon writes that parody invites us "to view genres critically, to make ourselves aware of the ways in which texts are constructed," and that, as a result, it can "challenge the authority of dominant texts."[16] Parody is also complicit in the continued dominance of such texts through its attention to them, but can raise questions about the texts that otherwise remain unaddressed. Lima states, for example, that his "favorite random reference" in *Enchanted* is that the "troll from the opening animation wears a collection of Disney Princess dresses as his loin cloth. He even wears two purple seashells as earrings. They're [*The Little Mermaid*] Ariel's shell bra!"[17] Decked out in remnants of past Princess attire and with Prince Edward trailing behind him, the self-aware troll ("I supposed to eat you") reads more as a tired device to effect a traditional and narrow feminine destiny than the exciting precursor to Giselle's happily-ever-after. The very possibility of creating a complete Disney Princess narrative in under eight minutes—the length of the animation from when the pop-up book opens to when Giselle and Edward ride into the sunset—pokes fun at the formulaic nature of the genre. When parodied in this way, the romanticized "medieval" of Disney's early Princess narratives looks more like the vernacular understanding of the medieval as not just laughably, but also dangerously, backward in comparison to modern reality.

Rehabilitating the Princess narrative depends in part upon negotiating away that dimension of Disney's medievalisms in order to privilege the histories of childhood memory over medieval history and the history of medievalisms. After parodying the medievalisms of its early Princess films (as if to reject them), *Enchanted* uses them to create neomedievalisms that reconcile contemporary values with nostalgic recollections of the Disney canon. Such a process involves abandoning or reimagining those undesirable elements of the "medieval" fairy tale that hamper its integration into the viewer's contemporary identity. Writing of the racially problematic *Song of the South*, Sperb contends that "there are at least two 'pasts' operating—the historical pasts (not) represented in the film, and the personal pasts of fans remembering *Song* as an experience from their childhoods." He notes that the film retains enduring popularity among fans in spite of its troubling representation of race relations in late nineteenth-century America, in large part because of the fans' affective relationship to it: "Because they enjoy the film, because *Song* fills them with pleasure and even love, nasty political implications are not just overlooked; they become impossible for fans who are so unambiguously positive in their emotions."[18] The possibility of creating new meaning out of memories of a text implies a gathering and sorting (conscious or not) that reorders reality.

From the start, *Enchanted* is more concerned with a multimediated approach to collecting and rearranging than with any kind of historical accuracy. The film opens with Giselle using household objects to construct the likeness of the prince she saw in her dream the night before, an allusion to Aurora's dream at the start of *Sleeping Beauty* ("Once Upon a Dream"). Giselle builds the life-sized sculpture from bits and pieces of everyday life, including books, bottles, a small pumpkin, a spade, a flowerpot, a broom, and other fairy-tale-appropriate—that is to say, familiar but plausibly preindustrial—items. Its heroic posture echoes the statue of Prince Eric that Ariel discovers and falls in love with in *The Little Mermaid*, but Giselle's idol is more humorous than noble because of its bric-a-brac construction. Meanwhile, her collecting of mundane objects also recalls Ariel's secret horde of human knick-knacks, so that *Enchanted*'s gathering and placing of references creates another layer of metaphor in Giselle's building. This creative act foreshadows Giselle's self-determining ability to fashion her own reality when she arrives in New York; in this she displays the dexterity of the poaching reader, the fan producer, and the makers of *Enchanted*, who all manipulate existing material to yield new meanings.

Baudrillard asserts that Disney is "in the process of capturing all the real world to integrate it into its synthetic universe, in the form of a vast 'reality show' where reality itself becomes a spectacle ... where the real becomes a theme park."[19] *Enchanted*'s move from the animated fairy-tale realm to live-action New York is a fictional representation of this process, with Giselle leading the way as Disney's ambassador: a princess/fairy godmother who can transform the mundane into a neomedieval fairy-tale realm. She translates New York City into such a space and the camera sees with her eyes, "poaching" existing fragments of the city and editing them together to reveal Manhattan as a neomedieval landscape. As Susan Aronstein and Robert Torry note, *Enchanted* "works immediately and continually to deny the putative opposition between Andalasia and New York, fantasy and reality, by representing New York as replete with indices of the marvelous, hints of an available, if at times unnoticed, realm of imaginative possibility."[20] The material culture of the Middle Ages serves as key evidence of this overlap, especially the emblematic castle that is also symbolic of Disney's cinematic enterprise. Aronstein and Torry cite a number of "castles" that the camera identifies in Manhattan when Giselle explores the city with Robert and Morgan, including Robert's apartment building, the Paterno at 440 Riverside Drive, which confirms Robert's status as a modern-day Prince Charming. The camera lingers on a number of potentially castle-like constructions in and around Central Park, and the final Kings and Queens Ball sequence is held inside the neo-Gothic Woolworth Building in lower Manhattan. The gables and spires of the building's roofs create a pseudo-medieval setting for the dénouement, in which Giselle and Robert do battle with Narissa, transformed into a dragon. I contend that the camera's (and Giselle's) selective looking in the film models how to use reality to construct a neomedieval Princess narrative out of one's own life.

This approach may, at times, require a willful rejection of evidence against neomedieval readings of the everyday. When Giselle arrives in New York, for instance, she remains fixed on a single goal: finding "the castle." When she catches sight of a billboard for "the Palace Casino," which sparkles with the image of a pink and blue cartoon castle, choral music swells and she rushes towards it. Giselle cannot gain entry, but her credulous pounding at the castle "door" is rewarded by attracting Morgan and Robert's attention. Morgan instinctively recognizes Giselle's identity, asking Robert why there is "a princess on the castle billboard." Robert, who represents the cynicism and pragmatism of (masculine) adult reality, dismisses Giselle as another simulation, calling her an "advertisement. It's a mannequin." Morgan, however, insists, "she's really there!" and darts out of their cab to approach Giselle. Within moments of meeting, Giselle falls from the billboard scaffolding into Robert's arms, the camera angles visually echoing her fall into Edward's embrace in the animated opening of the film. Giselle's reading of the billboard as a real castle and Robert's reading of her as a mannequin, a simulation, are equally incorrect. And yet it is Giselle's belief in the possibility of castles in a modern, live-action landscape—and Morgan's belief in the possibility of Princesses—that initiates the major romantic narrative of the film.

"Reality" conforms to Giselle's beliefs, and she and Robert unwittingly reenact iconic moments from the Disney canon throughout the live-action portion of the film. Like Cinderella, birds help Giselle prepare her dress for housecleaning, and her reflection floats up in a bubble as she sings and scrubs the floor. When Queen Narissa (Susan Sarandon) appears in New York, she casts the same dark silhouette as the witch Maleficent does in *Sleeping Beauty*, and Robert and Giselle's dance at the Kings and Queens Ball mirrors the motions of the Beast and Belle in *Beauty and the Beast*. These visual cues are more than homages to previous films; they also carry implied emotional meaning derived from their original contexts. Jenkins writes that "[e]ntertainment content isn't the only thing that flows across multiple media platforms. Our lives, relationships, memories, fantasies, desires also flow across media channels."[21] Thus, Giselle and Robert's postures in a Central Park rowboat recall the unspoken desires of Ariel and Eric's boating trip in *The Little Mermaid*, and by visually echoing the Italian restaurant scene from *Lady and the Tramp*, the film virtually guarantees that this human couple will also share a first kiss. Disney's cinematic history serves as shorthand for Giselle and Robert's budding romance, the references becoming less satirical and more earnest as the plot develops. When Giselle falls senseless at the bite of a poisoned apple at the ball and Robert attempts to revive her with "true love's kiss," these recycled Disney tropes are no longer presented as comedic. As Giselle adapts to the "real world," it also adapts to her, reforming itself into a neomedieval realm suitable for a modern-day/ fairy-tale Princess.

The Princess narrative is itself a neomedievalism that builds upon and responds to earlier Disney Princess films. As Kathleen Coyne Kelly and Tison Pugh write, the cinematic Middle Ages "has been historically recast as a place and time of an intransigent and romanticized vision of heterosexuality": "moderns have ... metonomized the clichéd materialities of a certain kind of medievalism—the knight in shining armor, the damsel in distress—as heterosexual."[22] The Disney Princess narrative's patriarchal vision likewise imagines heterosexual love and marriage as the most desirable outcome of a woman's life, giving rise to the conflation of fairy tales, the Middle Ages, and heteronormative romance in the popular imagination of the Disney brand. Jack Zipes writes of what he calls Disney's "civilizing mission" through the rewriting of fairy tales for its films. He notes the studio founder Walt Disney's heavy involvement in the making of *Snow White*, which "follows the classic sexist narrative about the framing of women's lives through male discourse."[23] In spite of—or perhaps because of—their antifeminist bent, Disney's Princess narratives afford a certain measure of pleasure to women and girls who live in patriarchal societies. In this, they echo the work of early English romances, which, as Helen Cooper argues, "do not offer any revolutionary attack on conventional sexual morals or a patriarchal system of dynastic inheritance, but they do repeatedly show women exerting their freedom within the system."[24] Giselle's desire for Robert enables her to question and reject her initial engagement to Edward, and her adoption of some contemporary ideas about love (and, perhaps, female possibility) result in her taking on the role of the prince when she attempts to save Robert from the Narissa-dragon. This exertion of freedom is acceptable within the neomedieval construction of Princess culture, as is Giselle's launching of a career in the closing montage of the film. These navigations within the structures of patriarchy allow Giselle some control and identity, but her Princess narrative remains intact: Giselle's life, formerly framed by Edward, is framed by Robert by the end of the film.

Cory Grewell suggests that the postmodern culture that enables neomedievalisms also informs some neomedievalisms' antagonistic response to that culture. Neomedievalism, he argues,

> is a form of medievalism that is intrinsically linked to late twentieth- and twenty-first-century advances in technology, and ... is distinguished from previous forms of medievalism by its multi-culturalism, its lack of concern for history, and its habit of imagining the medieval through the lens of previous medievalisms. I would add that it constitutes a particular response—or responses—to postmodernism, the construction of fantastic universes of good and evil being perhaps only one among many.[25]

The reassertion of patriarchal narratives may be another, especially in the case of *Enchanted*, in which Disney's commercial enterprise is at stake. Consumerism hovers behind the live-action sections of *Enchanted*, demonstrating that, in the neomedieval Princess narrative, American-style capitalism can replace the "pre-modern" economies of Disney's fairy-tale realms. Buying power even stands in for some kinds of magic, as becomes evident when Giselle decides to attend the ball at the last moment but, like Cinderella, has nothing to wear. She turns to Morgan, whom she finds outfitted like a fairy godmother in toy fairy wings and holding a toy wand, surrounded by pink Princess-style merchandise. The girl assures Giselle that she knows "something better than a fairy godmother," and pulls out one of Robert's credit cards. Morgan demonstrates that well-directed money is the neomedieval solution to Giselle's classic fairy-tale problem: like entry to the ball (which is ticketed), magical transformations can be bought. This is a powerful assertion for Disney to make; as part of the film's model for how to transform reality in the image of a Disney fairy tale, it encourages not only recalling and celebrating Disney films but also purchasing products. *Enchanted* also takes advantage of the emotional connotations of shopping as a gendered ritual, pausing in the montage of buying and beautifying long enough for Morgan to ask Giselle if their trip is what "going shopping with your mother" is like. Thus female bonding—especially the bond of mothers and daughters—becomes part of finding a "prince" in the neomedieval universe, and both are enabled by commercial consumption. This collecting of commodities (Giselle and Morgan wield armloads of pink and white shopping bags) joins Giselle's selective viewing and rearranging of reality and the camera's dexterity with Disney and medieval references to read as a kind of transcendent power: in this case, a particularly feminine one. By imbuing shopping with feminine power, Disney asserts a woman's ability to create her own neomedieval Princess narrative (which itself is a negotiation of patriarchal society) through consumer activity. Such a reading is problematized by the fact that the credit card is Robert's, which reasserts the woman's subordinate position to male economic power. The flexibility of neomedievalism opens up an alternate possibility for Giselle, however, presenting her as a producer as well as a consumer in the closing montage of the film. This happily-ever-after depicts Giselle at work in Andalasia Fashions, a store that sells princess-style dresses for young girls. The shop relies on Giselle's skill for reworking the material of the modern world into neomedievalisms, which she initially demonstrates (to Robert's frustration) when she makes gowns for herself from Robert's curtains and linens. Giselle's new career is indicative of her "modern" understanding of female possibility, and indicates her investment in the kind of neomedieval fairy-tale universe that makes room for both female autonomy and capitalism. However, Giselle's talent as a seamstress is part of her Princess identity, and thus she acquiesces to a patriarchal system that privileges those feminine skills that relate to the domestic sphere. This vision of neomedieval Princess culture delineates the desirable boundaries of female ambition, while the film also refutes visions that threaten patriarchal hierarchies. For instance, the first time that Morgan appears onscreen, Robert gives her a book called *Great Women of Our Time*, saying, "I know it's not that fairy-tale book you wanted, but this is better." He points out that his then-girlfriend Nancy is "a lot like the women in your book" as a way of introducing his "rational" plan to marry her. The scene creates an opposition between rationality, Nancy, and a universe where women function outside of patriarchal models on the one hand, and love, Giselle, and patriarchy-friendly "fairy-tale" femininity on the other. Morgan becomes a contested object in this battle, a child who in her Romantic innocence "naturally" desires fairy tales but is being unwillingly socialized against them.

Jacqueline Rose argues that adults insist upon the idea of childhood innocence as a way of assuring our own stable relationship to a "knowable" world: in this view, the child has "special access" to "a primitive or lost state," and represents "something of a pioneer who restores these worlds to us with a facility and directness which ensures our own relationship to them is, finally, safe."[26] In *Enchanted* this "lost state" is the atemporal neomedievalism of Disney's fairy-tale worlds: when Robert's assistant informs him that she cannot find information about Andalasia, she suggests that rather than "a country, or a city," Andalasia is "more like a state of mind." Morgan's intrinsic attraction to this state of mind and recognition of its medieval trappings is what brings Giselle into her and her father's lives. Giselle's ability to reconcile this worldview with adult modernity, meanwhile, is what enables her triumph over Nancy and Narissa, the film's symbols of unhappy female ambition, and facilitates her transformation of Robert and Morgan's family into a model of nuclear domesticity.

*Enchanted* thus celebrates female intuition and creativity so long as they do not undermine the patriarchal structures of Disney's previous Princess films, damaging these films' legacy (Disney's brand) and economic potential. *Enchanted* instead advocates for a feminine agency that is characterized by its upbeat, positive energy and makes do with what's at hand rather than criticizing the existing system. In this it echoes the gender divide between the genres of fan videos made by men and women: Jenkins reports that "the overwhelming majority of fan parody is produced by men, while 'fan fiction' is almost entirely produced by women." In particular, "[i]n the female fan community, fans have long produced 'song videos' that are edited together from found footage drawn from film or television shows and set to pop music."[27] This is not to say that all such videos affirm the narratives supplied by the original source material; Francesca Coppa argues that in "vidding," as this art form is known, "editing is not just about bringing images together; it is also about taking mass-media images apart."[28] The music is integral to this reconstruction: "the song tells the spectator how to understand the montage the vidder has constructed. Vids are therefore a form of in-kind media criticism: a visual essay on a visual source."[29] *Enchanted*'s musical homage to Disney may be read as a kind of tribute to female fan techniques that emphasizes the romantic and celebratory, elevating these over the cynicism of "masculine" parody.

The closing montage of the film supports such a view, recasting visual cues from the parodic opening animation as part of a celebratory "vid" that reveals the characters' romantic and commercial successes and the triumph of neomedieval Princess culture. As in most vids the song is essential to understanding the larger text; this sequence uses country singer Carrie Underwood's "Ever Ever After," a song dedicated to making the connections between Disney-style fairy tales and everyday contemporary life. The opening notes begin as the camera pulls back from Giselle and Robert on the roof of the Woolworth Building. The uplit spires recall the castle from the Disney logo, a citation of the film's early scenes that is strengthened by a wipe that folds the image down as if it were a page in a pop-up book. The scenes that follow are all separated by the same kind of transition, which turns both live-action and animated images into "pages" in a single pop-up "book." In the first scene, Edward tries Giselle's forgotten shoe onto Nancy's foot, and as they discover that it is "a perfect fit," the lyrics of Underwood's song begin: "Storybook endings, fairy tales coming true, / Deep down inside we want to believe they still do." Nancy and Edward rush to the manhole in Times Square that leads back to Andalasia, and as they jump down together and into an animated wedding scene, the lyrics urge, "Let's just admit that we all want to make it to / Ever ever after." Nancy flings away her Blackberry at the altar (it shatters before a crowd of curious animals) and then dips Edward into a kiss, becoming, like Giselle, a neomedieval Princess who exhibits joyful agency within her patriarchal romance. As the song continues, subsequent scenes unfold to reveal Andalasia Fashions bursting with young customers in princess dresses ("Start a new fashion, wear your heart on your sleeve, / Sometimes you reach what's real just by making believe," the lyrics assert) and book signings for Nathaniel and Pip's autobiographical works. Nathaniel's *My Royal Pain* appears to chronicle his release from Narissa's *femme fatale*-style domination, while Pip's *Silence Is Not Golden* recounts the indignities of his inability to speak while in New York. Attractive females (young women in Nathaniel's case and sultry-eyed woodland animals in Pip's) attend them and look on admiringly as they sign books for long queues of customers, underscoring the secondary characters' sexual and economic success in their "ever ever after." The final scene features Giselle, Robert, and Morgan dancing in their Manhattan apartment, as if to the music of Underwood's song. As the camera pans out of the window and past the ornate exterior of the building, the voice of the narrator from the beginning of the film returns to announce, "and so they all lived happily ever after." The shot appears to fold into the last page of the animated manuscript from the start of *Enchanted*, and Underwood samples a line from Giselle's "True Love's Kiss" song as the conclusion to "Ever Ever After."[30]

The multimediated approach of the montage recalls the breadth of Disney's transmedia empire as it evokes the pop-up book, animated and live-action cinema, the music video, the American country music genre, and fan-made online videos. It assumes the viewer's ability to move between media to derive a single meaning from the vid's many fragments: in this case, the continued relevance of Disney's Princess narratives and their patriarchal underpinnings, transformed into neomedievalisms for everyday life. This "vid" not only pays tribute to *Enchanted* and previous Disney Princess films, but it also echoes the female fan videos that Jenkins writes can "explore undeveloped subtexts of the original film, offer original interpretations of the story, or suggest plotlines that go beyond the work itself."[31] *Enchanted* renders the collisions from its tagline, which seems to promise readerly agency and a violent choosing and cutting that critiques the standard reading, into integration, culminating in a "mashup" song video that is entirely continuous with the standard reading. Disney's co-opting of the form deflates the genre's potential for subversive rewriting of the canonical film text, collapsing the critical metatext (i.e., the song video) into the canonical film text itself.

While *Enchanted*'s transition from masculine parody to feminine homage can be framed as a defeat of masculine cynicism and an assertion of a certain "girl power," it implies a femininity that is always already there, if repressed: a childlike femininity (figured by Morgan) that "naturally" desires a heterosexual Disney Princess narrative. The importance of *Enchanted*'s neomedievalism, as distinct from medievalism, lies in the way that its effacement of time naturalizes this model of female desire that the film constructs. The ahistoricity of neomedievalism thus not only proposes the possibility of seamlessly integrating Princess fantasy and capitalist postmodernity, but also retroactively discovers in the viewer's past the atemporal patriarchal fantasy that, as Carrie Underwood sings, we (women) should "just admit that we all want," ushering in a posttemporal, heavenlike "ever, ever after." The historical incongruities brought into relief by the "colli[sion]" of "real" and "animated" worlds, which constitute *Enchanted*'s neomedievalism, are leveraged into a refusal of history that makes the "once upon a time" both timeless and universal.

Walt Disney Pictures announced in late 2010 that *Tangled*, which is based on "Rapunzel," would be its last traditional Princess film for the foreseeable future.[32] This major shift seems to herald the end of Disney's iconic Princess culture and to repudiate the work that *Enchanted* does to rehabilitate the fairy tale for contemporary audiences. However, *Enchanted*'s postmodern approach to fairy tale, narrative, and Disney's archival material opens the door for other enterprises to continue exploring the brand's neomedieval possibilities. As of the date of this chapter's completion, for example, the ABC television network is midway through its first season of *Once Upon a Time*, a drama about fairy-tale characters cursed by an evil queen to lead "normal" American lives. The show, which is produced by Disney, places original Disney characters like Jiminy Cricket alongside classic fairy-tale figures and joins their stories in a new narrative that moves between fairy-tale universe flashbacks and present-day "reality" (both in live action). At the end of 2011 *Once Upon a Time* was the most popular Sunday night show on American television with adults aged 18–34, and with both women 18–34 and women 18–49.[33] Like *Enchanted*, *Once Upon a Time* encourages viewers to be textual poachers, actively seeking out the neomedieval possibilities in mundane modernity and recombining them to reveal the hidden Disney Princess narratives embedded in everyday life.

**Notes**

1. Carol Robinson and Pamela Clements,"Living with Neomedievalisms," *Defining Medievalism(s) II*, ed. Karl Fugelso (Cambridge: Brewer, 2009): 55–75. As Robinson and Clements note, this use of "neomedievalism" is markedly different from that explored by Bruce Holsinger in *Neomedievalism, Neoconservatism, and the War on Terror* (Chicago: Prickly Paradigm, 2007). I intend no reference to Holsinger's use of the term.
2. The film makes no reference to the similarity between Andalasia's name and the Spanish region of Andalucía, or to the Muslim nation in medieval Spain (Al-Andalus).
3. Henry Jenkins, *Convergence Culture* (New York: New York University Press, 2008).
4. For analysis of the differences in Princess culture during these eras, see Rebecca-Anne Do Rozario, "The Princess and the Magic Kingdom: Beyond Nostalgia, the Function of the Disney Princess," *Women's Studies in Communication* 27.1 (2004): 34–59.
5. Henry Jenkins, *Convergence Culture*, 2–3.
6. Carol Robinson and Pamela Clements, "Living with Neomedievalisms," 56.
7. Carol Robinson and Pamela Clements, "Living with Neomedievalisms," 64.
8. Jean Baudrillard, "Disneyworld Company," trans. Francois Debrix, *Liberation* (March 4, 1996); Web, accessed April 19, 2011.
9. Carolyn Dinshaw, *Getting Medieval: Sexualities and Communities, Pre- and Postmodern* (Durham: Duke University Press, 1999), 185–86. Dinshaw also explores the homophobic and homoerotic connotations of the medieval in this scene. Although beyond the scope of this essay, it is worth noting that *Enchanted* also flirts with such implications in its characterizations of Edward and Nathaniel. They each serve as the butt of homoerotic jokes, including several that play with the idea of a man desiring or seeking a "prince."
10. Henry Jenkins, *Textual Poachers* (New York: Routledge, 1992), 23. See also Michel de Certeau, *The Practice of Everyday Life*, trans. Steven Rendall (Berkeley: University of California Press, 1988).
11. Henry Jenkins, *Convergence Culture*, 3.
12. Jason Sperb, "Reassuring Convergence: Online Fandom, Race, and Disney's Notorious *Song of the South*," *Cinema Journal* 49.4 (2010): 25–45, at 26.
13. Rob Carnevale, "*Enchanted* – Kevin Lima Interview," *IndieLondon*; Web, accessed April 30, 2011.
14. Chuck Tryon, *Reinventing Cinema* (New Brunswick: Rutgers University Press, 2009), 151.
15. Rob Carnevale, "*Enchanted* – Kevin Lima Interview."
16. Chuck Tryon, *Reinventing Cinema*, 155.

17. Amy, "20 Questions with *Enchanted*'s Kevin Lima," *PopGurls* (December 6, 2007); Web, accessed April 30, 2011.
18. Jason Sperb, "Reassuring Convergence," 35 and 41. It is worth noting that the span of the *Enchanted* narrative across both cel animation and live-action footage invokes *Song of the South*'s weaving of animated Uncle Remus tales into its nostalgic live-action frame story.
19. Jean Baudrillard, "Disneyworld Company."
20. Susan Aronstein and Robert Torry, "Magic Happens: Re-Enchanting Disney Adults," *Weber: The Contemporary West* 26.2 (2010): 41–54, at 49.
21. Henry Jenkins, *Convergence Culture*, 17.
22. Kathleen Coyne Kelly and Tison Pugh, "Introduction: Queer History, Cinematic Medievalism, and the Impossibilty of Sexuality," *Queer Movie Medievalisms*, ed. Kathleen Coyne Kelly and Tison Pugh (Farnham: Ashgate, 2009), 1–17, at 3–4.
23. Jack Zipes, *Fairy Tales and the Art of Subversion*, 2nd ed. (New York: Routledge, 2006), 193 and 203.
24. Helen Cooper, *The English Romance in Time* (Oxford: Oxford University Press, 2008), 222.
25. Cory Grewell, "Neomedievalism: An Eleventh Little Middle Ages?" *Defining Neomedievalism(s)*, ed. Karl Fugelso (Cambridge: Brewer, 2010), 34–43, at 40.
26. Jacqueline Rose, *The Case of Peter Pan, or, The Impossibility of Children's Literature* (Philadelphia: University of Pennsylvania Press, 1993). 9.
27. Henry Jenkins, *Convergence Culture*, 159.
28. Francesca Coppa, "An Editing Room of One's Own: Vidding as Women's Work," *Camera Obscura* 26.2 (2011): 123–30, at 124.
29. Francesca Coppa, "Editing Room," 123.
30. The merging of these songs encourages audiences to realize that Underwood's singing career is itself a kind of neomedieval princess narrative: raised on an Oklahoma farm, she rose to stardom by winning the reality television talent show *American Idol* in 2005. Disney has built a relationship between its own brand and *Idol*'s image as a purveyor of modern-day dreams, opening "The American Idol Experience" at Disney's Hollywood Studios in the Walt Disney World Resort in 2008. This attraction allows park guests to compete for a "Dream Ticket" to bypass the queue at a regional *American Idol* audition.
31. Henry Jenkins, *Convergence Culture*, 160.
32. Dawn Chmielewski and Claudia Eller, "Disney Animation Is Closing the Book on Fairy Tales," *Los Angeles Times* (November 21, 2010); Web, accessed May 6, 2012.
33. Robert Seldmanm "ABC's *Once Upon a Time* Is Sunday's #1 Entertainment Show with Key Women," *TV by the Numbers* (December 12, 2011); Web, accessed January 5, 2012.

# A SELECT FILMOGRAPHY OF DISNEY'S MEDIEVALISMS

*Aladdin.* Dir. Ron Clements and John Musker. 1992.
*Atlantis.* Dir. Gary Trousdale and Kirk Wise. 2001.
*Beauty and the Beast.* Dir. Gary Trousdale and Kirk Wise. 1991.
*Cinderella.* Dir. Clyde Geronimi and Wilfred Jackson. 1950.
*Enchanted.* Dir. Kevin Lima. 2007.
*Fantasia.* Dir. James Algar, Samuel Armstrong, Ford Beebe Jr., Norman Ferguson, Jim Handley, T. Hee, Wilfred Jackson, Hamilton Luske, Bill Roberts, Paul Satterfield and Ben Sharpsteen. 1940.
*Fantasia 2000.* Dir. James Algar, Gaëtan Brizzi, Paul Brizzi, Hendel Butoy, Francis Glebas, Eric Goldberg, Don Hahn, and Pixote Hunt. 1999.
*Hercules.* Dir. Ron Clements and John Musker. 1997.
"How to be a Sailor." Dir. Jack Kenny. 1944.
*The Hunchback of Notre Dame.* Dir. Gary Trousdale and Kirk Wise. 1996.
*Hunchback of Notre Dame II: The Secret of the Bell.* Dir. Bradley Raymond. 2002.
*A Kid in King Arthur's Court.* Dir. Michael Gottlieb. 1995.
*A Knight in Camelot.* Dir. Roger Young. 1998.
*The Little Mermaid.* Dir. Ron Clements and John Musker. 1989.
*Mulan.* Dir. Tony Bancroft and Barry Cook. 1998.
*Pocahontas.* Dir. Mike Gabriel and Eric Golberg. 1995.
*Pirates of the Caribbean: The Curse of the Black Pearl.* Dir. Gore Verbenski. 2003.
*Prince of Persia: Sands of Time.* Dir. Mike Newell. 2010.
*The Princess and the Frog.* Dir. Ron Clements and John Musker. 2009.
*Princess of Thieves.* Dir. Peter Hewitt. 2001.
*Robin Hood.* Dir. Wolfgang Reitherman. 1973.
*The Rocketeer.* Dir. Joe Johnson. 1991.
*Sleeping Beauty.* Dir. Clyde Geronimi. 1959.
*Snow White and the Seven Dwarfs.* Dir. David Hand. 1937.
*Song of the South.* Dir. Harve Foster and Wilfred Jackson. 1946.
*The Sorcerer's Apprentice.* Dir. Jon Turtletaub. 2010.
*The Story of Robin Hood and His Merrie Men.* Dir. Ken Annakin. 1952.
*The Sword in the Stone.* Dir. Wolfgang Reitherman. 1963.
*Tangled.* Dir. Nathan Greno and Byron Howard. 2010.

*Tarzan.* Dir. Chris Buck and Kevin Lima. 1999.
*Toy Story.* Dir. John Lasseter. 1995.
*Treasure Island.* Dir. Byron Haskin. 1950.
*Treasure Planet.* Dir. Ron Clements and John Musker. 2002.
*Unidentified Flying Oddball.* Dir. Russ Mayberry. 1979.
*Who Framed Roger Rabbit.* Dir. Robert Zemeckis. 1988.

# SELECT BIBLIOGRAPHY

Addison, Erin. "Saving Other Women from Other Men: Disney's *Aladdin*." *Camera Obscura* 31 (1993): 5–25.

Akerman, James, and Robert Karrow, ed. *Maps: Finding Our Place in the World*. Chicago: University of Chicago Press, 2007.

Allan, Robin. *Walt Disney and Europe: European Influences on the Animated Feature Films of Walt Disney*. Bloomington: Indiana University Press, 1999.

Ameli, Saied, Syed Mohammed Marandi, Sameera Ahmed, and Arzu Meral. *The British Media and Muslim Representation*. Wembley: Islamic Human Rights Commission, 2007.

Anderson, Ken. "Walt Disney Productions' All Cartoon Feature *Robin Hood*." *Official Bulletin of IATSE* (Winter 1973–74): 24–26.

Aravamudan, Srinivas. "The Adventure Chronotope and the Oriental Xenotrope." *The Arabian Nights in Historical Context*. Ed. Saree Makdisi and Felicity Nussbaum. Oxford: Oxford University Press, 2008. 235–63.

Aronstein, Susan. *Hollywood Knights: Arthurian Cinema and the Politics of Nostalgia*. New York: Palgrave Macmillan, 2005.

—— and Nancy Coiner. "Twice Nightly: Democratizing the Middle Ages for Middle-Class America." Verduin 212–30.

—— and Robert Torry. "Magic Happens: Re-Enchanting Disney Adults." *Weber: The Contemporary West* 26.2 (2010): 41–54.

Artz, Lee. "Monarchs, Monsters, and Multiculturalism: Disney's Menu for Global Hierarchy." Budd and Kirsch 75–98.

Ayres, Brenda, ed. *The Emperor's Old Groove: Decolonizing Disney's Magic Kingdom*. New York: Peter Lang, 2003.

Bagrow, Leo, and R. A. Skelton. *History of Cartography*. Rev. ed. London: Watts, 1964.

Bailey, Martin. "The Discovery of the Lost Mappamundi Panel: Hereford's Map in a Medieval Altarpiece?" Harvey 79–93.

Bakhtin, Mikhail. *The Dialogic Imagination*. Trans. Caryl Emerson and Michael Holquist. Austin: University of Texas Press, 1981.

Barber, Richard. "Introduction." *King Arthur in Music*. Ed. Richard Barber. Cambridge: Brewer, 2002. 1–8.

Baudrillard, Jean. "Disneyworld Company." Trans. Francois Debrix. *Liberation* (March 4, 1996). Web. 19 Apr. 2008.

———"The Precession of Simulacra." *Simulacra and Simulation.* Trans. Sheila Glaser. 1981. Ann Arbor, MI: University of Michigan Press, 1994. 1–42.

———*Simulations.* Trans. Paul Foss, et al. New York: Semiotext[e], 1983.

Beard, Richard. *Walt Disney's Epcot Center: Creating the New World of Tomorrow.* New York: Abrams, 1982.

Beck, Jerry. *The Animated Movie Guide.* Chicago: A Cappella, 2005.

Behmler, Rub, ed. *The Adventures of Robin Hood.* Madison: University of Wisconsin Press, 1979.

Bell, Elizabeth, Lynda Haas, and Laura Sells, ed. *From Mouse to Mermaid: The Politics of Film, Gender, and Culture.* Bloomington: Indiana University Press, 1995.

Belsey, Catherine. *Critical Practice.* London: Routledge, 1980.

Bettelheim, Bruno. *The Uses of Enchantment: The Meaning and Importance of Fairy Tales.* 1976. New York: Random House, 2010.

"Bibbidi Bobbidi Boutique." disneyworld.disney.go.com. Web. 12 Dec. 2010.

Bolter, Jay, and Richard Grusin. *Remediation: Understanding New Media.* Cambridge: MIT Press, 2000.

Booker, Keith. *Disney, Pixar, and the Hidden Message of Children's Films.* Santa Barbara: Praeger, 2010.

Bourdieu, Pierre. *The Field of Cultural Production.* Cambridge: Polity, 1993.

Bradford, Clare. *Unsettling Narratives: Postcolonial Readings of Children's Literature.* Waterloo: Wilfrid Laurier University Press, 2007.

Brode, Douglas. *From Walt to Woodstock: How Disney Created the Counterculture.* Austin: University of Texas Press, 2004.

Broggie, Michael. *Walt Disney's Railroad Story: The Small-Scale Fascination That Led to a Full-Scale Kingdom.* Virginia Beach: Donning, 2006.

Bruce, Alexander. "Princesses without a Prince: A Consideration of Girls' Reactions to Disney's 'Princess' Movies." *Children's Folklore Review* 28 (2005): 7–21.

Budd, Mike, and Max Kirsch, ed. *Rethinking Disney: Private Control, Public Dimensions.* Middletown: Wesleyan University Press, 2005.

Butler, Judith. *Gender Trouble.* 1990. New York: Routledge, 1999.

Byerly, Alison. "The Uses of Landscape." *The Ecocriticism Reader.* Ed. Cheryl Glotfelty and Harold Fromm. Athens: University of Georgia Press, 1996. 52–68.

Campbell, Narelle. "Medieval Reimaginings: Female Knights in Children's Television." *Screening the Past* 26 (2009): 4. Web. 22 Aug. 2011.

Carnevale, Rob. "*Enchanted* – Kevin Lima Interview." *IndieLondon.* Web. 30 Apr. 2011.

Cecire, Maria Sachiko. "Medievalism, Popular Culture, and National Identity in Children's Fantasy Literature." *Studies in Ethnicity and Nationalism* 9.3 (2009): 394–409.

Chaucer, Geoffrey. *The Riverside Chaucer.* Ed. Larry Benson. 3rd ed. Boston: Houghton Mifflin, 1987.

Cherewatuk, Karen. *Marriage, Adultery, and Inheritance in Malory's* Morte Darthur. Cambridge: Brewer, 2006.

Chmielewski, Dawn, and Claudia Eller. "Disney Animation Is Closing the Book on Fairy Tales." *Los Angeles Times* (November 21, 2010). Web. 6 May 2012.

——— "Disney Restyles 'Rapunzel' to Appeal to Boys." *Los Angeles Times* (March 9, 2010). Web. 30 Nov. 2010.

Churchill, Winston. *Birth of Britain, Vol. 1. 1956–58*. London: Weidenfeld & Nicolson, 2002.

Cocteau, Jean. *Entretiens sur le cinématographe*. Ed. A. Bernard and C. Gauteur. Paris: Pierre Belfond, 1973.

Cohen, Jeffrey. *Medieval Identity Machines*. Minneapolis: University of Minnesota Press, 2003.

Cooper, Helen. *The English Romance in Time*. Oxford: Oxford University Press, 2008.

Coppa, Francesca. "An Editing Room of One's Own: Vidding as Women's Work." *Camera Obscura* 26.2 (2011): 123–30.

Crafton, Donald. *Before Mickey: The Animated Film, 1898–1928*. Chicago: University of Chicago Press, 1993.

Culhane, John. "Snow White at 50: Undimmed Magic." *New York Times* (July 12, 1987). Web. 14 Apr. 2012.

Davies, Gill. "Nature Writing and Eco Criticism: Reading T. H. White in the Twenty-First Century." *Critical Essays on T. H. White*. Ed. Gill Davies, David Malcolm, John Simons, and Debbie Sly. New York: Mellen, 2008, 157–77.

Davis, Amy. *Good Girls and Wicked Witches: Women in Disney's Feature Animation*. Eastleigh: Libby, 2006.

de Certeau, Michel. *The Mystic Fable*. Trans. Michael Smith. Chicago: University of Chicago Press, 1992.

——— *The Practice of Everyday Life*. Trans. Steven Rendall. Berkeley: University of California Press, 1988.

Dinshaw, Carolyn. *Getting Medieval: Sexualities and Communities, Pre- and Postmodern*. Durham: Duke University Press, 1999.

Do Rozario, Rebecca-Anne. "The Princess and the Magic Kingdom: Beyond Nostalgia, the Function of the Disney Princess." *Women's Studies in Communication* 27.1 (2004): 34–59.

Dragonetti, Roger. *Le Mirage des Sources*. Paris: Seuil, 1987.

Driver, Martha, and Sid Ray. "Preface: Hollywood Knights." *The Medieval Hero on Screen*. Ed. Martha Driver and Sid Ray. Jefferson, NC: McFarland, 2004. 5–17.

Ducille, Anne. "Dyes and Dolls: Multicultural Barbie and the Merchandising of Difference." *Differences* 6.1 (1994): 48–68.

Dunlop, Beth. *Building a Dream: The Art of Disney Architecture*. New York: Abrams, 1996.

Ebert, Robert. "Snow White and the Seven Dwarfs (1937)." *Chicago Sun-Times* (October, 2001). Web. 14 Apr. 2012.

———and John Culhane. "Snow White at 50: Undimmed Magic." *New York Times* (July 12, 1987).

Eco, Umberto. *Travels in Hyperreality*. Trans. William Weaver. New York: Harcourt Brace Jovanovich, 1986.

Edgerton, Gary, and Kathy Jackson. "Redesigning Pocahontas: Disney, the 'White Man's Indian,' and the Marketing of Dreams." *Journal of Popular Film and Television* 24.2 (1996): 90–98.

Edson, Evelyn. *Mapping Time and Space*. London: British Library, 1997.

Edwards, Elizabeth. "The Place of Women in the *Morte Darthur*." *A Companion to Malory*. Ed. Elizabeth Archibald and A.S.G. Edwards. Cambridge: Brewer, 1996. 37–54.

Edwards, Leigh. "The United Colors of *Pocahontas*: Synthetic Miscegenation and Disney's Multiculturalism." *Narrative* 7.2 (1999): 147–68.

Eisner, Michael. *Work in Progress*. New York: Random House, 1998.

Ellis, Erle. "Stop Trying to Save the Planet." *Wired Science* (May 6, 2009). Web. 6 May 2012.

Faden, Eric. "Crowd Control: Early Cinema, Sound, and Digital Images." *Journal of Film and Video* 53.2/3 (2001): 93–106.

Flinn, John. "Snow White and the Seven Dwarfs." *Variety* (December 28, 1937). Web. 14 Apr. 2012.

Fjellman, Stephen. *Vinyl Leaves: Walt Disney World and America*. Boulder: Westview, 1992.

Fradenburg, Louise. "'Voice Memorial': Loss and Reparation in Chaucer's Poetry." *Exemplaria* 2.1 (1990): 169–202.

Freud, Sigmund. *Totem and Taboo*. New York: Norton, 1950.

Gabler, Neil. *Walt Disney: The Triumph of the American Imagination*. New York: Knopf, 2007.

Garrard, Greg. *Ecocriticism*. Abingdon: Routledge, 2004.

Geer, Jennifer. "J. M. Barrie Gets the Miramax Treatment." *Children's Literature Association Quarterly* 32.3 (2007): 192–212.

Gilland, Joseph. *Elemental Magic: The Art of Special Effects Animation*. Massachusetts: Focal Press, 2009.

Giroux, Henry. *The Mouse That Roared: Disney and the End of Innocence*. Lanham: Rowman & Littlefield, 1999.

Gordon, Bruce, and David Mumford, ed. *A Brush with Disney: An Artist's Journey Told through the Words and Works of Herbert Dickens Ryman*. 2nd ed. Santa Clarita: Camphor Tree, 2002.

Grant, John. *Encyclopedia of Walt Disney's Animated Characters*. New York: Harper & Row, 1987.

Grellner, Alice. "Two Films That Sparkle: *The Sword in the Stone* and *Camelot*." Harty, *Cinema Arthuriana* 118–26.

Grewell, Cory. "Neomedievalism: An Eleventh Little Middle Ages?" *Defining Neomedievalism(s)*. Ed. Karl Fugelso. Cambridge: Brewer, 2010. 34–43.

Grossman, Kathryn. "From Classic to Pop Icon: Popularizing Hugo." *French Review* 74.3 (2001): 482–95.

Gutiérrez, Gabriel. "Deconstructing Disney: Chicano/a Children and Critical Race Theory." *Aztlán* 25.1 (2000): 7–46.

Guyot, Jacques. "France: Disney in the Land of Cultural Exception." Wasko and Phillips. 121–34.
Haas, Charlie. "Disneyland Is Good for You." *New West* (4 Dec. 1978): 13–19.
Hall, Millicent. "Theme Parks: Around the World in 80 Minutes." *Landscape* 21 (1976): 3–8.
Hall, Stuart. "Who Needs Identity?" *Identity.* Ed. Paul du Gay, Jessica Evans, and Peter Redman. London: Sage, 2000. 15–30.
Harty, Kevin J., ed. *Cinema Arthuriana: Twenty Essays.* Rev. ed. Jefferson, NC: McFarland, 2010.
——— *The Reel Middle Ages: American, Western and Eastern European, Middle Eastern, and Asian Films about Medieval Europe.* 1999. Jefferson, NC: McFarland, 2006.
———"Robin Hood on Film: Moving beyond a Swashbuckling Stereotype." *Robin Hood in Popular Culture.* Ed. Thomas Hahn. Cambridge: Brewer, 2000. 87–100.
Harvey, P. D. A., ed. *The Hereford World Map.* London: British Library, 2006.
Heng, Geraldine. *Empire of Magic: Medieval Romance and the Politics of Cultural Fantasy.* New York: Columbia University Press, 2003.
Hiaasen, Carl. *Team Rodent: How Disney Devours the World.* New York: Random House, 1998.
Higham, Charles. *Errol Flynn: The Untold Story.* Garden City, NJ: Doubleday, 1980.
Hugo, Victor. *Notre-Dame of Paris.* Trans. and ed. John Sturrock. 1831. London: Penguin, 2004.
Hurley, Dorothy. "Seeing White: Children of Color and the Disney Fairy-Tale Princess." *Journal of Negro Education* 74.3 (2005): 221–32.
The Imagineers. *The Imagineering Field Guide to Disneyland: An Imagineer's-Eye Tour.* New York: Disney Editions, 2008.
Jackson, Kathy. *Walt Disney: A Bio-Bibliography.* Westport: Greenwood, 1993.
Jankiewicz, Pat. "The Two Rocketeers." *Starburst* 156 (August 1991): 12.
Janzen, Jack, and Leon Janzen. "Disneyland Souvenir Maps, 1958–1965." *E-Ticket Magazine* 18 (1994): 4–7.
Jeffords, Susan. *Hard Bodies: Hollywood Masculinity in the Reagan Era.* New Brunswick: Rutgers University Press, 1994.
Jenkins, Henry. *Convergence Culture.* New York: New York University Press, 2008.
——— *Textual Poachers.* New York: Routledge, 1992.
Jhappan, Radha, and Daiva Stasiulis. "Anglophilia and the Discreet Charm of the English Voice in Disney's *Pocahontas* Films." Budd and Kirsch 151–80.
Kelly, Kathleen Coyne, and Tison Pugh. "Introduction: Queer History, Cinematic Medievalism, and the Impossibility of Sexuality." *Queer Movie Medievalisms.* Ed. Kathleen Coyne Kelly and Tison Pugh. Surrey: Ashgate, 2009. 1–17.

Klugman, Karen. "The Alternative Ride." *Inside the Mouse: Work and Play at Disney World*. Durham: Duke University Press, 1995. 163–79.

Knapp, Peggy. "The Work of Alchemy." *Journal of Medieval and Early Modern Studies* 30.3 (2000): 575–99.

Knight, Stephen. *Arthurian Literature and Society*. London: Macmillan, 1983.

——— *Robin Hood: A Complete Study of the English Outlaw*. Oxford: Blackwell, 1994.

——— *Robin Hood: A Mythic Biography*. Ithaca: Cornell University Press, 2003.

Koenig, David. *More Mouse Tales: A Closer Peek Backstage at Disneyland*. Irvine: Bonaventure, 2003.

——— *Mouse Tales: A Behind-the-Ears Look at Disneyland*. Irvine: Bonaventure, 1995.

——— *Mouse under Glass: Secrets of Disney Animation and Theme Parks*. Irvine: Bonaventure, 1997.

——— *Realityland: True-Life Adventures at Walt Disney World*. Irvine: Bonaventure, 2007.

Konstam, Angus. *Piracy: The Complete History*. Oxford: Osprey, 2008.

Korkis, Jim. *The Vault of Walt: Unofficial, Unauthorized, Uncensored Disney Stories Never Told*. Lexington: Ayefour, 2010.

Kurtti, Jeff, and Bruce Gordon. *The Art of Disneyland*. New York: Disney Editions, 2006.

——— *The Art of Walt Disney World*. New York: Disney Editions, 2009.

Lerner, Alan Jay. *The Street Where I Live*. London: Hodder & Stoughton, 1978.

Lester, Toby. *The Fourth Part of the World: The Race to the Ends of the Earth, and the Epic Story of the Map That Gave America Its Name*. New York: Free Press, 2009.

Lewis, C.S. *The Discarded Image*. Cambridge: University of Cambridge Press, 1987.

Leyda, Jay, ed. *Eisenstein on Disney*. Trans. Alan Upchurch. London: Methuen, 1988.

Linn, Susan. "A Royal Juggernaut: The Disney Princesses and Other Commercialized Threats to Creative Play." *The Sexualization of Childhood*. Ed. Sharna Olfman. Westport: Praeger, 2009. 33–50.

Lupack, Alan. "An Enemy in Our Midst: *The Black Knight* and the American Dream." Harty, *Cinema Arthuriana* 64–70.

——— *The Oxford Guide to Arthurian Literature and Legend*. Oxford: Oxford University Press, 2005.

——— "*The Once and Future King:* The Book That Grows Up." *Arthuriana* 11.3 (2001): 103–14.

——— "Valiant and Villainous Vikings." *The Vikings on Film*. Ed. Kevin J. Harty. Jefferson, NC: McFarland, 2011. 46–55.

——— and Barbara Tepa Lupack. *King Arthur in America*. Cambridge: Brewer, 1999.

Lupack, Barbara Tepa, ed. *Adapting the Arthurian Legends for Children: Essays on Arthurian Juvenilia.* New York: Palgrave Macmillan, 2004.
——— "Camelot on Camera: The Arthurian Legends and Children's Film." Barbara Lupack, *Adapting* 263–93.
Ma, Sheng-mei. "Mulan Disney, It's Like, Re-Orients: Consuming China and Animating Teen Dreams." Ayres 149–64.
Mackie, Erin. "Welcome the Outlaw: Pirates, Maroons, and Caribbean Countercultures." *Cultural Critique* 59 (2005): 24–62.
Magill, David. "Spectacular Male Bodies and Jazz Age Celebrity Culture." *Framing Celebrity.* Ed. Su Holmes and Sean Redmond. London: Routledge, 2006. 129–43.
Manovich, Lev. "'Reality' Effects in Computer Animation." *A Reader in Animation Studies.* Ed. Jayne Pilling. London: Libbey, 1997. 5–15.
Marin, Louis. *Utopics: Spatial Play.* Trans. Robert Volrath. Atlantic Highlands, NJ: Humanities, 1984.
Marling, Karal, ed. *Designing Disney's Theme Parks: The Architecture of Reassurance.* New York: Flammarion, 1998.
Martin, Adrian. "The Long Path Back: Medievalism and Film." *Screening the Past* 26 (2009): 7. Web. 22 Aug. 2011.
Martin, Karin, and Emily Kazyak. "Hetero-Romantic Love and Heterosexiness in Children's G-Rated Films." *Gender & Society* 23.3 (2009): 315–36.
Mattingly, Cheryl. "Becoming Buzz Lightyear and Other Clinical Tales." *Folk* 45 (2004): 9–32.
McCallum, Robyn. "Identity Politics and Gender in Disney Animated Films." *Ways of Being Male.* Ed. John Stephens. London: Routledge, 2002. 116–32.
Monmonier, Mark. *How to Lie with Maps.* 2nd ed. Chicago: University of Chicago Press, 1996.
——— *No Dig, No Fly, No Go: How Maps Restrict and Control.* Chicago: University of Chicago Press, 2010.
Moore, Alexander. "Walt Disney World: Bounded Ritual Space and the Playful Pilgrimage Center." *Anthropological Quarterly* 53 (1980): 207–18.
Moore, Lucy. *Liberty: The Lives and Times of Six Women in Revolutionary France.* London: Harper Perennial, 2007.
Morgan, Pamela. "One Brief Shining Moment: Camelot in Washington D.C." Verduin 185–211.
Morris, Rosemary. *The Character of King Arthur in Medieval Literature.* Cambridge: Brewer, 1982.
Morton, Tim. *The Ecological Thought.* Cambridge: Harvard University Press, 2010.
Mumford, Lewis. *Technics and Civilization.* New York: Harcourt, Brace, 1963.
Nadel, Alan. "A Whole New (Disney) World Order: *Aladdin,* Atomic Power, and the Muslim Middle East." *Visions of the East: Orientalism in Film.* Ed. Matthew Bernstein and Gaylyn Studlar. New Jersey: Rutgers University Press, 1997. 184–203.

Neale, Steve. "Pseudonyms, Sapphire and Salt: 'Un-American' Contributions to Television Costume Adventure Series in the 1950s." *Historical Journal of Film, Radio and Television* 23.3 (2003): 245–57.
Neff, Heather. "Strange Faces in the Mirror: The Ethics of Diversity in Children's Films." *The Lion and the Unicorn* 20.1 (1996): 50–65.
Newman, Kim. "The Robin Hood Collection." *Video Watchdog* 160 (Jan.–Feb., 2011): 68.
Oakeshott, Michael. *On History and Other Essays*. Oxford: Blackwell, 1985.
Pérez, Aida. "*Shrek*: The Animated Fairy-Tale Princess Reinvented." *Fifty Years of English Studies in Spain*. Ed. Ignacio Martinez, et al. Santiago de Compostela: Universidade de Santiago de Compostela, 2003. 281–86.
Pinchot, Gifford. *The Training of a Forester*. Philadelphia: Lippincott, 1914.
Pinsky, Mark. *The Gospel According to Disney: Faith, Trust, and Pixie Dust*. Louisville: Westminster John Knox Press, 2004.
Prime, Rebecca. "'The Old Bogey': The Hollywood Blacklist in Europe." *Film History* 20.2 (2008): 474–86.
Reel, Jerome. "Good King Arthur: Arthurian Music for Children." Barbara Lupack, *Adapting* 217–42.
Robinson, Carol, and Pamela Clements. "Living with Neomedievalisms." *Defining Medievalism(s) II*. Ed. Karl Fugelso. Cambridge: Brewer, 2009. 55–75.
*The Rocketeer Official Movie Souvenir Magazine*. Brooklyn: Topps for Buena Vista Pictures/The Walt Disney Company, 1991.
Rose, Jacqueline. *The Case of Peter Pan, or, The Impossibility of Children's Literature*. Philadelphia: University of Pennsylvania Press, 1993.
Roth, Matthew, "Man Is in the Forest." *In-Visible Culture* 9.9 (2005). Web. 19 Aug. 2011.
Ruskin, John. *The Electronic Edition of John Ruskin's Modern Painters*. Ed. Lawrence Woof. 1846. Web. 16 May 2012.
——— *Modern Painters, Vol. 1: Of General Principles and Truth*. Boston: Estes & Lauriat, 1894.
Sammond, Nicholas. *Babes in Tomorrowland: Walt Disney and the Making of the American Child, 1930–1960*. Durham: Duke University Press, 2005.
Scarlett, George, and Dennie Wolf. "When it's only make-believe: The Construction of a Boundary between Fantasy and Reality in Storytelling." *New Directions for Child and Adolescent Development* 6 (1979): 29–40.
Schaffer, Scott. "Disney and the Imagineering of Histories." *Postmodern Culture* 6.3 (1996): 1–34.
Shewman, Den. "Pirates of the New Sensibilities: Terry Rossio and Ted Elliott." *Creative Screenwriting* 10.4 (2003): 48–52.
Simpson, Roger. *Radio Camelot: Arthurian Legends on the BBC, 1922–2005*. Cambridge: Brewer, 2008.
Smith, Dave. *Disney A to Z: The Updated Official Encyclopedia*. New York: Hyperion, 1998.
Solomon, Charles. *Enchanted Drawings: The History of Animation*. New York: Random House, 1994.

Sperb, Jason. "Reassuring Convergence: Online Fandom, Race, and Disney's Notorious *Song of the South*." *Cinema Journal* 49.4 (2010): 25–45.

——— "'Take a Frown, Turn It Upside Down': Splash Mountain, Walt Disney World, and the Cultural De-rac[e]-ination of Disney's *Song of the South* (1946)." *Journal of Popular Culture* 38.5 (2005): 924–38.

Stephens, John. *Language and Ideology in Children's Fiction*. London: Longman, 1992.

Stevens, Dave. *The Rocketeer: The Complete Adventures*. San Diego: IDW, 2009.

Surrell, Jason. *Pirates of the Caribbean: From the Magic Kingdom to the Movies*. New York: Disney Editions, 2005.

Swanson, Mary. *From Swedish Fairy Tales to American Fantasy: Gustaf Tenggren's Illustrations, 1920–1970*. Minneapolis: University of Minnesota Press, 1986.

Takolander, Maria, and David McCooey. "'You Can't Say No to the Beauty and the Beast': *Shrek* and Ideology." *Papers: Explorations into Children's Literature* 15.1 (2005): 5–14.

Telotte, J. P. "The Changing Space of Animation: Disney's Hybrid Films of the 1940s." *Animation* 2 (2007): 245–58.

——— *The Mouse Machine: Disney and Technology*. Chicago: University of Illinois Press, 2008.

Thomas, Bob. *Disney's Art of Animation: From Mickey Mouse to Beauty and the Beast*. New York: Hyperion, 1991.

——— *Walt Disney: An American Original*. New York: Walt Disney Company, 1976.

Thomas, Tony. *Errol Flynn: The Spy Who Never Was*. Secaucus: Carol Publishing, 1990.

Thompson, Raymond. "The Ironic Tradition in Four Arthurian Films." Harty, *Cinema Arthuriana* 110–17.

Tiffin, Jessica. "Review: *The Emperor's Old Groove*." *Marvels & Tales* 18.2 (2004): 329–31.

Towbin, Mia, Shelly A. Haddock, Toni Zimmerman, Lori K. Lund, and Litsa Tanner. "Images of Gender, Race, Age, and Sexual Orientation in Disney Feature-Length Animated Films." *Journal of Feminist Family Therapy* 15.4 (2003): 19–44.

Trigg, Stephanie. "Transparent Walls: Stained Glass and Cinematic Medievalism," *Screening the Past* 26 (2009). Web. 22 Aug. 2011.

Tryon, Chuck. *Reinventing Cinema*. New Brunswick: Rutgers University Press, 2009.

Turchi, Peter. *Maps of the Imagination: The Writer as Cartographer*. San Antonio: Trinity University Press, 2004.

Umland, Rebecca, and Samuel Umland. *Arthurian Legend in Hollywood Film*. Westport: Greenwood, 1996.

Veness, Susan. *The Hidden Magic of Walt Disney World*. Avon: Adamsmedia, 2009.

Verduin, Kathleen, ed. *Medievalism in North America*. Cambridge: Brewer, 1994.

Wallace, Michael. "Mickey Mouse History: Portraying the Past at Disney World." *History Museums in the United States: A Critical Assessment*. Ed.

Warren Leon and Roy Rosenzweig. Champaign: University of Illinois Press, 1989. 158–82.

*Walt Disney Imagineering: A Behind-the-Dreams Look at Making More Magic Real.* New York: Disney Editions, 2010.

*Walt Disney World: The First Decade.* Walt Disney Productions, 1982.

*Walt Disney's Robin Hood and His Merrie Men: The Story of the Film Based upon the Screen Play by Lawrence Edward Watkin and Adapted by Edward Boyd.* London: Wm. Collins Sons, 1952.

Walt Disney Company. *Disney Princess: The Official Princess Website.* Disney.go.com. Web. 30 Nov. 2010.

Warner, Marina. *From the Beast to the Blonde: On Fairy Tales and Their Tellers.* New York: Farrar, Straus, & Giroux, 1994.

Warner, Sylvia Townsend. *T. H. White: A Biography.* London: Cape, 1967.

Wasko, Janet. *Understanding Disney: The Manufacture of Fantasy.* Williston, VT: Blackwell, 2001.

Wasko, Janet, Mark Phillips, and Eileen Meehan, ed. *Dazzled by Disney? The Global Disney Audiences Project.* London: Leicester University Press, 2001.

Watts, Steven. *The Magic Kingdom: Walt Disney and the American Way of Life.* Boston: Houghton Mifflin, 1997.

Weill, Sabrina. "An Eco-Princess Mani-Pedi" and "Little Princess, All Made Up." *Confessions from the Castle.* Disney.go.com. Web. 12 Dec. 2010.

Wells, Paul. *Animation and America.* New Brunswick: Rutgers University Press, 2002.

——— "'Thou Art Translated': Analysing Animated Adaptation." *Visions of the East: Orientalism in Film.* Ed. Matthew Bernstein and Gaylyn Studlar. New Jersey: Rutgers University Press, 1997. 199–213.

West, John. *The Disney Live-Action Productions.* Milton, WA: Hawthorne & Peabody, 1994.

White, Hayden. *The Content of the Form.* Baltimore: Johns Hopkins University Press, 1987.

White, T. H. *The Complete Once and Future King.* London: HarperCollins, 1996.

——— *Letters to a Friend: The Correspondence between T. H. White and L. J. Potts.* Ed. François Gallix. Gloucester: Sutton, 1984.

White, Theodore H. "For President Kennedy: An Epilogue." *Life* (December 6, 1963): 158–59.

Whitley, David. *The Idea of Nature in Disney Animation.* Aldershot, Hampshire: Ashgate, 2008.

Wilford, John. *The Mapmakers.* New York: Knopf, 1981.

Williams, Pat, with Jon Denney. *How to Be Like Walt: Capturing the Disney Magic Every Day of Your Life.* Deerfield Beach, FL: Health Communications, 2004.

Williams, Raymond. "The Idea of Nature." *Problems in Materialism and Culture.* London: Verso, 1997. 67–85.

Willis, Susan. "The Family Vacation." *Inside the Mouse: Work and Play at Disney World*. Durham: Duke University Press, 1995. 34–53.
Wohlwend, Karen. "Damsels in Discourse: Girls Consuming and Producing Identity Texts through Disney Princess Play." *Reading Research Quarterly* 44.1 (2009): 57–83.
Wood, Denis. *The Power of Maps*. New York: Guilford, 1992.
——— *Rethinking the Power of Maps*. New York: Guilford, 2010.
Wood, Naomi. "Domesticating Dreams in Walt Disney's *Cinderella*." *The Lion and the Unicorn* 20.1 (1996): 25–49.
Worthington, Heather. "From Children's Story to Adult Fiction: T. H. White's *The Once and Future King*." *Arthuriana* 12.2 (2002): 97–119.
Worthington, Marjorie. "The Motherless 'Disney Princess': Marketing Mothers Out of the Picture." *Mommy Angst: Motherhood in Popular Culture*. Ed. Ann Hall and Mardia Bishop. Santa Barbara: ABC-CLIO, 2009. 29–46.
Wortzel, Adrianne. "Sayonara Diorama: Acting Out the World as a Stage in Medieval Cartography and Cyberspace." Harvey 415–21.
Zipes, Jack. "Breaking the Disney Spell." Bell, Haas, and Sells 21–41.
——— *Fairy Tales and the Art of Subversion*. 2nd ed. New York: Routledge, 2006.
Zukin, Sharon. *Landscapes of Power: From Detroit to Disney World*. Berkeley: University of California Press, 1991.

# BIOGRAPHICAL NOTES ON CONTRIBUTORS

**Susan Aronstein** is professor of English at the University of Wyoming. She is the author of *Hollywood Knights: Arthurian Cinema and the Politics of Nostalgia*, as well as several articles on medievalism and popular culture, including Disneyland, Excalibur Hotel, *Monty Python and the Holy Grail*, and *The Da Vinci Code*.

**Martha Bayless** is associate professor of English at the University of Oregon, focusing on the intersection between literature and culture in the Middle Ages. She is the author of *Parody in the Middle Ages: The Latin Tradition*, as well as numerous articles on Anglo-Saxon, Latin, and Celtic literatures.

**Clare Bradford** is professor of Literary Studies at Deakin University in Melbourne, Australia. Her books include *Reading Race: Aboriginality in Australian Children's Literature* (2001), which won both the Children's Literature Association Book Award and the International Research Society for Children's Literature Award; *Unsettling Narratives: Postcolonial Readings of Children's Literature* (2007); and *New World Orders in Contemporary Children's Literature: Utopian Transformations* (2009).

**Maria Sachiko Cecire** is assistant professor of Literature at Bard College. Her publications include "*Ban Welondes*: Wayland Smith in Popular Culture" in *Anglo-Saxon Culture in the Modern Imagination* and "Medievalism, Popular Culture, and National Identity in Children's Fantasy Literature" in *Studies in Ethnicity and Nationalism*.

**Allison Craven** is senior lecturer in the School of Arts and Social Sciences, James Cook University of North Queensland, Australia, where she teaches film, communication, and children's literature. She has published on Disney film, gender and globalization, children's literature and education, and Australian film and cinema.

**Amy Foster** is associate professor of History at the University of Central Florida where she teaches courses in the history of science, technology, and medicine. She is the author of *Integrating Women into the Astronaut Corps: Politics and Logistics at NASA, 1972–2004*.

**Rob Gossedge** is a lecturer in medieval English Literature at Cardiff University. He has recently published articles and book chapters on Arthurian literature, the Robin Hood tradition, formations of British European and American medievalism, Catholic novelists, and the rise of militarism in the early nineteenth century.

**Kevin J. Harty**, professor and chair of English at La Salle University in Philadelphia, has published widely in the areas of medieval studies and medievalism, especially on cinematic representations of the Middle Ages. His most recent book is *The Vikings on Film*; previous publications include *The Chester Mystery Cycle: A Casebook*, *The Reel Middle Ages*, *King Arthur on Film*, and *Cinema Arthuriana*.

**Kathleen Coyne Kelly** is professor of English at Northeastern University. She is co-editor (with Marina Leslie) of *Menacing Virgins: Representing Virginity in the Middle Ages and Renaissance*, co-editor (with Tison Pugh) of *Queer Movie Medievalisms*, and author of *A. S. Byatt* and *Performing Virginity and Testing Chastity in the Middle Ages*.

**Erin Felicia Labbie** is associate professor of English at Bowling Green State University, where she specializes in medieval studies and literary and critical theory. She is the author of *Lacan's Medievalism* (2006), as well as articles about medieval studies and psychoanalysis.

**Ilan Mitchell-Smith**, assistant professor of English at California State University at Long Beach, teaches courses on medieval literature and culture. His research focuses on modern American representations of gender and identity in the Middle Ages and on violence and masculinity in chivalric literature and culture.

**Tison Pugh** is professor of English at the University of Central Florida. He is the author of *Queering Medieval Genres* and *Innocence, Heterosexuality, and the Queerness of Children's Literature*, and the co-editor of *Race, Class, and Gender in "Medieval" Cinema* and *Queer Movie Medievalisms*.

**Paul Sturtevant** is a PhD student of the Institute for Medieval Studies and the Centre for World Cinemas at the University of Leeds. His research examines the influence of cinematic depictions of the medieval world on the public understanding of the Middle Ages.

**Stephen Yandell** is associate professor of English at Xavier University in Cincinnati, Ohio, where he teaches classes in Chaucer and early English literature. His publications include the edited collection *Prophet Margins: The Medieval Vatic Impulse and Social Stability* and essays on Oxford's Inklings.

# INDEX

*101 Dalmatians* 120

Adam and Eve 28, 33, 61, 66, 68–69
*Adventures of Robin Hood, The* (film) 134, 137, 144, 145
*Adventures of Robin Hood, The* (television series) 136
*Aladdin* 8, 83–85, 89–92, 180, 182, 184, 209, 210, 211–13, 216, 219, 220, 237, 244
Alger, Horatio 9, 184, 218
Anderson, Hans Christian 116
Anderson, Ken 139
animation 97–113, 189, 227, 230–32, 239, 243, 245–46, 259 n.
Annakin, Ken 133, 135–38
*Apple Dumpling Gang, The* 161
Ariel (*The Little Mermaid*) 15, 171, 179, 180, 186 n.
*Aristocats, The* 139
*Atlantis* 232, 237
Aurora (*Sleeping Beauty*) 15, 171, 179, 180

*Bambi* 126, 194, 197
*Bandit of Sherwood Forest, The* 134, 145–46
Barrie, J. M. 4
Baudrillard, Jean 1, 25, 199
Baum, L. Frank 161
Baxter, Tony 11
*Beauty and the Beast* 88, 175, 177–78, 180, 182–83, 212, 231, 233, 243, 244, 251

Bedard, Irene (voice of Pocahontas) 221
Belle (*Beauty and the Beast*) 15, 171, 177, 179, 180, 182
Belsey, Catherine 200
Bettelheim, Bruno 188 n.
Bilson, Danny 144
*Black Shield of Falworth, The* 128
Blair, Mary 196
Blake, William 121
Bloom, Orlando 7
Boadicea 148
*Book of Merlyn, The* 117
Booker, Keith 115
Boorman, John, *Excalibur* 120
Borges, Jorge Luis 23 n.
Bourdieu, Pierre 173, 187 n.
Bretherton, Howard 134
Bridson, D. G. 118
Britten, Benjamin 118
Brode, Douglas 202–203
Burton, Richard 119
Butler, Judith 172, 176, 187, 188 n.

Camelot 153, 152, 163, 164
*Camelot* (1967 film) 119
*Camelot* (1982 film) 119
Cameron, James, *Avatar* 196
*Candle in the Wind, The* 117, 118
*Captain Blood* 144
Carroll, Lewis 23 n.
Carter, Angela 181, 188 n.
Chapman, Graham 203
Chaucer, Geoffrey 106–109

Cinderella (character) 15, 171, 179, 180, 186 n.
*Cinderella* (film) 88, 180–83, 212, 244, 245, 251, 256
Cocteau, Jean 200
Cohen, Jeffrey J. 181
Cohl, Emile 102
Columbus, Christopher 163
*Connecticut Yankee in King Arthur's Court, A* (novel) 15, 116, 120, 128–29, 133, 153, 161–64
consumerism 1–5, 14, 16, 25, 52, 58, 62, 67–68, 173–75, 186, 198, 213–15, 221–23, 244–45, 253–54
Coppola, Francis Ford 126
Curtis, Tony 128
Curtiz, Michael 134

Dalton, Timothy 145
Davis, Marc 198
Davis, Martin 29
de Certeau, Michel 97, 106
de Haviland, Olivia 135, 144
De Meo, Paul 144
de Worde, Wyken [sic] 135
Deeping, Warwick 127
Depp, Johnny 8, 69
Disney Parks
  Adventureland 10, 30, 61–62
  advertising campaigns 57, 59–60
  Animal Kingdom 201
  Bear Country 31
  Bibbidi Bobbidi Boutique 7, 50–51
  cast members 24, 34–35
  castles 14, 86
    Cinderella Castle 50–52, 133
    Sleeping Beauty Castle 42, 44–45, 62, 68, 133, 245
  Critter Country 68–69
  Disneyland Paris 165
  dystopia, as 1
  Epcot 24, 154
  fairs and expositions and 22, 155, 166 n.
  Fantasyland 30, 42, 47, 63–66
  Frontierland 30, 61
  Future World 166
  Hong Kong Disneyland 155
  hyperreality in 22, 23, 25
  lines 24
  Magic Kingdom 154, 155, 166 n.
  Main Street USA 21, 30, 32, 60–61
  maps 21–38
  nature and 200
  New Orleans Square 67
  time and 61
  Tokyo Disneyland 155
  Tom Sawyer Island 22, 23, 32
  Tomorrowland 62, 69, 153, 155, 157, 166 n.
  Toontown 31, 69
  transportation in 25, 29, 31
  Walt Disney World 23–25, 32, 35, 155, 194
  wienies 31, 47
  World Showcase 24
Disney Princesses 2, 15, 49–53, 79, 81–83, 85–86, 171–88, 236
  aristocracy and 180
  bad boys and 183–85
  children's play and 174–75
  chivalric code 183
  clothing 87–88, 210–21
  ethnicity and 178–79, 209–22
  fairy tales and 4, 81–83, 86
  fatherhood and 173, 181–83
  franchise 85–86
  innocence and 179
  mash-up 248, 256–57
  merchandise 243, 253
  Middle Ages and 171–72
  motherhood and 178, 179
  narratives 246, 252, 254, 256, 257, 259 n.
  Orientalism and 227, 236, 237, 240
  Pirate and Princess Parties 6–7
  website 171–72, 186, 214–18, 222

*See also Aladdin*; Ariel; Aurora;
   *Beauty and the Beast;* Belle;
   Cinderella (character);
   *Cinderella* (film); consumerism;
   Disney Productions; gender;
   Jasmine; *The Little Mermaid*;
   Mulan (character); *Mulan*
   (film); Pocahontas (character);
   *Pocahontas* (film); *The Princess*
   *and the Frog*; Rapunzel;
   *Sleeping Beauty*; Snow White
   (character); *Snow White and the*
   *Seven Dwarfs*; *Tangled*; Tiana
Disney Productions
   accents in 218–19
   "Book" film opening 86, 245–46
   Castle Logo 216, 243, 245, 250
   costumes, medieval 86–88, 161–63
   Disneyfication 153–62
   Distory 2–3, 154, 156, 161
   historical context 12–13, 105, 111, 155–67, 201, 203, 236
   innocence and 5, 233, 254
   landscape and 33–34, 83–85, 90–91
   music in 246, 255–56, 259 n.
   nation and 84, 91
   nature and 120–21, 189–203
   pedagogy and 79–81, 121–25
   Pixar 239
   polytemporality and 32–33
   psychological viewing of 80
   race and ethnicity in 90–92, 210–21
   science and 122–23
   time and 16, 98, 101, 105, 108, 226, 227
   Walt Disney Studios 153, 158, 159
Disney Rides 62–70
   Astro Orbiter 155
   Carousel of Progress 61
   Haunted Mansion 67
   It's a Small World 22–23, 24
   Jungle Cruise 22
   Living with the Land 154
   Matterhorn Bobsled 22
   Mission Space 155

monorails 25
Peter Pan's Flight 65–66
Pirates of the Caribbean 10–11, 67–68, 69–70, 245
Rocket to the Moon 156
Skyway 35
Snow White's Scary Adventures 64–65
Space Mountain 155, 166 n.
Spaceship Earth 154
Splash Mountain 70
Disney, Roy 103, 154
Disney, Walt 41, 47, 55, 101, 103, 115, 153–55, 157, 158, 160, 162, 176
   *Atlanta Journal* editorial cartoon about death of 133
   design (Disneyland) 58, 60, 63
   inspiration (for Merlin) 122
   populism of 164
   technological enthusiasm of 154, 160, 165
Disneyland (park) 21–26, 29–33, 35–36, 133, 154, 156, 166, 194
   consumption and 57–58, 71–72
   dedication of 154–55
   Fantasyland 30, 42, 47, 63–66
   Frontierland 30, 61
   history and 60–61, 68
   memory and 59
   New Orleans Square 67
   opening day 61–62, 63, 66
   pedagogy and 57–72
   pilgrimage centers, as 57–72
   pirates, and 69–70
   rides 62–70
   *See also* Disney Parks; Disney Rides
Douglas, Gordon 134
Dukas, Paul
   *L'Apprenti Sorcier* 107, 109
Dyer, Richard 179, 188 n.

Earle, Eyvind 48, 176, 196
Ebert, Roger 192
Eco, Umberto 25, 29

Edson, Evelyn  12
Eisner, Michael  201
Eleanor of Aquitaine  136–37
Ellenshaw, Peter  31
Elliott, Ted  8
Ellis, Erle  201
*Enchanted*  16, 243–58
Engle, Joseph  159
Erben, Dr. H. F.  144
*E-Ticket Magazine*  32

Fair Unknown  173, 184, 185
fans  247–48, 255
*Fantasia* (1940)  14, 97–109
*Fantasia 2000*  97–109
Finch, Peter  136–37
*First Knight*  9
Fjellman, Stephen  11, 12, 23, 154
Fleischer, Max  102
Flynn, Errol  134, 137, 144, 145
Fox, Atkinson  193
Frazer, James George  126
Freud, Sigmund  98
Fullerton, Charles  159
Fuqua, Antoine  148

gender
  convergence culture and  244–45
  cultural norms  172, 186
  Disney fairy tales and  40, 53, 87
  heterosexual romance  176, 180–81
  heterosexuality  173, 176, 178–82, 252, 257
  homoeroticism  258 n.
  homophobia  258 n.
  marriage  213, 217, 218, 220, 221
  masculinities  10, 81–82, 183, 211, 220, 221
  nature and  196–97
  roles  5–6, 9–10, 40, 53, 71, 87–88, 133–36, 146–48, 172–76, 179
  sexuality and  172, 183
  work and  186
Geoffrey of Monmouth, *Historia Regum Britanniae*  110, 117
*Gertie the Dinosaur*  190

Gilliam, Terry  126
Giroux, Henry  3, 174, 182, 187 n., 188 n.
Goldberg, Whoopi  133
Gregory the Great  59, 66
Grellner, Alice  115
Grimm, Jacob and Wilhelm  5, 40, 81, 86, 116, 174–75, 181, 187 n.

Haber, Heinz  156, 157
Haise, Fred  159
Hall, Stuart  5
Harris, Neal  57
Harris, Richard  119
Hartley, Paul  32
Helwig, Marianne
  *The Sword in the Stone* (1939 BBC radio drama)  118
  *The Sword in the Stone* (1952 BBC radio drama)  118
Hench, John  33
Heng, Geraldine  172, 187 n.
Henri, Robert  191
*Hercules*  237
Hereford Cathedral  22, 27
Hereford map  22, 25, 27–29, 31–35
Hewitt, Peter  133, 145–48
Hiassen, Carl  34
Hinch, John  196
"How to Be a Sailor"  12–13
Hugo, Victor. See *Notre-Dame of Paris*
*Humorous Phases of Funny Faces*  189–90
*Hunchback of Notre Dame, The* (Disney film)  16, 225–42
*Hunchback of Notre Dame, The*, live-action and other animated films of
  Dir. Wallace Worsley (1923)  226, 228, 229, 233, 234, 238
  Dir. William Dieterle (1939)  226, 228, 229, 233, 238
  Dir. Jean Delannoy (1956)  228, 229, 233
*Hunchback of Notre Dame II: The Secret of the Bell*  234–35
Hunt, Martita  136

# INDEX

*Ill-Made Knight, The* 117, 118
*Indiana Jones* franchise 143, 145
*Ivanhoe* (film) 128

Jasmine (*Aladdin*) 15, 171, 172, 179, 181, 182, 187 n., 210, 211, 213–14, 216, 217, 218, 219, 220, 236
Jenkins, Henry
  *Convergence Culture* 244, 248
  *Textual Poaching* 247–48, 250
John, Elton 121
Johnson, Joe 133, 143–45

Kammler, Hans 157, 166 n.
Kay, John 162
Kennedy, Jacqueline 119, 120
Kennedy, John F. 116, 119, 165
Kimball, Ward 154, 155, 156, 157
King Arthur (character) 133, 138, 161–64, 195
*King Arthur* (film) 148
Knapp, Raymond 188 n.
*Knight in Camelot, A* 129, 133
*Knight's Tale, A* 9
Knightley, Keira 146–48
*Knights of the Round Table, The* (film) 128
Kolve, V. A. 61

*Lady and the Tramp* 252
*Lancelot-Grail Cycle* 117
Lerner, Alan Jay, and Frederick Loewe 119
  *Camelot* (musical) 116, 119
Levin, Henry 134, 145–46
Lewis, C. S. 29
Ley, Willy 156, 157
*Lion King, The* 126
Lipartito, Kenneth 159
*Little Mermaid, The* 172, 180, 182, 183, 212, 244, 249, 250, 252
*Living Desert, The* 194
Logan, Joshua 119
Lucian 109
Ludwig II of Bavaria 42–43, 44–45, 54 n.

Lupack, Alan 121
Lupack, Alan, and Barbara Tepa Lupack 115

Maid Marian 135–37, 139–40
*Man and the Moon* 156
*Man in Space* 15, 153, 154–58, 160, 165
*mappaemundi* 22, 25–26, 29–33
Marin, Louis 1, 23, 31, 32
Marling, Karal 57, 72 n.
*Mars and Beyond* 156
Martin, Karin 180, 188 n.
*Mary Poppins* 120
Mayberry, Russ 161
McDowell, Malcolm 146–48
McKim, Sam 22, 30–35
Meador, Joshua 196
medieval
  art 59–60, 62–63, 65
  backwards 247, 249
  barbaric 173, 177–78
  idealized nature as 189–207
  romanticized 161–65, 173
Merlin (Merlyn) 82, 99, 104, 105, 110, 115, 117, 122, 124–25
mermaids 33–34
*Merry Adventures of Robin Hood, The* (novel) 137–38
Mickey Mouse 3, 34, 54, 58, 60, 97, 99, 103, 110, 190
modernity 89, 99, 101, 104–107, 128
Moore, Alexander 58, 59, 66
morality plays 62
Mordred (character) 163, 164
Morgan, Hank (character) 161, 163, 164
Mulan (character) 15, 172, 179, 181, 187 n., 210, 216–22, 236
*Mulan* (film) 180, 209, 213, 220, 221, 232, 243, 244

neomedievalism 243, 244, 247, 250, 252–54, 256, 257, 259 n.
Neufeld, Michael 156, 157
Neuschwanstein. *See* Ludwig II of Bavaria

Newton, John 134
Nichols, Stephen 60
*Notre-Dame of Paris* by Victor
 Hugo 225–26, 227–29, 230,
 234, 237, 238

Oakeshott, Michael 2
*Once and Future King, The*
 1958 volume 116, 122
 1996 complete volume 117
*Once Upon a Time* 257–58
Owen-Crocker, Gale 161

Parrish, Maxfield 193
pastiche 83, 215, 226, 231, 234
Peet, Bill 120, 122
Perrault, Charles 5, 115, 187, n., 196
*Peter Pan* 4
*Piers Plowman* 135
Pinchot, Gifford 194
*Pinocchio* 112 n.
piracy 4–13
*Pirates of the Caribbean* (film) 7–10, 70
Pixar. See Disney Productions
Pocahontas (character) 15, 171, 172,
 178, 179, 180, 187 n., 210,
 212, 215–19, 221, 236
*Pocahontas* (film) 178–79, 180, 181,
 209, 212, 244
*Prince of Persia: Sands of Time* 240
*Prince of Thieves, The* 134
*Princess and the Frog, The* 181, 183,
 184, 209, 213, 218, 219, 221
*Princess of Thieves* 133, 134, 145–48
*Prose Merlin, The*, attributed to Robert
 de Boron 127
*Pulp Fiction* 247
Pyle, Howard 116, 127, 137–38

race. See Disney Princesses
Rackham, Arthur 193
Rapunzel (*Tangled*) 15, 179, 181, 185,
 187 n.
Rathbone, Basil 137, 144
Redgrave, Vanessa 119

Reitherman, Wolfgang 133, 138–43
Reynard the Fox 138
Reynaud, Charles-Émile, *Pauvre
 Pierrot* 189, 190
Reynolds, Kevin 148
Rice, Joan 135–37, 147
Richard of Haldingham 27, 34
Robin Hood (character) 15, 117, 127,
 133–52
*Robin Hood* (animated film) 133, 134,
 138–43
*Robin Hood, Prince of Thieves*
 (film) 148
*Rocketeer, The* (film) 133, 134, 143–45
*Rocketeer, The* (graphic novel) 143
*Rogues of Sherwood Forest* (film) 134
*Roman d'Éneas* 116
Rose, Jacqueline 6
Rossio, Terry 8
Roth, Matthew 189
Ruskin, John 189, 190
Ryman, Herbert 30–31

*Saludos Amigos* 29
*Seal Island* 194
*Shaggy D.A., The* 161
Sherman, George 134, 145–46
*Shrek* (films) 8, 81–82, 174,
 187 n., 196
"Sir Gyro de Gearloose" 129
*Sleeping Beauty* 15, 88–89, 175, 176,
 181, 183, 189, 196–98, 212,
 244–46, 250, 251
Smith, Michael 154
Snow White (Character) 171, 180,
 186, 212, 217
*Snow White and the Seven Dwarfs* 15,
 138, 172, 175, 179, 181–83,
 188 n., 189–95, 212, 239, 244,
 249, 252
Solomon, Charles 196
*Son of Robin Hood* (film) 146
*Song of the South* 70, 236, 248–50
*Sorcerer's Apprentice, The* 14, 97–111
Sotto, Eddie 22

## INDEX

Sperb, Jason 70
*Star Trek* 159
*Stardust* 159, 160, 161, 163
*Steamboat Willie* 190
Stephens, Dave 143
Stephens, John 182, 188 n.
Stevenson, Robert Louis 4, 134
*Story of Robin Hood and His Merrie Men, The* (film) 133, 134, 135–38, 146–47, 152
*Suite de Merlin* 126
Surrell, Jason 11
*Sword in the Stone, The* (film; also known as *Merlin the Enchanter* and *Merlin and Mim*) 15, 115–31, 133, 138, 231, 233, 245
*Sword in the Stone, The* (novel) 116–17, 119, 122, 126

*Tales of Robin Hood* (film) 134
*Tangled* 172, 183, 185, 188 n., 257
*Tarzan* 232
Tate, Don 161
Tchaikovsky, *The Sleeping Beauty* 196
Tenggren, Gustaf Adolf 193
Tennyson, Alfred, *Idylls of the King* 117, 126–27
Thomas, Bob 176, 188 n.
Thompson, Raymond 115
*Three Little Pigs, The* (animated film) 139
Tiana (*The Princess and the Frog*) 15, 172, 179, 181, 184, 187 n., 210, 213, 216–19, 221, 223
Tiffin, Jessica 175, 187 n.
Tiling, James 134
Todd, Richard 134, 135–37
*Toy Story* 239
*Treasure Island* (film) 29, 134–35
*Treasure Planet* 237

*Très Riches Heures* 196
*True-Life Adventures Series* 194
Truly, Richard 159
Turner, Victor 58
Twain, Mark 15, 116, 127
 See also *A Connecticut Yankee in King Arthur's Court* (novel)

Underwood, Carrie 255–56, 259 n.
*Unidentified Flying Oddball* 15, 129, 153, 158–65
Uther Pendragon (character) 117

Viollet-le-Duc, Eugène Emmanuel 43–44, 55 n.
Von Braun, Wernher 156, 157, 160, 165, 166 n.

Wagner, Richard 118
Wallace, Mike 60, 154
*Walt Disney World: The First Decade* 10
*Walt Disney's Disneyland* 60
Warner, Marina 188 n.
Watts, Steven 193
Wells, H. G., *The Time Machine* 202
White, Hayden 3
White, T. H. 115–31
White, Theodore H. 119, 121
Wilson, Stuart 146–48
*Witch in the Wood, The* 117, 119, 126
Wohlwend, Karen 174, 187 n.
*Wonderful Wizard of Oz, The* 161
Wood, Naomi 174, 175, 187 n.

Yasgur, Max 204
Yen-sid 99, 105, 107–109
Young, Roger 133

Zipes, Jack 115

Printed in Great Britain
by Amazon